Praise for *Dangerous Markets*

"Financial crises are hardly limited to the purview of central bankers and regulators. The authors skillfully demonstrate that financial crises offer both peril and promise. A 'must read' for top management of any global company, whether a financial or a nonfinancial institution."

> *Ronald P. O'Hanley*
> *Vice Chairman, Mellon Financial Corp.*

"Based on their vast experience in financial crises around the world during recent years, the authors have developed an impressive review of the origins of and solutions to financial crises. The cost of such crises can be minimized and the path to recovery established earlier if bankers, other corporate executives, and public finance officials take advantage of this effort and apply the lessons learned from their significant work."

> *Charles H. Dallara*
> *Managing Director, Institute of International Finance, Inc.*

"*Dangerous Markets* is a 'must read' in the current global environment for all serious investors and senior executives. The McKinsey authors bring a unique practitioners' perspective to the challenges of anticipating, managing, and succeeding in financial crises, and close with an intriguing call for leading private sector players to step up their role in promoting new market standards and structures to help avoid future financial crises and minimize their potential impact."

> *Robert R. Glauber*
> *Chairman and CEO,*
> *National Association of Securities Dealers, Inc.*
> *former Under Secretary of the U.S. Treasury Department*
> *former Harvard Business School professor*

"The authors address an issue of enormous importance in today's volatile world. They emphasize the critical role that the management of financial institutions can play, not only in leading their own institutions through choppy waters, but in helping shape the development of more robust financial systems."

> *Peter Sands*
> *Group Finance Director, Standard Chartered Bank*

"Barton, Newell, and Wilson provide new and important insights into financial crises based on their extensive and successful work with private financial institutions and with governments. They offer clear and persuasive guidance on how best to avoid crises, how to see them coming, and what to do when they happen. This is best-practice counsel from three leaders in the field. They have worked in the trenches, and bring a vital private sector perspective."

Martin N. Baily
Senior Fellow, Institute for International Economics
former Chairman of the Council of Economic Advisers

"The book results from a fresh and imaginative approach to financial crises in the past few years, particularly from a corporation's standpoint. The insights are precious to top executives as well as to regulators and academics; in fact, the book provides a very skillful demonstration of the value of the dialogue between all interested parties on the issue of financial crises. Since the focus of such crises is now moving toward nonfinancial corporations, the book becomes even more timely and important."

Gustavo Franco
Partner, Rio Bravo Investimentos
Professor of Economics, Pontífica Universidade Católica
former Governor of the Central Bank of Brazil

"As a member of the private equity investment community, I recommend *Dangerous Markets* to all members of the world business community. Their insights provide valuable lessons which if applied can make the world markets much more efficient and stable."

Steven Lee
Partner, Lone Star Fund

"Based on their unparalleled experience consulting during financial crises, Barton, Newell, and Wilson offer a fresh perspective on such episodes. The microeconomic focus—as opposed to the conventional macro view—provides important new insights into the difficult art of forecasting and surviving these storms."

Dr. José A. Scheinkman
Chaire Blaise Pascal de l'État et de la Region Île de France
Theodore Wells '29 Professor of Economics,
Princeton University

DANGEROUS MARKETS

Managing in Financial Crises

DOMINIC BARTON
ROBERTO NEWELL
GREGORY WILSON

John Wiley & Sons, Inc.
New York • Chichester • Weinheim • Brisbane • Singapore • Toronto

Library of Congress Cataloging-in-Publication Data

Barton, Dominic.
    Dangerous markets : managing in financial crises / Dominic Barton, Roberto Newell, Gregory Wilson.
        p.   cm.—(Wiley finance series)
        ISBN 0-471-22686-6 (cloth : alk. paper)
        1. Crisis management.   2. Financial crises.   I. Newell, Roberto.   II. Wilson, Gregory.   III. Title.   IV. Series.
    HD49.B367   2002
    338.5'42—dc21

2002009965

Printed in the United States of America

10   9   8   7   6   5   4   3   2   1

To my wife, Sheila, and my children, Fraser and Jessica
Dominic

To my wife, Tamara, and my children, Laurence, DeNeen, and Tatiana
Roberto

*To my wife, Beejay, my children, Sarah and Christopher, and in memory
of my parents, Paul and Lorayne S. Wilson*
Gregory

contents

preface

WHY MANAGE FINANCIAL CRISES PROACTIVELY?

Financial crises are simply too important and too costly to shareholders and societies to leave unmanaged. There is no question that there are *real* dangers in financial crises: Companies go bankrupt, management teams are fired, investors lose their money, employees lose their jobs, pensions disappear, deposits are frozen in time, personal savings get depleted, civil unrest increases, public riots can break out, contagion spreads across political borders, secondary effects appear such as higher risk premiums in other unsuspecting countries, and, finally, governments fall—as they did in Indonesia, Ecuador, Russia, and Argentina in recent years.

Too often, we see companies and entire sectors of an economy that are consistently destroying shareholder value year after year, sowing the seeds of a future crisis. Too often, we find fundamentally weak banking systems, especially in emerging markets where the banks play a disproportionate role in the national economy compared to less volatile capital markets. Too often, these weak national systems are linked inefficiently to global capital markets, increasing the cost of capital locally to all borrowers—individual consumers, businesses, and governments alike. Too often, we see weak corporate governance or inadequate accounting and transparency. Invariably, we find weak financial regulators who lack both the needed skills and political independence to do their jobs adequately. Too often, weak national systems are hooked up to the global capital markets before they are ready, and a lot of money flows in under misguided assumptions, increasing the potential for crisis.

Consequently, financial crises are occurring more frequently, with costs that are measured by as much as one-quarter or one-half of a nation's GDP. They also have long time horizons, measured in years, not months. At different levels, contagion is now a fact of life in the world. Moreover, there is no end in sight. We believe firmly in the net benefits of dynamic market forces and globalization, but the collision of these forces with weak economies and weak financial systems exposes the rot lying below the surface in many countries and, in our view, will only increase the rate and intensity of crises in the future.

That's why financial crises need to be managed.

Yet, too many companies and too many countries fail to manage their crises proactively: Unfortunately for shareholders and taxpayers, they react day-to-day and usually lack a viable plan to navigate their way out of the financial storm that has engulfed them. Crises are often seen as random, catastrophic events, yet every client with whom we have worked regrets not having been prepared adequately. Crises are not going away.

From our global perspective, we see at least two major benefits to managing a crisis proactively. First, there are real financial savings by minimizing the crisis resolution costs imposed on these same shareholders and taxpayers. Second, there are real competitive benefits as well, if executives can act swiftly before or after a crisis hits to seize new opportunities and secure a winning position as economic growth returns in the post-crisis world. Consequently, both companies and nations have a huge economic self-interest in getting crisis management right. While some elements seem out of control, many are manageable with the proper planning and resources.

Managers in the midst of a financial crisis have an undeniable self-interest in survival and protecting their shareholders. Since financial crises can rob a country of years of needed economic development, policymakers have an equal self-interest in preserving GDP growth on behalf of the societies they represent. With the right combination of vision, leadership, strategy, courage, and operational and financial capabilities, however, executives can manage crises to optimize their competitive or national self-interest: Crisis resolution costs can be minimized; crisis durations can be shortened; corporate and national solvency can be restored more quickly; competitive positions can be enhanced; financial systems can be saved and reset for the global world in which we live; and economic growth can be restored and sustained. However, it takes commitment, skills, toughness, and hard work.

Just as executives have a clear self-interest in actively managing financial crises, they also have options that they can exercise.

For a moment, imagine two huge power stations supplying electricity to a neighborhood. Suppose you live in a house that receives power from one of these stations. If your house has up-to-date wiring, with the proper system of circuit breakers and controls, you can use all your appliances at the same time to cook your food, heat your home, and run your computer with little fear of electrical harm. Perhaps a light bulb will go out, or one circuit breaker will blow, but overall the house will not have major electrical problems and the risk of a major mishap is low.

If, however, the house's wiring is faulty or out-of-date with modern building codes, then you risk melting your entire electrical system, and perhaps even setting your house on fire. Of course, you can choose not to operate on the power grid, as have North Korea and Cuba, for example. In that case, however, you will not be able to obtain the electrical power you need to run your home.

In addition, your situation may be complicated by the fact that you can be affected directly by your neighbors if their wiring system isn't up to the proper code. If they overload the system or have faulty wiring, the entire neighborhood could be set on fire. Each house needs to have its wiring inspected regularly to manage power flows and surges, and the power stations in turn need to manage their systems effectively to ensure that they are delivering power safely and efficiently.

So it is with the modern global financial system. In this analogy, the power stations are predominantly the financial hubs in the United States and the United Kingdom, although national financial systems act as their own generators and substations that link end users to the ultimate providers. The electricity is the huge flows of capital and liquidity now available to individuals, companies, and governments from those financial centers. The houses with modern wiring that are up to current code are those companies, investor groups, pension funds, and nations equipped with strong economic and financial fundamentals to withstand sudden power surges or outages. Those houses with poor wiring operating under outdated codes are those companies and nations at risk during these times.

Globalization and market forces can either reduce or expand possible options, but executives still have options that they can exercise to influence the direction, depth, and pace of crisis resolution in their companies and reforms within their markets. They do not, however, have options that can stop financial evolution without negatively affecting their company's economic well-being. This is especially true in countries experiencing a financial crisis. In fact, the challenges in crisis countries may be more complex, and their solution space even more severely limited.

In our judgment, therefore, executives have at least three basic options to consider as they manage a crisis.

1. **Default to the pre-crisis status quo.** First, executives can default to the pre-crisis status quo. Some companies and countries do, but this step usually means reverting to the old ways of doing business and a mostly closed financial operating system that results in a high-cost, crisis-perpetuating, low economic growth model.
2. **Muddle through.** Second, executives can simply muddle through a financial crisis with reluctant strategy, operational, and policy adjustments. They typically commit only to marginal change, tinkering with broken ways of conducting business, smoothing over the underlying core issues, making some concessions to liberalizing markets and the emergence of the global operating system architecture. If they are lucky,

they may buy time. Yet they will most likely face unresolved issues that will come back to haunt them.

3. **Capture new strategic opportunities.** Finally, CEOs and other senior managers can opt to fundamentally challenge old assumptions and rebuild their companies and economies. While there are dangers and there are threats, fresh opportunities are also created as new market realities set in over time. This third option can maximize a company's economic effectiveness by linking directly with the world's most efficient financial operating systems and securing access to capital at the lowest possible cost. In turn, sustained real economic growth should be the long-term reward.

From our perspective, the executives who want to win and secure a sustainable position in the post-crisis endgame owe it to themselves, their shareholders, and other constituencies to choose option 3, just as policymakers owe it to taxpayers to choose option 3 in the name of restarting economic growth as soon as possible and safeguarding the financial system from further crisis. The costs of options 1 and 2 are simply too high to accept.

Regardless of the preferred option, neither CEOs nor policymakers can avoid responding immediately to crisis and longer-term market forces. *Dangerous Markets* is designed to assist all senior executives to manage in a national financial crisis while preparing to compete in a global marketplace. While policymakers often are forced to take the public lead when a crisis hits, the private sector—particularly those companies and institutions that see themselves as part of the backbone of the new economic system that emerges from the crisis—has an equally important stake in managing financial crises sooner rather than later.

Initially, both companies and countries are paralyzed, then CEOs and policymakers are overwhelmed with too much to accomplish, and typically there is no road map to help them manage a crisis and rebuild. Frankly, we found ourselves scrambling initially to pull together lessons learned from other crises and our own client work in other crisis countries, and wondering if we had all the right insights for clients and if we had the right countries to compare.

Dangerous Markets is our recommendation for that road map. It is written for all managers—CEOs, executive operating managers, investors of all kinds, public officials, and anyone else who has a self-interest in anticipating, weathering, and prospering in a financial crisis. There are certain general principles and action steps that we always recommend in the early days of a crisis, such as being better prepared, understanding and managing your cash position, minimizing your operational risk, conducting scenario planning, preparing to divest unproductive assets, and maintaining the confidence of key stakeholders. Next, corporations need to be prepared to reinvent themselves and to attain a new vision building on five strategic discontinuities: changes in regulatory regimes; competitor strengths; customer needs; organizational capacity for change; and changing social values. Finally, among other things, executives need to build specific skills and drive corporate governance practices to world-class standards. This road map, however, must be tailored to meet each unique set of national challenges and opportunities. We know that there is no single magic solution for each and every company or country.

WHY WE WROTE *DANGEROUS MARKETS*

This crisis management guidebook, *Dangerous Markets,* is written from a microeconomic and practitioner's perspective. It is drawn from McKinsey & Company's extensive client work globally and our significant Firm-funded research into the causes and impact of financial crises. It is not an academic treatise, nor does it necessarily address all crisis-related topics for all occasions.

Rather, we have drawn upon our practical crisis management work for the private and public sectors in numerous countries. Our journey together began with Dominic and Greg leading McKinsey's team that served the Canadian Task Force on the Future of the Canadian Financial System in 1996 and 1997. Greg then helped a McKinsey team serving the Thai government sort through the wreckage of that country's finance companies. Dominic happened to move to Korea on the eve of the Asian financial crisis, and he, Jungkiu Choi, and Greg led our work for the crisis-born Financial Supervisory Commission. Dominic also became heavily involved in several business turnaround situations as well as engagements helping stronger companies that were determined to use the crisis as an opportunity to leapfrog their competitors.

Later, they joined other McKinsey colleagues in Singapore, where McKinsey served the Monetary Authority of Singapore (MAS) and the Financial Sector Review Group, working beside private sector participants in the quest to turn Singapore into an Asian financial center. In Indonesia they were joined by Roberto, who helped other McKinsey colleagues serve the Indonesian Bank Restructuring Agency (IBRA) reset its strategy and organizational structure after the first two unproductive years of its existence. There, too, our practice was involved in serving several major Indonesian companies during the crisis.

Financial crises were unfortunately not confined to Asia. In 1998 Greg got a call from Roberto to join him in Jamaica where multiple McKinsey teams were assisting the Ministry of Finance and the Financial Institutions Asset Corporation (FINSAC), Jamaica's bank restructuring agency and asset management corporation, to implement solutions that Roberto and others had applied first in the United States, as part of the S&L crisis, and later in Mexico. Just as the crisis was breaking in Ecuador, Roberto and Greg traveled there to a series of meetings with the former president, Jamil Mahuad, to assist Ecuador's new Agencia de Garantía de Depósitos (AGD). They also later helped other colleagues in Colombia serve the Fondo de Garantías de Instituciones Financieras (Fogafín), the Colombian bank restructuring agency, by conducting a diagnostic and bank recapitalization program before a real crisis hit there. We have also served private and public sector clients, individually and collectively, in numerous other countries.

Our roles and the timing of our involvement have varied widely. In some financial crises, we had limited involvement in the early stages at the policy level, but we were always actively involved with our private sector clients. This was the case with Ecuador and Colombia, for example. In both of these situations, we assisted with the initial diagnostic work that allowed us to observe firsthand the responses that these two countries subsequently crafted. Despite our best efforts, Ecuador's embedded problems eventually turned into a systemic financial sector crisis, and thereafter we were involved with helping to pick up the pieces with the failed banking system. In Colombia, we were pleased to see that the government acted to prevent serious damage to the banking system, and while there were still significant costs to be paid, the government's preemptive action prevented a systemic crisis.

In most cases where we have played an advisory role, our involvement came later, but still early enough that the key assignments focused on minimizing the potential costs. This was the case in Korea, Jamaica, Colombia, Indonesia, Thailand, and Mexico, where we became involved after these countries already had suffered crises engulfing a significant proportion of the banking system and assets in the real economy.

In some cases, we helped countries create new financial sector visions after intense iterative processes involving all stakeholders. We also have assisted governments in devising performance contracts and investment guidelines that have been used when selecting specific institutions (alternatively called "backbone" banks or "anchor" banks) that were targeted to be part of the new financial system. In addition, we have crafted turnaround strategies for failing banks in Asia, South America, Europe, and the United States.

Moreover, we have spent considerable energy helping create new institutional capabilities to minimize the cost of financial crisis failures, both in the private and the public sector. Specifically, these capability-building engagements included: preparing turnaround programs for troubled banks; developing "bad banks" and/or capabilities to manage nonperforming loan portfolios; defining strategies to manage and dispose of other nonbanking assets; and preparing privatization programs to dispose of both bank and nonbank corporations.

Finally, we have done extensive work helping countries develop strategies and recommendations not only to stabilize their financial economy, but also to reset new financial systems that become linked efficiently with the larger global marketplace and therefore are better equipped to sustain stable economic growth. In these cases our roles generally have been centered around: creating new supervisory capabilities to oversee the performance of banks and other financial intermediaries; preparing policy recommendations for regulatory and legal change; helping to strengthen corporate governance structures; and developing capital markets to lower the overall cost of capital and improve financial market efficiency. We have drawn most of the lessons described in subsequent chapters from this real-world experience.

In contrast to the many academic studies or official reports from international financial institutions, our goal has been to use McKinsey's top management approach and frontline experience to offer some unique perspectives, case examples, and practical solutions, and an actionable, strategic blueprint that our clients can tailor to meet their specific needs. When we were first drawn into this important work—down in the trenches beside crisis management leaders—we found that few were fully prepared, including us. There were no textbooks to pick up and read.

We learned by doing—in at least twelve countries, many with similar problems, all different. We have been teargassed and forced in some cases to travel with armed guards. We have worked through bank holidays, been swept up in street demonstrations and riots, and forced at times to evacuate our client's work site. At still other times, we were the target of labor agitation and abuse due to our role in bank or company restructuring. Every day of a crisis has been a new adventure for us, some more exciting than others.

We also found several heroes who inspired us and encouraged us as we took this journey. In Korea, Hun Jac Lee, the first chairman of the new Financial Supervisory Commission, was the right man at the right time to guide Korea's early crisis response. Y.O. and Y. S. Park, the brothers running the Doosan Group, and Jung-Tae Kim, the CEO of Kookmin Bank, were also inspirations to us. In Singapore, Deputy Prime Minister Lee Hsieng Long, the head of the MAS, had the vision to seize the opportunities that the surrounding crisis in Asia offered to the city-state to become a leading financial center in the region. Brian Quinn, the former deputy governor of the Bank of England and head of bank supervision, has been an inspiration and valuable thought-partner.

From the United States, Frank Cahouet and Keith Smith, the former CEO and CFO respectively of Mellon Bank, have leveraged their considerable U.S.-based bank turnaround talents in Korea as well, lifting the aspirations and skills of banks there. In Chapter 6, they also kindly shared their full story of Mellon Bank's successful turnaround, which they led in the late 1980s after their equally successful turnaround of Crocker National Bank in California.

Timothy Hartman, the former vice chairman and CFO of NationsBank (formerly North Carolina National Bank) in the United States also shared his insights about NCNB's novel but successful entry into lucrative new markets in crisis conditions in the late 1980s under the leadership of former CEO Hugh McColl. We also learned from Robert Lehman at FAMCO during the U.S. Resolution Trust Corporation (RTC) cleanup of the S&L mess.

We assisted Jorge Castellano, head of Fogafín, to craft plans to turn around floundering institutions in a program that worked so well that a systemic crisis was avoided. In Mexico, we partnered with Guillermo Acedo of Bancomer, building a "bad bank" that was so successful that it became a model for work that we later carried out in Argentina, Brazil, Jamaica, and Colombia. In Jamaica, Patrick Hylton, FINSAC's managing director, faced extremely difficult and at times dangerous problems in that poor, crisis-wracked country, but managed to emerge as a guiding light and true public servant.

Moreover, we have also benefited from extensive McKinsey-funded research in a project we called the Future of the Global Financial System, led by two visionary Firm directors: Lowell Bryan and Ted Hall. We learned from several McKinsey teams who analyzed various aspects of the evolving structure and trends in the global financial system. We also developed twelve in-depth crisis country case studies that served as a helpful learning device to study past and current crises.

In the final analysis, we decided to capture our journey in writing for three reasons. First, we have a responsibility to our clients to deliver high-value consulting services, and the general lessons we have learned can be transferred to the direct benefit of other noncompetitive clients that we serve in the future. Second, we have a responsibility to our Firm to codify the deep knowledge that only practical experience and expertise can bring to the table. Finally, having lived through a number of these financially devastating crises that often destroy a generation of economic growth, we truly believe that there is a moral imperative to share our best thinking with a global audience in the hopes of helping to avoid financial crises in the future and reducing the frequency, duration, and costs of future financial storms wherever they may hit.

Dangerous Markets, therefore, should be considered a road map for those companies and those countries that either elect—or are forced—to take this journey. We present a practitioner's view based on real client work at the center of financial crises in numerous countries. While we offer our thoughts from a broad, deep, and current client perspective, we recognize that we certainly do not have all the answers. The nature of financial crises makes them continuous learning experiences.

Dominic Barton   *Roberto Newell*   *Gregory Wilson*

acknowledgments

Our journey has been a tremendous team effort. Many of our colleagues at McKinsey & Company and other experts outside our firm have played a valuable role in helping to make this project a reality.

We are indebted to the leadership of McKinsey's Global Strategy Practice, which has supported our efforts along the way. Our colleagues—Horst Beck, Lowell Bryan, Dick Foster, Ken Gibson, Ted Hall, and Peter Sidebottom—provided the initial overall support from McKinsey's Future of the Global Financial System project and encouraged us onward at every stage of this multi-year project. They deserve our sincere thanks for their encouragement.

In addition to the three of us, several former and current colleagues are also primary contributors to various sections or sidebar discussions, and they, too, deserve our highest gratitude for joining us on this adventure and for being true partners in our discovery process: Maria Blanco, Jungkiu Choi, René Fernández, George Nast, Emmanuel Pitsilis, Gervase Warner, and Mark Wiedman deserve a special thank you from each of us. A special thanks as well goes to Brian Quinn, the globally respected former head of bank supervision at the Bank of England, who has worked closely with us in several countries and added his thoughtful insights to our research and client work.

We also had the benefit of expert outside comments and suggestions along the way from some of the leading economists inside and outside McKinsey during the early stages. From McKinsey, we benefited from the advice and counsel of our McKinsey Global Institute (MGI) colleague Martin Baily, currently a senior fellow at the Institute of International Economics (IIE) in Washington, D.C., and a former Chairman of the U.S. Council of Economic Advisers. We also benefited greatly from the comments and suggestions on our early research by Professor Richard Cooper, the respected economics professor at Harvard University and noted author, and Professor José Scheinkman, a highly regarded author and economics professor at Princeton University. These three distinguished economists helped push our thinking throughout our research, and we have greatly valued the opportunity to learn from them. We also learned a great deal from Patrice Thys, an executive at Interbrew, who led much of its successful international expansion, often in countries that were in crisis. We also have benefited greatly from our discussions and work with David Scott at the World Bank,

Jonathan Fiechter, formerly at the World Bank and now Senior Deputy Comptroller of the Currency for International and Economic Affairs, and Arne Berggren, formerly of the Swedish Finance Ministry, with whom we worked in Thailand and Korea. Dr. Heungsik Choe and Dr. Buhmsoo Choi, formerly of Korea's FSC, deserve our thanks for their assistance during the early days of the Korean crisis.

Other colleagues from around the world made valuable contributions based on their relevant client work and aided our analysis and understanding along the way: Luis Andrade, Rick Arney, Hugo Alfredo Baquerizo, Doug Beck, Larry Berger, Tab Bowers, Andrés Cadena, Mauricio Camargo, Michael Carpenter, Emre Deliveli, Didem Dincer, Goktekin Dincerler, Andrey Dutov, Diana Farrell, Gonzalo Fernández-Castro, Lisa Finneran, Alex Gouvea, Thomas Grant, Eliza Hammel, Cherry Hui, Aly Jeddy, Marcien Jenckes, Sanjay Kalpage, Yuko Kawamoto, Myunghee Kim, Peter Lee, Eberhard von Löhneysen, Jacqueline Luo, Antonio Martínez, Carl McCamish, Colin Meadows, Alan Morgan, Leo Puri, Jaana Remes, Daniel Reséndiz, Gonzalo Rios, Carlos Rodríguez-Porcel, Andrew Sellgren, Joydeep Sengupta, Simen Simensen, Hans-Martin Stockmeier, Katherine Switz, Charlie Taylor, Ben Tsen, Carlos Vara, Roland Villinger, and Mark Watson. We also owe a debt of gratitude to the hundreds of McKinsey associates who have been on our client service teams who have helped us in many countries in crisis.

In the final months, we were greatly assisted by two of McKinsey's truly outstanding business analysts, Sarah Fox in Washington, D.C., and Paul Lee in Seoul, who helped us get the facts right, checked all of our data, and contributed to our own thinking in our working sessions with them.

Finally, this book would not have been possible without the superb help of three outstanding individuals who excel at what they do: Susan Lund, Ph.D. in economics, a former McKinsey associate and now a *McKinsey Quarterly* editor, who has been a constant thought partner with us from the earliest days of this project; Juanita Allen, our trusted McKinsey assistant and enthusiastic supporter, who provided all of the logistical and technical support over several years and labored through multiple drafts in our collective pursuit of a high-impact book; and finally, our external editor, Erik Calonius, who has helped us to fulfill our aspirations and deliver the best book possible to our readers.

Everyone deserves our deepest gratitude and thanks for their significant individual contributions. While so many played a valuable role, the views expressed in this book are those of the authors; they do not represent the views of McKinsey & Company, Inc., or any of its partners.

CHAPTER 1

Introduction to
Dangerous Markets

On January 1, 1997, South Korean President Y.S. Kim proudly announced that the nation's economy had grown by 7.1 percent in 1996. While slightly less than the growth rate in 1995, the new numbers confirmed that this Asian tiger—the world's eleventh largest economy with such power-houses as Hyundai, Samsung, and Daewoo within its borders—was still a formidable financial contender in the global economy.

To be sure, Korea's currency was stable. It benefited from a slight budget surplus. Unemployment was only 2.5 percent. Korea's average debt rating by Moody's was A-1. Yet, on the sunny day of Kim's pronouncement few observers realized that the dark clouds of a financial storm were already looming on the horizon. There were problems in the real economy, where industry-wide value destruction—companies unable to earn their cost of capital—had been increasing since 1994. The storm clouds billowed, with weaknesses apparent in Korea's banking sector, which earned very low returns, lacked real risk management skills, and was loaded heavily with destabilizing nonperforming loans (NPLs) to the country's family-owned conglomerates, with many of the loans directed by Korea's Ministry of Finance and Economy.

By that fall, Korea had become engulfed in the throes of a full-blown financial storm. Growth slowed to 5 percent for the year, tumbling to a neg-ative 6 percent the following year. Unemployment rose to 8 percent in 1998. The banking system melted down, forcing the government to intervene, first in the merchant banks and then the commercial banks, initially costing 15 percent of its gross domestic product (GDP) to recapitalize the banking sys-tem. The Korean stock market lost half its value from one year earlier. The International Monetary Fund (IMF) and the World Bank intervened with massive funding, policy mandates, and technical assistance.

By the end of the year, thousands of union members were battling police, with tear gas wafting over parts of Seoul. Meanwhile, pickets ringed some of the shipyards, pouring yellow paint over strikebreakers as they smashed their way into work riding bulldozers. Chaos in Korea had become a fact of life.

In the end, the financial damage was tremendous. Yet, equally disturbing was the fact that the storm had arisen either unseen or ignored. No executive in either the private or the public sector had been monitoring the underlying economy sufficiently, looking for the earliest warning signs of a crisis. Nor had anyone adequately prepared the country with a strategy for survival and return to economic prosperity, the best efforts of the precrisis Presidential Financial Reform Committee notwithstanding. Instead, a devastating crisis seized control—cascading ruin from corporations, to banks, into the rest of the private sector—eventually affecting the personal fortunes of millions of people. It was a disaster that shook South Korea to its core and captured the attention of the rest of the world.

FINANCIAL STORMS ARE DESTABILIZING

Unfortunately, Korea is not alone. Throughout the world, financial storms are increasingly frequent. In the 1970s, it was the Latin American debt crisis and its impact on banks. In the early 1980s, Chile and Morocco were hit. In the late 1980s, it was the United States, in the form of the savings and loan associations (S&L) crisis. In the early 1990s, it was Sweden, Finland, Norway, and most of the transitional socialist economies. In 1994–1995, it was Venezuela, Brazil, and Mexico; in 1997, Thailand, Indonesia, and several other Asian countries were consumed. In 1998, Russia's default sent tremors that had an impact as far away as Brazil.

In 2001, Argentina's former economic minister, Domingo Cavallo, was given extraordinary powers to manage the looming financial crisis, only to be overtaken by events, as the fiscal imbalance and short-term foreign borrowings spilled over into the banking system and eventually the streets of Buenos Aires during the *corralito* (freezing of customer bank deposits) and the banking "holidays" (bank closings) in early 2002. In Japan, meanwhile, Prime Minister Junichiro Koizumi struggled to clean up Japan's sinking banks and pork barrel spending that were crippling the economy. In Turkey, Economic Minister Kemal Dervis announced a hard-fought deal with the IMF and the World Bank to institute fifteen market-oriented changes to its financial and economic system, in return for $10 billion in new loans. As we write this book, these countries and others as diverse as Indonesia, India, China, Argentina, Ecuador, Jamaica, Russia, and many parts of Africa continue to struggle with severe financial problems that in our view are destabilizing and guaranteed to increase market volatility.

Financial crises create the conditions for dangerous markets.

We also have seen the human face of crises. In Ecuador and Argentina, we have seen middle-class savers, trying to withdraw their life's savings, beating futilely on the doors of banks that have been closed for a bank holiday in the midst of a national liquidity crisis. In 2002, Argentina is experiencing a breakdown not just of its financial system, but its political institutions and social order as well. In Indonesia, we have witnessed shop owners struggling to save their businesses in the middle of Jakarta street riots, when the currency collapsed, with several successive governments rising and falling in search of effective, long-term solutions. In Korea and most recently Japan, we have seen dedicated employees bowed by the weight of layoffs and joblessness. Sadly, we have read news accounts of suicides directly tied to the very real impact of financial crises upon individual lives.

Consequently, there is an urgent need to end, or at least significantly reduce, the impact of future financial crises. In our global and increasingly interconnected world—where financial mismanagement leads rapidly to economic destruction, lost growth, and diminished national and individual wealth—there is no credible alternative to taking action. Dangerous markets can spawn financial crises, and vice versa: Both need to be either prevented or, if already in progress, managed much more effectively.

FINANCIAL CRISES CAN BE UNDERSTOOD, ANTICIPATED, MANAGED, AND PREVENTED

Conventional wisdom and the bulk of academic literature lead many executives to believe that financial crises are difficult to predict. Conventional wisdom also argues that strategies for survival are hard to pre-plan, since the reasons for these financial meltdowns are specific to a nation, its culture, and its politics. Those conclusions would lead managers to believe that the elements of a financial storm are impossible to understand, prevent, and manage until the storm actually hits.

We disagree. Based on our experience, we believe that the warning signs of trouble *are* common from nation to nation. To be sure, there are some regional and national variations. Yet, there are also common patterns of buildup and meltdown. For this reason, we also believe that financial crises can be foreseen, their magnitude can be estimated, precautionary steps can be taken to prevent crises, strategic options can be devised and implemented, and corrective measures can be taken to lessen the storm's ultimate impact. Leaders with the foresight to observe and react effectively can manage a crisis strategically *before,* as well as after, it hits.

Given the likely increasing frequency, the unacceptable socioeconomic costs, and the heightened danger of rapid global contagion from one crisis to the next, it is imperative that we take a step back and evaluate the true causes of these events and what executives can do to manage them. Only through such a systematic understanding of financial crises can solutions be found and problems managed effectively.

WHAT THIS BOOK IS AND IS NOT

Dangerous Markets is intended primarily for executives in the private and public sectors who are battling with the unique challenges posed by financial crises. While we have a point of view about why crises happen and what can be done to avoid them, this book should be especially useful for practitioners managing the day-to-day consequences of crises. Readers, consequently, will understand how to recognize crises developing and what to do to devise tactics and strategies that make it possible for companies to survive and thrive in a crisis. This book has a second purpose, which is to urge the private sector to step up and take a much more proactive role in helping to strengthen the global financial system. We provide our view on initiatives that the private sector can pursue to design standards and build safeguards that complement the measures being devised and implemented by governments and multilateral organizations.

    Dangerous Markets is intended as our contribution to the policy debate about the redesign of the global financial system architecture that also is needed desperately. Readers will note that while this book presents points of view about policy issues, its primary purpose is much more pragmatic and focused. The goal is to help those individuals charged with the responsibility for managing companies, banks, and asset management corporations to manage crises more successfully. If it is successful in making their tasks less onerous and their achievements more tangible, then it will have succeeded in its goal.

WHO NEEDS TO READ *DANGEROUS MARKETS*?

Having served both private and public sector clients on crisis-related engagements extensively over the past five years, we think there are at least five major categories of readers in both developed and emerging market economies who have a direct self-interest in reading *Dangerous Markets*: first, CEOs and senior management teams at banks, other financial institutions, nonbank corporations, and family-owned businesses; second, boards of directors; third, investors of all types, including large institutional investors, pension funds, mutual funds, and foreign direct investors such as private equity firms and corporates investing in businesses in other countries; fourth, public policy officials, including ministers of finance, central bankers, heads of bank supervisory and restructuring agencies, officials at multilateral financial institutions, and legislators who must approve changes in laws that result from the crisis; and finally, the extended policy establishment, including journalists, academics, political analysts, and other thought leaders and decision makers.

Senior Management

We believe that CEOs and their senior management teams will find *Dangerous Markets* useful from their own self-interest of saving their companies—banks and nonbank companies alike—and capturing significant strategic opportunities during a financial crisis. Executives need to understand how global forces at work in the financial markets are changing their local and international competitive landscape and affecting their cost of capital.

Managers need to know whether their own firms and the industries in which they compete are destroying shareholder value. They need to understand crisis warning signs better than most currently do and take the necessary precautions such as aggressively managing their cash position, shoring up their distribution systems, leveraging their intangible assets, shedding noncore physical assets, and enhancing needed risk management and other skills. CEOs and their senior management teams need to know how to position themselves for the post-crisis endgame and seize the strategic opportunities that arise in all crises. Often, the most urgent task for new owners is to turn around a failing bank or company, bringing in a new management team when the old one fails in a crisis situation.

Boards of Directors

Boards of directors at healthy companies, failing companies, and those in between will need to read this book. Boards of directors, including those of family-owned businesses, need to understand the same global forces at work, the same crisis warning signs, and where management needs to focus its attention. Boards can be critical preventive mechanisms to avoid crises. In the worst case, if a company destroys shareholder value and does not take adequate steps quickly to reverse the trend with a new strategy or better operational performance, then the board needs to step in to exert its authority over management on behalf of all shareholders.

Boards need to know what management's tactics should be in the early days of a crisis and what its strategy is to ensure a winning endgame position three to five years after the crisis subsides. Moreover, boards need to understand the increased value of good corporate governance and transparency to investors, regulators, and other stakeholders. Boards typically need to intensify their defense of shareholders' interests in a crisis environment.

Investors of All Kinds

There are many kinds of investors with many different investment strategies around the world, but they all need to understand many of the same things that boards of directors need to know. Most savvy investors understand the forces at work globally or locally, depending on their portfolios, but too few have a rigorous strategy in place for understanding and analyzing crisis warning signs that could ultimately lead to future losses. Many fail to see the warning signs of shareholder value destruction embedded in the real microeconomies of the countries and major sectors in which they invest.

Investors need to be able to determine whether current management teams are up to the task of executing the tough tactics demanded in the first hundred days of a crisis and whether an effective crisis and post-crisis strategy is in place that will position the company to secure a winning endgame role. Is management looking at all the right strategic opportunities to take advantage of regime-shifting events? What kinds of changes in corporate governance and accounting are underway that will enhance the value of the company? Should investors exit while they have some prospect of recovering part of their investment, or should they invest more to take full advantage of the strategic opportunities that crises present that may not have been there before?

We also believe that investors as a group have an important role to play in driving necessary changes to help strengthen the overall global financial architecture and should be much more proactive in this regard.

Public Officials

Public officials at both the national and international levels need to read *Dangerous Markets* to get a better sense of the dynamics and powerful changes that occur in the private sector when a financial storm is unleashed in their countries or their financial sphere of influence. Senior finance ministry officials, central bankers, financial regulators, heads of restructuring and workout agencies, and international civil servants at the IMF, the World Bank, the regional development banks and the International Finance Corporation (IFC), the Bank for International Settlements (BIS), the Organization for Economic and Cooperative Development (OECD), the Association of Southeast Asian Nations (ASEAN), and other international bodies need to have a deeper understanding of the drivers and potential solutions of a financial crisis at the microlevel, not just at the macrolevel where most of their attention historically has been focused.

Many public officials are often thrust into a financial crisis suddenly, without the proper skill sets or experience base to do their part to manage a crisis on behalf of the constituencies they are supposed to represent—the taxpayers around the world who typically don't have a direct voice in crisis resolution. Officials scramble for best practices and lessons learned, but there is not a lot of material available and not a lot of time to read it. Many of them reinvent the wheel each time a crisis hits.

Extended Policy Establishment

Finally, those members of a country's extended policy establishment should also be interested in *Dangerous Markets*. As thought leaders and decision makers in their own right, journalists, academics, political analysts, foreign policy experts, labor union leaders, and other interested individuals should find this book to be a useful road map as well. Their professions and lives are often directly affected by financial crises, and they have the same need to understand the warning signs, know what management teams in both the real and financial economy need to do to survive and manage in a crisis, and ultimately contribute to the dialogue about the need for better standards and safeguards to prevent future crises as the other four groups of stakeholders.

In the pages that follow, we present our views about how to *anticipate, manage,* and *prosper* in financial crises. Many of these views go against conventional wisdom. We provide CFOs and their management teams, investors, boards of directors, public officials, and the extended policy establishment with a practitioner's perspective on the means by which they—as executives caught in the swirl of a financial storm—can see warning signs and survive, execute the correct tactics, devise new competitive strategies, and embrace new standards and safeguards for their post-crisis future.

PART I: UNDERSTANDING FINANCIAL CRISES

Financial crises are occurring with increasing frequency and devastating costs, resulting in financial shocks that cause widespread corporate failures and fundamentally change both industry structures and national economies forever. Moreover, crises can destabilize the global financial system as well, and have a direct impact on people's will to support reforms leading to more open economies dependent upon the efficient functioning and integrity of markets.

In Chapter 2, "Recognizing New Global Market Realities," we begin with a review of the frequency, duration, and costs of financial crises. While it is nearly impossible to tally the total costs of financial crises over the past two decades, we know these costs have been staggering—measured in trillions, not billions, of dollars.

These gigantic costs fall into two categories. First, there are the direct, immediate costs of a crisis—which are almost always borne by taxpayers in an allocation of pain: intervening, closing, and recapitalizing failed banks; paying off depositors and sometimes other liability holders; experiencing the surge in corporate and personal bankruptcies; and funding social programs such as extended unemployment benefits and retraining programs. Second, there are the indirect opportunity costs that are even more difficult to quantify and are probably more important than the direct costs in the long run because they either can be avoided or managed to reduce their impact: asset repricing in both the financial and real economy that can take years to work through an economy; unemployment and underemployment; postponed and forgone business investments; and forgone personal savings and consumption. Regardless of their total, these costs are simply unacceptable, especially since they often can be avoided and, ultimately, better managed.

Furthermore, we believe that financial crises will continue to be more frequent, more costly, and—regrettably—longer lasting for two basic reasons. First, with the increased globalization of capital markets, there is also the increased risk of contagion, aided by the breakdown of boundaries between national financial markets and the growing linkages of the world's financial markets. Second, the long overdue market liberalization of many economies is often naively designed and then poorly managed, which in turn "plugs" countries into a global, competitive market for which they are unprepared. The trend toward more open, integrated economies shows no signs of stopping, nor should it. If the markets fail to introduce additional safety buffers or if public policy initiatives fail, then the consequences of these two factors become inevitable: more crises.

As a result, we believe that financial crises—left unanticipated and unmanaged—will continue unabated in the future and potentially will be even more damaging than in the past. We see large problems brewing in Japan, China, India, and elsewhere that could have significant geopolitical and economic consequences.

■ ■ ■

Crises result mostly from failings in the microeconomy and more specifically the failings of complex financial systems. They are typically spawned by the interaction of problems in the real economy and the banking sector, even though macroeconomic forces clearly can lead to financial crises, as they have most recently in Argentina. The earliest warning signs of impending crisis, therefore, will be found not just in macroeconomic indicators, but rather appear first as microeconomic weaknesses.

In Chapter 3, "Using Crisis Dynamics to See Growing Risks," we describe how a financial storm builds up and then breaks upon a nation's economic landscape. There are five elements that contribute to the storm: the real economy; the financial sector; the macroeconomy; international money and capital flows; and asset pricing. When these elements are in balance, the economy generally runs well, but when any of the same elements fall out of balance and affect other elements, the conditions become ripe for a financial storm.

There are several forces that can set this imbalance in motion. We believe that the most important is chronic, real sector underperformance, leading to a gradual erosion of the value of assets over time, when companies fail to earn an adequate return above their cost of capital. These dynamics can be caused by much needed but poorly executed market liberalization, where aggressive reforms are introduced that outpace the economy's ability to absorb them. Unsustainable imbalances can also build up in the financial systems of countries with the uneven opening up of the market to foreign capital flows or deregulation in the financial sector. This fact is especially true if managers lack the risk management skills to discern between good and bad loans, which leads to mounting losses in the loan portfolio and very poor returns in banks. Imbalances can also arise as a result of unsustainable macroeconomic policies, such as untenable fiscal deficits, overvalued currencies, and too rapid credit growth in the economy fueled by either foreign funding flows or unsustainable monetary policies.

Whatever the specific causes, the pattern we have seen over time starts with trouble in the real and banking sectors and then builds until either external shocks (such as the currency attacks suffered by Thailand in 1997) or internal shocks (such as the bank runs by depositors in Ecuador in 1998 or Argentina in 2001) finally trigger a full-blown crisis. Unfortunately, this pattern of cause and effect is often overlooked or ignored until it is too late. By recognizing early warning signs in the banking and real sectors and analyzing their potential impact, managers can spot financial crises before they build to value-destroying levels in their companies or their countries.

PART II: EARNING THE RIGHT TO WIN

Financial crises can be anticipated and better managed tactically in their early days, based on the learnings that we take away from our client work in both the private and public sectors. Unfortunately, many companies and countries too often respond to financial storms reactively— too late, with too few resources, and without the required skills to be effective in minimizing the direct and indirect costs of a crisis.

As we explain in Chapter 4, "Managing the First Hundred Days," executives need to play their best cards. There are five tactical measures that executives need to execute successfully in the first hundred days of a crisis. First, executives need to understand and maximize the company's cash position: Cash is their ace in the hole. Managers need to maintain liquidity at all costs. Second, managers need to identify and minimize operational risk. Since both supplies and supplier relationships typically are interrupted, often for long periods of time, executives need to make plans to manage inventories and find alternative suppliers, either locally or overseas. Third, rigorous scenario planning is required as the crisis unfolds to anticipate a range of events and then plan the optimal reaction to them. Fourth, managers also need to review the company's business performance thoroughly and be prepared to divest assets to get cash and/or because they are not part of the company's post-crisis, long-term strategy.

Finally, in the face of extreme uncertainty, bold leadership, vision, and strategy also are required to preserve and protect the most fragile crisis commodity: the confidence of employees, customers, creditors, investors, depositors, and regulators alike. As Frank Cahouet, the retired CEO and chairman of U.S.-based Mellon Financial Corporation and chief architect of its successful turnaround in the late 1980s, says: "Managers need a strategic plan and a great story to tell in any turnaround situation." Management's ability to communicate effectively with all stakeholders will help it win in the early days of a crisis.

■ ■ ■

Financial crises are periods of significant strategic opportunity for those executives and investors who fully understand regime-shifting events and their new degrees of freedom to gain a competitive advantage during a crisis. Crises are not necessarily just periods of unmitigated value destruction.

In Chapter 5, "Capturing Strategic Opportunities After the Storm," we assert that once the early days of a crisis have subsided, managers need to turn their attention quickly to setting a new strategic direction and building their institutions for the future. While many managers think that financial crises have only financial downsides and no competitive upside, we know from experience that crises represent huge opportunities for companies to gain a strategic advantage competitively as entire industries are both restructured and revalued and economies are transformed. The challenge is to identify opportunities early, and then act on them with superb execution.

Fast movers with a clear vision, a credible strategy, sound corporate governance, and access to capital can secure a winning position in a post-crisis competitive environment. In the wake of the U.S. banking and S&L crises in the late 1980s, for example, Hugh McColl, the former chairman and CEO of North Carolina National Bank (NCNB), developed a vision of nationwide banking in the United States and saw strategic opportunities to enter lucrative new markets such as Florida and Texas, which previously had been off-limits due to arcane and protectionist banking laws. The Texas banking crisis helped to break down these old laws. By working aggressively with the FDIC to buy failing banks and S&Ls in new geographies and build new business lines in asset management and loan workouts, NCNB paved the way for its national transformation to NationsBank and its eventual merger to become BankAmerica.

Hyundai purchased Kia in the early days of the Korean crisis and reached an 80 percent market share in Korea. Thanks to its aggressive post-crisis strategy, Korea's Housing and Commercial Bank (H&CB), now Kook-min Bank after their merger, increased its market capitalization from roughly $300 million in 1998 in the wake of the Korean crisis to a pre-merger value of $2.8 billion in October 2001. In February 2002, its post-merger market capitalization was approximately $12 billion. Moreover, there are plenty of other success stories to tell where management has had the foresight, courage, and execution capabilities to seize the strategic opportunities that a crisis produces.

New strategic opportunities like these are created because crises typically change the entire competitive landscape. Crises often unleash what we refer to as the "five degrees of freedom"—previously accepted boundary conditions that are literally swept away in a financial storm. These five degrees of freedom include: regulatory regimes; competitor strengths and posture; customer behavior and needs; organizational capacity for change; and social values. For example, regulations on competition and market conduct usually change. Competitive rankings change as well; it is not uncommon for a list of the top ten companies in a given industry to shift dramatically after a crisis. The behavior of customers changes, too, as they get the opportunity to sample new products and services from new providers. Society's values also can change; it took a crisis, for instance, for Koreans to begin to welcome substantial foreign direct investment.

Winners recognize that nearly everything affecting strategy can change during a crisis. To maximize the value of these five degrees of freedom, successful executives will move deliberately along several fronts. First, they set a vision for the company's future; winning executives look beyond mere survival and see opportunities in a crisis. Second, they set aggressive performance aspirations. Third, winners strike during a crisis to find unique and regime-shifting acquisition opportunities, which they then seize rapidly, transforming their companies along the way. Finally, they execute effectively and efficiently.

PART III: MANAGING UNIQUE BANKING RISKS

*Bank turnarounds demand a significant, multi-year change manage-
ment commitment and have certain universal principles that apply
regardless of country or culture. With a renewed and talented management team, banks with a franchise value can be turned around in cost-
effective ways to the long-term benefit of shareholders and competitive
positioning for the post-crisis future.*

In Chapter 6, "Driving Successful Bank Turnarounds," we explore why
bank turnarounds, which are commonly needed after a financial crisis, are
huge change management efforts, focused on the basic building blocks of
superb risk management, organizational efficiency, and operational excellence. Rather than rocket science, turnaround situations are basic nuts and
bolts exercises. Moreover, a bank turnaround is a bank turnaround, regardless of the country. There clearly may be different laws and cultural issues to
consider, but in our experience the basics are the same around the world.

Successful bank turnarounds require vision, leadership, and dogged and
disciplined execution, as we have seen in the cases of Mellon Bank in the
United States, Christiana Bank in Norway, or Banca Serfín in Mexico. The
necessary vision and leadership, however, were lacking in the case of
Ecuador's Filanbanco, which is now defunct after an unsuccessful turnaround attempt in an extremely difficult national environment.

Additionally, capital needs to be replenished and cash has to be aggressively managed to maintain needed liquidity during the critical turnaround
phase. Balance sheets must often be shrunken down and assets reduced, and
a core business focus must reign, if, of course, there is a real business there.
Failure to ask this question can lead to value destruction, both at the company level and more broadly. Depositors, investors, and creditors must be
reassured of the bank's continued improvements. Current earnings must be
jump-started and operating costs must be cut, often dramatically.

Governments, too, are usually the first ones to face the difficult issues of
bank turnarounds. Often by default, they inherit a failed bank, and immediately need to protect depositors while deciding what to do with the rest of
the bank's franchise and the NPLs that invariably have caused the bank failure in the first place.

■ ■ ■

*When credit workout programs are carefully managed and executed,
the costs of crises can be reduced significantly, as recovery rates on failing assets can be maximized, many bad loans can be salvaged, and
stronger loan portfolios can be built.*

Chapter 7, "Minimizing Costs Through NPL Recovery Excellence," describes how to do this, by setting up asset management corporations (AMCs) to manage troubled assets and aggressively launch nonperforming loan workouts. The truth is that companies do not have to wait for the government to set up a central AMC to manage bad assets for them. There is much that companies can do on their own, including setting up their own "bad" banks. In our judgment, getting this aspect of crisis management right can mean as much as a 25 to 35 percent improvement in recovery returns.

Experience has taught us that the units charged with maximizing the recovery value of troubled loan portfolios cannot perform miracles—all they can do is minimize the costs by maximizing the recovery value. Writing off all bad assets and rebuilding capital early are key success factors to put past problems behind the current management team as soon as possible, as Mellon Bank and many other U.S. banks did in the 1980s. To succeed, they require excellence in recovery capabilities. There are three critical steps that must be followed by management to be successful: diagnose and segment the NPL portfolio; develop tailored strategies for NPL recovery; and build a strong, separate organization to recover the NPLs.

For governments, there are special issues to consider such as establishing a clear mandate, ensuring the right balance of governance and oversight, and maintaining a high level of accountability and transparency. The NPL recovery experiences of Sweden and Norway are excellent case studies coming out of the financial crises in Scandinavia in the early 1990s.

PART IV: BUILDING FOR THE FUTURE

Financial crises present the private sector with a unique opportunity and a financial self-interest in resetting the basic standards and safeguards that should prevent or reduce the impact of future crises on shareholders, customers, and employees.

In Chapter 8, "Strengthening System Safeguards," we begin the final part of our book by arguing that crises in fact afford individual companies and firms with opportunities to reset their financial policy environments. Standards and safeguards can be strengthened along all three levels of a comprehensive crisis prevention safety net—self-governance; market supervision; and government regulation—which we believe is essential to protect economies from crises.[1]

The first opportunity is in corporate governance, which is a core component of the first tier of our safety net. Effective boards provide a good "check and balance" on management activities. Today, global investors demand good corporate governance. They expect disclosure, transparency, management accountability, and ultimately a strong commitment to shareholder value through sound corporate governance, and they will pay for it. Effective boards act as a first line of defense to value-destroying activities in the private sector. Our series of McKinsey surveys, in fact, reveal that investors would pay a premium of as much as 30 percent for well-governed companies in emerging markets. Moreover, our ongoing research reveals that executives in emerging markets can expect as much as a 10 to 12 percent improvement in their company's market value in exchange for improving corporate governance along multiple dimensions. As a consequence, the private sector has a real self-interest in enhancing corporate governance standards following a crisis.

Deep and efficiently functioning capital markets comprise the second tier of our crisis prevention safety net. The private sector can also influence capital market reforms, including pension fund reforms. It can help promote the strengthening of domestic capital markets, especially debt markets. A vibrant market for corporate control, one in which a company can be taken over and bought and management replaced if it fails to perform in ways that increase shareholder value, will also enhance an economy's resilience to crisis. Such reforms are necessary since well-managed companies need to raise investment capital at the lowest cost. Effective capital markets can have several benefits, including channeling funds to their most appropriate use, providing better pricing of differentiated risks and more timely repricing of financial assets, and attracting a more robust mix of investors that play important but different roles in an economy.

In this third tier, private sector leaders can also influence the direction of a new regulatory and legal landscape that emerges after a financial storm. There must be clear supervisory and examination policies and processes. There also must be well-drafted, transparent, and neutral statutes and codes for general business law, investor protections, creditor rights, and financial transactions integrity. These legislative changes and legal codes must be administered well, with adequate judicial review and other protections against abuse. Speeding up bankruptcy proceedings and resolving disputes between and among creditors and debtors more quickly are critical. Reexamining the relationship between law, regulation, and supervision is also required.

■ ■ ■

Finally, the private sector must step up collectively and play an even greater role in shaping a new, more market-based global financial architecture that will minimize and prevent future crises and lay the foundation for less dangerous markets and more sustained economic growth.

We believe that investors and intermediaries need to explore the creation of a new, market-driven financial architecture, with global standards and safeguards that are as broad in scope and ambitious as the old Bretton Woods Agreement, but which are driven primarily by the private sector.

In Chapter 9, "Designing a New, Market-Driven Financial Architecture," we come to the conclusion that private sector leaders in both developed and emerging market economies—financial market makers, fund managers, private equity investors, direct foreign investors, and intermediaries such as leading investment and commercial banks—have a self-interest in robust and resilient financial markets to deliver shareholder and customer value and a global financial system that is safer, less dangerous, more efficient, and more effective at preventing future crises.

The private sector cannot afford to stand back and wait for the existing protagonists, such as the IMF, the World Bank, or the G-7 nations, to sort out needed crisis prevention measures on their own. The costs are too high and their speed of action is too slow. Moving to a new, world financial order has to include active involvement and leadership by private sector leaders in decreasing the frequency, duration, and costs of financial storms in the future. For instance, moving under private sector leadership to a single set of prudent, fair, and systemic standards and safeguards across multiple dimensions could have an enormous impact, not only on the global financial architecture but also on entire nations and the societies they represent.

Moreover, there is much that leading companies and their senior executives can do to set their own standards of business conduct, governance, and transparency. There is nothing to stop the leading institutional investors and pension funds, for example, from significantly accelerating how they manage by, and report their compliance with, those same standards in the course of their normal business. Organizations such as the International Corporate Governance Network (ICGN), the Institute of International Finance (IIF), and the International Accounting Standards Board (IASB), among others, are making significant strides, but more action needs to be taken to make standards and safeguards more effective and more credible—with real market incentives for success and equally strong penalties for failure.

For example, what if there were universally accepted, enforceable standards to determine when banks fail, so that depositors and taxpayers could be protected more than they are today? What if there were a groundswell to strengthen local capital markets and more efficient linkages to the financial hubs to lower the cost of capital to all end users—consumers, small businesses, large corporations, and governments alike? What if the governance, transparency, and accounting standards to list on either one of the world's two financial hubs were universally accepted as the new standards enforced globally in all markets? Suppose everyone could agree on the key skills and sets of experiences that CFOs and their risk management teams must have to help manage any company? What if there were private insurance for loan portfolios to take the pressure off underfunded and poorly designed national deposit insurance schemes?

All of these ideas are not just academic questions; rather, they are ideas that need to be discussed and debated by those private sector leaders with the greatest degree of self-interest in preventing future financial crises. We believe that these same leaders can seize the moment and start to create a new, global financial architecture that promotes sustained economic growth while avoiding financial crises.

We will advance this position one step further. In our view, the process or mechanisms to ensure a more effective global financial architecture could easily include the forming of a self-governance market mechanism to determine what standards and which safeguards will guide financial market behavior and commitments to shareholders and customers.

On a global scale, a financial market self-governance organization (SGO) would go a long way from our perspective to set and monitor these standards and become a central database for information, education, and skill transfers. The agenda we recommend contains a starting point for standards in an effort to reduce the dangers and costs that financial crises impose on companies and societies alike.

■■■

Of course, there are other components of our vision to manage financial crises effectively and lessen their future impact. In the following chapters, we describe what our practical consulting experience has taught us about surviving and prospering in financial storms. These are the real world lessons that we believe will make individual companies, national financial systems, and, ultimately, the global financial order safer from financial crises, more resilient and resistant to dangerous markets, and more conducive to supporting real economic growth and development in the years ahead.

Understanding Financial Crises

CHAPTER 2

Recognizing New Global Market Realities

On September 16, 1992, financier George Soros challenged the British government to one of the highest-bidding poker games in history, betting that the British had overvalued the pound relative to the German deutsche mark and other European currencies. With an investment of $10 billion, Mr. Soros won, forcing the devaluation of the pound—and walking away with a $950 million profit.[1]

Mr. Soros is still known as "the man who broke the Bank of England," but the effect of his actions went farther than a single man and a single event. Prior to this event, the reserves of the major central banks around the world were thought to be enough to counteract any movement in currency values. Mr. Soros proved that the power and volume of daily currency trading had far outstripped the reserves of central banks. Indeed, that power shift from governments to private financial markets had occurred years before—in 1986 (Figure 2.1).

Today, as we enter the twenty-first century, we are far from the days of the Bretton Woods Agreement, when markets were stabilized by fixed exchange rates and capital mobility was strictly regulated. Since the collapse of the Berlin Wall in 1989, the combination of economic liberalization, rapidly falling communications and transportation costs, new digital technology, the adoption of global standards for business, and increased mobility of capital has swept away historic market barriers. Larger, ever more integrated global markets have replaced closed national ones, and the familiar geographically defined market and industry structures are in flux. Businesses can now build on new economies of specialization, scale, and scope, both within and across countries.

Nowhere have these changes been more dramatic than in the world's financial markets. Formerly closed, tightly controlled financial systems that were dominated by banks (and often governments) have been replaced with free-flowing capital across borders. Decisions are no longer in the hands of

FIGURE 2.1   Daily currency trading overwhelms central bank reserves.

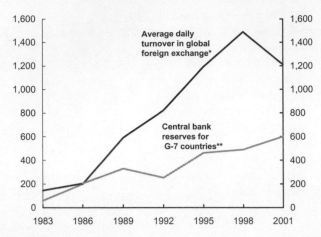

$ Billions

*Foreign exchange turnover includes spots, outright forwards, and foreign exchange swaps
**Total reserves minus gold; G-7 countries include Canada, France, Germany, Japan, Italy, UK, and US
Source: Central Bank Survey of Foreign Exchange and Derivatives Market Activity, BIS; IMF—
International Financial Statistics; literature search

the few, as the Bank of England learned, but rather in the hands of millions of individual issuers and investors, primarily large institutional investors. Markets, led often by mavericks like Mr. Soros, reward the winners and ruthlessly cull the losers. The use of financial derivatives has skyrocketed, both to hedge risk and to magnify potential gains or, inadvertently, losses. New types of financial contracts are being developed continuously to isolate and price specific risks and trade on future financial streams. Around the world, physical assets are increasingly becoming securitized and traded.

This new financial landscape has many benefits. Investors have more ways to diversify their portfolios and earn higher risk-adjusted returns. Those with the appetite can now take on many new types of risk; those without can hedge risk or sell it altogether. Cash-strapped companies can tap into a larger pool of global capital, unlimited by the paucity of financial capital in their own countries, and lower their cost of capital by doing so. Over the 1990s, the risk premium associated with both bonds and equities declined across nearly all asset types: capital was getting cheaper. Although this trend has reversed in the last few years and has perhaps overshot its equilibrium value, we believe that the long-term trend is toward cheaper capital as markets become more efficient.

More important, from our perspective, is the fact that many emerging markets have opened up their financial systems to the world of global capital.

Almost without exception, however, they have done so without the appropriate market infrastructure and standards in place. Bank supervision, accounting and governance practices, and legal protections were all insufficient to permit the efficient, stable functioning of financial markets. As a result, financial crises are now more frequent, more costly, and have more spillover effects on businesses and investors outside the crisis nation. Looking ahead, it is clear that we are now in a new era of financial instability, in which crises are an increasingly common part of the landscape. No manager—and particularly those operating in dangerous markets—can afford to dismiss or underestimate the risks.

In this chapter, we examine the empirical evidence on the frequency and cost of financial crises that have led us to our admittedly rather bleak view. We then turn to why crises are on the rise, and look at the dynamics following financial market liberalization that engendered the crises. (See Box 2.1: What Is a Financial Crisis?) In fact, we believe that there are two main reasons why financial crises occur more frequently today than in the past.

BOX 2.1: WHAT IS A FINANCIAL CRISIS?

Financial crises are admittedly difficult to define and often have no precise beginning or end. A World Bank staff report defines them as financial events that eliminate or impair a significant portion of a banking system's capital.[1] We believe, however, that crises have two fundamental dimensions: One is financial, the other is panic, which often is the trigger.

First, debilitating and massive shocks to bank liquidity, payments systems, and solvency are obvious characteristics of financial crises. Typically, there can be a crisis of liquidity and cash flows, in which depositors cannot withdraw their money and companies cannot get the credit they need to run their operations simply because banks have exhausted their cash reserves. There can also be disruptions in the payments system, in which everyday settlement and clearances of consumer and business transactions grind to a halt, become difficult to unwind, and place those expecting cash at the end of the day in the unfortunate position of being unsecured creditors overnight. There also can be a crisis of solvency if banks are forced to write off huge losses and equity capital is significantly impaired or lost. Any of these problems in an individual bank does not necessarily constitute a crisis; but it only takes a few large, failing institutions or a group of smaller ones (e.g., Thai finance companies, Korean merchant banks) to lead to a systemic panic.

(continued)

> *Second, panic strikes—a sudden and dramatic loss of depositor and investor confidence is often the precipitating event.* In Ecuador in 1998, depositor confidence quickly reached crisis proportions when banks could not meet their customers' demands for currency and the central bank reserves were depleted; customers' deposits were frozen and effectively confiscated; a week-long bank holiday ensued when people could not get their funds out of their banks. Argentina faced a similar meltdown in confidence in 2001 and 2002, with ugly street riots and public demonstrations by angry depositors swept up in that country's fiscal and currency problems that finally impaired its financial sector.
>
> When both the financial and panic dimensions collide, they set off a chain reaction and a country begins to spiral downward, as panic and the loss of confidence increases problems in the banking system as well as the real economy at the microeconomic level. Contagion between countries occurs as well.

The first is simply that more and more emerging markets are linking up with the global financial system, and many of them are doing so before ensuring that the appropriate safeguards and standards are in place (e.g., accurate accounting and transparent financial reporting, adequate risk management and asset-liability management skills, good corporate governance, adequate market regulation). In tandem, the greater liquidity of capital markets in developed countries increases the depth and reach of crises across developed and developing markets alike.

The second reason is that the large and rapidly growing global financial system is much more interconnected and closely integrated now than at any time in the past, making it more susceptible to contagion. In other words, except in cases like North Korea and Cuba, one can no longer "wall out" adverse situations in one part of the financial system.

All of this leads us to conclude that "you can run—but you cannot hide." In today's interlinked global economy, no one is safe from the destruction of financial crises. The warning signs must be recognized, and you must prepare for the storm.

INCREASING RISK OF FINANCIAL CRISES

The number of financial crises around the world has risen over the last twenty years, and even more sharply over the last ten years. During the 1980s, the World Bank counted forty-five major systemic banking crises. These are crises in which most or all of the banking system capital is wiped out.[2] In the 1990s, there were sixty-three major banking crises—an increase of more than 60 percent. Moreover, this trend has been fueled by dramatic increases in the number of crises in emerging market economies, especially in Latin America, in Asia, and in the transitional socialist countries in Eastern Europe and former Soviet bloc countries that have been moving from state-run economies to more market-oriented financial regimes.

Back in the 1980s, major financial crises were relatively rare. Latin America was hit with a string of crises stemming mostly from macroeconomic mismanagement and weak financial systems. In the United States, thousands of undercapitalized, poorly regulated savings and loans associations (S&Ls) went belly up as a result of imprudent real estate and other commercial lending problems, and ultimately had to be bailed out by taxpayers.

In the 1990s, there were major crises in every corner of the world, from Thailand and Korea, to Russia and the transition economies of Eastern Europe, to Mexico and Brazil. These banking crises, which included banking system meltdowns and major currency devaluations in industrialized countries such as Norway and Sweden, resulted in a tremendous loss of economic growth.

Conventional wisdom has it that financial crises subside in a few years; the government steps in to bail out the solvent banks and liquidate the failed ones, depositors are offered guarantees, and the IMF and World Bank may give new loans to repay creditors. Conventional wisdom also defines the direct costs of a crisis as the new costs that are being assumed, but this is not often the case. A more correct interpretation would be to think of the losses as "sunk" costs and the so-called direct costs as a transfer payment from taxpayers to depositors in a banking crisis. Using this optic, it is the political process of allocating pain between citizens in an economy that is being observed. Nonetheless, to the external observer, normalcy appears just around the corner. Eventually, the crisis headlines in the press die down, or at least move from the front page to the business section of the local newspaper. Indeed, about one-third of crises fit this description.

Yet, many more financial crises have a very long tail: More than one-half of all financial crises of the last two decades have lasted four years or more. Jamaica in 2002, for instance, is in its eighth year of financial crisis, while Indonesia is in its fifth year, both with lingering problems left unmanaged. After the 1998 financial crisis and currency devaluation, it took four years before Russian banks could again issue international bonds.[3] In countries like Japan and Indonesia, the lack of political will to resolve crises has allowed them to drag on and on. In other countries like Turkey, the same lack of political will results in recurring crises that materialize every few years. This raises other types of costs that need to be considered: costs that relate to the forgone growth of the countries afflicted by financial crisis. Since these will be new costs and can still be avoided, it is important to do everything possible to resolve the crisis expeditiously to avoid these additional costs.

Financial Storms' Costs Are Escalating

Financial crises are a staggering drain on economies because of the direct costs of bailing out the financial system and the even more important cost of lost growth, both of which need to be managed and avoided. The direct costs of a financial crisis alone—or the costs to taxpayers of guaranteeing deposits and recapitalizing the banking system—are enormous (Figure 2.2). Even the lowest costs to taxpayers are estimated at roughly 4 to 5 percent of the national GDP in Sweden and the United States. In Korea, for instance, the government has already spent $125 billion in direct costs to stabilize the financial system, equal to roughly 35 percent of GDP, according to a Bank of England study. In Mexico, the equivalent cost was approximately $75 billion or about 20 percent of GDP.

In the developing world, taxpayers' costs can rise to a range of as much as 30 to 40 percent of GDP or more in countries like Chile in 1981 or Thailand in 1997 (42 percent), and up to as much as 50 to 55 percent in Argentina in

FIGURE 2.2   Crisis costs are staggering.

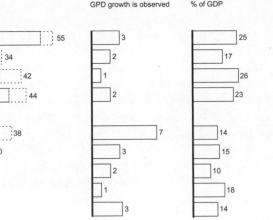

[1]Ranges represent differing estimates from two reports cited
[2]For those crises that have not yet subsided (Indonesia, Korea, Jamaica, Colombia, and Turkey) duration is calculated through 2002.
[3]Difference between average GDP's growth rate during crisis period and steady-state growth rate; economic literature suggests that in steady-state economic growth should be equivalent to population growth
Sources: Caprio, Gerard and Daniela Klingebiel, "Episodes of Systemic and Borderline Financial Crises," World Bank, October 1999. Hogarth, Glenn, Ricardo Reis, and Victoria Saporta, "Costs of Banking System Instability: Some Empirical Evidence," Bank of England, 2001; McKinsey analysis

1980 or Indonesia by 1999, when the bank recapitalization began. Bank of England research finds that over the last twenty-five years, banking crises have cost an average of 15 to 20 percent of GDP.[4]

In Asia, where many financial storm clouds are still gathering, the potential cost is staggering. A 2001 estimate by Ernst & Young puts the value of nonperforming loans in the region at about $2 trillion, an increase of about one-third in just two years.[5] The situation in individual nations is equally threatening. In China, nonperforming loans represent an estimated 44 percent of GDP; in Malaysia, 50 percent; in Indonesia and Korea, 15 percent. Japan is estimated by Ernst & Young to have at least $1 trillion in NPLs. We believe the size of the NPL problem is growing in Asia at an estimated rate of about 6 to 10 percent annually. Assuming an average recovery rate of 38 percent, which is average for the world, this will cost Asia roughly $1.2 trillion to resolve. If taxpayers bear this burden as they have in other countries, the pain of what must still be allocated is enormous.

These direct costs are bad enough, but the more important costs in our view, and the ones rarely discussed, are the costs of lost opportunities and economic growth. These are the costs that come when liquidity dries up, lending stops and deposit transactions freeze, and real assets abruptly reprice. Businesses and banks—both good and bad—fail, and both consumer demand and investment can remain depressed for years. In Korea, for example, we peg the lost growth opportunity at about 17 percent of GDP. In Mexico, it was about 10 percent, while in Sweden, we estimate it was about 5 percent.[6]

The last few years have brought us problems that continue to multiply. Now, in a globally linked economy, the crisis of one nation often becomes the crisis of another. After the Russian default in August 1998, for instance, bond yields skyrocketed in virtually every bond market in the world. As a result, Brazilian companies faced interest rates that were 1,300 basis points higher than previously. In the United States, meanwhile, start-up firms found that they could not issue bonds at *any* interest rate. In an interconnected global capital market, events in one market ripple inexorably out to others.

More Financial Storms Are Brewing

The increasing frequency and costs of financial crises are troubling enough. Yet, we also believe that more potentially big financial crises are now smoldering underground and may someday ignite.

This type of precrisis situation can burn slowly for years, with equally devastating effects on the economy. An overt crisis has not broken out— that is, bank runs are not visible, the payments system continues to function, and bank losses are contained just as inefficiencies are perpetuated—but there are signs nevertheless of financial duress that are of crisis proportions.

These signs include many insolvent banks, too rapid loan growth, and non-performing loans as a significant percentage of GDP—and subsequently constrained credit as a result. All it will take is a crisis of confidence to erupt and tip the situation into a full-fledged crisis.

Japan is an example. It has not yet had a sudden financial panic as we write this book, but that is in large part because the government has continued to prop up many large banks that would otherwise have gone under. In effect, taxpayers have continued to bail out failing banks.

The problem began in 1986 and peaked in 1989, when Japanese banks were badly hit by the collapse of the stock market and the real estate market. They were holding large portions of stock and had made numerous real estate loans that went bad. Yet, the banks and government did little to resolve the problem, refusing to restructure the financial sector and continuing to pour in new money to prop it up. With few investment alternatives, Japanese savers have not demanded their deposits. Given the lifting of blanket protection on time deposits in April 2002, however, observers should keep an eye on gold purchases. By now, there are at least an estimated $500 billion to $600 billion in nonperforming loans, and it will cost taxpayers at least 15 to 20 percent of GDP to recapitalize the banks.[7]

In 1999, the Japanese government began to take some of the steps necessary to resolve the crisis: Hokkaido Takushodu Bank failed and Long-Term Credit Bank was nationalized and then sold to a foreign private equity group—Ripplewood Partners. Several other major banks merged, but they have yet to address the bulk of NPLs.

Why don't these pre-crisis situations flare into the open like so many others? Most of these countries, like China and India, have tight control over their financial systems and depositors have no real choice about where to put their money in the current environment. Foreign competition for deposits is limited or nonexistent. Governments also implicitly guarantee the system, and many banks are considered "too big to fail." As a result, nearly insolvent banks are allowed to muddle on, ignoring their nonperforming assets. In China's case, however, this situation will begin to change as its WTO commitments phase in over the next five years starting in 2002 and new competitors are allowed in the financial system.

Crises Can Be Recurring

Other financial crises flare up periodically. Turkey has seen a repetition of currency and banking crises since 1994. A combination of uneven liberalization, large fiscal deficits, and a reliance on short-term, unhedged foreign currency loans sparked the initial 1994 crisis. The Turkish lira lost half its value in the first three months of that year, and the central bank lost more than half of its currency reserves futilely trying to defend it. The economy was plunged into recession, with GDP falling by 6 percent and inflation reaching three-digit levels. International banks withdrew more than $7 billion, adding to the liquidity crunch. The Turkish central bank and finance ministry calmed the waters with halfhearted measures, closing a few small banks and starting to bring its fiscal deficit under control. Yet, Turkey failed to address the underlying problems with both its economy and its banking system, so by 2000 it was once again faced with the ugly specter of a full-blown crisis. It is only as of this writing, in early 2002, that Turkey is starting to manage the lingering structural problems of its banking system as it moves to meet the requirements for membership in the European Union.

Like the smoldering pre-crisis situations described before, recurring crises result mainly from a lack of political resolve—and perhaps under-standing—of how to manage the situation aggressively. In nearly all cases, these countries refused to admit there was a fundamental underlying prob-lem in their banking systems. Turkey, for instance, largely papered over its problems after its 1994 crisis. As a result, all it took to spark it again in 2001 was the collapse of a single, mid-sized bank—Demirbank. Once one bank went down, investors began to worry about the health of other banks as well. Savvy observers can feel the heat and smell the smoke, even when they cannot see the flames raging out of control.

Executives in many countries consequently will be forced to manage their way through financial crises for a long time to come. Financial crises in far-flung nations can affect a company's financing, supply chain, growth plans, and overall strategy. In such a world, managers everywhere must understand clearly what causes financial crises to erupt, how to see the warning signs and then take the necessary precautions, and finally how to respond quickly and decisively once a crisis hits.

WHY FINANCIAL CRISES ARE ON THE RISE

Why are financial crises more frequent today, and with more widespread effects, than at any time since World War II? The answer is simply that financial markets have been liberated from strict government control, and poorly functioning markets, as we know, can spawn crises. This is especially true in developing countries that lack the many safeguards that ensure proper financial market functioning, such as adequate banking supervision, transparent accounting and financial reporting standards, bank resolution machinery, good bankruptcy law and shareholder protections, and vigilant investors and corporate governance structures that have the information and the authority to challenge and watch over management. In retrospect, no one now doubts that many emerging markets opened their doors prema-turely to foreign capital flows, as foreign investors looked the other way, showering these countries with money in hopes of high returns. As a result, this capital flow helped to create the problem: The "better" the macroeconomic policies, the greater the capital inflow, leading to macroeconomic laxity. At the same time, national financial markets are becoming increasingly interconnected, so a banking crisis in Thailand that no one outside the country may have noticed fifty years ago is felt keenly by thousands of foreign investors and shareholders, and foreign banks from Japan to Germany to Korea take a hit.

Financial Markets Are Entering a New Era

From after World War II until the end of the 1960s, the combination of regulation, lack of capital mobility, diverse standards, and the limits of technology created geographic barriers in the global economy and financial markets.[8] Nations strictly regulated competition between banks and other types of financial institutions, and many, such as Germany and Japan, used their financial systems to directly promote export industries and protect domestic producers and distributors. Economies operated largely within national borders, and the main form of exchange between nations was the trade of goods and the money needed to finance that trade, which grew quickly starting in the 1950s. Because central banks controlled the money supply and exchange rates, full-blown financial crises in the post-war era were almost unknown, particularly crises with repercussions on other national markets. When problems arose, they were typically limited to a single bank failing as a result of imprudent lending.

All of this began to change after the breakdown of the Bretton Woods system of fixed exchange rates in 1971–1972. At that time, the developed countries in North America, Europe, and Japan adopted a floating exchange rate system and began liberalizing their capital accounts and allowing cross-border financial investments. At the same time, they began deregulating their national financial institutions to allow more competition and new forms of financial activity. The 1970s and 1980s saw steady growth of capital flows across borders, including rapid growth of international banking credit, but it was limited mainly to the industrialized economies.

By the time the Berlin Wall fell in 1989, a new era of financial markets had begun, with the loss of national control over interest and exchange rates as well as the rapid advances in digital communications that enabled globalization. The barriers that used to define local, regional, and national financial markets began to erode. Emerging markets and transitional economies from the former Soviet bloc joined in the financial liberalization efforts and opened up their financial systems to foreign capital flows, typically with the explicit encouragement of the IMF and the World Bank. Capital flows moved swiftly all over the globe, reaching the farthest corners.

The explosion of cross-border capital flows vividly illustrates this change, as lenders and investors have sought higher returns in foreign markets. In 1980, gross annual cross-border equity and bond transactions were just $51.5 billion (Figure 2.3). By 2000, that figure had grown to $1.8 trillion—an annual compound growth rate of 20 percent. At the same time, cross-border bank lending increased from $416.5 billion to nearly $1.8 trillion as well. The number of companies issuing equity shares on foreign stock exchanges, almost all in New York and London, rose from just 242 in 1990 to over 2,070 in 2000, and the amount raised over that period grew by a factor of 20, from $16 billion to $316 billion. The international debt market, in which companies from around the world issue bonds denominated in foreign currencies, increased from roughly $800 billion in 1980 to $5.6 trillion in 2000.

Moreover, the growth and consolidation of debt, equity, bank credit, and foreign exchange markets are not haphazard. Two markets have coalesced into hubs for the financial activity of the entire world. One of these is located in New York, the other in London. Together, they account for the lion's share of the world's financial transactions, and countries' economies plug into one or the other of these two centers (Figure 2.4).

Most companies and financial intermediaries of the rest of the world's economies are faced with the decision of choosing which of these two hubs to use; there are other hubs, such as Frankfurt and Singapore, but they are much smaller. Consequently, the structure of financial markets is also gradually but inexorably setting de facto standards for financial operations

FIGURE 2.3   Cross-border capital flows expand significantly.*

$ Billions

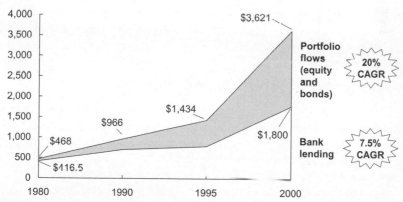

*Absolute value of capital inflows
Source: IMF—International Financial Statistics; McKinsey analysis

FIGURE 2.4   Two self-reinforcing capital market hubs have emerged.

$ Billions
Example of cross-border trading in equities, 1997

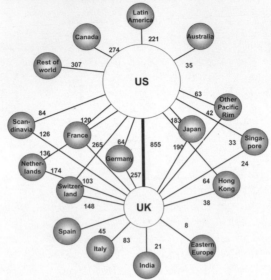

Source: IMF; McKinsey practice development

around the globe. These emergent standards define critical aspects of financial transactions, including: financial flow prices and costs; the mechanics of conflict resolution, which more and more are based on the contract law and courts of the United Kingdom and New York; financial product and service design; disclosure practices and accounting rules; listing criteria to access capital markets; corporate governance rules, and so on. The primacy of New York and London in the world's financial markets extends to other dimensions and has even contributed to the role of English as the unofficial language standard for business.

Emerging Markets Are Linking to Global Capital Markets

Beginning in the 1980s in Latin America and gaining steam over the 1990s, emerging markets began to liberalize their capital accounts and open their doors to foreign investors to access the growing flows of foreign capital. This reform set the stage for the ensuing financial crises, because these countries lacked the necessary market infrastructure and safeguards.

To make matters worse, the financial systems of emerging markets are dominated by banks rather than by equity and bond markets (Figure 2.5). In the United States, banks provide only 25 percent of the external funding used by the private sector, while equity and bond markets provide the

FIGURE 2.5 Banks still dominate domestic intermediation in emerging markets.

Composition of outstanding private sector liabilities
Percent

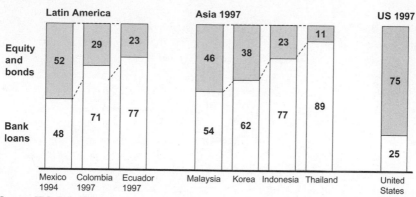

Source: IFC; BIS; IFS

remaining 75 percent. In emerging markets in Asia, Eastern Europe, and Africa and—to a lesser extent—South America, this proportion is typically reversed, with banks providing the vast majority of external funding. Capital markets are surprisingly underdeveloped in these countries, even after adjusting for differences in GDP per capita (Figure 2.6).

FIGURE 2.6 Capital market development varies across countries.

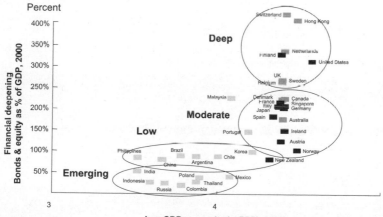

*PPP = purchasing power parity; log GDP per capita is used rather than GDP per capita as the log scale shows consistent percentage change in income, regardless of the absolute level of income
Note: The same clusters emerge when using a variety of other definitions of financial deepening
Source: WEFA; BIS; FIBV; WDI; IMF; McKinsey analysis

Capital market deepening is a function of several factors. First among these is the level of public sector debt. Other factors also weigh in, especially the impact of the legal regime governing a country's financial systems. Research done by McKinsey shows that, all else being equal, common law countries develop deeper capital markets, probably because this more practical, case-based law allows jurisprudence to grow more organically with the requirement of markets than does the law of other legal regimes. Strong and well-defined processes for conflict resolution seem also to weigh in on the development of capital markets, with deeper development occurring where these mechanisms are better defined. Finally, the legal rights of external stakeholders were also found to be key in determining the depth of financial markets. Legal environments that protect minority shareholders' rights to have a voice and creditors' rights to their investments are associated with more intermediated funding to the private sector. Ultimately, the financial deepening seems to be tied to choices that countries make regarding these issues. The choice is not without practical consequences.

From the perspective of financial system stability, banking is inherently risky. It involves taking short-term deposits but giving out both flexible and fixed-rate, longer-term loans. In many emerging markets, the problem is compounded when banks fund themselves with short-term, foreign currency borrowing and then give out long-term, domestic currency loans. In addition to a maturity mismatch between their assets and liabilities, they also face a currency mismatch. Banks' corporate customers sometimes take the currency risk to enjoy lower interest rates—and live to regret it.

Banks concentrate, rather than diversify, risk because they absorb the entire default risk of each borrower to whom they lend. Instead of the anonymous, arm's-length transactions that occur between equity and bond investors and a company, bank loans are highly individualized transactions between a single bank (or small group, in the case of syndicated lending) and a borrower. This opens the door to potential conflicts of interest in lending—violations of loan-to-one-borrower and affiliate lending rules—and relies heavily on the risk assessment skills of the institution. In the 1980s, the structure of the global financial system changed by virtue of the incorporation of the underdeveloped and vulnerable financial systems of emerging economies. The danger was reciprocal: Emerging markets were suddenly faced with the challenge of managing the powerful energy transmitted by the world's financial hubs and the developed markets' financial systems had to reciprocate and smooth the effect of the increased volatility of this action.

Hot Bank Lending Contributes to Volatility

Volatile global capital flows like the ones in Thailand are often blamed for "causing" financial crises. Based on our research, this view is simplistic, and ignores the true causes of financial crises, as we explain in Chapter 3.

Still, there is no doubt that global capital has been highly volatile and has been one factor contributing to many financial crises. Surprisingly, foreign bank lending historically has been more volatile than cross-border investments in equity and bond markets.[9] The five Asian crisis countries, for example, received $47.8 billion in foreign bank loans in 1996. This inflow turned into a $29.9 billion *outflow* after the crisis began in 1997, a turn-around of more than $75 billion. Inflows into local equity and bond markets fell by half, but remained positive. A year later in Russia, foreign bank lending again proved to be the money that most quickly fled the country. During the late 1990s, annual swings in the total amount of foreign bank lending—and thus higher volatility—were far larger than the swings in either portfolio bond or equity flows (Figure 2.7). Volatility was actually greater in the developed markets than in the emerging markets.

These private capital outflows did have significant impacts on crisis countries. They put downward pressure on local currencies—although in Asia in 1997 at least as much currency pressure came from local investors and companies—and contributed to a liquidity crisis.

FIGURE 2.7   More volatile bank lending applies worldwide.

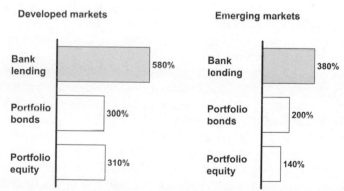

Volatility* of annual capital flows, 1996-2000

Developed markets		Emerging markets	
Bank lending	580%	Bank londing	380%
Portfolio bonds	300%	Portfolio bonds	200%
Portfolio equity	310%	Portfolio equity	140%

*Measured by the coefficient of variation (standard deviation divided by average size of flows for each country). Figure reported is the average for 75 countries. Excludes outliers, which occur when capital flows to a country average out to near zero for the period. Outliers are Finland for bank lending, and Iceland and Singapore for portfolio bonds. Results normalized against the average standard deviation of 1991–95 equity flows.
Source: IMF—International Financial Statistics, 2001; McKinsey analysis

Why is foreign bank lending so volatile? Many people assume that all bank loans are long-term, project-based finance that by definition cannot be withdrawn abruptly. While this may have been true in the past, it is decidedly untrue now. Today, international bank lending is often in the form of short-term, interbank loans. At the end of 1997, after the Asian crisis had begun, more than 55 percent of cross-border bank loans worldwide had maturities of less than one year. In Thailand, two-thirds of loans had maturities of less than one year, and the vast majority of foreign bank lending went to banks and finance companies.

Short-term loans are advantageous to banks because when trouble brews, they simply refuse to rollover these loans and cut lines of credit. Because bank loans are illiquid, fixed-margin assets, they adjust to changing economic conditions through quantity rather than price. A bank that is closely monitoring its loan portfolio can avoid a default if it believes a borrower is in trouble by simply cutting lending.

Bonds and equities, in contrast, adjust to changing market conditions primarily through price rather than quantity. Losses are realized immediately, so an investor cannot avoid losses by selling. Rather, investors have an incentive to hold on to the investment and wait for prices to rise. Banks, however, each have an incentive to be first out the door, and this incentive to act in unison amplifies volatility.

Ironically, the global banks in the worst shape had the greatest incentive to lend to emerging markets, to reap potentially high returns. Faced with a mountain of bad debt at home and very low returns overall, Japanese banks became the largest lenders to Thailand and the rest of Southeast Asia. By June 1997, they had extended $97.2 billion in loans to the region, while U.S. banks had extended only $23.8 billion. Large French and German banks, prompted by stagnant domestic markets and nimble, smaller bank competitors, also became prominent lenders to the region.

For a time, emerging market lending was highly profitable for the banks. Japanese banks could raise funds in the interbank market and then lend to East Asian and other banks at a spread of 150 to 200 basis points, assuming currencies did not move too much, and would make a substantial running profit. Their difficulties at home, however, made them highly sensitive to potential losses, prompting the massive withdrawal of credit to the region at the start of the crisis. Of the roughly $17.5 billion decline in lending to Southeast Asia between June and December of 1997, $10.5 billion in loans was withdrawn by Japanese banks, which grew more cautious at rolling over short-term Eurodollar advances to Southeast Asian borrowers.

Far from being the staid institutions of days past, banks today are at the forefront of driving the hot money in the financial system. When a country like Thailand faces a sudden capital outflow of $8.1 billion in just three months, its already precarious local financial institutions are going to crumble, causing widespread bank and business failures.

Banks, however, are not alone in their potential power to destabilize emerging markets. Institutional investors—asset managers from mutual funds, pension funds, and insurance companies, and traders from investment banks and hedge funds—also wield enormous clout. Together, they controlled nearly $35 trillion in assets as of 2001. Certainly, only a tiny fraction of this goes into emerging markets in any given year; foreign net investments in all emerging markets were just $135 billion in 2001.[10] Still, these flows are large compared to the size of many individual emerging market financial systems.

Although emerging market investing is currently somewhat out of vogue—capital flows to developing countries peaked in the period 1995 to 1997 at twice the level of 2001—it undoubtedly will return again. In part, this is simply due to the demographic shift that requires saving for retirement, and the inexorable search for higher returns among investors, particularly in the more developed countries. Moreover, in coming decades a significant portion of the world's economic growth is projected to come from emerging markets. Together, the actions of institutional investors could thus easily create enormous volatility, especially in small emerging financial markets.

Systemic Risk Potential Has Increased

Other sources of financial market instability today are the growing linkages between the large banks and other financial intermediaries, in the form of repurchase agreements and loan guarantees. Even as recently as the U.S. S&L crisis of the late 1980s, thousands of individual S&Ls and banks could fail without threatening to bring down other institutions or cause a wide spread systemic failure. Today that is no longer the case, and the failure of one player can lead to devastating losses for others.

Consider what happened to Long-Term Capital Management (LTCM) after the 1998 Russian crisis. After enjoying years of spectacular returns (over 40 percent in 1995 and 1996), its hedge fund grew to $4.8 billion in capital, including $1.9 billion from the fund's sixteen partners. LTCM used these assets as collateral to borrow from banks to increase the size of the market bets it was making, and by the summer of 1998 it had an estimated $100 billion of financial trades on its books. After Russia defaulted, bond yields in many markets defied historic patterns. In particular, the spread between various maturities of U.S. Treasury bonds widened to unprecedented levels. LTCM had highly leveraged bets (on the order of 20:1) placed in many markets, particularly U.S. Treasuries. As losses started to mount, they found themselves short of cash to meet margin calls and faced with the possibility of unwinding many of their positions at huge losses.

Who were the major lenders and investors in LTCM that stood to lose dramatically if LTCM was forced to start selling? Among others, they were the major global investment banks, many of whom themselves were reeling from large losses in Russia. They feared that if LTCM started unwinding a large number of trades, it would further depress a wide array of asset markets. So a group of Federal Reserve officials and fourteen Wall Street bank managers got together to discuss a solution, and subsequently the banks devised a private sector solution to aid LTCM with more capital in return for a controlling stake in the fund. At the end of the day, LTCM lost $4.4 billion of investors' money: $1.6 billion from its own partners; $700 million from Union Bank of Switzerland; and $2.1 billion from other investors, including major New York and European banks.[11]

The LTCM debacle was resolved in an orderly manner with a private sector solution, at no taxpayer expense. Private investors acted together to avoid a worse outcome for all involved, and in many ways the market functioned exactly as it should have. In another respect, however, the world had once again changed forever: With increasingly complex linkages between markets and big players, the failure of a single large player now poses potential systemic risks to other players far beyond itself.

The recent bankruptcy of Enron has had similar repercussions far beyond its direct shareholders and employees. The Dow was hit significantly, losing over 400 points in a two-day period following the bankruptcy, as the market reflected concerns about other companies having transparency issues. More than $33 billion in market capitalization was lost in these two days. This jolt in turn led to repercussions on many local exchanges around the world, including Seoul, Hong Kong, Singapore, and others.

In an increasingly interconnected global financial system, what happens to one player in one country can create shockwaves that travel the world. Some shocks will result in systemic crises; others will not. Following the LTCM example, both market players and supervisory officials will have to work hand in hand in the future to contain isolated events and prevent systemic breakdowns.

YOU CAN RUN, BUT YOU CAN'T HIDE FROM CRISES

A financial crisis that occurs far away may give senior managers a false sense of security; after all, the crisis happened in another country. Yet, one of the stark realities of a rapidly globalizing world is that you can run, but you cannot hide. When a financial crisis hits one country, it can complicate business strategy, operations, and financial results for companies around the world—even those without operations in the crisis country.

Consider the aftermath of the Russian crisis. In August 1998, the Russian government unilaterally restructured payments on its Gosudarstvennye

Kaznacheyskie Obiazatelstva (GKO) bonds, essentially going into default. This move spread panic in bond markets throughout the world, as investors who faced big losses in Russia sought to dump other risky investments. Interest rates in all types of bonds—emerging market bonds, corporate bonds, government bonds—jumped in response (Figure 2.8). Rates on emerging market index bonds jumped by more than 500 basis points. Prior to the Russian default, Brazil for example paid roughly 6 percent on its government bonds. Just after the crisis, however, that yield soared to more than 18 percent. Even some issues of the venerable U.S. Treasury bond—which is widely considered the safest bond in the world—saw demand dry up.

Price volatility after the Russian default spilled over into corporate bond markets as well. Companies with lower credit ratings saw their interest rates soar by 500 basis points or more. For many borrowers, credit was unavailable at any price. New emerging market bond issues fell from $17 billion for the month of April 1998, four months before the crisis, to less than $0.5 billion in August 1998, the month of the Russian default.[12] U.S. corporate high-yield bond issues fell by more than half, from $54.3 billion to $17.6 billion. Companies and borrowers of all stripes—whether or not they had anything to do with Russia itself—saw their cost of debt skyrocket. Stock markets were affected too, as investors shied away from risk.

Although earlier financial crises caused some repricing of risk outside the crisis country, the size and breadth of the market response to the Russian crisis are new phenomena. The Mexican crisis in 1994–1995, for example,

FIGURE 2.8 Risk spreads increase globally after Russian default.

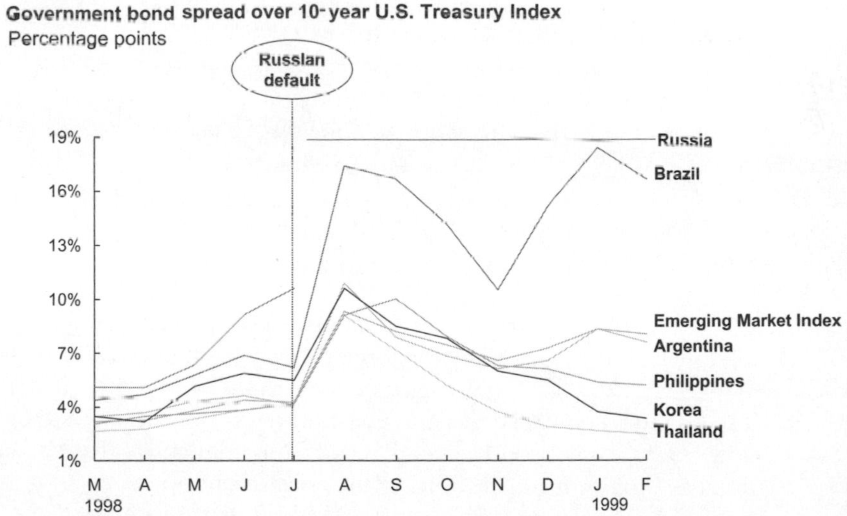

Government bond spread over 10-year U.S. Treasury Index
Percentage points

Source: IMF; Bloomberg; McKinsey analysis

caused a repricing of risk only within Latin America. Other emerging markets, such as those in Asia, were not affected. The Asian crisis of 1997 caused more widespread repricing of risk, but its effect was still limited to emerging market borrowers. Neither developed country government debt nor corporate debt was affected.

What was different about the Russian crisis that caused such widespread ripple effects? The answer has little to do with Russia, and everything to do with how international financial markets operate. In extremely risky investments like Russian GKOs, there were relatively few investors interested. Pension funds, for instance, are typically restricted from holding much in noninvestment-grade assets. When there are only a few large investors, their actions can more easily reinforce one another and have repercussions in markets around the world. What happened in the aftermath of the Russian crisis was not an anomaly and could well happen again.

Consider a hedge fund that had bought Russian bonds and used them as collateral to borrow funds to invest in mortgage-backed securities. After the Russian default, the value of its collateral fell and its bank would have called for more cash to be put into its margin account. The hedge fund might have unwound some of the mortgage-backed securities trades, depressing prices in that market. That act alone may not have been enough. So it would have unloaded other securities it was holding, lowering prices in those markets as well. This is exactly what would have happened, until investors with no connection to Russia suddenly discovered that the price of their investments was plunging.

Clearly, the opportunity cost of lost growth from a financial crisis is higher in a world in which distant markets can be affected.

Companies can also be exposed increasingly to crisis risk through the impact on their operations abroad. A financial crisis that puts one player out of business can have serious repercussions across the value chain to suppliers and customers around the world. Daewoo, for example, was a major car producer in Poland. When Daewoo went bankrupt after the Korean crisis began, it hit Polish workers and managers hard—so hard, in fact, that one of Daewoo's Polish subsidiaries, DMP, filed for bankruptcy in September 2001, and the other, FSO, is still facing financial difficulties in 2002.

Daewoo's bankruptcy illustrates another hard truth about globalization: Bankruptcy workouts—and resolution of financial crises—become far more complex. Daewoo had over 240 banks and major creditors from over ten different countries involved in the workout negotiations—and many had different sets of bankruptcy law. Sorting out the repayment of Argentina's massive $150 billion default, on the other hand, will entail potentially even more creditors, although most of its bonds were written under New York law, which will simplify matters. In past crises, such as the U.S. S&L crisis or the Swedish crisis, most of the participants in workouts were from the affected country and just one set of laws applied. In the patchwork global capital market of today, no such set of uniform standards exists. We believe this is a critical issue, which we address in Chapters 8 and 9.

Consider the fallout from the latest financial crisis in Turkey. Beginning in November 2000, there has been a growing crisis of confidence in the Turkish financial system after the failure of Demirbank—the ninth largest private bank in Turkey—sparked fears of a more widespread, and undeclared, nonperforming loan problem. As the Economist Intelligence Unit reported in 2000: "As in the Japanese banking sector, there is a great fear of revealing the true extent of the rot. There are rumors of up to twenty more banks in serious trouble."[13] Over the next year, bank failures continued, the lira plunged to a new low against the dollar, while inflation climbed to three-digit levels. Yet, companies halfway around the globe were affected. Procter & Gamble in Cincinnati, Ohio, was forced to issue a profit warning and watch its stock price fall 5.2 percent in one day (Turkey was P&G's twelfth largest market). Akso Nobel, the large Dutch pharmaceutical and chemical company, watched its first quarter 2001 earnings drop by 11 percent.

In a globalizing world, no one is immune to financial crises, and events in one corner of the world have far-reaching effects. Thus, strong ripples in the private sector are transmitted throughout the entire global economy. As we write this book, most financial observers and many managers on the front lines are worried about events not only in diverse countries such as Turkey and Japan, but also China, which agreed in 2001 to liberalize its financial system and economy as a condition of its World Trade Organization (WTO) membership. Moreover, you do not have to be in the front lines to be at risk; even a company's retirement plans (e.g., 401(k) retirement plans in the United States) are likely to be affected by financial crises overseas.

LOOKING AHEAD

Going forward, we believe that crises will continue on at least at their current pace. Many of the world's emerging market financial systems are still young and fragile, lacking the regulation, standards, transparency, and depth needed to ensure stability. As these countries plug into the system, volatility and crises will be nearly unavoidable. Furthermore, major bankruptcies and accounting fraud in more developed markets also will have significant repercussions in other markets.

Financial crises, therefore, are going to be part of the business landscape for the foreseeable future, and executives need to understand that volatility is likely to increase in the near term as a result. The first step is understanding in more detail why crises occur and how executives can spot the warning signs, which are the subjects of Chapter 3.

CHAPTER 3

Using Crisis Dynamics to See Growing Risks

Just before dawn on July 2, 1997, Bangkok's top bankers were awakened and summoned to a 6:30 A.M. meeting at a low-rise building facing Bankhumpron Palace, as the ornate Bank of Thailand headquarters is known. As the group gathered nervously, they were informed that after months of resistance, the government was abandoning the Thai baht's peg to the U.S. dollar. When the markets opened a few hours later, panic ensued. The baht dropped 15 percent against the U.S. dollar, signaling an economic crisis that soon swept across Thailand and the rest of Asia, with repercussions felt around the world.

For all the drama behind the unraveling of Thailand's economy, however, the elements of the storm had been building quietly for years. An early sign of a crisis brewing was the mid-1996 collapse of the Bangkok Bank of Commerce. The failure of the bank exposed years of highly questionable banking practices. Then, Somprasong Land, a company that had turned thousands of acres of swampland into suburban housing, became the first real estate company to default on its international bonds.[1] Other scandals and failures followed. Before long, foreign bankers began calling in their loans. Hedge funds and other investors, sensing weakness in the economy, began selling the baht short. Thai companies, fearing that the currency was on the brink of devaluation, started dumping the baht for dollars. The baht's drop occurred shortly thereafter.

Neither Standard & Poor's nor Moody's predicted the severity of the Thai financial storm.[2] Even the IMF, on the eve of the crisis in the summer of 1997, praised Thailand's "remarkable economic performance" and "consistent record of sound macroeconomic performance."[3] By the fall of 1997, of course, its cheery predictions were left twisting in the wind. Seasoned observers—whose task it is to identify problems before they boil over into crisis—all missed the signs of trouble in Thailand. They had also missed them elsewhere, as can be seen, for example, in Mexico's 1994–1995 financial crisis (Figure 3.1).[4]

How could the experts have been so wrong? How could they not have seen the financial storm approaching? We believe it is because most experts doggedly followed conventional wisdom, which told them to watch the government's choice of exchange rates and the management of fiscal and monetary aggregates to sense the approach of a crisis.

To be sure, macroeconomics matters, as the crisis unfolding in Argentina in 2002 demonstrates beyond any doubt: Argentina's crisis in 2001–2002 was set in motion by an unsustainable fiscal situation which led to the government's default on $141 billion in debt, a significant devaluation of the peso when the link to the dollar was eliminated, and a freeze on deposits, all of which triggered the banking crisis. Yet, based on our research, we believe that most of the warning signs of financial storms lie in *microeconomic* conditions, which we believe presage the arrival of financial crises long before they have built up into cataclysmic events.[5] For this reason, we assert that monitoring the microeconomic conditions—with relatively simple metrics—in addition to tracking macroeconomic indicators will not only help one track the probable course of a crisis, but also indicate *where* it will strike, and even roughly *when* it may strike.

FIGURE 3.1 Rating agencies were surprised by the Mexico crisis.

Interest rate spread of Mexican bonds over U.S. Treasuries

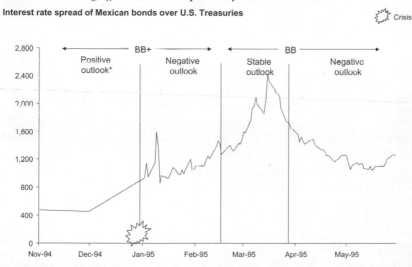

*Ratings outlook assesses the potential direction of the credit rating over the intermediate to longer term; it takes into consideration any changes in the economic and/or fundamental business conditions of the country.

Source: Standard & Poor's

In the rest of this chapter, therefore, we take a look at these microeconomic conditions as well as the macroeconomic conditions that contribute to a financial crisis. We first describe the chronology of a crisis, and then take a closer look at the dynamics involved. Finally, we describe the elements of the economic system that are often crisis triggers, starting with the real economy, followed by the financial sector, and ending with the macroeconomic and external catalysts.

THE CHRONOLOGY OF A CRISIS

There is a pattern in the unfolding of most crises. Most financial crises begin with weakness in the real sector, specifically in the inability of businesses to sustain efficient and profitable performance. This is often due to the closed nature of the economy, in which directed lending, the lack of real competition, and poor corporate governance are tolerated, often over a long period of time. It can also happen in mature economies in individual sectors (e.g., the U.S. savings and loan crisis of the mid-1980s). These structural weaknesses are often revealed when the government attempts to integrate the country into the global economy in one bold stroke. It is often too much, too soon.

Next, misguided lending fans the flames. In all the crises we have seen, financial institutions not only continued their lending to these increasingly unstable corporate entities, but *increased* their lending to them—sometimes dramatically. We have also seen them move away from their areas of expertise into high-risk corporate and consumer lending. Poor banking skills are at the heart of most of these missteps, but they are exacerbated by questionably close relationships between the banks and their debtors, pressure by the government to lend money to facilitate economic development, and the lack of caution that comes when deregulation and a wave of foreign capital wash into the economy. All of these actions lead to a rapid and unsustainable buildup in bad loans.

In this stage of the crisis, the regulatory system—which should prevent such problems—either fails completely or is inadequate to correct the problems. The regulators are civil servants who frequently lack the skills to manage a booming economy—let alone the power to face off against the financial institutions, which may be arbitraging the regulations and hiding the true extent of their problems.

The final stage comes when macroeconomic policies and exogenous shocks set off the crisis. Macroeconomic policies—mostly those setting exchange rates and fiscal policies—often determine the timing and magnitude of the crisis. External shocks, meanwhile, serve as crisis triggers. In some cases they are exogenous (as in El Niño's effect on the Ecuadorian economy) and in others they are internal (as in the rapid loss of depositor confidence in Argentina after years of economic mismanagement).

With this pattern in mind, any financial crisis becomes easier to understand.

In the Thai crisis, for instance, as early as 1992 the real sector was already underperforming. Momentum leading to the crisis built up when Thailand liberalized its financial system in an effort to give domestic investors access to offshore funds. In doing so, the government made the momentous mistake of keeping the baht pegged to the U.S. dollar, which in turn encouraged foreign bankers to flood the country with short-term credit, which overheated the Thai economy. With seemingly little risk of devaluation, Thai financial institutions borrowed freely and imprudently in dollars to make baht loans without hedging the currency mismatch.

Many of these loans went into real estate deals, another very common feature of bubbles, leading to eventual collapse and subsequent crisis. Soon, property values were rising rapidly. The Thai financial institutions, loosely regulated and lacking the necessary credit skills, accepted inflated property values as the basis for new loans. The stock market was also spiraling upward, fed by foreign and domestic investors who ignored clear signs that the corporations were in trouble.

Confidence in the Thai economy, however, was quietly eroding. In the spring of 1997, investors began to pull out their money. That act was followed by a run on the banks that depleted the central bank currency reserves. When the government floated the baht in July, the storm hit for real. Finance companies—which sometimes had as much as 60 percent of their assets in nonperforming loans—toppled. Businesses collapsed and Thailand's economy lay in ruins.

Thailand's story is not unique. In one crisis after another, we have found a similar pattern of gradual buildup in the corporate and banking sectors, followed by a triggering event in the macroeconomy.

In Mexico's crisis, for instance, the banking system was also fueled by excess liquidity. That in turn encouraged the banks to lend generously to the private sector. But at the same time that the corporate sectors were being fed by the credit boom, they were simultaneously suffering from a flood of imports, leading to performance problems long before the crisis. (See Box 3.1: Mexico: Dynamics of a Crisis.)

This, paradoxically, was caused by government policies that began in 1989 when much of the economy was privatized and liberalized, followed a few years later by the NAFTA trade pact with Canada and the United States. These changes were all necessary and caused confidence in the Mexican economy to rise dramatically. They also encouraged the foreign lending boom that eventually led to the overvaluation of the Mexican peso. Like Thailand, Mexico's government did not see the imbalances building in its economy, and was blindsided by the crisis that hit at the end of 1994.

BOX 3.1: MEXICO: DYNAMICS OF A CRISIS

In 1989, Mexico began an economic reform program that culminated in the signing of the North American Free Trade Agreement (NAFTA) in late 1993. As part of that program, the financial sector was liberalized and opened to foreign competition, and eighteen state-owned banks were privatized. The new bank owners, many of them inexperienced, paid a high price: 202 percent of book value on average. (U.S. banks were selling then for 120 percent of book value.) The new owners sought to recoup their investment through rapid expansion.

At the same time, the banks found themselves awash in funds—thanks to the elimination of reserve requirements, an increase in deposits (in part prompted by the confidence the reforms inspired), loose monetary policy, and foreign borrowing. As restrictions were lifted, the Mexican banks' foreign borrowing, partly encouraged by the country's pegged exchange rate, actually trebled. A significant proportion of foreign loans were coming due in 1995 and denominated in dollars, leaving the banks vulnerable to changes in the exchange rate or in the opinion of foreign investors.

Banks, in turn, made some loans to Mexican companies in dollars, apparently reducing the banks' foreign currency exposure. But many borrowers didn't have dollar revenues, thus creating a significant credit risk for these banks. Not surprisingly, a lending boom ensued: Domestic lending as a percentage of the gross domestic product grew from 16 percent in 1989 to 39 percent in 1994.

As credit expanded, the balance of the banks' loan portfolios shifted away from traditionally safe borrowers—notably the government and large corporations. Budget surpluses caused the government's share of borrowing to shrink to 3 percent from 30 percent, while large corporations turned to newly available bonds, equities, and foreign loans. Banks filled the void by lending to lower-rated corporations, small businesses, and consumers, but didn't have the credit analysis skills required to screen them. Bank regulators failed to monitor the risks arising from these new types of lending.

Fundamental shifts in the economy caused a further deterioration of loan portfolios. Positive economic growth rates hid the fact that many Mexican companies, faced with new competition, were in trouble and failing to earn their cost of capital. Yet lending to them continued. On the eve of the crisis in 1994, had Mexican banks valued their portfolios at market prices, they would have registered at least $25 billion in loan losses—equivalent to 5 percent of the GDP and enough to wipe out all the equity in the banking system.

The crisis erupted in 1994, when political instability and rising U.S. interest rates eroded investor confidence in Mexico, breaking the pegged exchange rate.

Mexico also held an election in 1994, and it was not a good year: During the campaign, one of the leading candidates was assassinated, and in an unrelated incident a rebellion broke out in Mexico's Chiapas region, thus undermining investors' confidence. Interest rates and foreign debt repayments soared while credit dried up and many companies went bankrupt.

Sweden offers a similar pattern. From a history of tight bank regulation, the Swedish financial sector was deregulated in 1985. The removal of lending restrictions triggered aggressive lending by foreign and domestic banks, much of it going directly into real estate.[6] Before long, property values were soaring. In 1989, Sweden liberalized its capital restrictions and citizens were allowed to invest in assets abroad.[7] Many bought property outside the country, borrowing in foreign currencies with lower interest rates.

Against this mounting problem, the Swedish economy was being eroded by a growing trade deficit, partially fueled by real exchange rate appreciation. In addition, the government's policy of pegging the exchange rate encouraged creditors to take unhedged loans in foreign funds. Because the pegged currency masked the true exchange rate risk, borrowers obtained what appeared to be "cheap" foreign currency loans with little thought that the krona would ever depreciate.

It took just a few swift measures by the Swedish government to make the storm clouds coalesce: In 1992, in an attempt to protect the exchange rate in the face of international turmoil, the government imposed a new tax system and introduced a more restrictive monetary policy. The new tax system favored saving rather than borrowing, thereby reducing interest payment deductibility. These measures led to a sharp decrease in inflation and large after-tax increases in real interest rates. As a result of this, the real estate market plummeted, and that, in turn, resulted in a flood of nonperforming loans. By the early weeks of 1993, the krona had lost 25 percent of its value, and foreign capital was fleeing Sweden for safer havens.[8]

In these examples and others, we see two important benefits from having a better understanding of crisis dynamics and what causes financial storms. First, by understanding the fundamental causes of financial storms, we hope that their sudden impact, high cost, and prolonged duration can be minimized. Second, by recognizing that the seeds of a financial storm grow first and foremost in the real and banking sectors, we hope that executives can see the warning signs of a storm early—in time to make informed decisions that help to shelter their companies from the fury of the storm.

In Appendix 3.1: Ten Warning Signs of a Financial Crisis, we summarize ten warning signs that we believe serve as a barometer of crisis buildup and, if faithfully reviewed, can help executives prepare for financial storms. In addition to these warning signs, being part of the informal "inner circle" can help executives gather useful crisis-related information as well. (See Box 3.2: A Dinner Party for Eight.)

BOX 3.2: A DINNER PARTY FOR EIGHT

"I Heard It Through The Grapevine" is not just a classic rock hit, it's also how some of the best-informed people in financial markets complement the information readily available from other sources. In one crisis after another, we have found that the "inner circle" recognized the coming of a financial storm and made their moves in advance of the rest of the market. Just knowing that a bank's loan portfolio is far worse than it acknowledges, for instance, is a critical piece of information. Or that the foreign borrowing of a major bank has just been cut off. That news indicates that the foreign market is getting the jitters about the economy.

It may be hard for an outsider to get into the inner circle, but anyone serious about avoiding financial storms should make an attempt. For this reason, we suggest hosting as many dinner parties as possible and inviting the "right" people, those who—with a wink or a nod—may confirm that a formerly friendly market is becoming a dangerous one. The guests might include:

1. **Knowledgeable local banker,** from a leading local bank, preferably one with a deep understanding of the corporate sector and the local money market
2. **Foreign commercial banker,** preferably one involved in corporate and/or institutional banking with knowledge of the interbank market
3. **Economist working for the central bank,** preferably one involved in foreign exchange operations or local money market activity
4. **Independent economist,** who tracks the local economy, preferably one affiliated with no party, or with the opposition party

5. **Local correspondent** with *The Financial Times, The Economist,* or *The Wall Street Journal,* who is preparing an article on the state of the economy
6. **Independent political analyst,** generally a professor or political scientist, who understands the ins and outs of the current political system
7. **Member of the opposition party,** who understands the state of the economy and what leaders of the opposition think of the current situation
8. **Prominent local businessperson,** who knows the corporate sector well enough to interpret how key sectors will fare in the event of a sudden disruption in economic activity.

Ask them what they think of the current situation and then—listen! Is there a crisis brewing? Are key corporations in good shape? Are their balance sheets robust? If there were a crisis, would it engulf all the banks, or just some? Does the government have a plan for action? Are they satisfied with the quality of the leadership team that would address the problem were it to materialize? Will the IMF, the United States government, and other critically important governments support the economy over a rough spot?

A dividend that you might earn: In return, one of them might invite you to dinner.

THE DYNAMICS OF A FINANCIAL CRISIS

In the preceding section, we described a chronology that paints the broad strokes of financial crises. Financial crises, however, are complex events, and to understand them you must disaggregate their complexity into manageable parts. Faced with this, we ultimately developed a dynamic representation of the economy consisting of five loops. Each loop corresponds to a part of the economy, and each must be operating in a sustainable way while simultaneously interacting with the others in a delicate balance for the economy to continue to grow. Otherwise, it could collapse. These dynamic loops are: the real economy (corporate) sector; financial intermediation; government macroeconomic policy; international money and capital markets; and asset pricing (Figure 3.2).

FIGURE 3.2   Dynamic economic loops drive financial crisis.

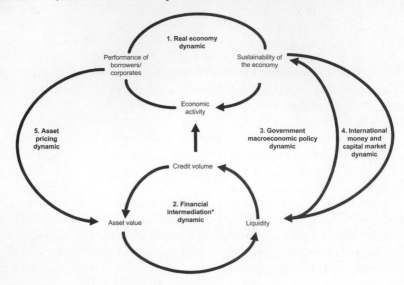

*Includes nonbank financial intermediaries
Source: McKinsey practice development

THE CORPORATE SECTOR: ASSESSING VALUE DESTRUCTION

We have found that value destruction in the real sector is one of the fundamental causes and earlier warning signs of a financial crisis. In most of the cases we have seen, the real sector was suffering economic losses, gradually destroying itself for years prior to the crisis. At the same time, risk in the portfolios of the financial intermediaries funding these businesses was gradually—and sometimes, rapidly—mounting. If left unchecked, this dangerous confluence could easily spiral into a financial crisis. Conversely, we found that countries that did not go into crisis (such as the United States) did not show value destruction in the real sector but, rather, value creation. (See Appendix 3.2: Estimating Value Destruction in the Economy.)

This weakness in the real sector is *the* common theme in crises worldwide. In Mexico and Argentina (and most of Latin America, as well as Turkey and Sweden), corporations that failed to perform well were exposed through well-intentioned market reforms that heightened competition to levels that they previously had not faced. As a consequence, many of these same corporations went into an even steeper decline as part of a necessary but painful free-market therapy.

In other cases, such as Japan, Korea, Thailand, and Indonesia, the companies were sheltered somewhat from direct foreign competition, but they still suffered from traditional industry structures and misguided industrial policies that encouraged overinvestment in key sectors and protectionism which lulled domestic corporations and caused them to delay needed changes. In still other cases, such as China, Russia, Romania, and the Czech Republic, the real sector suffered because of decades of government intervention in the economy.

In each case, the performance problems of the corporations are made evident by the fact that their return on invested capital (ROIC) was insufficient to cover their weighted average cost of capital (WACC). That a few corporations should be failing at any point in time is not surprising. In fact, it is actually a normal manifestation of a healthy economy's transformation over time, or what economists since Schumpeter have referred to as the process of "creative destruction." When this is the case for a significant number of the leading companies of a country, across the breadth of the entire economy, however, crisis conditions could be building.

In Korea, for instance, corporations were able to cover the pre-tax cost of debt in only four of the fifteen years preceding the crisis (Figure 3.3). To put this in the proper perspective you must understand that the electronics sector, and to a lesser extent the steel industry, skewed the average by far

FIGURE 3.3   Value was destroyed in most Korean industries.

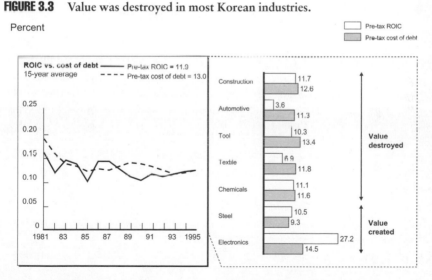

*ROIC = NOPLAT (net operating profit less adjusted taxes)/invested capital
Source: Bank of Korea; McKinsey analysis

outperforming the rest of the industry. In the Korean economy, then, only two sectors created value. All the rest were using capital inefficiently. Korea's failure is even more apparent when its average ROIC of less than 12 percent is compared to that of the United States, where the average ROIC during the same period was almost 19 percent.

A similar but much more dismal story emerges when one examines Mexico in the four years preceding its 1994–1995 crisis (Figure 3.4). During this entire time, its companies destroyed more value than they created. Only telecommunications earned a return higher than its after-tax cost of debt, and that sector's performance was heavily influenced by Telmex, which was operating as a monopoly, had a stranglehold on long distance service, and benefited from regulated rates. Overall, Mexico's corporate sector performance was far lower than its WACC—lower even than Korea's. (See Appendix 3.3: Why Corporate Sectors Underperform in Crisis Economies.)

Timing Crises by Tracking Interest Coverage Ratios

Tracking value destruction in the real sector does raise a problem, however. When does value destruction signal a crisis, rather than merely a sluggish economy? To solve this problem, we have found the need for a more finely tuned metric—the interest coverage ratio (ICR). ICR, which also is used by Standard and Poor's in its ratings of companies, is calculated by dividing

FIGURE 3.4   Most Mexican companies destroyed value prior to the crisis.

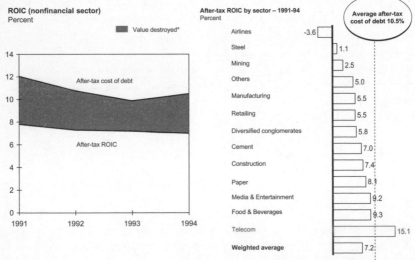

*Conservative estimate based on spread over after-tax cost of debt
Source: Bloomberg (sample of 120 companies); IMF; McKinsey analysis; Standard & Poor's

FIGURE 3.5 Corporate sector's ability to service debt decreased prior to crisis.

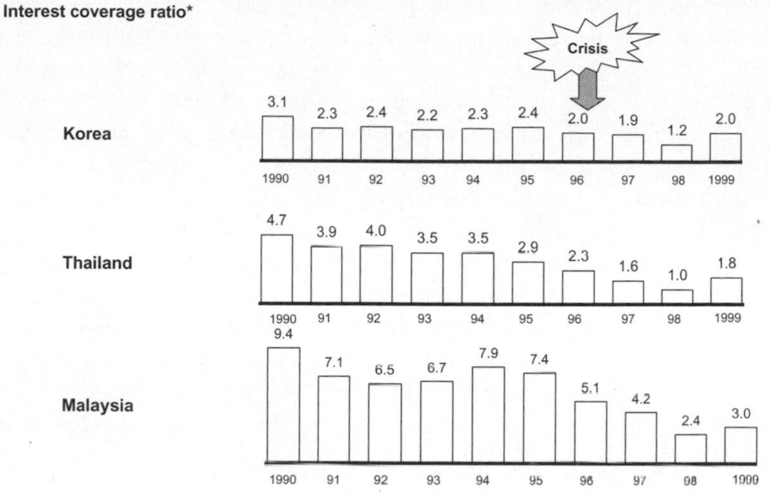

Interest coverage ratio*

*Interest coverage ratio is calculated as EBITDA/interest payments of the same time period
Source: Bloomberg; McKinsey analysis

projected EBITDA (earnings before interest, taxes, depreciation and amortization) by the projected cost of paying the interest on the debt of the company over the same time period. Working with the value destruction database of a few countries, we found that when ICR dipped below 3.0, the debt-service capacity of the key industries of the corporate sector was exhibiting growing fragility (Figure 3.5).[9] When the indicator fell to 2.0 or below, we read it as indicating almost certain problems in the loan portfolios of financial institutions. To be sure, a level of 2.0 for an individual company does not necessarily signal immediate distress, but when an entire corporate sector has such a low debt-service capacity, the system has little room left for error. Standard & Poor's provides ICR medians for the various debt rating categories (AAA to CCC) by industry sectors.

Other Crisis Warning Signs

There are two other tools to use as crisis-tracking indicators. The first is a high debt-leverage ratio. This indicator is simple to estimate—it requires dividing the sum of bank debt and bonds by shareholder equity. Generally, levels under 50 percent are easily borne, but as these mount and get closer to 100 percent, the vulnerability of companies is high. In the Korean case, long before the crisis, debt-to-equity ratios had grown far beyond what prudence dictates. For instance, on the eve of the crisis the average ratio for the top twenty chaebol stood at 425 percent, far higher than was sustainable.[10]

The second test of the sustainability of corporate sector growth requires an assessment of the quality of corporate governance. This is a judgment call, of course, but we think it can be made by asking four tough questions: In the economy in question, are corporate disclosure rules well-defined and commonly practiced? Do minority investors have well-defined legal protections? Are the fiduciary obligations of corporate boards well-defined and established? Do independent board members have significant roles in board decision making?

The United States and the United Kingdom are supposed to have the best financial practices in the world. The recent U.S. public debate, however, highlights the importance of protecting minority shareholders and having independent boards, audit committees, and transparent financial disclosure practices. Poor corporate governance has been a factor in every crisis we have studied. While good governance practices help corporations achieve a higher performance level, the real impact of poor governance practices is expressed in a more indirect way: When governance practices are poor, the risks borne by minority shareholders and creditors are disproportionately high. Hence, if other signs suggest that a storm is brewing, companies operating in countries with weak governance practices should pay especially close attention.

THE FINANCIAL SECTOR: BANKS IN DISTRESS

When real sector ROIC begins to slip, an increasing number of companies have difficulty finding the cash to repay their debts. With all the doubts about company accounts, cash is one of the most telling indicators of trouble ahead. This, in turn, puts tremendous pressure on banks, whose performance begins to slide as nonperforming loans begin to rise, as was the representative case of Mexico (Figure 3.6).

Interpreting the Warning Signals for Banks

The potential impact on banks, whose loan portfolios are dominated by failing real sector companies, is intuitively obvious. Nonetheless, actually tracking and measuring the impact of the real sector's problems on banks is another matter altogether. Unfortunately, understanding the full extent of the problems in banks' balance sheets is obscured by accounting practices and transparency issues. Moreover, to interpret the full impact of the real sector's problems on the loan book requires them to be marked-to-market, which is almost never the case until a crisis occurs. The size and breadth of banks' problems generally cannot be known until after the fact, when a full accounting forces them to the surface. Hence, estimating the true extent of banks' problems *before* the fact requires interpreting trends and accounting information.

FIGURE 3.6　　As performance slides, NPLs rise.

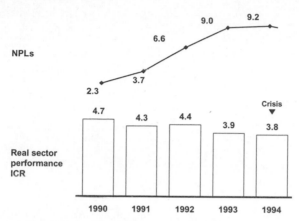

NONEXHAUSTIVE

Mexico, ICR percent NPLs*

* NPLs are calculated as percentage of total loans
Source: IFS; Bloomberg; McKinsey analysis

Tracking Nonperforming Loans[11]　　The trend ratio of NPLs to total loans is a powerful sign of bank problems when credible and timely data are available. An NPL portfolio of 1 percent of total assets signifies probable write-offs of about 5 percent of bank capital, depending on the bank's provisions. Using this as a yardstick, NPLs of 1 percent and rising[12] can signal trouble, whereas levels of 5 percent invariably signal significant problems. The trend is also important: Rising NPLs, regardless of their level, signal problems. The good news is that regulators and bankers carefully monitor NPLs. The bad news, however, is that unless disclosure practices are strongly enforced by regulators and accounting firms, the NPL levels that are reported are usually unreliable. The reason for this is that banks have a strong incentive to underreport their NPLs. Reporting them accurately, after all, would force the bank to increase the funding of its bad-loan reserves, which would then lower its earnings. Accurate reporting might also shrink the bank's loan portfolio, which would then compel the bank to raise additional capital to replace its loan losses. It could also trigger supervisory intervention. Hence, banks have strong incentives to underreport the true extent of the problems on their portfolios; for this reason, too, some countries' banking systems manipulate the meaning of an NPL to remove some of its sting.

　　Investors and managers cannot necessarily count on external auditors and regulators either. They can be fooled, and their accounting invariably comes too late. Thus, even in financial systems where regulators are respected for their skills and perspicacity, accounting of probable loan losses should be suspect.

To make matters worse, we have found that the greater the problems in the loan portfolio, the greater the incentive to lie about their quality. This has led us to take this kind of information with a grain of salt. For example, we routinely use a modeling technique that stress tests the health of banks by using loan-loss scenarios. In these analyses we assume that NPLs are understated by 25, 50, and 100 percent—and ex post audits typically bear out this skepticism.

In sum, what should be an important indicator of the health of banks is also sometimes the least reliable. Reported NPLs in countries with known problems, therefore, should be viewed suspiciously until all of the facts can be assembled and analyzed. While we maintain a healthy skepticism about the accuracy of NPL reporting, we also invariably track it, looking for patterns and trends. We read the published reports and listen to the opinions of the experts, even when their opinions are based on little more than impressions. In addition, we also track other indicators.

Other Indicators of Banking System Health   To track the health of the banking system, we recommend four other indicators:

1. High rates of growth of the loan portfolio are used frequently to illustrate the health and vitality of a banking system. This measurement must be applied cautiously, however. Sustained credit booms with high growth rates put systems under serious strain and frequently can lead to banking system

FIGURE 3.7   Colombian banks' loan growth outpaces sector economic growth.

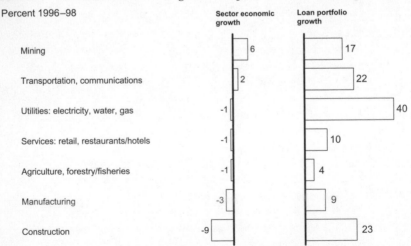

Source: Asociación Nacional de Instituciones Financieras (ANIF); Asobancaria; McKinsey analysis

failures. Indeed, a common pattern in the period leading up to a financial crisis is rapid loan growth. Figure 3.7 shows one such case: The rates of growth of the loan portfolio to the least healthy sectors of the Colombian economy outpaced the growth of credit to healthier sectors during the two years prior to that nation's crisis.

2. ROA (return on assets) calculations also are used commonly as metrics of banking system health. In our judgment, levels close to or below 1 percent indicate that the system is barely matching the normal profit levels of developed economies. Figure 3.8 shows data for Colombia's banking system during the period leading up to the 1998 crisis. Similar information for Korea's banks shows that the ROA fell from 0.62 percent in 1994 to negative 1.06 percent in 1997. Moreover, asset values are questionable in many developing countries for the reasons noted above.

3. Capital adequacy ratios that fall below 10 percent are also worrisome, especially in emerging markets. It is important to examine the definitions and requirements for tier-1 and tier-2 capital (and how these relate to NPLs), since these can vary across countries. In 2001, for instance, Mexico's regulators still allowed tax losses to carry forward and be counted as bank capital. This definition would have been acceptable if the Mexican banks had somehow been guaranteed future profits. Since the capital had yet to be earned, however, this was a dubious practice.

4. Net interest margins are also useful indicators. When this indicator drops under 200 basis points, we become concerned. When they fall below this level, it is very difficult for banks to earn sufficient returns, given their cost structures and capital investments, which are other indicators.

FIGURE 3.8 Colombia's declining bank profitability signals problems.

ROA, percent

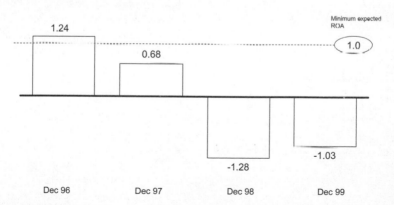

Source: Asobancaria; Superbancaria; McKinsey analysis

Banking system indicators provide less timely warning signs than do those of the real sector of the economy. Consequently, predictions of financial crises that are based solely on them are less insightful and robust than predictions based on a combination of banking and corporate sector indicators.

Why Banks Fail

After many years of working to counter the effects of financial crises, we have developed a point of view about why banks fail. The simple causes, in our opinion, are traceable to errors made while underwriting loans.

However, this answer is not very satisfying in itself and it leads to more questions, such as: Why were these underwriting errors made in the first place? What impacts do special conditions that are generally not present in more developed and stable markets have in these bank failures? Do these banks operate in dangerous markets?

Bankers operating in economies hit by financial crisis recognize that corporate sector underperformance places enormous pressure on banks. They can trace the effects of real sector underperformance on their loan portfolios. Since loan portfolios in most countries are kept on the balance sheet, without being marked-to-market, it is nearly impossible for bankers (or regulators) to fully and fairly assess the value of their portfolios—and the state of health of their banks. Moreover, because the banks themselves provide the lion's share of financial intermediation in these countries, the capital market trading that would force visible repricing in a more advanced economy generally does not exist. In crisis conditions, many banks simply will not recognize the extent to which their asset values have declined, since they fear a collapse of confidence.

Even those who knew before the crisis that they were on perilous ground, and who could have possibly reshaped their portfolios, generally did not. As we showed in Figure 3.7 above, Colombian bankers deepened their commitments to the very companies whose declining performance was threatening them. This phenomenon is common in many developed economies as well.

Old Game, New Game

Before the globalization of economies, the old banking game had been about channeling funds to businesses in a closed economy. In most of the emerging market countries we studied, banks historically had relatively little choice regarding to whom they lent, for which projects, or at what rates. Their role was to create a deposit base, then lend the funds (as well as those borrowed or granted from overseas) to the government and strategic sectors of the economy, often as directed by the government or the banks' conglomerate owners. Banks and financial intermediaries were not expected to make much money lending. Nor were they considered risk takers. After all, their debtors faced little or no competition, and in any case would not be "allowed" to fail. Given these parameters, banks, not surprisingly, built enormous systems for taking deposits based on numerous local branches. They also built large bureaucracies for working with government—in fact, many banks took on the feel of a government agency themselves.

In countries dominated by high inflation and frequent currency devaluation, banks also developed skills in buying and selling foreign exchange (often an exclusive legal right) and taking advantage of the spread between these treasury activities and the negative real interest rates they paid out on their deposit base. Banks, like their real economy cousins, were products of their controlled-economy environment.

Reform, however, changed this environment radically. First, as barriers to entry were removed and ownership laws restructured, new domestic and international banks and nonbank lenders entered the sector, intensifying competition for the most attractive borrowers. Second, as deposit and loan rates were deregulated, banks in many countries were allowed to price risk for the first time, which required a whole new set of skills.

Third, lending practices were significantly liberalized, allowing banks to decide to whom to lend, and for how much, again requiring a new set of underwriting skills. Fourth, BIS capital adequacy regulations were broadly adopted, focusing attention on risk assets. In most emerging markets this caused increases in the resources available to lend, which in the past had been tied to other balance sheet indicators (especially cash reserves).

Fifth, intermediaries were allowed to borrow money from abroad, in foreign currency, providing significant additional liquidity and opening up a new area of currency risk. Sixth, in some cases, lower fiscal deficits and access to low-cost funds through international capital markets and from foreign market entrants caused a "crowding in" effect. As government took a smaller proportion of their domestic loans, banks were left with excess liquidity to deploy, including times when lax monetary policy may be in place to give a country's liberalization a chance to flourish.

Almost overnight, banks were playing a very different game. Now they were free to grow their loan books for scale, while simultaneously ensuring that they could recover their funds. They were flush with resources borrowed overseas, much of it loaned on a short-term basis in foreign currency. They also experienced lower reserve requirements that effectively increased their lending liquidity yet again. They faced competition for their traditional "safe" government and conglomerate customers, many of whom were no longer "safe" due to real economy reform.

Banks had to broaden their base to include new customer segments, and were required to choose for themselves which customers were good bets, at what rates, and with which product instruments. As competition increased, they were also required to run their own operations for profit, but faced difficulties in streamlining their bloated structures dramatically. In sum, they needed new rules and new skills.

The Failure to Adapt to Market Conditions

Most banks were not up to the new game. Four reasons help to explain their failure: weak credit skills, cozy and directed lending practices, rational expectations built on the old game, and the drive for new earnings.

Weak Credit Skills   Credit skills had never been important to banks in most of these countries, and thus they were never developed or rewarded. As a result, when the underlying conditions changed, local banks were starved for talent and forced to place increasingly important lending decisions in inexperienced, unskilled, and unsupervised hands. The requisite credit culture simply did not exist.

In many economies, deficient credit skills were among the biggest issues leading to financial crisis. In the case of a Mexican bank, for example (Figure 3.9), much of its bad loan portfolio was flawed at origination. Only 5 percent of its NPLs could be traced to events in the macroeconomy beyond the bank's control.

Directed Lending   Many banks in these countries had been either part of a conglomerate, controlled directly by the government, or established by government with a charter to foster the growth of some sector of the economy.

FIGURE 3.9   Poor credit skills lead to destabilizing NPLs.

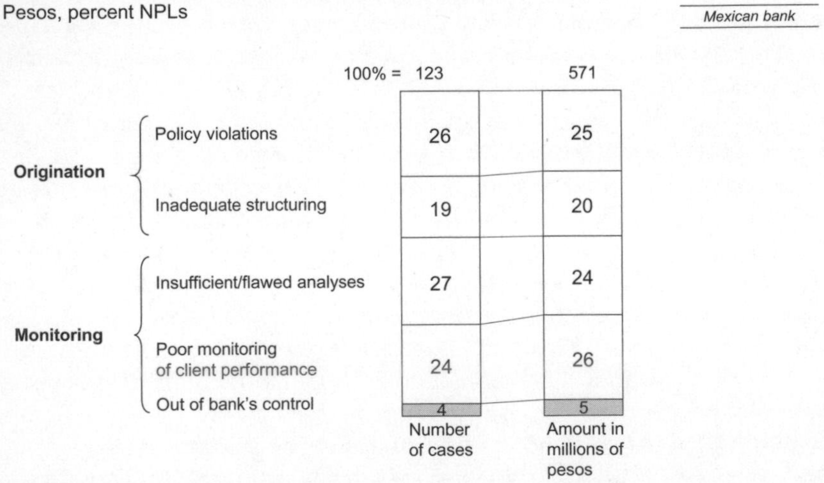

Pesos, percent NPLs

Source: McKinsey client analysis—Mexico

They were set up as facilitators of development, not as profit generators, and their lending practices reflected these relationships and objectives.

Conglomerate-owned banks in Ecuador and Jamaica, for example, existed solely to further the conglomerate's growth objectives. For these reasons, assets in one company were used to guarantee loans in other companies, often regardless of the creditworthiness of the companies or the expected investment returns. Banks within the group made loans based on these guarantees, or in some cases with little or no guarantee at all. In such cases, loans were based on group-level strategy decisions and government policy objectives, rather than more legitimate underwriting guidelines.

State-owned development banks, such as Bancafé in Colombia, experienced similar pressures and made loans based on the needs of economic development and industrial policy, and often to state-owned or controlled natural resource and heavy industry entities.

Not surprisingly, conglomerate-owned banks tend to be poor performers. Even when deregulation freed the banks to lend to other parts of the economy, longstanding (often family) relationships continued to exert hidden pressure. A combination of coercion (such as the withholding of key licenses) and the inertia resulting from years of habit made these lending patterns difficult to break. In one case in Russia, for example, more than 75 percent of all bank loans went at preferential rates to bank-related companies.[13]

Rational Expectations Built on the Old Game   Ironically, even if a more rational credit policy had been established in Russia and elsewhere, the old corporate behemoths would have still received the lion's share of funds. After all, these old-line borrowers still dominated virtually the entire economy. They had long-established relationships and favorite "cronies" to substitute for their poor or nonexistent credit histories. From a banker's perspective, they presented a better risk than the new market entrants, which relied on unproven reforms and had yet to prove themselves.

The Frenetic Drive into New Markets   Even these behemoths could not absorb all the liquidity flowing into local banks, particularly when access to foreign capital was also available. Thus, as the corporate and government borrowers gained access to foreign bank lending, foreign direct investment (FDI), and capital markets, local banks began to be crowded out, and therefore began to look for new lending targets, including individuals and small and mid-sized businesses. The opportunities in these segments were large, as they had typically been previously underserved and underdeveloped. Now, with the advent of reform, they were growing rapidly. However, these segments were unsafe, at least for local banks.

The corporate middle-market is difficult for banks to assess, even in developed economies. In emerging markets, these difficulties are compounded:

Information on debtors is unreliable or nonexistent; virtually all relationships are new, with little credit history to help discern potential risk. Furthermore, the financial statements of such firms frequently lagged performance, are rarely audited, and are often inaccurate. In addition, it is often impossible to differentiate between the company and the individual owner. Thus, special skills are required to lend effectively to customers in this segment—and banks sometimes do not possess those skills.

In addition to commercial loans, there was a pent-up demand for consumer lending—in the form of auto loans, mortgages, credit cards, and other household durable loans. Most of the loans in these areas were too small to warrant individual analysis. Rather, they relied on underwriting techniques that depend on the historic performance of the borrower, not on his or her future cash flow. Unfortunately, most consumers in emerging economies do not have a consumer-lending history in any organized, commercially available form. There are no credit bureaus, and those that do exist tend to be woefully inadequate. Bankruptcy and claims information is inaccessible. All of this makes risk assessments and write-offs hard to manage.

Regardless of the risk, banks felt the need to find a home for the growing amount of resources on their balance sheets. Banks began a "race for the bottom" in their quest for market share, in which middle-market and consumer loan portfolios were often the fastest growing components of the total portfolio. In Colombia, for example, during the five years prior to the crisis, mortgage loans grew at an annual compounded rate of 19 percent, and commercial loans grew at 15 percent per annum.[14]

Watching the Descent into Unmanaged Risk

Banks—bewildered by the pace of change around them and determined to remain relevant in the evolving economy—often built their loan books to the sky. In so doing, they exposed themselves to a number of significant risks which varied in intensity by country. Chief among these, of course, was the risk of lending without the requisite borrower information or credit skills to evaluate individual loans (or to effectively monitor those loans once made). Also critical were the liquidity and currency risks inherent in the kinds of borrowing and lending that banks were doing.

Banks were borrowing short-term funds from abroad, often in foreign currency, and lending those funds domestically in longer-term instruments denominated in the local currency and sensitive to local economic conditions. Sometimes they loaned in foreign currency and the borrowers took the exchange rate risk, with disastrous results for them and the bank. Thailand's massive and ultimately disastrous move into property loans is just one example. Mortgages, with their long term structures, were being mismatched with deposits and other sources of bank funding with much shorter maturity. The mortgages, of course, were very sensitive to macroeconomic conditions. During a downturn, the value of real-asset collateral, such as housing and land, typically declines, creating a large number of defaults. In a country like Thailand, this situation created an exposure problem for lenders that in more developed financial markets is solved by securing and trading mortgage income streams and risk via derivatives. Yet, in Thailand no active markets existed for trading securitized loans. The banks assumed both the counterparty and liquidity risks.

In Thailand, investments fueled by Thai banks and finance companies created a tremendous real-asset bubble; property prices increased by 395 percent between 1993 and 1996.[15] The financial institutions funding the bubble were in turn funded by a massive increase in net foreign liabilities (roughly 52 percent per year, up to nearly $80 billion), fueled by a large number of new bank loans to the country (over $10 billion in the first half of 1996 alone).[16]

The wiring for contagion across countries also was being developed. For example, many merchant banks in Korea, funded with short-term money, were actively financing real estate and other investments in Thailand and Indonesia, attracted by the high returns, but they lacked basic hedging skills and were unaware of the implicit risks they were taking (Figure 3.10). To compound this situation, many Korean commercial banks and security firms had "guaranteed" these merchant banks and their foreign forays. This rising level of risk was replicated in sector after sector—and country after country. Poor credit skills, lack of arm's-length lending, rational "old-game" expectations, and a headlong drive for new sources of income ensured that credit mismanagement, risk mismatches, and misallocation of capital to less than optimal uses ran undetected or were ignored for some time. The interlinkages between countries and sectors also increased.

FIGURE 3.10 Korea's merchant banks: borrowing short, lending long overseas.

Merchant bank FX liquidity crisis, FX sources and uses, as of August 1997
Korean won, Trillions

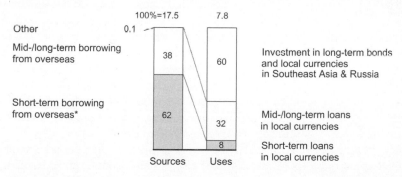

*Less than 1-year maturity
Source: Bank of Korea; McKinsey analysis

In the end, in Thailand and other crisis countries, weaknesses in the real economy, whose bad practices were being reinforced by the banks' lending behavior, begin to take their toll on bank performance. NPLs balloon upward, swelling quietly to between 15 and 35 percent of total loans in the countries surveyed, and bank returns on equity drop. As a result, bank balance sheets and income statements become uglier and uglier. Credit from overseas continues to flow for the time being, driven by reform euphoria, rosy economic projections, and lower interest rates in the developing world. Increasingly, however, the system is a house of cards.

The Failure of Regulation and Regulators

The failure of banks to control their destiny is compounded by the inability of regulators to understand the building imbalances in the financial system and to move quickly enough to head off disaster. Regulatory weakness in most countries, we have learned, is rooted deeply in both the skill levels of the regulators themselves and the structural flaws in the system.

Even in the civil service organizations of many developed economies, bank supervision is an unsung vocation. Like other civil servants, regulators are compensated far below their private sector counterparts rather than in line with the extraordinary returns that quality bank supervision provides to an economy. They are generally promoted by seniority rather than by performance. The incentive, therefore, is to *last* in the job, rather than to *excel* at it. This reward system tends to discourage regulators from expressing suspicion about a bank's P&L or balance sheet, or in other ways "rock the boat." Forbearance becomes the norm. To be sure, regulators in developed countries are helped by the existence of board oversight and capital market-related scrutiny (equity analysts, self-regulating entities, and active price signaling), but their existence is still sometimes viewed as secondary.

Making matters worse are the political powers of conglomerate, state-owned, and other private banks controlled by elite families. In some countries, the regulators are often drawn from the same tight social circles as the bank leaders they are regulating. To top it off, regulators are rarely lauded for their successes, but often vilified for their failures. While the continued operation of the banking system produces few heroes, its collapse provides many villains. As a result, quality regulators in emerging markets have historically been few and far between.

In addition to the difficulty in attracting top talent, the bank supervisory function in many countries suffers from a number of structural problems. These include: the absence of stronger private sector safety nets (appropriate governance practices and capital market-related scrutiny); moral hazard; the lack of coordination among regulators of different financial service industries; opaqueness of information; the overwhelming impact of technology;

and the inadequacy of banking and accounting rules, sometimes fueled by competitive pressure among national financial systems for international customers. They also are sometimes limited in financial resources and their political independence within the government.

Given these issues, most emerging market regulators are completely unprepared for the storm brewing in their financial sectors.

The powerful dynamics driving both the real economy and the financial sector, then, continue to reinforce one another in a negative spiral reflected in the declining health of bank portfolios. Regulatory and management weakness help ensure that bank leaders themselves are often unaware of the extent of their problems, and that regulators are in no position to arrest the decline. Over time, the concentration of bank loans in increasingly underperforming sectors of the real economy, combined with the rapid expansion of unskilled lending to new segments, take NPLs well beyond the breaking point—anywhere from 16 to 35 percent of total assets at the time of crisis.

Regulators are often unaware of the magnitude of the problem until it is enormous. When the full measure of its danger finally hits them, they face a painful dilemma. Many banks were linked through loans and cross-guarantees, making effective concentration even greater. Perception of their health is tightly correlated in the eyes of foreign and domestic investors, depositors, and creditors, so that one failed bank could possibly undermine the credibility of the whole system.

In most cases, therefore, shutting down a major bank would be tantamount to shutting down funding to the economy, strangling the many corporations that are dependent on loans to meet operating budgets, including payrolls. This action would destroy their ability to repay loans to other banks, which would already be under pressure as dwindling confidence had reduced volume and destroyed their credit, touching off the very crisis that regulators sought to avoid.

As we look back at countries in crisis, then, we see regulators and bankers caught in what rapidly becomes an unstoppable decline. Trapped by the consequences of any potential action, as well as by their own skill deficits, mindset, and, for many, stake in the existing system, they are in a dilemma. By and large, their reaction is to do nothing.

UNDERSTANDING THE IMPACT OF MACROECONOMIC CATALYSTS, FOREIGN FUNDING, AND ASSET BUBBLES

As we said earlier, the unstable atmospheric conditions underlying a financial storm are composed typically of inefficiencies in the real economy, financial sector instability, and ineffective regulatory supervision. Now, macroeconomic policies—particularly surrounding exchange rates—increase the instability of the system and ultimately cause the storm to intensify. They also can play a significant role in determining how long the resulting storm will last, and what the severity and the duration of the crisis will be. Since exchange rates are perhaps the most immediate triggers, we will focus on their implications first.

Impact of Exchange Rate Policies

Managed well, exchange rate policies help control inflation, enable domestic industries to develop and build an international presence, and attract foreign capital. Managed poorly, they can quickly increase prices, putting companies and whole sectors out of business by making them noncompetitive, and setting off crises in both the financial and real sectors. The truth is that virtually any "managed" exchange rate is by definition a distortion of the "market price" for a currency. Over time, the existence of a peg leads to increasing distortions. Between countries and within them, these distortions can affect the allocation of resources.

Managed rates also lead to the danger of sudden repricing, should pressure from investors and creditors ultimately overwhelm the ability of government to maintain a pegged rate. Every country we have studied employed fixed or crawling-peg exchange rates to control inflation, reduce the cost of capital, and improve terms of trade. In every case these currencies were suspected of being overvalued in the period leading up to crisis (Figure 3.11).[17] Overvaluation helps to cause currency attacks, forces interest rate policies that negatively affect banking system profits, and reduces banks' ability to manage the unfolding crisis and the negative impact of exogenous shocks.

FIGURE 3.11 Overvalued exchange rates often precede crises.

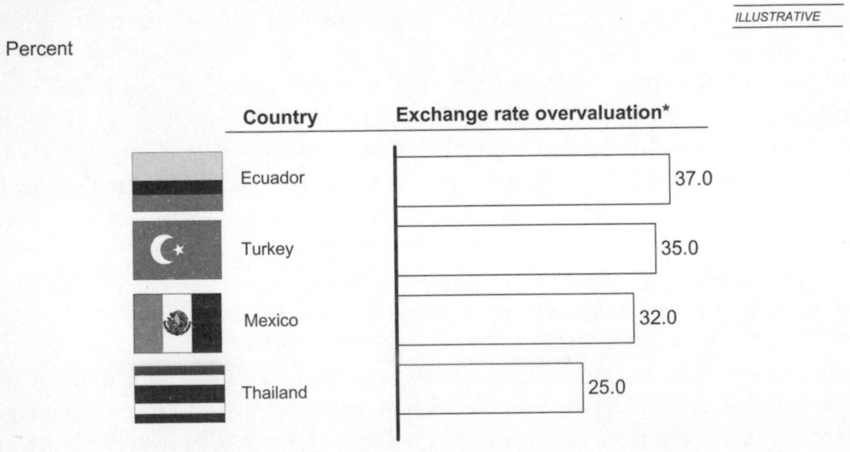

ILLUSTRATIVE

Percent

Country	Exchange rate overvaluation*
Ecuador	37.0
Turkey	35.0
Mexico	32.0
Thailand	25.0

*Overvaluation calculated by using PPP methodology, represents overvaluation on eve of crisis
Source: IFS; World Bank; McKinsey analysis

Pegged Exchange Rates and Overvaluation   For fixed exchange rate regimes to work, they—and the monetary and fiscal policies that underpin them—must be both believable and sustainable. Domestic investors want to know that the value of their investments will not drop in real-dollar terms. Foreign investors want to ensure that currency risk will not eat away at their returns. Domestic borrowers in foreign currency—including banks in the countries we examined—pray for stable currency, but they also hedge positions and take precautions to ensure that they are not too exposed to sudden depreciation. Lenders want to avoid increases in defaults due to increased debt servicing among their borrowers. Virtually every actor in the economy, therefore, closely watches exchange rates for the first sign of weakness. For this reason, the government tries to guard its stability fiercely.

Thus, the choice to peg exchange rates requires a heavy economic management and public relations burden for policymakers. They have to ensure not only that key product, factor, and financial market conditions are being met, but also that nervous investors and creditors *expect* them to be and to continue to be met.

Unfortunately, the relatively weak real economies of many countries cannot keep pace with the demands of the currency regime—and their currencies gradually become overvalued, the traded goods sector becomes uncompetitive, and the currency to which exchange rates are pegged (e.g., the U.S. dollar) goes out of alignment. In reality, it is the productivity of the U.S. economy and other countries that compete in traded goods that helps to influence the demands of the currency regime. The longer these policies are maintained, therefore, the deeper the distortion of supply and demand for the currency becomes. This danger only increases the government's commitment to a fixed-rate regime. However, most governments lead with a defense that first begins with interest rates and then with reserves.

Interest Rate Defense of Exchange Rates   In defending failing exchange rates, most governments begin by tightening interest rates. While this move tends to increase demand for the currency and thus props up its valuation, it has a number of negative effects as well. Government interest rate hikes increase the real rates paid by corporations, individuals, and government entities themselves, and quickly reduce aggregate economic activity as investment declines.

This decline affects banks in three painful ways. First, a slowed economy reduces the total demand for bank credit. Banks therefore see their book of new loans shrink. Second, weakened corporate and individual returns increase the number of NPLs, and banks see their profitability drop on outstanding loans. Third, rising money market rates ensure that the net spread on loans falls, further reducing bank profitability. Few policymakers appear to fully understand this tight linkage between interest rates and bank performance, and many others are caught unaware as their banks begin to lose ground. More sophisticated investors and creditors perceive this weakness, undermining the confidence that the government is trying so hard to engender.

Figure 3.12, drawn from our analysis of the Colombian crisis, displays the tight link between interest and fixed or pegged exchange rates. Prolonged periods of high interest rates weaken corporate sectors and financial intermediaries. Even if high rates are successful in holding off exchange rate depreciation, they nevertheless have secondary effects that can be equally devastating.

Currency Attacks   Even more devastating than the impact of increased interest rates is the unsustainability of an overvalued exchange rate. When a currency is perceived as being overvalued, and as expectations of devaluation build, market participants rush to save their investments before the currency collapses. Meanwhile, opportunists and speculators arrive to capture profit opportunities. These are the "currency attacks" that often trigger dangerous dynamics in both the real and financial sectors. In the real sector, devaluation drops real income and further weakens corporations' and individuals' ability to repay loans. The financial sector is then hit by a rapid increase in NPLs, as well as by increasing payment requirements as foreign-denominated loans become vastly more expensive.[18]

To make matters worse, at the first sign of devaluation in many emerging markets, the foreign interbank loan flows that historically have been so

FIGURE 3.12   Rising rates fuel Colombian banking problems.

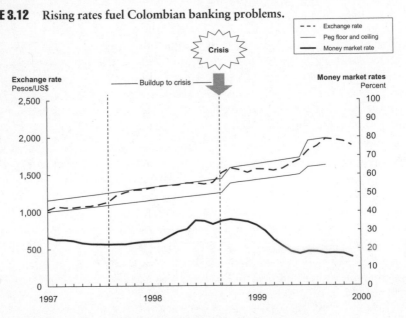

Source: Bloomberg; Banco de la República; McKinsey analysis

critical to financial solvency are typically the first to reverse and withdraw from an economy.[19] The result is a series of banks under increasing duress, faced with a liquidity crisis that can set off a broader financial crisis. Since governments will often burn up their reserves in an unsuccessful bid to stem the tide of this process, market forces will lead inevitably to a depletion of reserves, devaluation, or both—as Argentina's case and those of other countries have painfully shown.

Unfortunately, crawling pegs and mini-devaluation systems are bound by similar conditions as fixed exchange rates, and provide little relief from the dangers of overvaluation. As the currency becomes overvalued, the market tends to push governments through crawling peg triggers, forcing an accelerating series of controlled devaluations that merely inject political fanfare—and a loss of credible government promises—into the inevitable process of devaluation. Past experiences with these middle-of-the-road regimes prove these policies to be functionally the same as fixed rates. In fact, they may be even worse, as they tie themselves to a predetermined amount of devaluation, restricting the ability of policymakers to react to currency attacks.

The Role of Exogenous Shocks   The final process of disintegration often begins with exogenous shocks in the relevant country. Political events (the assassination of Mexican presidential candidate Luis Donaldo Colosio in March 1994 and the revival of the Chiapas crisis later that year), weather systems (the impact of El Niño in Ecuador), wars (the civil war in Colombia), and financial crises in other countries (the impact on Korea of the financial crisis in Thailand) all serve to undermine confidence in shaky exchange rates, weak real economies, and financial systems. In many of the cases we examined, the final push, in fact, was provided by an unexpected event that had nothing to do with the domestic financial system, but that nevertheless undermined confidence in the fragile economic status quo.

The Role of Internal Shocks   Finally, there are internal shocks. The most common internal shock is the rapid loss of investor or depositor confidence following the closure of one or more failed banks. The first sign may be when depositors rush en masse to their bank branches to withdraw their life savings. Unless sufficient liquidity—cash—is provided to stop the runs, a bank holiday may occur, further eroding already fragile consumer confidence. Left unmanaged, the bank holiday becomes a rout on the entire financial system and worsens the crisis, as was the case in Ecuador in 1998 or Argentina in early 2002.[20]

Effects of Other Macroeconomic Policies

Other macroeconomic conditions have a bearing on the health of the economy and the banking system. An especially important link exists between fiscal deficits and interest rates charged in money markets. Tracing the effects of fiscal deficits to banks' profits only requires remembering that the hikes in interest rates caused by fiscal crowding out have similar effects on corporate sector portfolios as do increases made to protect exchange rates, which lead to higher NPLs and lower bank profits. However, another interesting effect arises, because the crowding out of private borrowers leads to a change in bank portfolios. Generally, governments are thought to be better risks than private borrowers; however, governments also can default, but not before funding to the private sector dries up and causes financial distress.[21]

Figure 3.13 shows that during the period 1998–2001, Argentina's government crowded out private corporate borrowers from the bank market at higher and higher interest rates. Hence, during this period, banks' loan portfolios became more tied to the destiny of the government. When the government defaulted in early 2002, it pulled the banking system down with it.

We believe that crises like those of Argentina and Russia are relatively rare. In both of these cases, the route to crisis was defined almost exclusively by government behavior. However, there were some significant weaknesses and warning signs in the private corporate sector and state-owned banks. The other crises we have seen had both the private corporate sector and banks as the key instigators. Governments played a role, to be sure, but

FIGURE 3.13 Argentina's government crowds out private corporate borrowers before crisis.

$ Billions

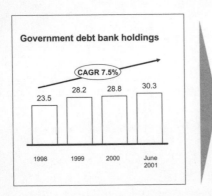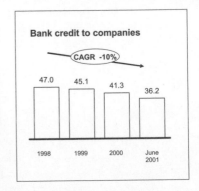

Source: Banco Central de la República Argentina; McKinsey analysis

their role was to trigger the crisis events, generally through mismanagement of macroeconomic policies rather than through their direct involvement in the conditions leading to crisis.

The Role of International Money and Capital Markets

In Chapter 2, we underscored the role of international money and capital markets in enabling the conditions that cause the buildup and triggering of crises. Since this subject has been amply covered previously, we only underscore key conclusions in this section.

We believe that in most crises foreign funding sources have roles more as catalysts than as prime movers. The institutions and investors that control foreign funding resources are clearly pursuing arbitrage opportunities in crisis-bound economies. While a few of these investors are large, generally the resources of any one player deployed against any particular situation will be a relatively small part of the total, both for reasons of risk diversification and other opportunities available. While George Soros is correctly perceived to have taken on the Bank of England and won, for instance, this type of incident is rare—though useful to politicians, investors, and bankers anxious to find scapegoats for problems of their own making.

Arbitrageurs play on the cutting edge of markets. As players on the margin who seek to take advantage of opportunities for trading currencies and financial instruments, their reactions to specific opportunities help to moderate price fluctuations. Their role is to seek price anomalies and to exploit them until they are exhausted. They run large risks in doing so, for if the anomaly outlasts them, then they lose a portion of the principal that they put at risk. For this reason, if they feel that a price in the market is sustainable they go elsewhere with their money. Their very nature makes them ephemeral participants in markets, always one trade away from being altogether gone from any market. Hence, their role is to take anomalous conditions and to exploit them for what they are worth. They are professional skeptics, always looking for signs of weakness.

In recent financial storms, international commercial banks—seeking to earn the higher returns available in emerging markets—have taken on a role as arbitrageurs. In this way, they have served as catalysts that cause sudden surges of funding to enter countries, only to reverse course and leave, causing a funding drought that eventually triggers a crisis. In every case, though, they are reacting to others' leads, and primarily to the signs of extreme optimism and distress that are displayed by economies on their way to crisis.

In the highly interrelated global economy, foreign funding will surge on good news, thus reinforcing the good news, and sputter with bad news, sometimes spiraling an economy into crisis as the bad news feeds more fund withdrawals, which lead to a steeper downward spiral. Knowing this, we believe that governments and companies should adopt strategies that allow the overshooting to be absorbed and countered.

In many emerging markets, however, there is an ingrained resistance against allowing the development of markets where risk positions can be traded, reflecting contending points of view about the sustainability of economic growth and the policies on which such growth is based. Thus, there are too few instruments with which to hedge risks and too few opportunities to take and express contrarian positions. As a consequence, doubts about the sustainability of a growth model turn into currency runs that are both more damaging and abrupt than is justified. As the world becomes more tightly linked, the points at which emerging economies interconnect with the rest of the world will need to develop further—until there is a rich variety of instruments with which to buffer and protect an economy from bouts of skepticism and concern about the sustainability of a growth path. In other words, many small corrections following a trend are much better for emerging markets than large, abrupt swings. This fact is as true during the initial period of growth as it is later when only downside risks are apparent.

The Impact of Asset Bubbles

Asset bubbles are present in several of the crises analyzed in this book.[22] In none of the cases that we have examined do they alone account for the crisis, although in several cases—including Sweden and Thailand—they were strong contributors to crisis conditions.

Bubbles are relatively rare and happen most frequently in nontradable goods, such as commercial and residential real estate, where supply grows slowly. They also happen in stock exchanges, generally due to exuberant feelings of optimism that are usually dissipated as information about the sustainability of a price run-up is made available.

Figure 3.14 shows the price bubbles in real estate and the stock exchange of the Thai economy. The Thai bubble was especially harmful because real estate developers used expectations about the effect of price increases on the value of their property portfolios to obtain financing. These pyramid-like schemes could not withstand the pressure that eventually was placed on them, and they collapsed when financiers became reluctant to provide additional resources to fund development.

Bubbles tend to be just as exaggerated on the way down as they are on the way up. In Jamaica, the bubble's burst caused the government workout agency to be the largest owner of commercial and residential real estate. The government had to slowly liquidate the portfolio or run the risk of having big blocks of real estate on the market, further depressing the value of its holdings. Consequently, real estate bubbles can take an especially long period to work out. This is also true of nonperishable assets whose technologies are

FIGURE 3.14 Asset bubbles preceded Thailand's crisis.

Index values for real estate and the stock market

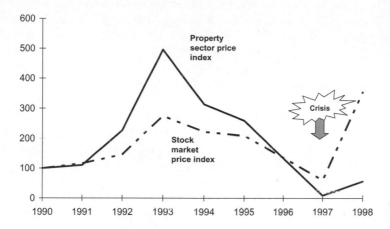

Source: IFS; Bloomberg; Datastream; McKinsey analysis

not rapidly evolving. The bubble that burst in the U.S. data and telecom market in 2001 is a good example. How long the effects of this event will last is dependent upon the pace of technological change. If these assets become obsolete rapidly, then new investments will start up in the industry soon, otherwise the amount of equipment—servers, switches, and computers—sitting around will depress the recovery of the sector.

■ ■ ■

In sum, financial crises are the result of the complex interaction of powerful forces at both the macro- and microeconomic levels. Our work suggests that the microeconomic foundations of financial crises have been seriously underestimated and understated as a primary explanation of financial crises. Underperforming corporations and inadequate banking practices create the conditions for crisis. Rapid increases in international money and capital flows, government policies, asset bubbles, and other exogenous and endogenous triggers usually act as catalysts.

CONCLUSIONS AND OUTLOOK FOR FUTURE CRISES

The process of tying emerging markets to the global economy offers great rewards to all, but it does not come without pain and cost, if these emerging markets are not ready or do not have adequate "immune systems" in place.

We believe that several significant crises might lie ahead. It is almost pre-ordained that this should be the case. As markets develop and expand to areas of the world in which they had not traditionally had a major role, it is highly likely that crises will grow in frequency as well as in magnitude and intensity.

The benefits of joining the world economy far outweigh the costs, but there is much that investors, managers, regulators, and governments can do to safeguard economies from crisis and to react intelligently when crisis conditions begin to manifest themselves.

Many observers believe that there might be at least three major financial storms brewing in the world economy. These are likely to be among the largest experienced to date:

1. Japan, which *The Economist* in early 2002 called the "non-performing economy," has delayed needed reforms for a very long time and caused enormous unresolved pressures to build in its banking system and macroeconomy.[23] The costs to the Japanese people and to the world of this continued inattention are likely to be bigger than anything previously experienced. (See Box 3.3: Japan: The Rising Cost of Delayed Reforms.)

BOX 3.3: JAPAN: THE RISING COST OF DELAYED REFORMS

The Japanese economy continues to stumble. Since its initial stock market crash in 1990, Japan has failed to develop a recipe for revitalization. Instead of tackling necessary reforms, the government has allowed a gradual decline, one that may now be reaching crisis proportions. This makes Japan a rather different case from some of the others that we have analyzed, since its problems are not masked by the overvaluation and enthusiasm of a growing economy. There is no asset bubble, the yen continues on a several-months' decline, and there is no excess of foreign funding as of this writing. However, the potential for crisis is evident in three of the five economic loops described in Chapter 3: the real economy, the financial sector, and macroeconomic policy.

Real Sector Economy   In the real sector, value destruction is evident, driven primarily by slumping demand and overcapacity. This is particularly true in the construction and retail sectors, and has led to an increased number of bankruptcies over the last several years. While bankruptcies are increasing, Japan's bankruptcy rate remains relatively low at 1.2 percent in 2000, just above rates observed in the U.S. and Germany (0.7 and 1.1 percent respectively).[1] This is due to a banking sector that continues to prop up companies that are not profitable by providing debt at exceedingly low interest rates (short-term interest rates approach zero percent).[2] These low interest rates (the result of Japan's current deflationary period) make value destruction in the Japanese economy undetectable through traditional analyses. However, using the opportunity cost of debt facing Japanese investors and financial institutions, value destruction is evident.

To make matters worse, Japan's productivity is also lagging. The Japanese are 31 percent less productive than Americans in terms of labor and 39 percent less productive in terms of capital.[3] Although Japan's labor and capital inputs have grown steadily, surpassing U.S. and European levels, its lower productivity levels have offset any potential positive impact on GDP growth.

Financial Sector   Japan's financial sector is also struggling. Taxpayers' funds are propping up weak banks and inefficient public financial institutions, and there is little incentive to solve the financial sector problem. It has been left "holding the bag" as companies have gone bankrupt instead of paying their debts. NPLs are currently estimated at $500 billion to $600 billion and increasing, well above the warning threshold.[4] As a result, the banking sector's ROA averaged −0.1 percent in 2000.[5] Moreover, given recent regulatory changes, the situation is unlikely to improve in the near term. As of April 1, 2002, the banking sector is required to record its equity holdings, which are often substantial, at market value. Since many of these equities were purchased at higher prices, banks will face significant losses. This change, coupled with changes in government deposit insurance, may cause investors and depositors to flee already shaky banks, although it is difficult to see any signs of capital flight as we write this book.[6] This transition moment could actually spark a currency depreciation if Japanese savers come to the conclusion that their savings would be safer in institutions outside of Japan than in other Japanese institutions.

Macroeconomy   From a macroeconomic perspective, Japan is plagued by deflation and depressed spending. A continuous fall in consumer prices and retail sales over the past two years has contributed to a fall

(continued)

in GDP both in nominal and real terms. The deflationary period itself can be attributed to government inaction following the collapsed asset bubble in the Asian crisis of 1997. In addition, the government's inadequate fiscal policies—low tax revenue compared to high spending— have contributed to a public debt that is 130 percent of GDP, and that is expected to rise above 140 percent in the coming year.[7] To date, Japan's government has avoided a fiscal crisis due to the unusually low interest rates. However, should interest rates on government debt rise to more empirically normal levels—about 6 percent—the true state of Japan's fiscal nightmare would be revealed. Doing so would show that Japan's debt would consume 28 percent of total government spending.[8] Japan's poor fiscal position has already prompted domestic credit rating downgrades by several ratings agencies, including Moody's and Standard & Poor's.[9]

Japan has muddled through its financial and economic problems for over ten years. Whether a crisis looms on the horizon is unclear, but many of the warning signs are flashing. The stalemate continues. The bad debt problem is both a real economy and a political problem, given the unwillingness to allow excess capacity to be eliminated and the fear of rising unemployment. Consequently, growth rates are likely to remain unattractive for years to come. Only time will tell whether the private sector and the government are ready and able to finally take the steps necessary to jump-start the economy—their track record to date, however, is not reassuring.

2. A similar, albeit smaller, storm might be taking shape in China, where years of rapid credit portfolio buildup to state-owned enterprises (SOEs) has created an NPL portfolio estimated at more than $600 billion to accrue.[24] The catalyst of a potential Chinese storm might be allowing Chinese depositors to move their deposits freely within China or make investments outside the country. (See Box 3.4: China: Plugging into the Global Economy.)

3. Another, fortunately smaller, event of similar characteristics might be taking shape in India, where decades-long protection accorded to inefficient SOEs might eventually lead to an economic reckoning. Here the likely precipitating event could be further trade liberalization that exposes ancient behemoths to more intense competitive pressure. (See Box 3.5: India: Seeking a Second Generation of Reforms.)

BOX 3.4: CHINA: PLUGGING INTO THE GLOBAL ECONOMY

Despite impressive economic growth and progress toward integration into the global economy, China might be prone to a future financial storm. Whether and when the storm materializes depends on several key factors, predominantly in the real sector and the financial loops of its economy, but the macroeconomy as well.

Using the information available on publicly traded companies, we find that there has been value creation in the real economy over the last five years, with the exception of 1999. These figures, however, probably mask problems in other parts of the economy as well. SOEs and other nontraded corporations are thought to have systematically destroyed value throughout this period, in large measure neutralizing the contributions of the healthier publicly traded companies. It is thought that 41 percent of SOEs are generating losses, as are 20 to 30 percent of Chinese private companies.[1]

The performance of the real economy is further hindered by a lack of available capital (despite high domestic savings rates that flow mostly into deposits) for commercially-driven firms that have the potential to create economic value. These companies are "crowded out" by lending to the less sustainable, but politically important, SOEs and by other "policy" lending targeted at developing or ailing sectors of the economy. By starving those companies that create value and subsidizing those that do not, China is further increasing its chances for financial problems in the future.

Financial Sector   The potential for problems is also evident in China's financial sector. According to Standard and Poor's, the Chinese banking sector is "technically insolvent."[2] Market estimates of NPLs are as high as 44 percent of GDP in 2001, largely due to the preponderance of lending to financially unsustainable SOEs.[3] As a result, the ROA of the banking system is a low .05 percent and ROE is 1.6 percent.[4] These metrics provide clear warning signs of problems brewing.

Solvency issues of the banking system notwithstanding, the liquidity of the financial system is very high. Annually, Chinese customers save 39 percent of GDP, continually replenishing the losses of the banking system.[5] Moreover, since the banking system has not been liberalized and capital outflows are strictly regulated, these high savings rates

(continued)

might continue to fund the questionable loans being made by the banking system. Although NPLs are estimated at 44 percent, when all is said and done the crisis might be contained by the unflagging willingness of the Chinese to save, especially if domestic depositors decide to maintain their savings in the banking system rather than move their resources elsewhere.

Macroeconomic   Macroeconomic factors are mixed and are also a cause for worry. As in Japan, as of 2002 China has experienced deflation for four years. Meanwhile, estimates of government debt are as high as 75 percent of GDP, fueled by potential state bank loan bailouts and pension liabilities.[6] Moreover, China, like many emerging economies, continues to lack transparent, market-driven "rules of the game," which are vital for future economic stability. Offsetting this are China's impressive growth of above 7 percent annually over the past decade, considerable trade surpluses and export growth, and one of the largest flows of foreign direct investment into any emerging economy, which has accelerated since its entry into the World Trade Organization. China's foreign exchange reserves currently are in excess of $200 billion.

Historically, China has been slow to address these critical issues, although WTO membership may force its hand to accelerate the necessary reforms to prevent a future crisis before it is too late.

The pressures building in these three economies and in those of many others are daunting. Liberalization is gradually reaching all of Eastern Europe, Southeast Asia, and Africa. Further deregulation is likely in the developed markets of Europe and North America as pension reform, bank deregulation, and financial services convergence continue. Moreover, the linkages between the world's economies are increasing, as corporations globalize, more institutions and individuals invest outside their own countries, and financial institutions become more interconnected through payment systems, syndicated loans, repurchase agreements, interbank lending, and capital market investments.

All of these events will keep managers busy tracking the crisis warning signs that are flashing in many dangerous markets. Executives also should start now to take the precautionary measures essential to weather the first hundred days of a financial storm.

BOX 3.5: INDIA: SEEKING A SECOND GENERATION OF REFORMS

Ten years ago the Indian government embarked upon reform, liberalizing the economy to open it to global markets. Today, this liberalization effort is showing mixed results. Despite strong GDP growth (averaging 5 to 6 percent annually), a reasonably low current account deficit (less than 2 percent of GDP), and ample foreign reserves (over $55 billion), an analysis of India's economy shows indications of distortions in three areas: the real economy, the financial sector, and macroeconomic policy. India is considering a "second generation of reforms" to further liberalize the economy and correct these market distortions, but if distortions remain unchecked, a financial crisis could emerge.[1]

Real Economy   In the real economy, steady value destruction has been evident over the past eight years. A comparison of ROIC with the cost of debt over the years 1995 to 2000 reveals a corporate sector unable to service its cost of debt (with ROIC averaging 8 percent compared to a cost of debt at 10 percent) as shown in Figure 3.15. This value destruction is due to the fact that 80 percent of available capital is directed at

FIGURE 3.15   Value is being destroyed in India due to capital misallocation.

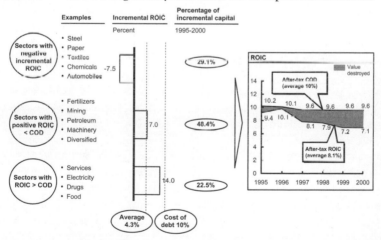

Source: CMIE; McKinsey analysis

(*continued*)

nonprofitable sectors, a trend that is unlikely to change in the near future due to government-directed lending regulations, high transaction costs, and depressed market conditions. Additionally, declining growth in the industrial sector, coupled with a reliance on the volatile agricultural sector (tied to unpredictable monsoons) that still accounts for 25 percent of GDP, have contributed to poor real economic performance. Finally, the corporate governance structure is in urgent need of reform—public sector banks are governed abysmally, family-owned businesses are still a mainstay in the private sector, and the voices of minority shareholders are frequently neglected.[2]

Financial Sector   The financial sector also appears weak—as of 1998, 46 percent of financial institutions had ROAs of less than 1 percent, and the banking average was 0.55 percent in 2001.[3] This poor performance of the banking sector is compounded by low productivity and a lack of fee revenue. Gross NPLs are estimated to be as high as 30 percent of total loans in the banking system and, as a result, it is likely that the banking system has already lost most of its capital and that profits are overstated. This is a consequence of poor credit risk skills in domestic banks as well as high levels of government-directed lending (40 percent of total loans are priority-sector directed).[4] Bank credit has been largely misallocated to nonprofitable sectors, including iron and steel, sugar, cement, and paper industries.[5]

Macroeconomy   Both the real and financial sectors are impeded by poor macroeconomic policies. The Indian government exercises significant ownership and control over the economy, directly owning 60 percent of assets in the real sector and 75 percent of assets in the financial sector.[6] In addition to a strong presence in the economy, the Indian government has been very active intervening in the economy through fiscal policy and monetary measures to maintain liquidity and the exchange rate, and to support weak institutions. In the past six years, over $6 billion in support has been provided to recapitalize weak banking institutions and force the merging of weak and strong domestic banks. Many observers are concerned about the quality of the government's spending.[7] In addition, as a result of such poor spending, central and state government deficits amount to approximately 11 percent of GDP.[8]

Despite weaknesses in the three areas mentioned above, the outlook for India is not all gloom. The economy has low foreign debt exposure and has been able to avoid a credit boom in the real sector. What is needed to turn around the distortions in the economy are more government and microeconomic reforms—more privatization and liberalization in the real sector and a lessened presence of the government in these same sectors, fewer requirements on government-directed lending, better corporate governance, and a greater reliance on market decisions to allocate savings.[9] Whether these reforms will occur in time to prevent a crisis remains to be seen.

APPENDIX 3.1: Ten Warning Signs of a Financial Crisis

No one would argue that financial crises are easy to predict. As one former IMF official conceded, "The IMF has predicted fifteen of the last six crises."[1]

Still, we believe that they are not *impossible* to predict. For this reason, we list below the ten best indicators (that we have found) of impending crisis. As we explain in this chapter, most come from the microeconomic side of the economy, not the macro side.

To be sure, judgment and common sense must be used to make sense of these warning signs, and care must be taken that the data from which they are drawn is accurate, timely, and complete. They may not be perfect, but they are the ones we typically use in our client work to form a judgment about the vulnerability of a financial system to crisis.

WARNING SIGNS IN THE REAL SECTOR

1. **Value destruction in the private sector.** When companies cannot make enough money to cover the cost of the money they have borrowed, a crisis may be brewing. The red light starts flashing when the return on invested capital (ROIC) for most companies in the country is less than their weighted average cost of capital (WACC).[2] This was the case in every crisis we have studied. ROIC data can be obtained for most large companies in any country, which because of their size and impact will reflect on the economy as a whole. WACC data is more difficult to obtain. Annual reports will provide information about the cost of debt; however, calculating the cost of equity requires estimating betas for individual sectors in each country, and these are rarely available from public sources. But you might not need to estimate WACC at

all. If you find that the cost of debt is equal to or higher than the ROIC, you can be sure that value destruction is happening in the corporate sector.

2. Interest coverage ratio. If the ratio between the cash flow and the interest payments of a company (the ICR) falls below two, that company may be facing a liquidity crisis; if this applies to the average of the top listed companies in a country, a widespread crisis could be impending. ICR data is easily available for most companies quoted in capital markets.

WARNING SIGNS IN THE FINANCIAL SYSTEM

3. Profitability of banks. An annual systemwide return on assets (ROAs) of less than 1 percent for retail banks and/or an annual net interest margin of less than 2 percent are often signs of a crisis. Banks publish accounting reports that contain the data needed to make both these calculations. Financial newspapers usually carry monthly reports of information required to estimate both of the indicators. Given the caveats noted previously about the reliability of these indicators, further careful analysis is often required to understand the true indicators, which can be different from the reported numbers.

4. Rapid growth in lending portfolio. When banks' loan portfolios grow faster than 20 percent per year for more than two years, we have found that many of those loans turn out to be bad, and can fuel a financial crisis. When Brian Quinn, former executive director of the Bank of England, sent out his supervisors to scrutinize banks, he told them to use the 20 percent figure as a rule of thumb for further probing. The information to estimate this can be obtained from the same sources used to calculate domestic banking ROAs as well as from central banks' economic indicators series, usually published monthly.

5. Shrinking deposits or rapidly rising deposit rates. When depositors start pulling their money out of local banks, particularly over two consecutive quarters, beware. This action is frequently a sign of imminent crisis. The IMF's International Financial Statistics report provides data on deposits for an entire country, although with a time lag. The same information issued by central banks comes monthly. The information can also be calculated using the data of individual banks, which is published monthly. Rates are primarily a function of domestic monetary policy. When individual banks are bidding up deposit rates above other competitors' rates to attract funds for more risky lending or to pay operating expenses, then the warning lights should be flashing as well.

6. Nonperforming loans. Ill-advised lending eventually ends up bloating nonperforming loan (NPL) portfolios. When true NPLs exceed 5 percent of total bank assets, the warning lights should be flashing red. The trouble is that banks often do not fully disclose NPLs until the crisis has hit, as noted above. Also, different countries have different definitions of "nonperforming loans."

Banks issue information on this as part of their reporting obligations, but the reports of private analysts and industry observers are very useful, especially when official reports are suspect. In any event, significant massaging of the data is required to develop an accurate picture of the real extent of credit losses.

7. **Interbank, money market borrowing rates.** When a retail bank is chronically short of funds, borrowing in the interbank market, or offering rates higher than the market in order to drag in funds, the market is, in essence, giving a vote of no confidence to the bank. The weakness of one bank can lead to contagion. Unfortunately, this warning sign is difficult to track. Data is usually available only from interbank dealers and brokers. But by plugging into the right dinner party conversations, you may get an early tip-off.

INTERNATIONAL MONEY AND CAPITAL FLOWS

8. **Term structure of foreign bank loans.** Many companies in emerging markets borrow from foreign banks in dollars, euros, or yen to lower interest rates. Banks, for their part, typically lend in short maturities to these companies. This creates both currency and maturity mismatches for the borrower. When more than 25 percent of foreign lending to a particular country has terms of less than a year, a warning light should be flashing since those loans are highly vulnerable to withdrawal in the event of a crisis. For the data on this, check the Bank for International Settlements in the *Quarterly Review: International Banking and Financial Market Developments,* which is available online at www.bis.org. It is often reported on a timelier basis by individual central banks.

9. **Rapid growth or collapse of international money and capital flows.** When foreign investors, through equities, bonds, and bank loans, pour money into a country that is neither productive nor well-managed, a credit binge results that may lead to a crisis. Such inflows can set the conditions for a crisis. We use the rule of thumb that when such inflows grow three times faster than the economy, conditions may be ripe for crisis. Crises also can be triggered by changes in the direction of the financial flows. This makes the tracking of funds flow a valuable gauge to the sustainability of the exchange rate as well as the exposure of companies and banks to currency risks. This data is also available from either the BIS report listed above or central bank reports, and is frequently available from other sources tracking the balance of payments such as the Institute of International Finance (IIF).

ASSET PRICE BUBBLES

10. **Asset price bubbles.** Asset price bubbles—and busts—occur the world over, but are particularly common in emerging markets where asset markets are thinly traded and the moods of investors can be volatile. Watch

for bubbles in real estate and the stock markets, but do not forget other luxury goods: cars, restaurants, clothing, and even such seemingly trivial services as the cost of upscale haircuts. As a rule of thumb, when we see asset price growth for any asset class over 20 percent annually for more than a couple of years, we see signs of a bubble building.

Appendix 3.2: Estimating Value Destruction in the Economy

Financial storms build up over several years. The most critically useful predictor of serious problems building in the economy is a time series of value destruction in the corporate sectors of the economy. We found that using a time series of value creation or destruction for the five years preceding a crisis helped us determine the dynamics of crisis buildup.

The most accurate method for calculating value destruction is to estimate the difference between ROIC and WACC for the corporate sectors. However, due to data availability and limitations, it is impossible to estimate value destruction for the full economy. Additionally, for most countries the data are not detailed enough to provide ROIC, or WACC calculations. Nevertheless, we were able to construct a methodology that provides a good approximation for value destruction in the economy, using data for the largest listed companies in each economy to construct aggregate estimates of AROA (adjusted return on assets) and cost of debt. The methodology we used, as well as lessons learned along the way, are outlined below.[1]

AROA is used as a proxy for ROIC, as the published data for most countries does not distinguish between different types of assets (the most accurate measure of ROIC calls for computing the return on operating assets only). Typically, Bloomberg can be used as the main source of information, providing balance sheet and income data from which the necessary data can be extracted. For each company in the sample set, after-tax AROA can be calculated as follows:

$$AROA = \frac{EBIT\,(1 - tax\ rate)}{adjusted\ assets\ (average\ of\ current\ and\ previous\ years)}$$

In this equation, adjusted assets are defined as total assets *minus* accounts payable *minus* excess cash and marketable securities *minus* long-term investments and other assets. Individual companies' AROAs are then averaged (weighted by asset size) to provide the sector-wide estimate of AROA. Some additional challenges that we encountered, and that should be considered when calculating AROA, are listed below.

1. Accounting practices varied over the five-year period for several countries, particularly in the areas of depreciation rules, other assets' line item requirements, cross-holdings reporting, and interest expense reporting. As such, it was impossible to calculate totally homogeneous time series.

2. Other country-specific situations affected how we interpreted the time series. For instance, some countries experienced high inflation rates, which affected the levels of the rates, while others did not. We controlled this by converting all figures to dollars at the prevailing exchange rates. Tax policies also changed during the five-year periods that we examined; we simply took this into consideration and moved on.

3. We also encountered challenges calculating the WACC time series for the companies in the countries that we analyzed, and thus used cost of debt as a proxy. Had full information been available, we would have calculated the betas of specific sectors and then used this information together with the after-tax cost of debt taken from the accounting information to calculate the WACC of the companies within the sectors and countries that we studied. While this information was not available, we were able to obtain the information that allowed us to calculate the after-tax cost of debt— admittedly a conservative estimate of the cost of capital due to the fact that cost of equity is always higher than cost of debt—for the companies in these countries' time series. We recommend doing this as well, as the advisability of estimating country-specific betas is questionable due to how thin the trading is in some markets, while there are also issues about using developed economies' betas in emerging markets.

4. After-tax cost of debt is calculated as a weighted average of domestic and foreign borrowing cost. The cost of domestic debt is equivalent to the domestic lending rate (which can be sourced from the IMF's International Financial Statistics; and the cost of foreign funding can be estimated based on foreign currency corporate bond yields).[2] The two costs are then averaged, weighted by the percentage of foreign funding in the corporate sector.

5. Finally, we had to settle on a method for aggregation across the years. Consistency in the time series would have required weighing the sectors of each country equally over the five-year period. But this was not possible because of data availability and because some companies came into existence while others disappeared over the five-year period. Instead of using constant weights for sectors, the annual weights were obtained using total assets for the year. Moreover, the total share of the economy accounted for by these companies varied over time and across countries, although in all cases they accounted for a large proportion of their respective economies. Although more sophisticated weighing techniques might add to the comparability of figures from year to year, due to practical issues we recommend following the approach we used.

APPENDIX 3.3: Why Corporate Sectors Underperform in Crisis Economies

Macroeconomic conditions can sometimes be so turbulent that the returns needed to compensate corporate investors for the risks they are taking soar. This generally happens when investors are not confident about the future, in terms of currency depreciation, inflation, or other conditions. However, in most economies very high risk premia usually manifest shortly before the storm hits; they are like the gale winds that precede hurricanes. Most cases of value destruction are more insidious and are caused instead by companies earning too low ROICs; they are either the legacy effects of structures and practices inherited from the past, or the unintended consequences of rapid and perhaps naive liberalization.

IMPACT OF LEGACY STRUCTURES AND PRACTICES

Globalization notwithstanding, most of the corporate sectors of emerging market economies—and even some of highly developed economies, such as the U.S. steel sector or the chemical sectors of Europe and Japan—are still dominated by legacy structures and practices of the past. Decades of economic protectionism and regulatory intervention caused the institutions and companies of these countries to be highly adapted to the economic paradigms of the period between 1930 and 1990. Economic interventionism and misguided policies caused weak competition in the heavily controlled markets. Years of misguided development policies, combined in many cases with greed, cronyism, and excessive influence, caused unwieldy and inefficient corporate sectors that absorb more wealth than they create. Change is coming rapidly to competitively exposed sectors in these economies; but modern, competitive industry structures and behaviors are still unevenly distributed and absent in isolated or protected sectors.

Tight relationships between regulators and the corporations they regulate also contribute to generally low standards of competition, as does directed lending aimed with few underwriting controls at existing incumbents, which provides funds with little or no incentive for performance.

Family- and state-owned conglomerate groups are still dominant in key sectors of these economies. Sheltered as they are from competition, and with notoriously weak corporate governance practices, there are no effective controls to counterbalance questionable investment decisions and poor business performance. The lack in many countries of alternative sources of funding (i.e., non-"group") reinforces this trend and makes it extremely difficult for new competitors to spring up. Moreover, the absence of a market for corporate control ensures that the system, inefficient as it is, rolls onward, its stewardship essentially unchanged.

Many of Korea's famous chaebol were profoundly implicated in every aspect of that country's crisis, but while the chaebol system was unique to Korea, combinations of family- and state-owned conglomerates and national "champions," national industrial policies, and the lack of a market for corporate control persist in most emerging market economies, including those of: Turkey, Indonesia, Thailand, Mexico, Brazil, India, China, and a whole host of countries that formerly were part of the Soviet economy. Most of these conglomerates chronically destroy value and rely heavily on the specific combination of political and economic realities of their own closed or heavily protected markets for their continuing operation; most of these contributed heavily to the buildup of crisis in their respective economies.

UNINTENDED CONSEQUENCES OF NECESSARY MARKET LIBERALIZATION

While the specific content, intensity, and speed of market liberalization programs varied in the countries we analyzed, the essential purpose of reform was to promote higher real economic growth by introducing stronger market disciplines to domestic markets, liberalizing key sectors, and lowering barriers to entry—all geared toward the conscious elimination of protectionism and exposure to new competition. The unintended consequence of liberalization, however, was rapid economic performance deterioration of the corporations that had made up the old, closed system. This happened in Mexico, Colombia, Ecuador, Korea, Thailand, and—to a lesser extent—Argentina and Turkey. Liberalization has also unleashed powerful effects in other economies, including those of Japan, China, and India (see accompanying boxes), where financial storms might be brewing but have not yet been unleashed by a combination of circumstances unique to each of these countries.

Reformers in these countries had strong and valid arguments for their actions: In the late 1980s and early 1990s, the demise of communism and the robust prosperity in the developed Western nations made many want to follow their lead. Motivated by ideological and intellectual conviction, by IMF and World Bank advice, or simply by pragmatism, many emerging nations in Asia and the Americas moved to "open" large swaths of their economies to maximize their share of growth.

Latin American countries aggressively pursued the full suite of reforms available while Asian countries generally focused on financial reforms and the opening of the economy via liberalization of current and capital accounts. The package of reforms had many of the intended effects. Mexico's case illustrates the patterns that affected many economies. During the first half of the 1990s, Mexico was widely viewed as the poster child for economic reform. Views on the changes under way in Mexico were so positive that the country was flush with foreign investment; its domestic savings rose and renewed economic growth and improved stability led to a period of rising standards of living and expectations.

Deregulation of markets through the elimination of nontariff barriers and "official prices," relaxation of foreign holding laws, and the encouragement of competition allowed both international players to enter and new domestic competitors to sprout up. The opening of the current and capital accounts through the liberalization of trade and the lifting of capital restrictions allowed new products and capital into markets that had long been protected. One law, for example, allowed foreign investment in most industrial sectors of up to 100 percent ownership, and similar changes affected virtually every part of the Mexican economy.

The changes in the structures of Mexican markets were nothing less than dramatic—leading to new competitive imperatives. Those that adapted successfully to the new environment lived to fight another day. Many more companies reacted slowly and skeptically and sustained competitive blows from which they did not recover. Dominant companies in almost every sector have either been wiped out or have started to decline irreversibly, defeated by the tactics of vastly superior competitors who honed their skills in markets where competitive conditions were far more intense than anything previously experienced in Mexico. The reforms of the 1990s were responsible for changes that gradually are wiping out the economic species lacking the skills and capabilities to succeed in the new conditions. Prestigious companies were also slowly being made redundant in every sector from abrasives to zippers. The unintended consequence of economic liberalism was a wholesale destruction of many corporations that came into being between 1930 and 1980.

The global economy operates by rules that require that companies extract returns on investments equal to or greater than their opportunity cost. When they do not do so, it is not just investors who lose; all agents in the economy pay a cost. Chronic value destruction must eventually be recognized, whether on the books of these same corporations, or as losses absorbed by financial intermediaries.

Earning the Right to Win

CHAPTER 4

Managing the First Hundred Days

As the first day of Thailand's financial crisis unfolded, the nation reacted with increasing alarm. "You could see that no one was in the mood to work," one Bangkok resident told *The New Straits Times*. "There was shock and worry on everyone's face."[1]

Fear gripped the nation. Finance companies shut their doors and shopping malls were vacated. Highway traffic dwindled. As the baht slid further that day against the dollar, things looked increasingly worse. "We suddenly found ourselves staring at a dark abyss," recalls the executive director of one large bank, "and left without many choices."[2]

Imagine yourself in their shoes. You arrive at the office to find that many of your key suppliers have shut down. Your bankers are calling with the news that they are cutting your credit lines. Your cash flow has suddenly dried up and, to top it off, strikers from the local labor union are staging a loud and nearly violent protest.

This is not an unlikely scenario. In most cases, chaos reigns as soon as a financial crisis hits a country. Consumers and businesses stop spending. Layoffs spread. The government fiscal situation worsens. Savings are depleted and anxiety sweeps the markets. Short-term loans are not rolled over and credit dries up, tipping even healthy companies into crisis. International banks cut their lines of credit and access to international capital markets is no longer possible. By this time, if not before then, investors are ready to flee. Many pull their money abruptly from the markets, making things even worse.

If management already had taken steps to prepare for a financial crisis while the skies were still blue, then the company may be able to tap into cash reserves or backup lines of credit, or immediately respond to issues in the supply chain. They also know which of their businesses are lean, fat, or dead weight, and thus what to keep or let go for extra cash, which potential buyers to approach, and which capital expenditures to postpone or cancel.

The reality, however, is that most companies are *not* prepared for financial crises, and most managers wrestle with the frustration of what appears to be an environment with very few options. Some executives panic, not knowing where to begin to manage their way out of the crisis. Although there is little that management can do to change the external conditions that drive a financial crisis, the way executives manage a number of tactical decisions in the first few days can make a material difference in the company's survival and fortunes. While the agenda can include literally hundreds of items, we believe that five tactical measures deserve top priority:

1. Understand and maximize the current cash position
2. Identify and aggressively minimize operational risks
3. Conduct rigorous scenario planning
4. Review business performance and prepare for divestitures
5. Maintain the confidence of key stakeholders.

In this chapter, we define each of these five measures, and describe how to implement them. We also explain how to build a crisis management organization, consisting of a "crisis czar," a "cash czar," and five "crisis response teams." Finally, we conclude with an agenda for the CEO, which includes ensuring high-quality management talent as well as sufficient management attention and dedicated resources to respond to the crisis.

In addition, we include a set of appendices to this chapter, which gives executives a deeper understanding of key management topics during the first hundred days of a crisis. Appendix 4.1: Painting the Picture of a Financial Crisis gives a detailed description of the four phases of a financial crisis so managers have a richer appreciation of what to expect when it hits. While *Dangerous Markets* is not a manual on risk management, we nevertheless believe that managers cannot ignore the importance of this broader topic across the entire corporate portfolio. In Appendix 4.2: How Companies Can Strengthen Funding Before a Crisis, we examine how companies can reduce their debt and strengthen funding sources before a crisis hits, thereby substantially improving their starting position. Finally, in Appendix 4.3: Using Scenario Planning in Financial Crises, we examine the important topic of scenario and contingency planning in greater detail.

TAKING FIVE TACTICAL STEPS WHEN A CRISIS HITS

We have seen many companies come and go during financial crises, but the winners are those with management teams who excel in five tactical areas in the early days of a crisis.

1. Understand and Maximize the Current Cash Position

Understanding the company's cash position is the first and most important step for management in weathering a financial storm. When a crisis hits, revenue streams and credit lines dry up. First, companies must understand their sources and uses of funds, asset and liability management, and ICR. Second, they must manage cash through inventories, accounts receivable, and accounts payable. One of our clients in Korea, for example, recalls from the 1997 financial crisis, "Almost every creditor was trying to walk away from us. They were cutting their credit lines drastically. Cash really does become king."

Ayhan Yavrucu, CEO of Alarko, a Turkish mid-sized holding company that has been through numerous crises over the past two decades, explains it another way: "Our company's approach to cash management is guided by our founder, Uzeyir Garih: 'Managing a business in crisis conditions is like juggling three balls. Two of them are rubber and can bounce back if you drop them—these are profitability and equity. The third is made of glass and will break if you drop it—this is cash.' "[3] Without knowing how much cash is moving in and out of the company, managers will never know how bad the bleeding is, where it is coming from, and what must be done to stop it.

Understanding the Company's Cash Position   During the first hundred days, three immediate actions are required to track a company's cash position: get a clear picture of its cash position; map out the sources of cash and look for any potential disruptions; and monitor the company's ability to pay off its debts by calculating its ICR.

First, management must get an immediate picture of its current cash position, broken out by business line, and update it on a daily basis. As basic as this seems, some managers fail to realize that profits do not mean cash. Profits, after all, can overstate or understate free cash flow, depending on factors like the number of days of accounts receivable or accounts payable, inventory positions, and amount of depreciation taken.

Tracking the company's cash position requires constant vigilance. In Turkey, for instance, chronic high inflation, reaching over 120 percent during the 1994 crisis, has forced Alarko to adopt a crisis approach in its everyday business activities. A large part of its revenues comes from sales of heating and cooling systems, second only to revenues from construction. Managers carefully monitor monthly reports from over 400 dealers for any issues with sales, inventories, and accounts receivable. "What matters is not just sales to the dealers, but *healthy* sales from dealers to end users," explains CEO Yavrucu.[4]

Alarko illustrates the importance of not just monitoring apparent cash flow, but also the actual major sources of cash—such as customer receivables, loans, commercial paper, and foreign exchange positions. During the Korean financial crisis, for example, one of our clients with over a thousand loan contracts had up to six or seven of them maturing on a single day. Under normal conditions, that might not be a problem, but in a financial crisis, credit, credit extensions, and reasonable interest rates may not be available. In addition, asset-liability mismatches (interest rate, currency, and maturity) can lead to severe internal liquidity crises, emphasizing the importance of monitoring both sides of the balance sheet and tracking cash flow on the income statement. We discuss asset-liability mismatches in greater detail in Appendix 4.2: in particular, how management can prepare in advance to reduce the threat of such mismatches on internal liquidity.

Even after the crisis hits, how well management understands potential mismatches can make a big difference. The Indonesian retail chain Ramayana, for example, recognized early during the Asian financial crisis that a currency mismatch—in the form of dollar-denominated leasing rates for eighteen stores and two warehouses—could become an even greater problem if the rupiah slid further, especially since 100 percent of its income was in rupiah.[5] Management worked quickly to fix the exchange rates in new and renewing contracts at an average of Rp 3,000 to the dollar for the whole of 1998. This turned out to be a wise move. Before the end of the year, the rupiah would fall to more than Rp 15,000 against the dollar.

These mismatches—interest rate, currency, and maturity—can occur simultaneously, as was the case with Samsung Corporation, a large trading company in Korea. When the crisis hit, Samsung Corporation had almost two-thirds of its total debt in current short-term borrowing with term structures of less than one year, and about 20 percent of this amount in foreign currencies. Corporate bond rates skyrocketed from 12.6 percent at the beginning of November to over 30 percent by year's end, and the Korean won depreciated by 75 percent. However, the company learned from this experience, and two years later Samsung Corporation's current short-term debt was down to less than 20 percent of the total, while its interest rate and currency exposures were much better matched.[6]

Finally, it is important to understand the company's ability to repay its immediate and near-term loans. Specifically, management must be able to calculate and monitor its ICR, the ratio of cash flow generated to the amount of debt interest payments that must be paid over the same time period.

Maximizing the Company's Cash Position Once management has determined the company's cash position, the next step is to move swiftly to maximize it. This action may include canceling or postponing spending on overhead, fixed assets, or advertising, for example. It also means actively maximizing cash across the three areas of working capital: inventories, accounts receivable, and accounts payable.

Inventories. Depending on the company's businesses, management may want to cut inventories, perhaps adjusting prices to reflect what might be plunging consumer demand or rising replacement costs.

We typically divide inventories into three blocks. The "A" block includes the fast-moving items, for which turnover is relatively high and carrying costs are consequently low; the "B" block is comprised of dated, slow-moving products, for which the carrying costs are fairly significant; and the "C" block is made up of products that have not sold for a long time. Management should do whatever they can to move the "B" and "C" inventories. However, the company needs to be more cautious about slashing prices on the "A" block merchandise: During a financial crisis, with its exchange rate fluctuations, executives may find that replacement costs are greater than what they had imagined. In fact, the company may want to increase prices.[7]

One way to dispose of slow-moving inventories is to manage them, along with underutilized assets (e.g., plant equipment, company cars, furniture), through a legally separate asset management company. When the crisis hit the Korean chaebol LG Group in late 1997, Yong Nam—then vice president of LG Electronics and head of the multimedia division, and now CEO of LG Telecom—set a target that the division find over $400 million in cash from the approximately $1.5 billion business. When he realized that none of his senior managers knew what their asset inventories and utilization levels were, he gave them two weeks to do their homework. By the end of that time, managers had accounted for "every screwdriver in the factory." They were surprised to discover that for some assets, utilization levels were as low as 10 percent. Nam then asked them to find ways to increase their cash position in each department.

Borrowing the workout concept from the banking sector, Nam created an internal "bad company" to aggregate inefficiently used assets within the company and sell them off externally, including to the local marketplaces in Seoul. Nam now believes that this dramatically sped up the disposal of unused assets, including slow-moving inventories. This and other initiatives—purchase cost reduction programs, layoffs, and divestitures—were so successful that the division ultimately realized its $400 million cash target within six months.

Accounts receivable. When it comes to accounts receivable, both merchandisers and service providers should work to lower the number of days receivable. This area can be a large potential source of cash, but an even larger drain on the company's cash position. This action means examining exposure to key debtors, developing strategies to respond to key risks, and executing quickly.

One food manufacturer in Asia segments its wholesalers by their financial condition and their preferred product manufacturer, in order to determine what kind of cash and credit policies to pursue. For example, if a wholesaler is financially strong and prefers the manufacturer's own products, then the latter works to support the former and extend credit lines. If, on the other hand, a wholesaler is financially weak and actually prefers a competitor's products, then the manufacturer does its best to limit its exposure by demanding payment in cash. This not only helps the manufacturer to manage its cash more strictly, but also to balance the cost of credit with concerns about loss of share among key wholesalers.

Managing credit risk requires that management find out what is needed to keep good-credit customers current. But it also means that for customers whose debt is beyond recovery, the company may need to do more than change its credit policies. Sometimes, it may need to get the merchandise back, or at least secure the loan or accounts receivable as quickly as possible.

When the Russian crisis hit in 1998, for instance, Roust, a company best known at the time for its alcoholic beverage distribution business, awakened to the realization that much of its stock sitting on shelves across the country might not be repaid. Fortunately, Roust rallied its sales force, and within several days pulled back most of its stock across the country. The company benefited from a favorable negotiating position vis-à-vis distributors because of its strong product portfolio. But it also realized early on that it should focus on wholesalers rather than supermarkets, since the former were less likely than the latter to make payments. Roust told its wholesalers that it would be glad to restock the products, but only if they paid in advance.

Accounts payable. Accounts payable is the third component of working capital. The main goal in this area is to increase the number of days payable, either by rescheduling payments or seeking price reductions from suppliers unless the payables are in foreign currency, in which case the company may want to pay on time or even prepay. As mentioned earlier, management needs to aggressively monitor the company's payments schedule to make sure that it is aware of any interest payments due or loans maturing. The options in accounts payable are typically much more limited than with accounts receivable or inventories, mainly because suppliers will likely be trying to improve their own receivables to guarantee cash for themselves.

Still, making the right moves at the right time can significantly benefit the company's cash position. Mexican supermarket chain Aurrera, for instance, reacted to the 1982 peso crisis by learning how to run a negative working capital situation, driven primarily by an aggressive accounts payable program. It negotiated special terms with suppliers that allowed it 60 to 90 days on accounts payable and minimized accounts receivable days, thus producing a negative working capital position. Aurrera was consequently able to self-finance its growth during the 1980s—a decade in which the rest of the Mexican economy stagnated—and the 1990s. The company was eventually bought by Wal-Mart in 1996 in a deal that was highly lucrative for Aurrera's private owners.

Like Aurrera, LG Electronics' multimedia division also realized negative working capital positions after strong efforts across all these elements of working capital in the first twelve months of the crisis. At first, no one knew anything about managing working capital, but Nam says, "This was simply something that had to be learned and done."[8] Nam trained his managers the best way he knew how—by asking lots of questions. Six months later, the first business unit achieved this goal, followed shortly thereafter by others. In fact, managers had gotten the concept down so well that some were telling suppliers that not until the final products were completely assembled would this division assume the suppliers' inputs as liabilities. Soon, vendors were even setting up their own warehouses at the company's production facilities. Today, Nam cites this as a key component of the division's crisis recovery.

Nam's experience illustrates another important lesson for managers: During a crisis, asking the right questions can make all the difference in a company's quest to optimize cash. Management should constantly review the company's options. For example, has the accounts receivable status of some customers been impaired? Would an adjustment of credit terms improve their recovery value? These are just some of the tough questions that must be asked.

In addition, management should ask if there might be significant opportunities to maximize cash in operational areas such as purchasing. There are standardized, ready-to-use processes that can help companies start to pull out between 8 to 12 percent of their total purchasing costs within six months. During the Asian financial crisis, all of our manufacturing clients realized substantial savings through purchasing improvement initiatives. Managers analyzed vendors and systematically categorized components by degree of specialization and importance to the production processes. One of them created an online, closed-network marketplace for supplier bidding that led to cost savings of over $100 million on an annualized basis.

2. Identify and Aggressively Minimize Operational Risk

During the early days of the Mexican financial crisis of 1982, senior managers at Banamex realized that if there were a run on the bank they might not have enough cash on hand to give to their depositors. This could cause a tragic cascading effect in which the depositors—believing that their money had either been frozen, devalued or, worse, expropriated—could panic. By midyear, the conditions had deteriorated even further. Branch managers were spending most of their time frantically reassuring depositors that their money was safe. Management realized that it absolutely had to meet the withdrawal demand.

There was a small problem, however. The bank needed to keep supplying the branches with money, but the number of armored cars available to do so was limited. The bank came up with a clever solution: It hired a fleet of off-duty ambulances to shuttle cash from bank to bank. The distribution plan worked, and the needs of depositors were met without interruption.

As the Banamex story illustrates, operational problems are common in financial crises. They are a priority that must be managed, with as much care and ingenuity as possible. Generally speaking, there are two elements to this: managing upstream and downstream links in the supply chain.

Managing Upstream Links   Supply chain interruptions are even more threatening during financial crises because, at the same time, the competitive landscape is rapidly changing, making one company's loss another's gain.[9] During the 1997 Korean financial crisis, one automobile company had a substantial portion of its parts suppliers go under. Without backup suppliers in place, it could not ramp up production for the export market after the devaluation of the Korean won. While their foreign distributors were begging for more cars to sell, some of the production lines in Korea were idle due to a lack of critical parts. The company managed to revive itself but never fully recovered its market position. It was bought out eventually stream by another domestic auto company that used the crisis to rapidly expand its global market share.

Suppliers are prone to the same liquidity issues that all companies face in financial crises. Doubts may arise about the ability of the afflicted parties to pay. Even those willing to extend credit may face the shutdown of the international payments system and correspondent banking lines, making further transactions impossible.[10] The consequences can be devastating; thus, the companies that rely heavily on suppliers may need to lend them a hand when a crisis hits. Ramayana, for example, used its favorable cash position during the Asian financial crisis to make early payments to some of its 2,000 suppliers, which helped keep them afloat until the banks were functioning again. In exchange, Ramayana received rebates from its suppliers, ranging from 3 to 8 percent, which allowed it to offset crisis-related increases to its cost of goods.

Because retailers and manufacturers in developed markets source many of their critical components from developing markets, the supply chain operations in those developing markets are of particular importance to them. Suppliers and shippers in developing markets will almost certainly face liquidity issues in a crisis, and may halt shipments of critical inputs unless they receive assistance.

During the Mexican financial crises of the 1980s, for example, Volkswagen helped out its suppliers by signing long-term contracts with them.

Although Volkswagen did not guarantee the loans, it provided the suppliers with the credibility they required to obtain financing. The company also helped suppliers negotiate with their labor unions, acquire land at a reasonable cost, and obtain tax incentives.

Managing Downstream Links   Financial crises can also impact the purchase of goods by affecting the purchasing power of consumers. This is particularly true of luxury items and goods whose purchase can be postponed. Furthermore, a breakdown in the domestic payment systems, as seen in Argentina in 2002, can devastate business by restricting the amount of cash in the economy.

At Alarko, for example, managers work closely with the company's dealer network to provide support during crisis periods. When the current crisis first hit Turkey at the beginning of 2001, for instance, they focused on identifying ways that the company could help support the financial needs of its dealers through more frequent localized promotions, higher margins to dealers, or longer payment terms. Alarko managed to keep a loyal and motivated dealer network. Currently in 2002, one year after the beginning of the crisis, managers are going through another round of dealer assessments to search for other ways in which the company can support them.[11]

During and before a crisis, management needs to have a better understanding of which customer and supplier relationships should be nurtured and which should be terminated. Using this information, it can refocus its marketing, sales, and pricing efforts on the most attractive geographic, product, and customer segments. This process is also important for helping companies prioritize with whom they need to communicate first during a crisis.

Making the most of the harsh, post-crisis landscape, of course, takes a lot of ingenuity. During the crisis, Ramayana found that it needed to cut costs and keep operating expenses under a targeted 18 percent. The company did this cleverly, working with its suppliers to use fewer print designs and accessories such as imported buttons from Taiwan and Korea, and to cut the amount of material in each article of clothing to save on the cost of fabric. At the same time, it decided not to raise its prices—to retain its lower-income and more price-sensitive customers—and thus endured a slight decline in its gross margins, which fell from 28.8 percent in 1996 to 25.9 percent in 1998.[12] Through this and other efforts, Ramayana was able to retain price-sensitive customers and continue to make a profit.

3. Conduct Rigorous Scenario Planning

Scenario planning is necessary to understand the effects of a financial crisis on the company's performance. These analyses give managers both a picture of the magnitude of further potential challenges as the crisis unfolds, and a set of contingency plans with which to respond. In addition to identifying threats, scenario planning also points out potential opportunities and helps create proactive strategies to capture them. The scenarios, which are typically a bundle of business drivers (e.g., GDP growth, cost of debt), are linked to the company's cash flow by a model. By shifting any of the input variables, companies can get a good view of what the immediate implications are for the business. During a crisis, scenario plans need to be revisited frequently as the external conditions change constantly, thus affecting the variables used. One of our Thai clients did this on a weekly basis during the height of the Asian financial crisis. For more detail on how we view scenario planning, see Appendix 4.3: Using Scenario Planning in Financial Crises.

Scenario planning enabled Banco Itaú to prepare for the macroeconomic change that eventually transpired in 1994. In the early 1990s, the bank, like other banks and corporates in Brazil, was making easy money in the hyperinflationary environment through float gains. Yet in 1992, Banco Itaú realized that the hyperinflationary ride would not last. It turned to scenario planning to plot its future course, and through the process realized that it had to boost its operational efficiency, develop better credit skills, enhance its credit position, and improve its risk management process to cope with the new economic realities.

Banco Itaú and some of its competitors in Brazil, such as Bradesco and Unibanco, applied their learnings to great success in future crises. They reached such advanced levels of asset and risk management, combined with rigorous scenario planning, that they not only prepared for, but took direct advantage of, future currency devaluations. During the 1998 financial crisis, for instance, these banks anticipated a float on the Brazilian real and took positions on the currency that significantly contributed to the 20 to 30-plus percent returns on equity.

Doosan Group, one of the oldest conglomerates in Korea, developed scenario planning processes right after the 1997 Korean financial crisis. It not only incorporated traditional demand driver and cost driver inputs, but also a variable called "stability of funding source." Doosan finances about 90 percent of its borrowings domestically, and has created an internal rating of the health of each funding source, reflecting the type of institution (i.e., bank, investment trust company, merchant bank, international bank, others) and its latest financial statements. Doosan estimates the percentage of its current borrowings that it might be asked to pay or prepay by financial institutions in trouble, thus enabling Doosan to better manage its liquidity risk. This type of active management of risk by consciously incorporating it into scenario planning can help companies more effectively manage their liquidity risk during a crisis.

So, How Bad Can It Get?

One of the most difficult aspects of scenario planning is setting the appropriate ranges on different variables. In particular, executives who have not lived and managed in a crisis may have difficulty developing an appreciation for how unnerving such a period can be. Conditions become so nasty that even relatively healthy corporations can be severely impaired and ultimately fail. Using the data from four financial crises (Mexico in 1994; and Thailand, Korea, and Indonesia in 1997–1998), we show the range of values of three critical economic indicators: exchange rate, GDP growth rate (representing aggregate economic activity), and interest rates. These three indicators provide a good sample of the breadth and depth of a crisis.

Real Currency Depreciation   Real currency depreciation is frequently the most spectacular of the crisis indicators (Figure 4.1). During the first two quarters following the crisis, the currency depreciated in all four sample countries. Equally important is the range of values. Six months into the Korean crisis, companies were facing a real drop in the value of their currency of "only" 32 percent; whereas Indonesian companies had lost 73 percent of the real purchasing power of their currency. Ultimately, real exchange rate depreciation settled at a level about 45 percent lower than it was in the period before the crisis. The terms of trade of the companies in these countries were seriously and permanently changed by the crisis. Companies that required

FIGURE 4.1   Currency depreciates after crisis hits.

Change in rate, index = 100, calendar year quarter

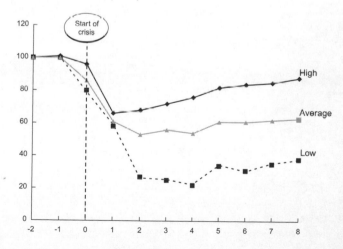

Note: Sample includes Mexico (1994Q4), Indonesia (1997Q3), Thailand (1997Q3), and Korea (1997Q4)

Source: WEFA; WMM; EIU; McKinsey analysis

low-cost imports to sustain their competitive position were crippled, whereas others who relied on export markets saw vast improvements in their competitive positions though not before experiencing significant pain, especially if they were carrying a significant debt load.

Real GDP Growth Rates   Real GDP growth rates also are affected dramatically. Consider the range of values shown in Figure 4.2. Corporations operating in Korea, for example, were affected most deeply by the crisis in the very short run. At annual rates, GDP in Korea dropped more than 20 percent during the first quarter of its crisis. Corporates selling goods to customers in that country suffered a decline analogous to the Great Depression in the United States. In another example, Thai companies also were under severe pressure immediately after the crisis outbreak, but conditions were not as severe in the very early days when GDP was stagnant during the first quarter. On average, however, the first year following a crisis is terrible. Negative growth rates were experienced by all of the countries analyzed in this book, and in the case of the sub-sample in Figure 4.2, the accumulated output losses were about 10 percent of GDP.

Korea and Mexico bounced back rapidly after the initial pummeling that each country suffered during the first four quarters after their respective crises broke out. Two years later, both of these countries had begun a turnaround process. Korea's recovery was driven by profound restructuring in its economy and admirable discipline in managing the challenges posed by

FIGURE 4.2   Real GDP growth rate gyrates after crisis.

Percent change, calendar year quarter

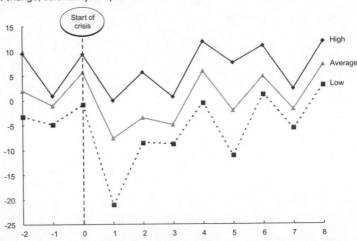

Note: Sample includes Mexico (1994Q4), Indonesia (1997Q3), Thailand (1997Q3), and Korea (1997Q4)
Source: WEFA; WMM; EIU; McKinsey analysis

the crisis, whereas Mexico was fortunate to have the wind of the U.S. economy at its back to complement the fiscal prudence of its government. Thailand and Indonesia have both taken much longer to recover from the aftereffects of their crises.

Real loan rates also vividly reflect the conditions that the crisis brings to bear on companies that operate in dangerous markets. As a group, the four economies in our sample saw real loan rate spikes in the first quarter after their crises erupted (Figure 4.3). Working hand-in-hand with the central bank, for example, Mexico's government applied extraordinarily stringent monetary and financial policies on the way to preparing the conditions to float the peso. This was a first step in reversing the exchange rate policies that Mexico had previously pursued, which had relied on a floating peg. Consequently, real loan rates surged to more than 45 percent during the first quarter of the crisis, although after that rates rapidly converged with the levels of the other countries in the sample, and eventually settled at levels somewhat lower, in part due to the success of floating the peso.

So, what would have happened to a hypothetical company operating in these markets? A quantitative example is useful to illustrate the effects of the first few months of the crisis. To do so, we will use the average values of the four countries at the end of the first quarter of each crisis.

Imagine a corporation selling all of its outputs in the domestic market of the crisis economy. Its sales rise and fall with the economy, as does the cost of servicing its debts, which are 50 percent of total assets—half in

FIGURE 4.3   Real loan rates rise then fall after crisis.

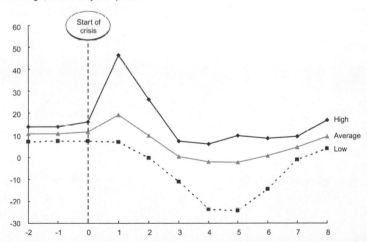

Percent change, calendar year quarter

Note: Sample includes Mexico (1994Q4), Indonesia (1997Q3), Thailand (1997Q3), and Korea (1997Q4)
Source: WEFA; WMM; EIU; McKinsey analysis

dollars and half in local currency. All of its sales are in local currency, which, like the Argentine peso prior to January 2002, was pegged at one peso to the U.S. dollar.

The results of this simple exercise clearly show the effects of not being prepared to withstand the possible effects of financial crises (Table 4.1).

As shown in the aforementioned figures, this scenario is not far-fetched, and stresses the importance of conducting rigorous scenario and contingency planning. Operating in dangerous markets can have enormous negative impacts on unwary investors. Businesses that operate exclusively in these markets are totally exposed to crises, and need to develop special survival skills of the sort displayed by the "local champions" discussed in Chapter 5. "Global players," however, are inherently advantaged by their geographic diversification—which ameliorates the risk of systemic crises—as well as by their access to lower-cost capital and more stable currency pools.

4. Review Business Performance and Prepare for Divestitures

In late 1996, Yong Oh Park, chairman and major shareholder of Doosan Corporation, realized that his company would survive only if it faced up to its declining performance and increasing debt. With almost $5 billion in

TABLE 4.1   Effects of a financial crisis on an otherwise healthy corporation

| | In constant pesos | | In dollars |
	Before	After	After
Balance Sheet Items			
Assets	100.00	100.00	61.35
Liabilities			
Domestic	25.00	25.00	15.34
Foreign	25.00	40.75	25.00
Total	50.00	65.75	40.34
Net worth	50.00	34.25	21.01
Profit and Loss Items			
Sales	100.00	92.40	56.69
COGS (70%)	70.00	64.68	39.68
EBIT	30.00	27.72	17.01
Operating costs	15.00	15.00	9.20
Interest (10%)	5.50	11.58	7.10
FX losses	0.00	15.75	9.66
Profits	9.50	−14.61	−8.96
Taxes (35%)	3.33	0.00	0.00
Net profits	6.18	−14.61	−8.96
Key Ratios (percent)			
ROA	6.20	−14.60	−14.60
ROIC	12.40	−42.60	−42.60

debt and about $700 million in additional debt accumulating each year, Doosan had reached the point where it simply could not generate sufficient cash from its operations to continue.[13] Park, the third-generation leader to run this family company, called an emergency meeting of all the key executives in the company. No one was allowed to leave until there was agreement on clear direction on a turnaround plan for the company.

After ten days, they finally agreed to an aggressive restructuring plan: Under the plan, costs in core operations would be reduced by over $300 million annually. Meanwhile, marginal assets and noncore equity stakes would be sold off to raise cash, including assets in 3M Korea, Kodak Korea, Coca-Cola Korea, Nestlé Korea, and Doosan-Seagram. The following year, cash flow from operations increased from a negative $402 million in 1996 to a positive $16 million. Management also arranged for backup credit and liquidity lines with major lenders, and changed its management ethic to become more professional and performance-driven.

When the crisis rocked Korea in November 1997, Doosan therefore was quite well prepared. Even though this example actually predates Korea's crisis, it illustrates the kind of actions required during the early days of a crisis. In June 1998, all of Doosan's subsidiaries managed to avoid virtual "death sentences" issued by the government to fifty-five companies that it considered unsustainable and for which workouts had been mandated.[14] Park reflects: "Without the family consensus for a drive to secure cash, Doosan would have gone bankrupt shortly after the outbreak of the 1997–1998 economic crisis, like Daewoo and other debt-heavy conglomerates."[15]

The Doosan example illustrates several of the required tactical measures, but particularly this one: When they have done the required scenario planning, they should be able to measure the performance of each business in terms of actual value creation, prepare for divestitures to rationalize the company business portfolio, and generate cash to help keep the company afloat.

In Korea, for example, we worked with another large conglomerate during the 1997 financial crisis to help rationalize its portfolio of over fifteen businesses. A simple analysis of value creation by looking at net profit (ROIC over WACC) provided a framework for prioritizing cash flow improvement programs and determining which businesses to shut down or divest (Figure 4.4). When debating which businesses to divest (Figure 4.5), management also evaluated the strategic importance of each business, as well as its potential for value creation (see Box 4.1: Evaluating the Strategic Value of Portfolio Businesses).

Working with the client, we helped them generate ideas to quickly improve the performance and assess the potential market values for each business. Figure 4.6 shows the range and impact of initiatives generated by the management team of a business unit in this particular conglomerate. Figure 4.7 shows the overall cash flow trend analysis for the group.

FIGURE 4.4   Value creation/destruction analysis is required.

Percent, current fiscal year
$ Thousands

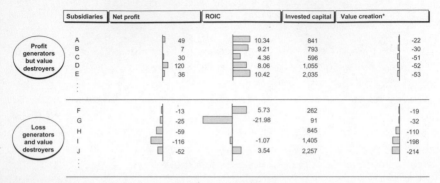

*Economic profit = (ROIC – cost of capital) × (invested capital)
Source: McKinsey analysis

FIGURE 4.5   Prioritization of restructuring efforts.

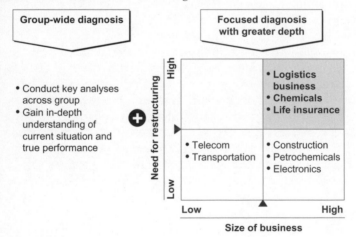

Source: McKinsey analysis

From firsthand experience, we have learned that many companies are able to restructure their portfolio to raise cash, even without affecting their revenues. In some cases, it may be the lavish corporate headquarters building, which houses redundant operations, that goes on the sales block, or poorly

FIGURE 4.6 Potential impact from operational improvements.

Airline company example
$ Millions

	Major levers	Key programs	Fiscal year 1	Total
Growth in current earnings	Revenue enhancement	• Tactical CRM	1~5	10~20
		• Market-based revenue stimulations	2~5	20~40
		• Channel-based stimulations	1~5	10~25
		• Innovative price and fee restructuring	15~20	85~105
		• Leverage noncore assets	1~5	10~20
	Nonpersonnel productivity improvement	• Marketing spend effectiveness	1~5	10~20
		• Purchasing and supply management	5~10	65~150
		• Catering and cleaning redesign	1~5	25~50
	Personnel productivity improvement	• Lean maintenance	3~5	20~30
		• Call center redesign	5~10	20~40
		• Quality management	5~10	40~50
			40~85	315~525

Source: McKinsey analysis

FIGURE 4.7 Cash flow trend analysis.

Fiscal years 1–5
$ Millions

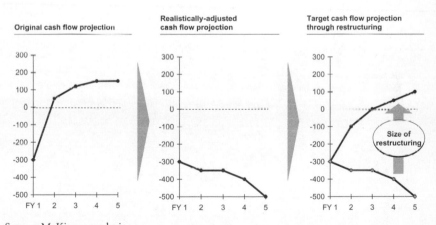

Source: McKinsey analysis

performing units, which have never been scrutinized closely before. Particularly in developing markets, where companies are often diversified, unfocused, and lacking competitive pressure, crises provide the opportunity to simultaneously reshape the company business portfolio and enhance profit.

Management needs to be diligent about balancing divestitures with a commitment to improving cash flow from existing businesses. In the aftermath of the 1994 peso crisis in Mexico, for example, one large bank combed through its businesses' operations looking for ways to boost cash flow. Eventually, it stumbled across a corporate backroom operation that it converted into a data processing center for foreign credit card issuers. The bank was able to generate positive operating revenues through that business that, although small compared to the total operations of the bank, were enough to save hundreds of jobs. (See Box 4.1.)

BOX 4.1: EVALUATING THE STRATEGIC VALUE OF PORTFOLIO BUSINESSES

The matrix in Figure 4.8 is a simple but powerful diagnostic tool that we use to help our clients evaluate how businesses in their portfolio stack up against each other in terms of their strategic value to the company. The horizontal axis is a fact-based understanding of a business's value creation potential on a standalone basis; that is, without any cross-subsidies. The vertical axis rates how good the business fit is with the tangible and intangible assets of the company. After placing each business on this spectrum, management needs to take a hard look at the ability of each business to extract real and sustained value over time. For some businesses, the company might be a "natural" (usually unchallenged) owner of an attractive, core business (top-right quadrant). For others, the company might be simply just one of the pack in a relatively unattractive business and ought to consider an exit strategy (lower-left quadrant).

FIGURE 4.8   Strategic evaluation of business portfolio.

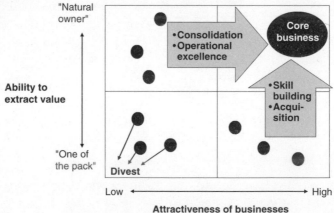

The tougher decisions come with respect to those businesses that fall somewhere between being the natural owner and clear divestiture candidates. In most cases, a dedicated business strategy is required to move these businesses into the top-right quadrant. Examples include consolidating to build scale and make a potentially core business profitable, or moving to operational excellence through a combination of talent acquisition (building or buying skills) and cost reduction.

5. Maintain the Confidence of Key Stakeholders

Companies that survive crises are often those most skilled at communicating with their customers, regulators, board members, employees, and especially shareholders and creditors.[16] The trust of shareholders and creditors, in particular, should be thought of as a valuable asset that, once lost, is very difficult to recover. Consequently, management must identify all of the company's creditors, including key suppliers, and take the initiative by launching a communications offensive to reassure them and retain their confidence.

When the Indonesian financial crisis struck in late 1997, for instance, the conglomerate Astra, known primarily for its car manufacturing operations, saw sales in the automotive industry plunge by more than 70 percent. In response, the company suspended its principal payments and announced that it would restructure debt across its thirty subsidiaries. Within months, the company put together its own creditor committee and started shuttling between Singapore, Jakarta, and Tokyo to negotiate with over two hundred creditors on thorny issues such as debt buy-backs. In June 1999, Astra and its creditors finally signed a deal that divided the debt into three tranches, each with different repayment schedules. This gave Astra some breathing room, and its creditors the assurance that they would not need to "take a haircut" on outstanding loans.

Over the next two years, Astra not only met its debt obligations, it also improved performance though salary cuts, voluntary layoffs, and the closing of nonstrategic distribution outlets. Investor confidence began to rebound. In the April 2001 issue of *Finance Asia,* Astra was voted "Best Managed Company," "Best in Investor Relations," and "Most Committed to Shareholder Value" in Indonesia. Astra was the only Indonesian conglomerate to effectively and professionally manage its debt obligations following the crisis.

Astra illustrates several principles of good crisis management. First, top management had an intelligent and clear understanding of the company's situation. They understood their debt position and knew exactly which subsidiaries were in trouble. Second, the company maintained frequent communications with critical creditors—most importantly, banks such as Chase, Sakura Bank, and Sumitomo Bank—who later cited the company's willingness to be transparent and honest with creditors as essential to the deal.[17] Finally, the company exhibited consistent behavior at critical decision-making points. It stood by its commitment to full disclosure and backed up its words with new efficiency measures and an improved investment strategy.

What and how much to disclose are very important decisions for managers during the first hundred days of a crisis. During crises, managers tend to respond reactively rather than proactively; thus, we recommend that to the extent possible they should consider early on what they are going to reveal to external parties. An important feature in all of the successful examples we have seen is that management should be candid and not overly optimistic. Executives in these success cases are comfortable saying that they do not know all the answers, but they clearly articulate the processes that they have under way to get the answers.

Russia's Alfa Bank provides another example of a company that was forthcoming about its troubles during a financial crisis. In the 1998 crisis, Alfa Bank was dedicated to making its payments to its customers. In the end, Alfa retained its customers' trust as well as their deposits—becoming the largest private bank in the country. A marketing slogan launched by Alfa soon after the crisis reminded customers and competitors that it had honored its commitments during the crisis: "We still make payments every day."[18]

Maintaining trust with customers is critical. One of our clients spent the first two months of the Korean financial crisis personally visiting every major customer in the multi-billion dollar company's registry. By taking each customer through the company's crisis recovery plan and addressing issues in-person and forthrightly, he reinforced these important relationships and built their confidence in the company's future prospects.

Communicating with regulators and government restructuring agencies is also important. Especially during crises, regulators can be a valuable source of information and, more importantly, have special M&A and workout powers. For this reason, both domestic and international companies need to actively manage the relationships they have with key regulators in all of the countries in which they operate.

Finally, and perhaps most importantly, managers and employees must be updated frequently on the rapidly evolving crisis. It is the front-line employees who, for example, interact directly with customers. If they are uncertain or doubtful about the company's prospects, then customers will be as well. In Indonesia in 1998, the new president director of Bank Central Asia (BCA), Djohan Emir Setijoso, focused intensively on reassuring employees through town hall meetings and constant communication. He believed that the key to rebuilding the liquidity position of the bank after the 1998 depositor run was securing the confidence of employees, thereby improving depositor retention rates. Declining employee morale is contagious and often requires a visible response by management—in both words and action—to turn the tide.

DEVELOPING A CRISIS MANAGEMENT APPROACH

Before tackling the five tactical measures listed above, management needs to develop a crisis management approach to the emergency, since by definition crises are not "business as usual." Crises are all-encompassing and are a time when companies need to pull together internally across the corporation, which is why we recommend using a highly structured approach. The core of this effort should be led by a "crisis czar," with strong support from a "cash czar" and five crisis response teams: the information, cash optimization, operations, scenario planning, and communications teams.

The crisis czar—usually the president, COO, or owner of the company—leads the overall restructuring program. When executives think of a crisis czar, they should think of someone with the vision and courage of Banthoon Lamsam, president of Thai Farmers Bank (TFB) and the first person in that country to successfully complete a bank turnaround. During the Thai crisis, he led his company in an aggressive write-off of nonperforming loans, which involved persuading the owning family to dilute its holdings in the company from 17 to 4.2 percent to recapitalize the bank. This allowed TFB to complete its write-offs a full year ahead of the required deadline of December 2000. As a consequence, *Business Week* magazine in 2000 named President Lamsam one of the stars of Asia.[19]

Or consider Yong Nam at LG Electronics or Y.S. Park at Doosan Group: Working six to seven days a week, they pushed their organizations for seemingly overaggressive short-term results while simultaneously keeping their eyes open for strategic opportunities. They were actively involved in both the planning and execution, negotiating with major suppliers, creditors, and potential buyers of parts of their businesses, and also calming and assuaging employees and customers. They were decisive, aggressive, and strong motivators of people.

Roustam Tariko also displayed the right leadership skills. When the Russian crisis hit in August 1998, Tariko moved his organization quickly to reduce major risks—such as recalling its valuable inventory of alcoholic beverages from the shelves of retailers around the country, pulling most of their stock back in three days—while at the same time identifying and acting on a major business opportunity to enter the consumer finance business in Russia.

If the crisis czar is the inspirational leader of the crisis team, the cash czar (often the CFO) is responsible for the company's critical cash management.

In the first hours of the crisis, it is the cash czar who cuts spending and radically reshapes the cash and working capital regimes. The cash czar must work swiftly and have the best people assigned to work on the team.

Once these two leaders are in place, the company needs to form five other sub-teams under them: the information, cash optimization, operations, scenario planning, and communications teams. Typically, the operations and communications teams would report to the crisis czar; while the information, cash optimization, and scenario planning teams would report to the cash czar. These crisis response teams typically range in total from as few as ten people to as many as forty or a hundred people, depending on the size of the company and the depth of change required. In larger conglomerates, they are often grouped together in a restructuring office or headquarters. In Korea, for example, during the first six months of the crisis, LG Group had about sixty people in its restructuring headquarters, Samsung Group had eighty people, and SK Group had about ninety people.[20] In Indonesia, BCA had twenty people in its core crisis team at the peak of the crisis in 1998.

Information Team   The purpose of the information team is to track the company's cash and debt situation. Its goal is to give the cash czar the most current and accurate picture of the company's cash and debt positions. This usually requires that the team balance the twin requirements of speed and accuracy by applying an 80/20 rule to the data. This team also works with the scenario planning team to provide the crisis czar with the overall performance targets and key milestones for the entire crisis management team.

This is also the team upon which the other four teams must rely to build their own assumptions. If the company's treasury group is a high-performing group, it should form the core of the team; otherwise, management should put the company's best financial talent in its place. Information technology skills are also needed since existing management information systems are not set up for managing through crises. In situations we have seen during a crisis, a major "quick and dirty" change is required to the management information system (MIS). During a crisis, the MIS is the CEO's navigational "dashboard" that provides him or her with the necessary warning signals to successfully steer to safety without a serious accident.

Cash Optimization Team   The mandate of the cash optimization team is simply to free up as much cash as possible. While the goal of the information team is to understand and anticipate cash requirements, the optimization team should view its objective as maximizing cash on hand: The managers' mindset should be that the company with the most cash wins in the post-crisis endgame.

For the cash optimization team to be successful, it must set stretch targets and specify timetables for cash generation. The cash optimization team should work with the operations team to help each business reach its targets, and share the lessons that it has learned with the rest of the company. Once the efforts show results, it should immediately ratchet up aspirations.

At LG Electronics' multimedia division, for example, senior managers instituted what they termed the "stretch 1-2-3" principle. Midlevel managers were asked to set targets and timelines, and as soon as they achieved their goal the process was repeated and the bar was raised. After three or four cycles, managers began "stretching" themselves, setting their own targets to take their units to the next level.

Operations Team   The operations team is composed of two sub-teams. The first, the supply chain sub-team, is tasked to manage the issues that crop up in the supply chain with the goal of minimizing disruptions and ensuring as smooth a flow of products and services to the end customer as possible. The second, the divestiture sub-team, is tasked to review and rationalize the company's business portfolio with the goal of creating as much value as possible from the business portfolio. It must therefore be prepared to design and monitor cash improvement initiatives that are too large for the cash optimization team to handle, such as divestitures of business units, even core businesses of the company, if necessary. This is clearly the largest and most diverse of the five teams, requiring people with unique skills and varied backgrounds.

Because of the nature of the task, this is the team that is most likely to encounter resistance from the business units and from senior managers themselves. It is therefore even more incumbent on the CEO, crisis czar, and cash czar to ensure that senior managers are on board in terms of what the company must do to optimize its cash position and business portfolio. It is important to reach this consensus *before* decisions are made on specific lines of business to divest, in order to get everyone on the same page of management's strategic game plan.

Scenario Planning Team   The scenario planning team pulls together the material from the other teams and generates scenarios that will help the company develop contingency plans. From the earliest days of the crisis, its goal is to reduce as much uncertainty as possible. If senior managers have confidence in the company's existing planners, then this group should continue as the scenario makers; otherwise, it should summon together the best strategic thinkers in the company.

Senior managers need to be frequently involved in this team's reports and rigorously test the underlying assumptions. Given the rapid fluctuation of financial indicators and other news during financial crises, reviews should be driven by key events instead of following a regimented structure of monthly or quarterly meetings. Managers should also practice stress-testing the scenario plans. At Emerson, for example, management consciously challenges planning assumptions with seemingly illogical conditions to test its outer limits.

Communications Team   The job of the communications team is to stay in close contact with key stakeholders: shareholders, customers, creditors, regulators, board members, employees and, of course, the media. It also must stay in contact with domestic and international financial markets. Its goal is to maintain stakeholder confidence in the company and its future prospects. Because of the very public nature of its task, close involvement by senior executives in the communications team is almost always required.

Frequent and honest communication is essential. One day after the September 11 terrorist attacks, for example, Phil Purcell, the chairman and CEO of Morgan Stanley (the largest tenant in the World Trade Center), sent out an e-mail to all customers expressing grief for the tragedy and assuring them that the company's business was continuing to operate and that their assets were safe. In addition to a broad communications effort, a few critical investors, creditors, suppliers, and customers need to hear more detail from top management, and the sooner the better. Consistency of message is also critical, which is why *all* communications must go through this team. Contradictions, obfuscations, and partial disclosures are almost always judged negatively and taken as evidence of management's inability to recognize the facts and manage them properly.

MANAGING THE CEO AGENDA

Once the crisis czar, cash czar, and crisis response teams have been established, the CEOs can move on to manage their own agendas. While the CEOs must be involved in many of the areas described above—negotiating directly with key creditors for a debt rollover, approaching key suppliers to increase volume, or overseeing a major acquisition or divestiture—they need to maintain a wider perspective that cuts across all of these areas. In particular, two items on that agenda stand out: ensuring talent quality and the dedication of sufficient management resources.

The first item on the CEO agenda is to make sure that the level of talent is up to the challenges of the crisis. Obviously, this is much easier to do if the company recognizes skill gaps before the crisis. During the crisis itself, companies often have to be resourceful at how they fill these needs. The finance role, in particular, is absolutely critical. At H&CB and Hanvit Bank in Korea, for example, the CEOs brought in experienced CFOs from outside Korea to act as tutors and advisors to their existing CFOs and management team. Not only did their experience help them identify problem areas more quickly, but they also played an instrumental role in real-time training and development of key leaders in the two banks.

This training and development included making sure that the existing CFOs understood the responsibilities of their position. This included: ensuring that a sound asset-liability management program was in place, as well as good management information systems and controls; instituting performance and capital management processes; and communicating the bank's business economics clearly to both internal and external parties. The experienced CFOs also taught senior management what to look for in future potential CFO candidates: public accounting background, strong understanding of the economics of the bank's business, broad business mindset, and good communication skills.

Roust used an aggressive talent acquisition strategy during the 1998 Russian financial crisis to help launch the country's first commercial lending company, Russian Standard Bank. CEO Roustam Tariko brought in Alexander Zourabov, the former chairman of what had been one of the largest banks in the country. Zourabov in turn purchased the banking license of another bankrupt bank. Tariko also brought in basically the entire top management team from Mezhkombank, another leading bank, who were attracted to the bank's business plan. Finally, he hired a vice president from the central bank as Russian Standard Bank's first CEO.[21]

As important as ensuring that the right skills and people are in place is quickly taking out leaders who do not cut it. Companies cannot afford to delay in these types of situations. Ironically, it is not so much the lack of skills that causes the problems, but the lack of drive, energy, and decisiveness.

With the right skills and people in place, the second agenda item that the CEO needs to manage is to ensure that the appropriate level of management resources is dedicated to the crisis management program. As we mentioned earlier, most companies whom we have served had dedicated, talented employees ranging from as few as ten to as many as eighty people totally focused on crisis management leadership roles.

At Mellon Bank, CEO Frank Cahouet and his team led by example, starting their days at 6:00 A.M. and working sixty-hour weeks. The entire top management team met twice a week, Mondays and Fridays, from 7:00 A.M. to 9:00 A.M., to ensure that the necessary turnaround planning was being carried out satisfactorily.

Crisis management is about more than just the frequency of meetings, however; it is about a fundamental shift in mindset and a total commitment by senior managers, a point that the Cahouet team understood and delivered by the personal example it set for the rest of the bank.

At LG's multimedia division for example, during the Korean crisis, Nam took a substantial cut in his compensation and switched his upscale company car to a lower-cost model. He also basically moved into the office. Six days a week, Nam slept at the office and went home only for one weekend day. He visited company facilities at 11:00 P.M., ate late-night meals with his managers, and for six months managed his division through the crisis day and night. "I essentially spent my whole life at the office," Nam recalls.[22] With such a visible commitment by the top leader in the company, employees came to realize that this was not just about securing the next bonus—it was about saving the company. Their collective commitment paid off, and in 2001 not only had the multimedia division survived the crisis, but revenues had increased from about $1.5 billion in 1997 to $4.5 billion in 2001.[23]

Obviously, the level of commitment will vary in each company and crisis. Still, it is important for the CEO to set the tenor of the crisis management approach and to foster a team spirit among managers. Ultimately, it comes back to the CEO to set the standard for the company and lead by example. (See Box 4.2: The Ten Commandments of Crisis Management, used by one of our Korean clients during the 1997 crisis.)

Leadership is a critical factor in both crisis prevention and management. Our observations from working alongside those executives who have been successful and unsuccessful in steering their organizations through crises suggest a number of common behaviors or characteristics.

First, these leaders set bold, measurable aspirations, as President Nam did at LG by setting targets of multiple increases in cash flow. As we will see in Chapter 6, the management teams at Mellon Bank in the United States and Christiana Bank in Norway, for example, set equally high targets for cost reduction and profitability in those critical bank turnaround situations.

Second, they are ruthless about ensuring they have the right people in the right place and are terrific at building effective leadership teams. They often will reach down within the organization, and outside the company if necessary, to ensure they have the best skills in place to drive critical initiatives. We have not been surprised to see 50 percent of leadership teams change during these episodes.

Third, these leaders are relentless on performance and results. They operate in a "no-excuse" mindset, where people are expected to make their numbers, without excuses and without a second chance. Leaders establish key performance indicators for all of their key people, receive timely information on those indicators, and ensure clear consequences (both positive and negative) for performance and nonperformance.

Finally, these leaders are totally committed themselves, focusing most of their energy on three fundamental tasks: driving the overall program; spending significant time with key customers, suppliers, investors, and employees; and communicating, listening, coaching, fixing, and cajoling people to push the envelope and meet management's aspirations and produce results. For most of these leaders, this has meant a significant change in lifestyle and many personal sacrifices for the duration of the effort.

BOX 4.2: THE TEN COMMANDMENTS OF CRISIS MANAGEMENT

How do you set the right tone for effectively conducting crisis management? One of our clients told us about the following "Ten Commandments" that his company has used to focus management on the measures needed to survive. Since then, we have used these common-sense rules in many situations, with excellent results.

1. Accept the seriousness of the situation
2. Deliver results, not plans
3. Be prepared for a tough, multi-year effort
4. Explore all plausible options in parallel
5. Commit 100 percent
6. Be decisive; don't delay tough decisions
7. Exercise top-down leadership
8. Remove key people who don't "get it" or who don't move
9. Tolerate no sacred cows
10. Stay focused until the job is done

■ ■ ■

By taking these steps, managers can help to ensure that their companies survive the first hundred days of a financial crisis and effectively manage its challenges—from cash shortages to supply chain disruptions to shaky stakeholder confidence. As we mentioned earlier, however, the ideal situation is when a company already has taken the necessary steps to prepare for a crisis before it hits; unfortunately, this is rarely the case. In fact, we asked a number of our clients who have been through financial crises what they would have done differently to be better prepared had they known that the crisis was coming. We share with you the insights we have gleaned from these retrospective discussions in Box 4.3: Preparing for a Financial Storm—While the Skies Are Still Blue.

BOX 4.3: PREPARING FOR A FINANCIAL STORM— WHILE THE SKIES ARE STILL BLUE

Surviving a financial storm is more than just battening down the hatches as the dark clouds roll in. It is building a ship beforehand that can survive rough seas. After speaking with dozens of companies that have been through financial crises—the vast majority of which operate in crisis-prone areas—we have arrived at five actions that senior executives need to take to prepare while the skies are still blue.

1. Keep an Eye Out for the Warning Signs

Remember that many of the warning signs of a crisis are visible, such as value destruction in the real sector, excessive short-term borrowings, declining bank profitability, asset price bubbles, or other clear financial mismatches. Monitor these warning signs regularly, and tap into informal sources of knowledge in your local business and political communities. Do not close your eyes and look the other way. *Do* scan the landscape for these warning signs—analyzing them using your best judgment—and encourage bad news to travel fast to enhance transparency.

2. Prepare the Management Mindset for a Crisis

Prepare the emotional fitness of your management team by building internal training programs around financial crises, especially if you notice storm clouds building. Hold a two-day senior management off-site workshop, under the context that a crisis scenario has just occurred, to define a crisis program—key actions, allocation of resources, and management approach. Critically evaluate these simulated decisions, and rework management approaches with external input. Study, evaluate, and codify responses, successful or otherwise, of peer companies in crisis countries. Give employees the option to debate issues related to the company's future. Likewise, include the input of analysts and industry observers when working to develop crisis-related contingency plans and management approaches.

3. Reduce Debt and Strengthen Funding Sources

Understand and increase your cash flow position, reduce debt, and strengthen funding sources. Track the amount of free cash flow that is being generated, and the interest coverage ratio. Reduce your overall debt load, lengthen loan maturities, and hedge currency and interest rate exposures. Diversify your funding sources and actively monitor the health of your creditors. Weigh the costs of these additional measures, and seriously consider establishing backup lines of credit before a crisis hits.

4. Safeguard Your Supply Chain
Understand how key suppliers and customers might be affected during a crisis, and build in safeguards to your supply chain. Examine plant operations and optimize their asset configurations before the crisis hits. For example, you may even want to consider the convenience of such radical measures as vertically integrating operations within each plant so that they can be more self-sufficient during a crisis, and thereby give management greater flexibility in its choice of responses (e.g., shifting production volume or human resources across plants). Less radical measures might include arranging backup supply lines for specialty inputs and consolidating suppliers of commodity inputs. If a critical component is currently sourced from a crisis-prone region, consider alternative sources. Finally, understand the health of downstream wholesalers and retailers, and prepare to act to protect critical links.

5. Put Basic Scenario and Contingency Planning Processes in Place
Consumer goods companies now routinely study Johnson & Johnson's excellent response to the Tylenol crisis in 1982, when seven people died as a result of product tampering and cyanide-laced tablets. Manufacturing companies hire engineers to identify safety risks and then take workers through a simulated safety crisis. Even school children conduct fire drills.

If your company operates in crisis-prone economies, you should take similar measures. We believe that financial crises require the same, if not a higher, level of attention and *preparatory* training by top management. Develop scenarios that incorporate multiple macro- and especially microeconomic parameters as we explained in Chapter 3, and make sure that these scenarios and contingency plans are thoroughly reviewed by senior executives. Ensure that an accurate and timely cash flow measurement system is in place and linked to the scenario plans. Run stress tests on scenario plans to see how they handle simulated crises.

Keep in mind what Jaime Augusto Zobel, the CEO of the Ayala group in the Philippines, has to say about the value of being prepared: "We are a 165-year-old company accustomed to being prepared and taking advantage of crises," he explains. "That is why we have survived and thrived."[1]

Finally, it is important for executives to realize that tactically managing the early days of a crisis not only increases the company's chances of survival, but also positions it to capture new strategic opportunities. In Chapter 5, we learn how companies that have earned this right to win then go a step further to secure significant advances for their shareholders.

APPENDIX 4.1: Painting the Picture of a Financial Crisis

It is crucial for managers to understand what to expect when a financial crisis hits, what actually happens in the first hundred days, and what are the typical next phases. Management teams that improvise solutions not grounded on a thorough understanding of financial crises are more likely to stumble in their efforts, and may even do more harm than good. Companies that survive crises do so because management clearly understands the risks and deploys resources in a timely manner where they will have the greatest impact.

To give executives a sense of rhythm and timing, we have found that financial crises can be broken down into four phases that have different themes: managing the initial liquidity crisis, returning to financial stability, restructuring the economy, and reentering the global marketplace. We first developed this framework while summarizing the Scandinavian financial crises of the early 1990s for our Korean clients in 1998, and have since applied it to other crises as well. We describe each phase briefly below, to give executives a sense of how badly a financial crisis can affect the economy.

Unfortunately, some countries do not make it through all of these four phases, become stuck in one of the early phases, and subsequently often go back into crisis.

One caveat that we have found: Good macroeconomic policies rarely emerge before there is political consensus and stability. Countries such as Indonesia, Japan, Russia, and Argentina demonstrate that financial crises can take a long while to resolve when the political situation is uncertain.

Phase 1—Managing the Initial Liquidity Crisis   The first phase is usually several months long and very acute. Most of the time, its first manifestation is a sudden currency depreciation accompanied by a liquidity crisis. The central bank raises real interest rates to stabilize and reverse currency flows as well as to lower inflation expectations. It may also choose to restrict the money supply further by selling bonds or increasing reserve requirements. Many financial institutions cut back credit lines and stop rolling over debt. Short-term interest rates skyrocket.

The implementation of a restrictive monetary policy has a significant impact on businesses in the short term. As interest rates rise, so do companies' existing debt burdens. In addition, higher interest rates limit companies' access to capital since it becomes unaffordable and banks may create a credit crunch because of the effects on their profits and losses. Managers need to either limit spending or find alternative sources of capital to offset the impact of increased interest rates on their businesses. Cash is short for everyone, bankruptcy tremors are rampant, and assets are repriced almost overnight to new, depressed-market prices while the cost of liabilities soars.

Under these conditions, there is also a crisis of confidence. Rumors and uncertainty abound, and the financial crisis crowds out all other news on the front page. Every dinner party discussion turns into an exchange of anecdotes that illustrates both the extent to which the economy is suffering and the almost obsessive but understandable involvement that every business-person must have with respect to current crisis events.

Phase 2—Returning to Financial Stability   After the first few months, the second phase starts in motion. By this time, the most vulnerable surviving companies are beginning to negotiate with creditors, and business operations have slowed down, sometimes quite significantly, in response to consumers adapting to the new environment by curtailing purchases and simply making do with less. Usually, this financial crunch can last anywhere from six to twenty-four months. Liquidity problems persist and sometimes increase (e.g., Argentina, Turkey), and bankruptcies continue. Payment systems are often deeply affected and adopt new channels and sometimes even new currencies, while banks are reorganized or taken over, awaiting resolutions that can take months or even years. Asset prices continue to head south, albeit less steeply than at the beginning of the crisis, and by now even the optimists acknowledge that recession has set in.

Figure A4.1A shows just how hard a financial crisis can hit an economy, but even these numbers do not give the full picture. Overshooting—prices moving past their long-term equilibrium level—is very common during the early months of crisis. Interest rates soar, in part due to monetary restrictions imposed by the central bank, but also as a reflection of the lack of confidence in the economy. Exchange rates plunge, and with this change come many dramatic effects. Overnight, companies that are significantly dependent on foreign trade blossom, as they export their way out of their problems—or die, if they rely significantly on foreign inputs or if overseas credit lines are pulled. The prices of shares in the stock exchange also gyrate wildly as investors reassess the circumstances of companies, for better and worse. Paradoxically, some companies even experience windfall profits from the repricing of accounts receivable, cash balances, or inventories.

How long these conditions last depends on many factors, some of them political. Figure A4.1B shows how various countries have restored economic activity over time, with some obviously faring better than others. Korea and Mexico stand out for their comparatively rapid recovery in the

FIGURE A4.1A   Credit crunches following financial crises.

Asian example
Percent, 1999 to 2000

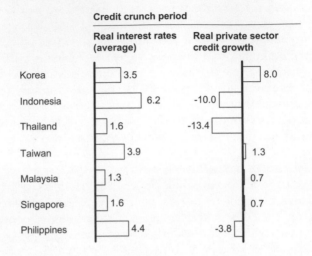

	Credit crunch period	
	Real interest rates (average)	**Real private sector credit growth**
Korea	3.5	8.0
Indonesia	6.2	-10.0
Thailand	1.6	-13.4
Taiwan	3.9	1.3
Malaysia	1.3	0.7
Singapore	1.6	0.7
Philippines	4.4	-3.8

Source: IMF; EIU; central banks

FIGURE A4.1B   Recovery from financial crises.

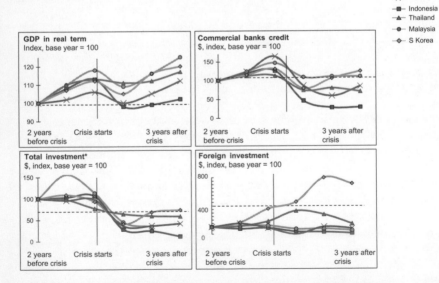

*Data source for Malaysia only covers total investment for manufacturing industry
Source: National Statistic Offices; BKPM; BI; Bank of Thailand; Bank of Korea; Bank Negara Malaysia; EIU

near term, although both countries still face lingering issues at the time of this writing. Much of this relative advantage is due to the collective response in Korea to its crisis, compared especially to other countries in Asia, and Mexico's unique trade relationship with the United States and Canada.

Phase 3—Restructuring the Economy   The third phase, which can last several years, is the beginning of the real long-term turnaround, with a restructuring of not just the financial system but the entire economy. The government focuses on establishing a sustainable foreign exchange regime, concluding negotiations with bank creditors, and establishing principles for long-term economic liberalization. In the private sector, businesses consolidate, industry structures shift and realign, and assets that pass through a restructuring agency are slowly redeployed into the real economy.

Setting an appropriate foreign exchange rate, given a country's economic context, is one of the most important policy decisions that a government will make after a financial crisis. It fosters economic stability by setting sustainable currency levels to help avert crises—to make sure that the government does not run out of money trying to prop up the currency—and limits inflation expectations. It also creates the conditions for growth by providing a stable environment for trade and investment.

BOX A4.1: METHODS TO STABILIZE THE EXCHANGE RATE

There are several policy methods a government can use to stabilize the exchange rate, and the chosen method may change over the short versus long term (for example, using a fixed currency peg in the short term to create complete exchange rate stability, and—two to three years later—floating the currency once stability has been achieved). These methods are briefly defined below.

1. **Fixed or floating currency peg.** Under a currency peg, the central bank commits to buying or selling the necessary amount of foreign currency to maintain the exchange rate level at which the currency is "pegged." Policymakers implement pegs because they achieve the dual objective of creating both real and perceived stability and allowing policymakers to retain some control over currency policy (as compared to adopting a third party's currency).

2. **Similarly, under a floating peg,** the central bank commits to supporting the currency within a predetermined band within which it is allowed to float against a chosen currency or a basket of currencies. Central banks deploy two strategies to support both fixed and floating

(continued)

pegs. Either they buy or sell their own currency to support the peg or they use interest rate policy to stimulate private currency traders to do so.

3. Floating exchange rate. Under a floating exchange rate, a central bank does not commit to maintaining the currency at a given exchange rate. Instead, it lets markets set the exchange rate through daily buying and selling. Because of their frequency, these adjustments are typically small and therefore not economically disruptive after an approximate equilibrium is reached. Before that point, currency values tend to gyrate wildly.

4. Currency board. Adopting a currency board has similar implications to a fixed exchange rate, if not more extreme. It sends a signal of even more binding commitment to prudent and austere macroeconomic policies because it more rigidly supports a given exchange rate. Governments choose to adopt currency boards because they provide the most short-term stability following a crisis. In the long term, however, they can be difficult to sustain and are therefore ultimately problematic.

5. Adopting the currency of another country. This is by far the most far-reaching example of the final foreign exchange mechanism and perhaps the most difficult to implement. The best example of this is dollarization; the adoption of the euro by European countries in January 2002 is another.

In addition to setting foreign exchange policy, policymakers focus on concluding negotiations to restructure bank debt. Prompt renegotiation of existing debt plays an important role in stabilizing the economy by lessening burdensome interest payments on the government to free up resources for other uses, and restoring the credibility and confidence of lenders, thereby increasing access to future capital. The process of restructuring debt following a crisis essentially allocates losses among the following key parties: creditor banks, international and domestic investors, bondholders, and the government. Because it is a zero-sum game, each party must fight aggressively to preserve its interests.

After addressing the critical issues of monetary and foreign exchange rate policy, governments focus on implementing needed fiscal discipline. Sound fiscal policy depends on crafting a government budget, which can be financed over time on a sustained basis. The budget allows government to meet obligations to international and domestic creditors as well as public stakeholders (e.g., pensioners) while decreasing its debt level. As a result, government often must either raise revenue or reduce spending accordingly.

Given the difficulty of balancing the budget during crises, governments often turn to supplementary mechanisms, such as privatization, to increase revenues. It is difficult to gain political support for these structural reforms in prosperous times, but it becomes more compelling during a crisis. While the sale of government assets in times of crisis yields lower prices, by the time they are actually sold few alternatives exist. As a result, privatizations under such circumstances are common. Other efforts to improve government finances through structural reforms include eliminating barriers to foreign competition in certain sectors, opening formerly protected areas for resource exploration (e.g., oil), and increasing private sector involvement in the pension system.

Given limitations, particularly in consumer demand and government spending, growth becomes highly dependent on bank lending for capital investment. Yet banks are unable to provide the stimulus for growth. They lack the necessary access to capital on which to leverage a loan portfolio. In addition, during this time banks are focused on important internal objectives, such as collecting nonperforming loans and internal restructuring. Finally, having just survived a financial crisis, banks are hesitant to risk lending to companies that are in the process of restructuring, as most are at this time. Bank managers are often shell-shocked and strongly risk-averse after a financial crisis. Their inability or unwillingness to provide needed economic stimulus is referred to as the "credit-channeling problem."

Managers experience the impact of this credit-channeling issue at the business level as they struggle to raise the necessary capital for their own businesses. Similar constraints affect their own suppliers and customers facing similar challenges. In addition, they have to demonstrate significant restructuring efforts to convince debtors to continue debt rollovers.

In many post-crisis countries, private sector credit fails to grow despite low real interest rates. As described above, this lack of available credit results from weak and poorly capitalized banking sectors, a scarcity of viable lending candidates, and high risk aversion. One solution to this situation is to have the government implement a credit guarantee program, as was done in Korea. Such programs have risks, however, which include the potential for moral hazard, delayed restructuring, and high fiscal costs. Because these risks have the potential to limit long-term economic stability, managers must ensure that they are effectively addressed by policymakers in the design phase.[1]

As these public reforms occur, bank lending resumes and more long-term capital becomes available, including an influx of new foreign capital looking for enhanced opportunities in a post-crisis, restructured economy. Companies build up operational excellence and revamp the internal performance ethic, and an active market for corporate control appears, along with more visible M&A activity.

Phase 4—Reentering the Global Marketplace   Finally, the crisis enters a fourth phase, marked by a renewed emphasis on harmonizing the economy in line with global market demands and standards. Managers now face lower inflation, less currency risk, and increased access to credit. They feel that business is finally "coming back" even if it has not returned to pre-crisis levels. GDP growth resumes, banking systems are rebuilt, and capital markets develop better linkages to global financial hubs. Manufacturing moves toward world-class standards, a growing service sector emerges, small and medium-sized businesses develop and change the competitive landscape, and foreign competitors increase the level of competitive intensity as well.

Now, government officials shift their focus from stability to growth. While the macroeconomic policies outlined above are critical to creating the underlying stability needed for economic growth, they alone are not sufficient to stimulate it. Growth depends on policies that focus on the business sector, including policies that promote world-class corporate governance standards, a domestic capital market that is linked efficiently to the global financial markets, a strong financial service supervisory regime, and improvements to the legal framework that usually results in the aftermath of a financial storm.[2]

APPENDIX 4.2: How Companies Can Strengthen Funding Before a Crisis

Operating on threadbare ICRs is like walking a tightrope; in a financial crisis, it is like walking that same tightrope in a storm. Consequently, it is crucial for companies to not only understand their cash position, but also to reduce their debt burden and strengthen funding sources before the crisis hits.

Emerson, for instance, runs a conservative balance sheet and refuses to increase its debt position despite criticism from some analysts. By minimizing its leverage, Emerson retains the ability to assume debt when attractive acquisitions become available. In addition, it avoids getting entangled in burdensome interest payments, which management learned from the recession of the early 1990s can be particularly onerous during economic downturns.[1] When a crisis hits and revenue streams are disrupted, defaults on interest payments can spell disaster for a company and serve as an invitation for creditors to seize control of assets, especially if its funding sources are not well diversified.

Similarly, the Turkish holding company Alarko prefers to stay away from direct plant, property, and equipment investments as much as possible. Instead, management prefers to lease buildings and equipment to provide a more balanced cash flow, avoid large upfront cash outlays, and ensure continuous technology upgrades of equipment. It also reflects their attention on the company's balance sheet, which as we mentioned in the chapter text needs to be managed closely alongside the cash flow and income statements.

Surprisingly, many companies have fundamentally sound businesses but are plagued by significant asset-liability mismatches. Three common mismatches are interest rate (floating versus fixed), currency, and maturity. Interest rate mismatches are much more important for banks—for whom managing this type of risk is the bread and butter of what they do—than they are for corporates. Yet, corporates can definitely be exposed to these mismatches, especially in developing markets and especially when operating primarily in non–U.S. dollar, local currencies (e.g., Thailand, Indonesia). Whereas dollar interest rates may only fluctuate within a narrow range of three to four percentage points over several years, short-term rupiah interest rates jumped from the mid-teens to over 70 percentage points in a matter of months during the Asian financial crisis. In particular, using short-term borrowings at floating rates to finance long-term capital expenditures creates interest rate exposure, in addition to currency exposure, if borrowings are in a foreign currency.

Currency mismatches occur when a company's assets are in one currency while its liabilities are in another. A company might receive revenues in pesos while servicing debt interest payments or supplier purchases in deutsche marks. In Thailand before the 1997 financial crisis, for example, finance companies were borrowing short-term dollar deposits at an annual interest rate of about 7 percent, converting the money into baht, and lending it again on the spot market at interest rates between 12 and 25 percent.[2] This was fine as long as the exchange rate remained stable, but when the baht was floated in July 1997 these currency mismatches forced over fifty finance companies into bankruptcy.

Currency mismatches, in turn, are often further aggravated by maturity mismatches. Maturity mismatches can occur when assets are structured on longer timeframes than liabilities, such as when debt interest payment or supplier purchase schedules come due much earlier than accounts receivable or other cash inflows, leaving a company especially exposed to the volatility of financial crises. In Korea, some industrial companies have been known to borrow using short-term, ninety-day promissory notes to fund significant, long-term capital expenditures—an extremely risky approach during the period before a financial crisis hits. In Indonesia before the 1997–1998 financial crisis, some financial institutions borrowed dollars in the short and medium term, swapped the dollars on the spot market for rupiah, and lent the rupiah to Indonesian corporations. In less than a year, the dollar-rupiah exchange rate, which had been reasonably stable for more than a decade, skyrocketed from less than 2,500 to over 15,000, leading to incredible losses.

To say that the consequences were entirely unexpected, though, would be less than completely fair. Between 1993 and 1997, the average debt-equity ratio in Korea was 520 percent, compared to 253 percent in Japan, 171 percent in the United States, and 120 percent in Germany. In 1997, the average debt-equity ratio of the top ten Korean conglomerates was just under 500 percent. Only one year later, the average fell to about 320 percent. The 1997 financial crisis taught the chaebol a painful lesson on the importance of reducing debt, one that they are still learning. In fact, the government—through its restructuring agency, the Financial Supervisory Commission (FSC)—mandated that all of the top thirty chaebol have debt-equity ratios of less than 200 percent by December 31, 1999, and prohibited asset revaluations (e.g., raising the value of their real estate holdings).[3] This was an important step. One executive recalls, "Every individual and management team got the message loud and clear: If you didn't meet the 200 percent target, you were in big trouble."

To manage against currency mismatches, management must first examine the asset and liability structures of the company's balance sheet and identify key exposures. How much of the company's liabilities are in foreign currencies, and which ones are particularly subject to volatile exchange or interest rates? What are the term schedules for debt-interest or other payments versus receipts? Management should also ask how much is hedged naturally, either in dollar inventories or dollar accounts receivable, or through the use of financial hedging instruments. In the Philippines, Ayala, which operates with a debt-equity ratio of about 90 percent, has about 80 percent of its exposure in dollars, but is virtually completely hedged with a mix of foreign exchange forward contracts and interest rate swaps.

Once management has assessed the situation, it can take action to reduce risks associated with these exposures. For interest rate exposures, management should consider negotiating fixed rates, if the creditor will consent, or using interest rate swaps. Companies should also consider availing themselves of currency forwards or options, when available. In addition, it can also pursue more natural hedges. Management can split up its balance sheet by currency and earmark dollar receivables to dollar payables on its pro forma financial statements. It can also match short-term liabilities to current assets, and negotiate with creditors to lengthen term structures when necessary and feasible.

These options, however, are a function of the depth and sophistication of local currency markets. Banks, for example, might not be willing to lend term rupiah, making it almost impossible to get a five-year fixed rate. In many emerging market economies, most funding comes from bank loans, and corporate bond markets are still relatively early in development. In the 2001 crisis in Turkey, for example, there were few financial instruments for companies to hedge against currency devaluations. Without a local currency forwards market, even the largest companies with private debt are hit hard because of their dollar-denominated debt. If a company recognizes the warning signs of an impending financial crisis, it might want to prepay its foreign currency liabilities to reduce its exposure—but this depends on its cash position.

Consequently, Alarko responded to the latest crisis in Turkey in 2001 with two changes in company policy. First, the company increased its target ICR by 50 percent to prepare for future financial crises (e.g., if banks call back loans or if receivables become an issue). Second, all new investments have been targeted for a fifty-fifty balance between equity and other financing. Management prefers international to local financing to ensure longer terms (Turkish bank loans are typically on term structures of less than one year due to high inflation and economic uncertainty), and it tries to use local short-term financing for bridge loans only, as necessary.

Because of these risks during financial crises, companies must improve their ICRs and reduce their debt to reasonable levels before a crisis hits. Companies need to consider shifting at least a portion of their debt from floating to fixed rates, diversifying their sources of funding, and lengthening term structures. All of these actions require an understanding of the company's debt and funding sources at a group level.

In addition, corporates and financial institutions should review their funding requirements and sources to ensure that they always have access to stable sources of funding at reasonable rates (which means diversifying before a crisis hits). Like Doosan, companies should seek backup lines of credit before a crisis, even though this requires that they pay a premium for the added security. These actions also usually require some asset-liability management experience. If their management skill portfolio is not up to the task, it is crucial to bring in the requisite talent as soon as possible to assume this responsibility.

APPENDIX 4.3: Using Scenario Planning In Financial Crises

Scenario and contingency planning are often neglected during financial crises, when time pressures and tremendous uncertainty push management's attention to seemingly more urgent tasks. From our experience, however, companies that have learned to incorporate these processes into their ongoing management processes have benefited greatly during crises, and many who did not have these processes in place eventually learned to do so. By setting ranges on multiple sets of "parameters" or variables, management can define a set of scenario outcomes to inform assumptions in the company's budgeting processes, forecast future cash flow trends, and help the company define crisis contingency plans.

The first step of selecting and setting ranges on parameters is often the most time-consuming. When creating and updating scenarios for financial crises, we recommend that management incorporate at least four sets of key parameters—macroeconomic, financial environment-related, industrial, and political/regulatory. Each of the four sets of parameters should be broken down individually and forecasted for change over time.

1. Take, for example, macroeconomic parameters, which typically include GDP growth, interest rates, exchange rates, inflation rates, and the current account balance as a percent of GDP. To populate a forecast table, management draws upon expert interviews, publications research, and questionnaires to assess the range of each of the parameters in terms of "most likely" and "less likely" outcomes. This is clearly a case where science and art shake hands, but the important thing is to remain as fact-driven as possible.

Defining the ranges on especially the macroeconomic parameters is an absolutely crucial part of the process—whether for financial crises or otherwise, scenario planning is only as useful as the ranges selected on different parameters. One company with whom we worked in Asia mentioned that despite their attempts at scenario planning, the outside financial situation got much worse than they had expected, in part because they had selected narrow ranges on their variables. In other words, "it was the market's fault" that they went into difficulty. The company has now learned to be much more aggressive and proactive (looking at other country case examples, carefully monitoring the external environment), and to be mentally prepared for a broader range of outcomes.

Working through the remaining three sets of parameters—financial environment-related, industrial, and political/regulatory—requires even more art, and more importantly, experienced, individual judgment.

2. For financial environment-related parameters, net flows of capital, which depend on a separate set of factors related to investor and depositor confidence, are critical for determining how bad the liquidity shortage will be. Sometimes, outflows from residents matter as much as inflows. In Argentina, for example, the complete lack of confidence due to the debt default, the currency devaluation, and the freeze on deposits (*corralito*) has led to an estimated 15 percent decline in the depositor base in the first quarter of 2002, coming on top of the 23 percent deposit outflow in 2001. This situation is affected more generally by the extent to which capital is available for investment, given constraints on bank lending following a crisis and higher interest rates. Capital constraints combine with asset-liability mismatches or the inability to liquidate assets quickly enough to influence the default rate. The default rate, in turn, can signal who is still likely to be standing at the end of the day, what the industry landscape will look like, and how long it will take to recover from the crisis.

3. Understanding the dynamics of industrial parameters is slightly more complicated. Among the four key sub-parameters—market demand and behavior, government policy toward domestic companies, speed of consolidation, and global competitor entry—market demand is the easiest place to start. Changes in market demand and behavior affect both domestic and foreign companies. A slowdown in consumer spending puts a squeeze on producers, and may push companies out the door. The response and timing of domestic and foreign companies affect the industry landscape by determining the speed of industry consolidation. Government plays a big part here as well, either by encouraging certain domestic companies to consider M&A or competing companies to make business swaps, or by opening the door to foreign companies such as through the lifting of foreign ownership limitations.

4. Finally, there are the political/regulatory parameters, which are divided into two groups: internal parameters, including the strength of political leadership, willingness to reform, and ability to reform; and external parameters, including labor unions or consumer groups, multilateral financial institutions such as IMF and the World Bank, and governments. So, for example, management must consider the potential for fiscal reform in their forecasts, which might include the adoption of a balanced budget or tax reforms. Management must also evaluate the extent to which government is putting in place the necessary legal and regulatory frameworks for a stable market economy (e.g., private property laws, corporate governance mechanisms). If managers do not perceive the government to be serious about such reforms (e.g., Japan, Venezuela, Argentina), then they should increase their assessment of market risk in their scenario planning.

These parameters provide a basic starting point for any company; each company should tailor the parameters or introduce new ones based on "killer risks" that are specific to the company's situation and could bring it down in the early days of a financial crisis. *For banks,* killer risks might include: failure by the central bank to act as a lender of last resort; regulatory intervention or takeover; or a catastrophic business failure in a subsidiary that could produce a contagion effect for the group at large. *For corporates,* the list includes: prospects for near-term debt rollovers or the complete severing of bank relationships; lack of investor confidence accompanied by dumping of stock; or a commodity price collapse in response to deflation (e.g., Japan) or price increases of key inputs, such as oil (e.g., Korea).

Second, after going through this exercise of setting ranges for all of the parameters, management can then define a limited set of outcomes. By assigning probabilities to each outcome—essentially bundles of different variables—it can prioritize which variables to use as key assumptions in the company's financial models, and also forecast future cash flow trends. Changes in the GDP growth rate might influence sales growth, or interest and inflation rates might affect the carrying cost of cash. Even qualitative parameters, such as political or banking system stability, work together with more quantitative figures such as consumer spending trends, to help set pricing and revenue assumptions. Any key variable that could put noticeable stress on the company's cash position in a volatile economic environment should be included. Examples include changes in demand conditions for the company's products and services (price and volume), operational risk factors (supplier pricing or margins to dealers), and funding conditions (e.g., financing variables across different countries, viability of supplier funding or consumer funding).

Finally, these outcomes provide something tangible, finite, and fact-based against which management can design contingency plans. How the scenarios predict interest rate changes, for instance, will affect expectations on cost of debt, and exchange rate fluctuations will influence the company's hedging strategy. Other questions include: Which assets could a company most easily divest to raise cash? Which plants or offices, if closed, would cut costs most sharply or preserve the most cash? Which products or services are least profitable and could be jettisoned? Conversely, what critical business lines and customer relationships must be preserved at any cost? In general, management should establish a contingency plan for each outcome. (This part of the process can take weeks to complete.)

Like Emerson, action plans should be developed based on best case and less likely scenarios, and reviewed by senior management. This review process helps senior executives integrate ongoing risk management into day-to-day tactical issues as well as longer-term strategy. Management needs to execute aggressively against each one, and bring in outside help when necessary, including accounting firms, law firms, and investment banks, to ensure that all of the required skills are available.

While some international companies may opt to use the Economist Intelligence Unit or other commercial country risk ratings, we recommend that companies also build and monitor their own scenarios for countries in which they have substantial operations. Many of the critical inputs are what we term "softer" variables, or information that is usually not published but is instead obtained through informal channels (see Box 3.2: A Dinner Party for Eight, in Chapter 3). On the other hand, if a company has only a minimal presence in a country, or entry into that specific country is not a key strategic priority, then it is better to use commercial risk ratings.

Successful scenario planning for financial crises ultimately requires seemingly plain ingredients. The first is excellence in financial forecasting and reporting processes. Without this, incorporating crisis-related variables into existing but malfunctioning models will not produce trustworthy, fact-based results. As in other operational areas, crises require that management first get the basics right. The second is quality of judgment. Defining the ranges on planning parameters requires experience, creativity, and owner-ship. At Emerson, former CEO Charles Knight required that division heads assume full responsibility for their own planning processes rather than handing it off to subordinates. Companies need to ensure that they have the right talent and proper alignment of incentives to ensure that scenario plan-ning is thoughtfully managed.

CHAPTER 5

Capturing Strategic Opportunities After the Storm

Soon after the financial crisis hit Thailand in July 1997, it was not long before the contagion swept through the rest of Asia. First came Malaysia and the Philippines, where before year's end the ringgit lost 56 percent of its value and the peso fell 53 percent, respectively. Then came Indonesia and Korea, where the rupiah lost 139 percent of its value and the won plunged by 121 percent. Even the mighty Singapore and Hong Kong dollars came under attack.[1]

While many foreign and domestic investors were pulling out of these dangerous markets, some realized that times of great uncertainty—when financial and competitive landscapes change almost overnight—are exactly when companies should seek out new strategic opportunities. Instead of running away, these managers went even deeper into their markets to rethink their strategies.

Douglas Daft, then head of Asian operations for Coca-Cola, was one of them. As the Asian crisis spread, Daft summoned his executives and a select group of academicians and outside advisors to an offsite in California. He invited this group of outsiders to expand the thinking of his executive team in a time of wrenching change. He wanted to seed his team's strategy and planning discussion with a debate on macroeconomic, trade, policy, and social issues, and he wanted all of his executives thinking with a broadly defined frame of reference. They discussed not only how Coca-Cola could manage short-term needs, but also how it could capture new growth opportunities and emerge from the crisis in a better position than before. He reminded them that the company had achieved one of its greatest breakthroughs in its international markets at the end of World War II, when it discovered new opportunities in the broken landscape of Western Europe and Japan.

How could Coca-Cola find an opportunity in the crisis to acquire some locally branded products? How will the regulatory regimes likely change? How should Coke's local divisions and bottlers work with new regulatory regimes to support reforms that could reduce import and retail trade barriers? How could the company change its distribution strategy in different regional markets, such as Korea, where getting into "mom-and-pop" retail stores was difficult, or China, where it lacked bottlers, or Indonesia, where it had few vending machines? Is there a breakthrough distribution strategy in Indonesia?

To answer those questions, Daft not only convened his group of advisors, but also started a monthly series of two-day, offsite workshops with internal managers to push those questions further and develop common viewpoints. Eventually, these strategic thinking sessions helped Coca-Cola significantly strengthen its position across Asia. In Korea, it completed the purchase of full control of its bottling business from Doosan and other bottlers in Korea, as well as in China, Japan, Malaysia, and the Philippines, in an attempt to rationalize the system. The company also shifted away from a country-defined market perspective to viewing the region as a whole, which was reflected in its development of a regional procurement business to aggregate purchases of aluminum, sugar, PET (for its plastic bottles), and coffee.

Coca-Cola is just one example of how companies can discover new opportunities in the months following a financial crisis. From our experience, two groups of companies have been and are very successful at doing this. The first is a set of international companies we will refer to simply as "global players." This includes companies such as Interbrew, Holcim, LaFarge, Renault, Johnson & Johnson, Citigroup, Unilever, Emerson, GE Capital, Newbridge Capital, and Lone Star. Given their global operations, which provide them with a diverse financial safety net, these companies clearly have the luxury of thinking strategically because their own survival usually is not at stake.

There is also a second set of companies that does well, and these are domestic companies. We will call them "local champions." This includes companies such as Banco Itaú in Brazil, Ramayana in Indonesia, Kookmin Bank in Korea, the Ayala Group in the Philippines, Alfa Bank and Roust in Russia, and North Carolina National Bank (NCNB, now BankAmerica) in the United States. Through a combination of insightful understanding of the environment in which they operate, winning strategies, and the ability to seize major discontinuities, these companies ended up winning significant market share and successfully expanding into new business lines in the wake of financial crises.

Both sets of companies capture strategic opportunities by doing three things right. First, they recognize that crises are times of radical change, and therefore significant opportunities become available. Former NCNB

CEO Hugh McColl clearly understood this starting point and leveraged it to gain entry into new U.S. markets during the Texas banking crisis in the mid-1980s, a powerful story that we review as a special case study at the end of this chapter (see Appendix 5.1: Leveraging Strategic Opportunities in Financial Crises: The Successful Story of NCNB).

Second, they completely assume away the boundary conditions that confined them before the crisis. Clever managers relax their operating assumptions about traditional boundary constraints in five key areas: the regulatory regime; the competitive landscape; customer behavior and needs; organizational capacity for change; and social values. They recognize that the rules have changed, which opens up new strategic opportunities.

Finally, global players and local champions share several common traits in the way that they execute against these opportunities. First, they set aggressive performance aspirations. Second, both types of companies search for merger and acquisition opportunities. Third, they respond to opportunities quickly. Lastly, they exhibit determined leadership. Leaders in times of crisis must be courageous, but implicit in their courage is a great sense of vision and commitment. In the deepest trough of a crisis, when the weary and the wary retreat, it is the visionary who searches and finds the best strategic opportunities and then acts on them to achieve the most valuable competitive gains.

RECOGNIZING SIGNIFICANT OPPORTUNITIES IN A CRISIS

From our last chapter, it may seem that managing in financial crises is all about tactical blocking and tackling against the downside risk, but this is only part of the post-crisis game plan. The other part is in gaining ground competitively. Consider the following examples from around the world.

Brazil. During Brazil's pre-1994 hyperinflationary period, Banco Itaú infused its trading and other operations with world-class technology and productivity improvements. When a series of financial crises hit Brazil between 1994 and 1999, Banco Itaú's processing superiority, improved risk management skills, and scale developed through acquisitions and greenfield expansion not only sheltered it from the storms but enabled it to grow despite adversity. It acquired several banks within Brazil, and also entered the Argentine market, the first Brazilian bank to start up retail operations there. Today, Banco Itaú remains Brazil's second-largest private bank, with the second-largest market capitalization ($8.5 billion in 2002 versus $3.2 billion in 1994) of all banks in Latin America.[2]

Thailand. Before the Thai crisis hit in July 1997, Holcim—one of the world's leading cement companies based in Switzerland—had been looking for expansion opportunities in Asia for over a decade. In 1998, in the wake of the Thai crisis, it finally found an entry point and purchased a 25 percent stake in the beleaguered Siam City Cement Corporation (SCCC). SCCC was a Thai conglomerate that sold an unfocused collection of goods ranging from cement to tableware. Holcim upgraded management skills and installed a new board of directors and turned SCCC into a focused cement and concrete company, in the process boosting its market capitalization five-fold (to $819 million) while dramatically reducing its debt, and increasing market share from 25 percent to over 30 percent by 2001.[3]

Philippines. In the Philippines, the Ayala Group used the Asian financial crisis to continue its evolution from a property developer into a conglomerate boasting the leading wireless telecom company (Globe Telecom), as well as one of the top banks in the Philippines (Bank of the Philippine Islands, or BPI). Globe Telecom made the courageous decision to continue investing heavily in its wireless network through the crisis, which eventually helped it secure a market leadership position. Meanwhile, BPI acquired a key competitor during the crisis to move from the fifth to the second largest bank in 2001, with $6.6 billion in assets.[4]

Korea. At the beginning of the Korean financial crisis in December 1997, Housing and Commercial Bank was a medium-sized, government-controlled bank moving from its mortgage-lending base into large corporate lending, with mediocre performance and a looming NPL problem. In September 1998, when a new CEO, Jung-Tae Kim, took over, its market capitalization was about $250 million.[5] Four years later, its pre-merger market capitalization stood at $12.8 billion.[6] Completely retail-focused and with world-class performance, the new Kookmin Bank became the first Korean bank to list American Depositary Receipts (ADRs) on the New York Stock Exchange.

In 1998, Chairman Louis Schweitzer of Renault committed his company to exploring expansion opportunities in Asia and other emerging markets, despite the chaos of financial crises. Three years later, in 2001, Renault had transformed itself from a European to a truly global car company with its alliance with Nissan in Japan and acquisition of Samsung Motors in Korea. Seizing new crisis-generated opportunities, Renault gained entry into Korea by buying control of Samsung's troubled car business. This move also gave them a platform for further growth in Asia, alongside their more publicly recognized entry into the Japanese market with Nissan.

Russia. Before the Russian financial crisis in 1998, Roust was a consumer goods distribution company that specialized in premium alcohol labels, including its own Russian Standard vodka. Three years later, Roust had become a holding company that also included Russian Standard Bank, the first retail bank in Russia focused on consumer lending, and Russian Standard Online, an online, business-to-business grocery distribution enterprise. In less than one year after opening in June 1999, Russian Standard

Bank was ranked 45 out of 800 banks in Russia in terms of capital.[7] In 2002, the bank is now one of the largest consumer lenders in Russia.

Yugoslavia. In 1994, taking one of the few civilian flights into Croatia and landing among twenty to thirty warplanes and with United Nations security forces monitoring the front-line positions of ethnic Serb and Croat army troops, Interbrew, a global brewing company based in Belgium, made the gutsy decision to acquire a 24 percent minority stake in Zagrebacka Pivovara, the largest brewery in the country.[8] GDP had declined by one-third over the previous five years, real wages had been cut by more than one-half, and financial markets were shallow and narrow, with just a few stocks and no bonds being traded.[9] Six months later, despite the unstable financial, legal, and political environment, Interbrew moved to a majority stake, and over the next several years increased its market share in Croatia from 28 to 40 percent. Today, in 2002, Interbrew—driven by a vision to rebuild the beer industry in the region—has secured a favorable position as a leading brewery in the former Yugoslavia with successful investments in Croatia, Montenegro, Slovenia, Bosnia and Herzegovina.[10]

United States. During the mid-1980s, NCNB was a growing, but still regional, bank focused on its branches in the southeastern United States, but with a grand vision of becoming the first nationwide bank, despite regulatory restrictions on geographic expansion. NCNB used the Texas banking crisis of 1988 to nullify a key regulatory constraint and enter that important market through the purchase of the biggest bank in Texas, First RepublicBank Corporation.

The Texas deal became an important building block for NCNB's future expansion and growth, and was enhanced by generous support from the FDIC. In 1991, it acquired the troubled Citizens and Southern National Bank in Georgia, and became NationsBank. Eventually, in 1998, NationsBank merged with Bank of America and took the BankAmerica name. Market capitalization for the bank had grown to $105 billion from $2.3 billion a decade earlier in 1988.[11] At year-end 2001, BankAmerica was the largest U.S. bank in terms of deposits ($360 billion) and the third-largest based on assets ($640 billion).

MOVING FROM BOUNDARIES TO GREATER DEGREES OF FREEDOM

Financial crises clearly offer companies significant new opportunities. Yet, how can CEOs and senior managers capture them? Looking back on our experiences, we believe that they can position themselves best by recognizing that in normal times, five "boundary conditions" exist for most companies that change slowly, if at all. As noted above, these boundaries are: the regulatory regime; the competitive landscape; customer behavior and needs; organizational capacity for change; and social values.

In times of crisis, however, these boundaries can change, often dramatically. Instead of limiting what companies can do, boundaries by necessity may shift and disappear; moreover, they become the means by which companies can improve their competitive position in the market. We will refer to these boundary changes as the "five degrees of freedom." By focusing on these degrees of freedom *before* the crisis hits, savvy executives can prepare themselves for strategic opportunities that emerge in the new competitive environment as the crisis unfolds.

1. Regulatory Regime

Regulatory constraints are embedded deeply in the core assumptions of most companies. During noncrisis periods, management tends to view these standards as immovable. What types of businesses or markets the company is allowed to enter, what kinds of products or services it can sell, how much market share it is "allowed" to capture—these are parameters that management typically assumes it can neither change nor control.

Companies that can think beyond the current regulatory regime will soon learn to benefit from crises and find new strategic opportunities. In Korea, there were certain bank mergers that would have been viewed as highly unlikely to receive approval from the Fair Trade Commission before the crisis because of the likely concentration in products and services, but were suddenly possible following the 1997 financial crisis.[12] H&CB, for instance, was able to merge in 2001 with Kookmin Bank, one of the largest banks in Korea. This merger increased H&CB's market share from 11 to 26 percent in deposits, from 29 to 44 percent in retail loans, and from 5 to 24 percent in corporate loans.

Liberalization of foreign ownership limits in the banking sector is one of the clearest examples of changing regulatory constraints in financial crises. In September 1999, Newbridge Capital, the U.S. private equity firm, received government approval to take a majority stake (51 percent) in Korea First Bank for $417 million.[13] Figure 5.1 shows the change in foreign ownership limits across eight countries in Asia, before and after the 1997 financial crisis. Throughout most of the major economies in Asia, the permitted ownership levels rose from less than 50 percent to 100 percent, except in Malaysia, where the increase was relatively small.

In Brazil, regulatory changes during the 1994 financial crisis opened up new markets for domestic and foreign financial institutions alike. In the asset management arena, the government set new rules that designated mutual funds as legally separate entities from banks to reduce the risk of fraud and prevent bankrupt banks from tapping into fund money. Meanwhile, credit card issuers were given freedom to work with multiple brands. These changes, along with increasing customer demand for new products,

FIGURE 5.1   Crises open markets.

Banking sector example

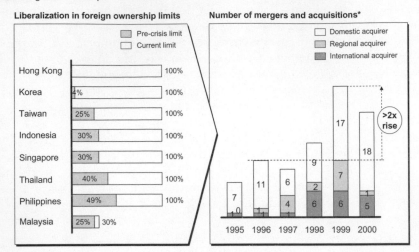

*Includes M&A led by other Asian banks; includes only mergers and acquisitions above $50 million in value
Source: Thomson Financial Data; central banks and regulatory services

led to rapid growth in both markets. Assets under management skyrocketed from a negligible level in 1994 and $8 billion in 1995, to $120 billion in 1996. Over the same two-year time period, the volume of credit card transactions also increased from $10 billion in 1994 to $26 billion in 1996.[14]

Regulatory changes during financial crises are not limited to emerging markets. The growth story of North Carolina's NCNB provides an example of a company that benefited from consistently probing and actively pushing its regulatory boundaries as a part of its corporate strategy.

Financial crises not only spur top-down changes in the regulatory regime, they also give companies leverage to influence change from the bottom up. In Japan in 1998, GE Capital established a $1.1 billion joint venture with Toho Mutual Life, a life insurance company that had gone into insolvency. During the bubble economy, it had aggressively sold savings-oriented products with high guaranteed interest rates. After the bubble burst, the value of this costly asset base fell as interest rates declined dramatically. Folding the operating assets of Toho Life into the joint venture, GE relaunched the enterprise as GE Edison Life. As a part of its purchase of Toho Life, GE Capital was required to recapitalize the old Toho Life to stabilize it to survive. A year later, however, Toho slipped into even more trouble and GE Edison agreed to take over the rest of its existing businesses. In exchange, GE Capital extracted an important concession by a ruling from the regulators, which agreed to adjust the assumed rate of interest on new policies from an unprofitable average of 4.75 percent to a more profitable (for insurers) average of 1.5 percent. GE Capital was able to use the situation to enter the Japanese life insurance market.[15]

Executives should never operate on the assumption that regulations cannot be changed, particularly during or shortly after financial crises. We know of one global credit card issuer that looked longingly at the Korean market, with over 25 million potential customers, but assumed that regulations on whether and how foreigners could enter the market would not change. When the Korean crisis hit, those regulations were thrown out the window. Unfortunately, the credit card company had not anticipated that move and, by not thinking aggressively, lost the opportunity to jump into the market and gain a first mover's advantage, as Warburg Pincus and Olympus Capital did with LG Capital and Korea Exchange Bank, respectively.[16]

2. Competitive Landscape

Financial crises can result in dramatic changes in the competitive landscape. Interest payment defaults, supply chain interruptions, loss of creditor or investor confidence—these events can topple leaders in an industry. We have often seen major shifts in the market position of companies during financial crises. For instance, in both Mexico following the 1994 peso crisis and Korea following the 1997 financial crisis, changes in the ranking of the top ten companies in those countries occurred twice as frequently after the crises, compared to before.[17]

During the 1994 financial crisis in Brazil, three of the top ten private banks went bankrupt. Two of them—Banco Nacional and Banco Econômico—were purchased, respectively, by two of their competitors: Unibanco and Banco Excel. The third, Bamerindus, was acquired by The HSBC Group, formerly The Hong Kong and Shanghai Banking Corporation.[18] Even more dramatically, almost all of the mid-sized banks in Brazil were wiped out during the hyperinflationary period in the early 1990s, giving greater opportunities to Brazil's big banks and any new competitors. Banking was a different business before and after 1994: those with strong fundamentals took advantage of the situation and prospered, while those who lacked the intrinsics required to succeed disappeared. In addition to gaining share at the expense of smaller banks, half of the rankings of the top ten banks changed over a six-year time period.[19]

In Russia, Alfa Bank emerged from relative obscurity before that country's crisis to become one of the largest banks in the country. In 1996, the bank was not even ranked among the top twenty banks in terms of asset size, half of which went bankrupt by 2001.[20] During the crisis, at the end of

1998, it had risen to sixth position. As the crisis unfolded, three of the five behemoths faltered, and Alfa continued to push forward. In this case, Alfa did three things that made the difference: It maintained open communications with its shareholders and customers; it steadfastly paid its obligations (the only Russian issuer to honor its Eurobond in full and on time); and it attracted great talent. In 2002, Alfa was recognized by *Global Finance* as the "Best Russian Bank."[21] Alfa is now Russia's largest privately held financial institution ($2.7 billion in assets in 2001), surpassed only by two state-owned banks, Sberbank and Vneshtorgbank.[22]

In the Philippines, meanwhile, the 165-year-old company Ayala took advantage of the Asian financial crisis to become a banking and telecom leader. During the crisis, Ayala convinced SingTel and others to continue investing heavily in Globe Telecom, a small telecommunications company with a critically important wireless license that Ayala had acquired several years earlier. While competitors were putting the brakes on new capital expenditures, Ayala continued aggressively building out the country's first digital wireless network on the GSM standard, spending $500,000 per base station. Within a few years, several of Globe's analog competitors went out of business, and Globe had established itself as the top wireless company in the Philippines.

Ayala was equally opportunistic in the banking industry. As the profitability of other banks declined sharply during the 1997 Asian financial crisis, Ayala's BPI, the fifth-largest bank at the time in terms of assets, used its cash reserves and the additional leverage afforded to it by its parent company to purchase one of its competitors, Far East Bank & Trust Company (FEBTC), and turn it around. FEBTC, then the seventh-largest bank with the number one trust banking business in the country, was put on the trading block because of its poor loan book and inadequate returns. In October 1999, BPI closed a deal to acquire FEBTC for $1.26 billion, creating BPI-Far East Bank, the second-largest bank in the Philippines in 2001 with $6.6 billion in assets.[23]

It is not just domestic companies, obviously, that benefit from crises. Switzerland's Holcim, for example, had been looking for a way to enter the Asian market for over a decade. As financial crises swept the region in 1997, Holcim's area manager recognized the opportunity for the company to finally make its entry through M&A. Several Asian cement manufacturers, burdened with debt, were becoming insolvent. Holcim used the crisis to purchase controlling stakes in cement companies in Thailand (SCCC) and the Philippines (Alsons Cement, Union Cement). This scenario repeated itself throughout Southeast Asia. Before the crisis, virtually all cement production in the region was locally-owned, whereas afterward, the majority is now foreign-owned.

3. Customer Behavior and Needs

Most marketing strategies are built on the presumption that customer behavior is extremely resistant to change. In other words, customer acquisition and switching costs are extremely high. During financial crises, however, this can change in a number of ways.

First, customers may exhibit a "flight to safety." In order to attract new customers during the Asian financial crisis, Korean banks placed advertising posters featuring their BIS ratios on public buses. In Indonesia and Japan, Citibank has reaped enormous benefits from this flight to safety. Following the Indonesian riots in May 1998, Citibank managers set up scores of "mini-branches"—low-cost banking outlets that consisted of basically an ATM and an attendant—in the four metropolitan centers of that country. The number of accounts rose 300 percent between 1998 and 1999. In Japan, Citibank has also benefited from customer concerns about trouble brewing in the local banking sector. Retail bank earnings for the company in that country grew by 60 percent in 2000 to $139 million. Citigroup Vice Chairman William Rhodes commented: "Sometimes when an economy is under the most stress, you get presented with the biggest opportunities.[24]

Government actions often trigger flights to safety, creating new opportunities. Argentina's November 2001 sovereign default caused $1.8 billion, or 2.3 percent of total deposits, to flee the banking system on a single day. Deposits declined by 23 percent in 2001. It is estimated that more than $100 billion has left the system in recent years. Argentina's problems have resulted in a complete breakdown of banking consumers' confidence. Since many citizens prefer to keep their funds outside the domestic banking system, new opportunities will be created for new entrants (e.g., retailers, offshore asset managers) with novel strategies.

Second, customers are more open to a change in their preferred institutions during financial crises. Every year, McKinsey & Company conducts a survey of customer behavior and needs in the personal financial services sector across the Asia-Pacific region. Since the 1997 Asian financial crisis, our survey results have shown an increase in the percentage of customers who are ready to change financial institutions—those that are receptive to foreign institutions, new services, and new channels, or are even already switching accounts. This trend was especially marked in Southeast Asia, where the financial crisis began. In Malaysia, for example, the percentage of change-ready customers increased from 7 to 34 percent between 1998 and 2000. The same figures for the Philippines were 8 and 31 percent, and in Singapore, 8 and 27 percent.

Ramayana, the Indonesian retailer, is an example of a company that was able to take advantage of a shift in consumer demand during a financial crisis. In general, financial crises often spark recessions and widespread bankruptcies and layoffs. Retailers and manufacturers that focus on bargains and lower-end goods can prosper. At Ramayana, sales during the five years preceding the crisis had been growing at over 30 percent per annum, and had doubled over the preceding two-year period. Despite its compelling financials, Ramayana rarely got much respect. After all, it was selling low-priced labels such as Marco Polo and Mr. Robinson, as opposed to the more expensive merchandise of its upper-scale competitors.

That lack of respect, however, began changing in August 1997, when the Indonesian rupiah depreciated dramatically and subsequently was floated, and the middle class saw its purchasing power dry up. It was a devastating situation that most people had never before experienced. Ramayana's managers responded by holding prices steady on their core products and offering cheaper goods, as well as smaller-sized, more affordable packages of basic food products such as rice, cooking oil, and sugar. Ramayana not only kept its current customers, it also attracted a new set of middle-income customers who shifted their purchasing downscale and to the Ramayana stores, and have continued to shop there even after the crisis. While nominal sales for high-end and large department stores declined, Ramayana's nominal sales figure increased 18 percent between December 1997 and December 1998, one of the worst periods of the Indonesian financial crisis.[25]

Finally, latent customer demand often becomes more apparent during financial crises. For example, sometimes customers participate in new markets simply because they are suddenly able to, due to crisis-driven regulatory changes. Regulatory change can unlock pent-up demand for new products, as was the case in Brazil with mutual funds and credit cards during the 1994 crisis. Following the 1999 crisis in that country, consumer credit as a whole witnessed significant growth in the aftermath. The lending figure, $13.1 billion in 1999 in constant 2000 dollars, increased to $18.1 billion the following year, and to $24.0 billion in 2001.[26] A similar phenomenon also has occurred in Korea since the 1997 crisis.

4. Organizational Capacity for Change

Financial crises allow management to drive organizational change much faster and more comprehensively than in normal times. Management can institute better procedures, change the power structure, right-size the organization, and throw conventional thinking out the window. People and organizational cultures are simply more willing to change during a crisis. They know that they may not have an alternative.

Before the 1997 financial crisis in Korea, for example, retail branch managers at many banks typically had acted as mini-CEOs, making all lending decisions at the local level. During the crisis, several banks made dramatic moves in centralizing credit decision making, effectively taking power away from branch managers. Such a move had been discussed prior to the crisis, but the crisis created the opportunity to make it happen. As a result, the banks that implemented the changes realized significant performance gains.

In fact, CEO Jung-Tae Kim used the crisis to drive sweeping changes through H&CB, much of which he explains would have been impossible before the 1997 crisis. Within three months of becoming CEO, he rightsized the organization by cutting back 30 percent of the organization's personnel. Kim was also able to make changes in compensation to demonstrate that the bank would be driven around shareholder value, not asset size. The first year, he personally took a salary of just 1 Korean won per year (about 0.1 U.S. cent), receiving the rest of his compensation in stock options. Kim reorganized the bank into customer-oriented business units versus functions and geography-based divisions, which made responsibility for and assessment of performance clearer in each of its business areas, and he increased the proportion of compensation based on performance.[27] These measures were unconventional in Korea, to say the least. In the wake of financial crisis, however, they became quite feasible.

Some of the organizational changes at H&CB occurred in line with a change in bank strategy. Kim reoriented the bank around retail banking to maximize its profitability, and consequently set to work to revamp the culture. He molded a true service culture in the bank, where employees previously were used to thinking of themselves as superior to customers. The bank also enhanced its personal and relationship banking activities by offering advanced training programs to its employees, increasing the number of personal bankers and relationship managers, and introducing additional customer service facilities at its branches.

We have found that these organizational changes were able to occur quickly not only because of anxiety within the company, but often because managers and employees simply realize that crises demand change. Ayala, for instance, had always prided itself on a social pact with its employees that promised a job for life. In the wake of the Asian financial crisis, however, Ayala's management realized that it would have to operate in even more uncertain times, and thus it had to refresh its talent pool to remain competitive. For these reasons, management took the unprecedented step of installing its first ever voluntary layoff program.

5. Social Values

Social values and public opinion also often change during financial crises. From our experience, there are four areas in particular where we see changes in values and opinion.

The first is in the perceptions of foreign companies and management. In Korea, for example, the public expressed little desire for foreign investment before the crisis. An opinion poll conducted in 1994 by the Korea Development ment Institute (KDI), a government think tank, showed that only 47 percent of Koreans were in favor of incoming FDI. During the Asian financial crisis, however, KDI conducted a similar poll in March 1998, which revealed that public opinion had changed dramatically, with almost 90 percent now in favor of FDI.[28]

This change in opinion was in part driven by a growing realization by business leaders of the need for not just foreign capital, but also transfers of technology and new management practices. Worried about the negative perceptions of foreign capital and ownership in Korea, President-elect Dae Jung Kim also played a key role, arguing for the importance of FDI in a series of "town hall" meetings across the country, and a publicly broadcast television program in January 1998. He stressed the need to foster a welcoming environment for foreign investment to create new job opportunities. Drawing on the example of the U.K.'s financial services and automotive industries— the Wimbledon effect, where few companies are British-owned but nonetheless create many well-paying jobs and attract leading players from around the world—President Kim reasoned that Koreans could also benefit from foreign investment. "It's very clear in an era of a global economy, we can't survive without foreign investment," President Kim said. "We must change our attitude toward foreign investment."[29] That argument was accepted, and between 1997 and 1999, FDI inflows to Korea increased from less than $7 billion annually to over $15 billion.[30]

Second, trust in public institutions may change during financial crises. Often, this involves state-owned enterprises and banks, regulatory authorities, or other government bureaucracies. It went even further in Thailand, for instance, when the Asian financial crisis and associated abuses of power in the government helped usher in a new constitution in 1997 that aimed to stem corruption, change the nature of competition among political parties, and localize many elements of government authority. According to a member of the drafting committee, the only reason the new constitution was passed by parliament was because of a popular backlash against the government and central bank for spending so much public money to defend the baht exchange rate policy.[31] Even though an extreme example, we have seen a similar erosion in the general level of trust in public institutions—and sometimes a corresponding increase in the trust of private ones—across many countries.

Third, we have seen drastic changes in compliance with international standards (accounting, transparency, corporate governance, and risk management). Take corporate governance, for example, a topic we examine in greater depth in Chapter 8. Many companies exhibit poor corporate governance practices before a crisis: lack of transparency and disclosure, few independent board directors, and limited protection of minority shareholder rights. Managers often complain, "Things are different here; Western standards do not apply."

When a financial crisis hits, however, corporate governance becomes one area in which companies quickly focus to regain investor confidence. In Korea, for example, the government mandated corporate governance reforms following the 1997 crisis, forcing the leading banks and chaebol to appoint a majority of outside independent directors and bring new transparency to committee and board activities.

In Indonesia, military officers, who had no previous business or banking experience, ran virtually all of the state banks' boards of supervisors before the crisis. This created a vacuum of responsibility for oversight of the executive management team. After the crisis, these figureheads were replaced by more skilled individuals who took on responsibility for auditing, risk, and compliance with other corporate standards.

Moreover, consumers may change their lifestyles dramatically following a financial crisis. This is driven by the widespread impact of financial crises and their immediate influence on individual pocketbooks.[32] McKinsey's Asia-Pacific personal financial services survey revealed that between 1998 and 1999 consumer attitudes toward credit underwent significant changes in certain crisis-affected countries. In Korea, the percentage of those who considered borrowing "unwise" declined from 46 to 26 percent.[33] The same figures in Malaysia were 52 and 42 percent, and in the Philippines, 55 and 45 percent.

In Korea, we have seen a number of work- and lifestyle-related changes follow from the 1997 financial crisis. Demand has been increasing for a reduction to the current 44-hour workweek, the longest among OECD member nations, to a 42- or 40-hour workweek. This has become a major point of contention in management-labor relations, and a highly politicized issue. There is also less loyalty to lifetime work commitments at a single company, and greater mobility that is reflected in the rising growth rate of employment agency services active in Korea. In the two years following the crisis, the number of new agencies grew twice as fast compared with the two years prior to the crisis.[34]

Finally, in Korea, we are witnessing a decline in public contentment with the adequacy of current education systems to prepare local workforces to compete in the global marketplace. McKinsey's work in education reform has revealed that the public has begun to realize that the move to a globally competitive, knowledge-based economy requires a distinct shift away from rote memorization to more analytical problem solving, open discussion and debate, and self-guided learning.

EXECUTING SUCCESSFULLY TO CAPTURE
CRISIS OPPORTUNITIES

Simply recognizing that the rules have changed and identifying opportunities created by the five degrees of freedom is not enough. Capturing new strategic opportunities during financial crises requires that managers set aggressive performance aspirations, continuously search for M&A opportunities, respond to opportunities quickly, and exhibit determined leadership.

1. Set Aggressive Performance Aspirations

The first step is to set and drive very aggressive aspirations. At NCNB, CEO Hugh McColl, CFO Tim Hartman, and their team used the Texas banking and S&L crises to fill in the company's franchise on the way to becoming the first truly nationwide U.S. bank. During the Asian financial crisis, Coca-Cola not only sought to increase market share in individual country markets, but also set goals to improve its position across the entire region. In addition, it had moved boldly out of its traditional carbonated drink market into new high-growth products, such as tea and coffee.

At H&CB, Kim's vision back in 1998 was to "become a world-class, top 100 retail bank in three years." Kim reinforced his vision with global benchmarks and real performance targets. He used Wells Fargo and Lloyds-TSB as benchmarks, and aimed to meet or beat an ROA of 1.5 percent and ROE of 25 percent. H&CB met those targets by cutting costs and reducing exposure to bad loans, paying greater attention to price-sensitivity analyses to optimize profit, reforming the management performance ethic, and refocusing strategy on retail banking. In his first two years alone, Kim launched over twenty performance improvement initiatives, including pricing strategy, retail credit scoring, reorganization, and branch sales stimulation, to name just a few.

Similarly, Russia's Roust launched Russian Standard Bank with the vision of becoming one of the leading banks in Russia and a pioneer in consumer finance. By the end of 1998, while most of the banks in the country were seriously ill or bankrupt, CEO Roustam Tariko recognized an opportunity to fulfill a longstanding ambition to invest in the banking sector. He realized that the bankrupt banks had left behind facilities and talent that could be easily acquired on the market—the only thing missing was money. Fortunately, Roust had the cash. Within half a year, he crafted a solid business plan, used it to hire the entire senior management team of one of the leading but failed banks at the time, and established Russian Standard Bank in June 1999. Though still in its early stages, Russian Standard Bank is one of the first movers in the personal financial services field, with about $100 million in its credit portfolio and increasing at a rate of several hundred percent per year.[35] Clearly, growth this fast can only be sustained for a limited time period, but it is indicative of the benefits of taking advantage of a unique circumstance. While banking competitors were barely hanging on or shutting their doors, Russian Standard Bank gained a lead of several years ahead of its eventual competitors.

2. Continuously Search for M&A Opportunities

Changes in one or more of the five degrees of freedom can lead to significant and new strategic opportunities. Yet, conventional wisdom argues for caution and prudence during crises, but the experiences of many successful companies clearly demonstrate the opposite: Financial crises present new and sometime unique, regime-shifting opportunities for companies to improve their market positions through M&A.

Consider the significant increase in M&A activity that typically accompanies a financial crisis. Between August and December of 1997, just as the Asian financial crisis was breaking, more than 400 deals totaling $35 billion were completed in Asia, an increase of more than 200 percent over the same period the year before.[36] These deals included M&A by both global players and local champions. M&A activity in the banking sector alone totaled $18.0 billion in 1998, compared to $5.3 billion in 1997 and $5.1 billion in 1996.[37] Figure 5.1 shows the increase in the number of acquisitions above $50 million in value, between 1995 and 2000, by both domestic and foreign companies.

In Indonesia, for example, Unilever took advantage of the cheap rupiah and basement prices for corporate assets to acquire four leading domestic brands and expand its operations. By 2001, net profits had grown five-fold to almost $90 million, and sales returned to precrisis levels. Today, at least one of its brands can be found in 95 percent of Indonesian homes.[38]

The biggest impact of increased M&A activity in crises is greater industry consolidation. Whole industries shift rapidly during crises, dramatically changing the competitive landscape. The Brazilian financial crises between 1994 and 1999, for instance, led to significant consolidation of the banking sector, with acquisitions led by both global investors and local champions. A correspondent shift in assets toward foreign banks and away from domestic, privately owned banks also occurred.[39]

Mergers and acquisitions during crises tend to be more difficult than normal, particularly due to high levels of uncertainty. Being successful requires three distinct actions. First, managers need to be ready to implement flexible deal structures. They also need to look for and "expect the unexpected," and take steps to actively manage these risks. Trust is important, especially for foreign companies that rely on a local partner, which means investing in local relationships long before the actual deal takes place. Second, companies can also manage these risks by carefully monitoring social and political conditions and their ramifications for potential deals, or actively building a portfolio strategy to manage crisis-related risk in different countries. Finally, managers need to be prepared mentally to leverage new and unique opportunities.

Implement flexible deal structures. Over the past decade, Japan has been in a smoldering-crisis mode, with major issues still unresolved and many observers such as *The Economist* and *The Financial Times* predicting another financial crisis looming.

Several companies, however, have been undeterred from entering. GE Capital, which has chosen to continue investing aggressively, is one of them. Its investment in Japan may seem counter-intuitive, but it is really based on a fundamental rationale: GE realizes it can use Japan's economic crisis not only to enter a market that has traditionally been hard to penetrate, but also to catch up with such longtime foreign rivals in Japan as AIG and Citibank, which have been there since World War II. In its 1997 annual report, GE boldly trumpeted: "The path to greatness in Asia is irreversible." Closing these deals, however, often requires being creative with deal structuring, as we saw in the Toho Life example, where the bad business stayed in Toho and a new, clean joint venture was established. Since 1990, GE Capital has completed over forty M&A, alliance, and joint venture partnership deals in Asia.

Interbrew provides another example. In early 1998, right after the crisis hit Korea, Interbrew was negotiating with Doosan over the sale of its beer business, Oriental Brewery (OB). There was much uncertainty in the market. No one knew how long it would take before the economy would begin to grow again. There was an unstable industry structure with a near-bankrupt competitor, and rumors of changes to liquor tax laws.

The two companies agreed on a set of three "triggers," or conditional payments, to bridge a gap in expectations of future value. The three triggers would lead to payouts if certain changes occurred to the industry or tax structure. By thinking creatively, Interbrew inked a solid "win-win" deal with Doosan in the midst of the crisis, managed the downside risk and upside potential, and successfully locked itself into a high-growth market. Had it not been for the crisis, Interbrew might not yet be positioned in Korea.

NCNB also recognized the opportunity to break new deal-making ground during the self-contained Texas banking crisis in the late 1980s. During that year, the failure of First Republic would become the largest and costliest in FDIC history: $3.9 billion. McColl and Hartman had set their sights on the largest Texas bank, but they only wanted the good bank that lurked within First Republic, not the bad bank that contained all of the non-performing assets. According to Hartman: "The FDIC owned the bad loans, not us." Ultimately, the FDIC agreed to segregate the roughly $12 billion in problem assets into a separate asset pool, and created one of the first bridge banks in U.S. history, which the FDIC owned and NCNB managed until it acquired full ownership of the good bank.

Expect the unexpected. Although financial crises create unprecedented opportunities, M&A deals—particularly cross-border ones—also present difficulties. Closing a deal or turning around a company still takes time, and managers will almost definitely encounter other issues. Making a merger profitable, for instance, is particularly hard when a financial crisis sparks an economic downturn.

Social and political tensions specific to the crisis can further complicate mergers. A scandal or employee backlash may arise unexpectedly, as a result of factors that drove the crisis to its tipping point, such as regulatory forbearance that allows bankrupt banks to continue to exist and exacerbate risk. The same "dinner party" concept that we raised in Chapter 3, of keeping an ear to the ground and tapping into informal sources of information, also is crucial for keeping managers informed of potential risks to their M&A deals.

Especially for foreign managers in an M&A deal, it is important to develop close relationships with local management, before the deal if possible. As an operating principle, Interbrew tries to spend time with the family members of family-owned companies to ease their concerns and craft mutually beneficial arrangements. The deal it closed with Doosan in the fall of 1998, for instance, was the result of conversations that began two years earlier. Interbrew's latest deal in Cuba, in 2002, was the result of relationships established more than five years ago. Remember, too, that Holcim spent ten years in Asia before it entered the markets there. Holcim's managers recall how important it was during that time to invest early in relationships, by walking the halls and getting to know the key people in the local industry.

In addition, some companies—such as GE Capital and Interbrew—have been able to manage risk by balancing M&A investments in both developed and developing markets, in effect diversifying their portfolio, a strategy that applies in both crisis and noncrisis situations. Over half of Interbrew's total volume, for instance, comes from mature markets in the Americas and Western Europe; the rest is from emerging markets in Central and Eastern Europe, and Asia. "This spreads our risk, in terms of region, country, and currency," Interbrew's annual report recently noted. "Emerging markets have the highest growth potential but carry the threat of economic and social fluctuations. Mature markets give us security and good margins, but the downside is limited volume growth. We need exposure to both, and now we have it."[40] Over the past decade, Interbrew has invested in at least ten post-crisis markets to drive this strategy, including Hungary in 1991, Croatia and Romania in 1994, Bulgaria and Mexico in 1995, Montenegro in 1997, Korea and Russia in 1998 and 1999, Bosnia and Herzegovina and Ukraine in 1999, and Serbia in 2001.

Diversification in this context, however, does not imply a random walk through crises. Instead, management needs to balance portfolio strategy with a clear picture of where the company wants to go in each market or region. For Interbrew, the investments in Yugoslavia only made sense in the bigger picture of expanding into Central and Eastern Europe. The investment in Zagreb was actually preceded by the acquisition in late 1991 of Borsodi Sorgyar, one of the largest breweries in Hungary.[41] Even with Yugoslavia at war near the country's borders, managers realized that this investment was part of a bigger regional and global strategy, which helped to frame the risks in a much larger context. Making twenty-four trips to the region within three months, managers closed the deal in October 1991, and put in place the first piece of its regional expansion strategy.

Leverage the opportunities. Despite the difficulties associated with successfully managing deals in the midst of financial crises, many crisis-inspired M&A transactions present new opportunities with mutually beneficial outcomes.

Consider Renault's acquisition of Samsung Motors, the Korean car company, in the aftermath of the Asian financial crisis. In late 1999, two years after the crisis first hit Korea, Samsung Motors was clearly in trouble: The company was in receivership, and production was halted through most of the year. The company had been in production for only two years, but was sorely crippled by a slowdown of the global automobile market, coupled with the financial crisis. Many key suppliers were either bankrupt or had stopped selling to the company. Total debt had reached $3.9 billion, against assets of $2.9 billion. To stay afloat, Samsung Motors had cut its workforce from 6,100 to 2,000 people. Conditions were so bad that Samsung Group Chairman Kun Hee Lee had to put in $2.3 billion of his personal shares in Samsung Life as a debt guarantee.[42]

In January 2000, Renault began discussions with Samsung Motors for a potential acquisition. Since 1998, the French carmaker had been looking to expand in Asia, despite the crisis that had swept through the region. Chairman Louis Schweitzer stated at the time: "Our strategy is pointed toward new, nontraditional markets. Renault is building plants in Turkey, Argentina, Colombia, Brazil, and Russia. But more international expansion will occur in Asia. The current crisis in the Asian markets presents us with more opportunities than problems."[43] Its alliance with Nissan in March 1999, for instance, gave it access to Nissan's distribution network in the United States and throughout Asia, superior production and engine technology to complement its own design capabilities, and enormous cost synergies.

In April 2000, Renault paid $570 million for a 70 percent stake in Samsung Motors. The acquisition gave Renault an entry point into the fast-growing Korean car market, as well as a relatively low-cost platform for producing small, dependable cars. Samsung Motors was kept afloat, and got new models and a stronger supplier network. In addition, Renault asked Nissan—which had been a key supplier for Samsung Motors since its beginnings in 1994, and had designed its factory in Pusan—to send in engineers to help with the turnaround. In 1999, production was limited to 2,100 cars. One year later, Schweitzer stated that he expected Samsung Motors to reach its breakeven production level of 150,000 units no later than early 2004.[44]

Leveraging new opportunities is not limited only to global players, but applies to local champions as well. When Indonesia's crisis exploded into rioting in May 1998, a number of Ramayana's stores, including the company's headquarters, were looted and burned to the ground, and 4,000 employees were displaced. Everything in the headquarters was lost—including all of the accounting records—except for a few computer disks.

Notwithstanding this terrible loss, the company fortunately had very little debt and began reopening some of the salvageable stores in July. The following year, it rebuilt more stores and constructed several new ones. It also began expanding outside of the main island of Java, where almost all of its stores were located before the crisis. The company found that with virtually no other competitors looking to expand—and a lot of people wanting to sell property—the crisis had created a buyer's market.[45] Consequently, Ramayana was able to secure very favorable terms on new land contracts, meanwhile providing the sellers with desperately needed cash.

3. Respond to Opportunities Quickly

In financial crises, the speed of business accelerates, and both opportunities and problems arise quickly. Where a bank may have one year to work out an NPL in ordinary times, during a crisis each month and even each day can make a critical difference. The acceleration of events penalizes companies that are slow to adjust and rewards those that are nimble and can adjust their strategies quickly.

Reacting quickly during the 1997 Asian financial crisis helped turn Asia into Citibank's fastest-growing regional profit center. In Indonesia, instead of pulling back from its operations there after riots erupted in the spring of 1998, managers flew *toward* Jakarta to craft a strategy to capture crisis opportunities. As middle-class Indonesian refugees were landing in Singapore, Citibank employees greeted them at the airport with signs that read, "Citibank will help you!" Over the next several years, Citibank invested over $200 million in Asia and opened seventy-four branches in eight countries. Between 1997 and 2001, building on its new platform in the wake of the crisis, the number of credit card accounts in the region doubled to seven million, making Citibank the largest issuer in Asia. In 2000, after-tax profits for retail operations in Asia grew 58 percent to $702 million, on revenues of $2.8 billion. One manager commented, "The crisis gave us opportunities that were beyond belief."[46]

One company that realized this during the Korean financial crisis was Lone Star Fund. After the crisis hit, Lone Star—one of the largest U.S.-based private equity funds since the U.S. S&L crisis in the 1980s—was the first to purchase real estate-backed nonperforming loans from the Korean Asset Management Company (KAMCO) in December 1998. The first portfolio of $467 million in loans sold at 36 percent of book value, or $168 million. Lone Star and KAMCO created a special purpose vehicle controlled and managed by Lone Star. The company spent several years working out the loans, and finally resolved the portfolio and closed the financial books in 2001, earning a very significant annualized return.

Being the first to take on the bad loans was not easy. Steven Lee, country manager for Lone Star in Korea, recalls, "No one had tested the liquidity of these assets in the market. It was a daunting due diligence task."[47] Competition was much more limited initially, but investors soon flocked quickly to Korea. When Lone Star bid for its first portfolio, for example, there were only three investors in the bidding pool. In June 1999, KAMCO's auction attracted over fourteen investors and the resulting price was higher.

In an environment where time is critical, strategy must be event-driven. Each new twist of circumstances must be met with a reevaluation of strategy and a review of a company's five degrees of freedom. A company must always know what changes need to take place for it to emerge as a winner. Moreover, it must know how to influence these five degrees of freedom. Winning companies, both global players and local champions, understand these tenets. They play them ahead of their competitors, constantly searching for changes in the regulatory environment, competitive postures, and other boundary conditions that will provide the break that they need.

4. Exhibit Determined Leadership

Finally, managers must exhibit determined leadership. If we were to describe the kind of leadership required in the months following a financial crisis, we could do no better than to profile the leadership that Kookmin's CEO Kim provided to his bank.

During Kim's first year at the bank, six months after the financial storm swept through Korea, many people thought his reforms were so radical that he would be fired within the first year. After all, Kim was demanding changes in all aspects of the bank that were still uncommon in Korea. This change included the introduction of corporate governance reforms, such as creating a board comprised mostly of outsiders when the government was still the largest stakeholder, and performance-based evaluations, which went against the traditions of Korean business. "He's not going to be around for much longer," some executives remarked. "It's simply too much, too fast."

Many critics said that Kim simply did not understand the culture of the bank. He did not respect its employees, they claimed. It was not easy for Kim. During his first few months at the bank, labor union activists even forced their way into his office and seized it for a week in protest of the changes.

Kim, however, had the courage of his convictions.[48] He refused to back down. Today, it is evident to both his friends and former foes that the turn-around program has been overwhelmingly successful. "I was skeptical like many others before. But looking back now, I realize that he understood the concept of triage very well," one observer reflected. "He prioritized issues quickly, and cut away the second- and third-level issues that would have otherwise bogged him down." Kookmin today commands more than 80 percent of the mortgage lending market in 2002. With a BIS ratio of 10.00 percent,[49] market capitalization of about $15 billion, and declining NPLs due to improved risk management and reduced chaebol exposure, it is known as one of the most successful and trusted banks in Korea.

In the best of cases, individuals rise to the occasion and display their best traits during financial crises. For many executives, a crisis gives them a burning platform and the opportunity to change the rules, to fundamentally change the company into what it will be for the next five to ten years. Companies with management teams that are visionary enough to see the opportunities in a crisis—where others only see chaos—and are determined to pursue and capture those opportunities can emerge from financial crises as winners.

■ ■ ■

Capturing strategic opportunities during financial crises requires even more courage, commitment, and skills than in a noncrisis environment. Keeping an eye on both crisis management tactics and potential strategic opportunities resulting from changes in the five degrees of freedom is difficult, but only part of the management challenge. What will set the company apart from its peers is management's ability to successfully execute against both strategic and tactical agendas simultaneously.

Based on our experience, we can imagine that executives in both domestic and foreign companies are closely looking at potential opportunities—through organic growth, acquisitions, or alliance partners—in countries such as China, Japan, India, and Argentina to name a few. They are managing their cash, conducting due diligence, building personal and business relationships, and otherwise preparing themselves for the day when countries get themselves into severe difficulty. When that day arrives, those companies that have made the right preparations in advance will be the first to move to capture unique, strategic opportunities arising from a crisis.

Leadership is a key part of a winning strategy: Individual people make it happen—or not.

APPENDIX 5.1: Leveraging Strategic Opportunities in Financial Crises: The Successful Story of NCNB

The story of North Carolina National Bancorporation (NCNB)—now known as BankAmerica since 1998—during the Texas banking crisis in the late 1980s is an amazing tale about aggressively pursuing an expansionist growth strategy, leveraging strategic and unique opportunities during a financial crisis, and being nimble enough to execute a plan few other banks could match, either in sheer aspirations or execution skills.[1]

NCNB began in 1961 in Charlotte, North Carolina, as a three-way bank merger of two "lockbox" banks owned by Jefferson-Pilot Insurance Company and American Trust Company of Charlotte, after the U.S. Bank Holding Company Act prevented nonbanking holding companies, including insurance companies, from owning banks. Immediately forced to compete with local heavyweights such as Wachovia and First Union, NCNB adopted an expansionist branch banking strategy and searched for small banks to fill in its market share in the limited geographic area of North Carolina, the only state in which it was allowed to compete in branch banking.[2] As an important corollary to its strategy, it opted to operate in a holding company model, consolidating the first two banks and centralizing other activities, including treasury functions, trust departments, investment activities, and corporate lending. At that time, banking across state lines had not yet been authorized and nationwide banking was just a dream.

CRISES PRESENT OPPORTUNITIES

Crises, however, present opportunities for expansion in new markets and better positioning to gain future competitive advantages. In October 1972, under the leadership of Hugh McColl, NCNB had the opportunity to acquire the failing Lake City Trust Company in Florida, a potentially profitable banking market previously off limits to out-of-state banks like NCNB. It did so, and gained a strategic platform from which to grow—a platform that other out-of-state banks could not replicate due to the existing prohibition on interstate banking and branching.[3]

Later, in June 1982, when several small bank holding companies in Florida—Gulf Stream and Exchange Bank—ran into difficulties, NCNB had the unique opportunity to once again leverage its trust company foothold that other foreign banks did not have, buy the banks, and increase its market share, becoming the fourth-largest bank in Florida and the largest bank in the southeastern U.S. NCNB also learned a valuable skill that would serve it well as part of its evolving acquisition strategy: how to successfully integrate the seventy-four bank branches it had scattered throughout Florida into a single bank, to gain the cost savings and customer convenience benefits of a single-product platform.

NCNB's audacity to push the law and use legal "loopholes" to find opportunities and gain entry into the lucrative Florida market helped to provoke the initial reconsideration of the prohibitions on interstate banking. Eventually regional compacts came into existence, in the South and Northeast, as a means of allowing local banks to grow into regional banks before nationwide banking emerged as a reality.

NCNB was at the forefront of pushing those changes, advocating the complete dismantling of outmoded restrictions on geographic competition. NCNB's vision was to become the first truly nationwide bank, a vision former Chairman and CEO McColl first emphasized in April 1987 while on a roadshow trip to Tokyo to sell the bank's stock. His strategy can be summed up as follows: Pursue aggressive branch banking expansion and consolidation of attractive markets, pushing the limits of existing laws to find new growth opportunities in unique ways that most banks would not even consider.

MOVING INTO TEXAS DURING THE BANKING CRISIS

In the fall of 1987, McColl and CFO Tim Hartman observed a downward turn in the Texas economy, a targeted market that was still off-limits to NCNB under existing law. Previously, the Texas economy had been supercharged for years with Eurodollar deposits funding huge energy and real estate deals throughout the southwestern United States. Meanwhile, the Texas economy began to soften and NCNB began to explore the acquisition of Allied Bank, which was showing signs of strain before others knew that there might be potential problems. Despite rigorous due diligence, "Our team just couldn't make the numbers work in the Allied loan portfolio," explained Hartman, "and so, to protect our capital and our shareholders, we walked away from the deal because of what we found." While it was not able to expand across state lines at that time, NCNB's appetite for growth in Texas did not go away, however. NCNB understandably made a strategic decision that it did not want to own the bad loans without some sizable protection.

By the spring of 1988, the situation in Texas had worsened, and Hartman's distrust of the numbers he saw coming out of the banks led him to a new tactic. McColl and Hartman decided not to waste any more time in Texas with numbers that they could not evaluate accurately. Instead, armed with a growing sense of the severity of the Texas situation, the small NCNB team including Frank Gentry, head of strategic planning, and Mark Leggett, the bank's chief Washington representative, headed to Washington, D.C. While there, they spent most of their time at the FDIC, exploring the strategic opportunities that might arise from the Texas banks that were starting to fail and coming into the FDIC's portfolio.

NCNB was convinced that the FDIC would soon own several large failing banks and their loans, and so from April to August 1988, Hartman and his colleagues became regular visitors to Washington, calling on the FDIC, the Comptroller of the Currency (the national bank regulator), and the Federal Reserve (the regulator of bank holding companies). NCNB had worked hard in previous years to increase its capital base and, unlike most other banks at the time, the senior management team proactively met with the regulators on a regular basis to keep them apprised of their current business plans and future strategy. As a result, NCNB was well-positioned with its regulators to launch its Texas expansion strategy.

NEGOTIATING THE DEAL

NCNB's strategy and tactics in the middle of the Texas banking crisis were about to pay off for its management and shareholders.

In 1988, First RepublicBank Corporation (First Republic) was the fourteenth largest U.S. bank and the biggest bank in Texas. It had forty subsidiary banks and more than 160 locations throughout Texas, and it owned a credit card bank in Delaware. It had 2.2 million depositors and held 20 percent of the loans made by Texas banks. Its trust department managed $50 billion in assets for more than 25,000 customers. First Republic, which was the result of a prior merger between RepublicBank and Inter-First Corporation in 1987, eventually had to recognize the problems in its troubled portfolio and posted $2 billion in NPLs representing 16 percent of its loan portfolio at year-end. Its public loan problems soon created new funding problems, leading to electronic runs on the bank and heavy borrowings from the Dallas Federal Reserve Bank. In March 1988, the FDIC had to intervene with open bank assistance, which took the form of a blanket guarantee of all deposits and liabilities and an injection of a $1 billion, six-month FDIC note.[4]

The next month, the FDIC received a proposal from NCNB to restructure the company's bank subsidiaries through a bridge bank that NCNB would manage for the FDIC on a fee basis. The FDIC board of directors rejected that proposal, but that did not stop the NCNB team. By then, other banks such as New York-based Citicorp and California-based Wells Fargo had also entered the negotiating picture, since Texas banks could not do so given their size and problems.[5]

The tactic that NCNB executed next demonstrates the nimbleness and aggressiveness that made its expansionist strategy a success in the middle of the Texas banking crisis. The FDIC was accepting bids for First Republic by July 25, 1988. NCNB quietly obtained two private tax rulings from the Internal Revenue Service, which amounted to roughly $1 billion in tax benefits if and when it acquired the First Republic banks.[6] More importantly, NCNB would be able to treat these tax rulings as a tax-free reorganization and therefore carry forward the losses from the failed banks to offset future income. These tax rulings allowed NCNB to outbid the other potential acquirers and offer the FDIC the best deal because it was at the least cost to the FDIC.

On the day of the transaction, NCNB displayed another one of its strengths that most other banks could not match. Early in its history, NCNB saw the value of hiring several hundred college graduates a year and putting them through a two-year training program to learn various aspects of the bank's business. Most banks did not have such a program. Moreover, NCNB had completed so many acquisitions over the years that it had developed its own successful blueprint for bank takeovers. When it came time to actually take over the failed bridge bank, NCNB had the talent and template to deploy roughly two hundred employees throughout the extensive branch network to be able to close the failed First Republic Bank on Friday night and reopen on Saturday morning as the new NCNB-Texas National Bank (TNB), using the acquisition experience that had worked so well in the past.

Ultimately, the failure of First Republic would be not only the largest U.S. bank failure but also the costliest in the history of the FDIC: $3.9 billion. NCNB had leveraged its management and operating capabilities during the crisis to gain a strategic advantage by entering Texas with the winning bid through a complex negotiation and transaction.[7] McColl and Hartman earlier had decided they only wanted the good bank that still existed within First Republic; they did not want the bad bank. According to Hartman, "The FDIC owned the bad loans, not us." Since NCNB was managing the bridge bank for the FDIC—NCNB-Texas National Bank under Hartman's leadership as chairman and CEO[8]—it eventually owned and also managed the special asset pool under a three-person oversight committee, composed of two senior FDIC officials and one NCNB-TNB employee.[9]

Under the terms of the asset management contract, however, the FDIC remained responsible for the decline in market values and for the servicing expenses of the special asset pool. NCNB-TNB received $2.2 billion from the FDIC for funding of the marked-to-market valuations on the bad assets and $1.9 billion for costs of the special asset pool and other deferred settlement costs. Losses on the FDIC's purchase of assets from the special asset pool were $113 million, with indemnification, legal, and other costs adding another $42 million, for a grand total of $4.3 billion.

By early 1989, however, NCNB-TNB also experienced its own funding problems, just like other Texas banks, and was forced to go to the markets to issue $300 million in preferred debt. Fortunately, this debt sold immediately and cured the bank's funding problems. At that point, NCNB had fulfilled its expansionist strategy in Texas: It owned a clean $15 billion asset bank that was growing, it had no NPLs, it was getting a monthly check from the FDIC for the special asset pool, and it was earning a roughly 150-basis-point spread on its investment assets, mostly U.S. Treasuries, over its deposit costs. Moreover, it still had a tax loss carryforward of approximately $1.0 billion, which helped NCNB's profitability when the economic slump hit North Carolina and the rest of the southeastern United States in 1989.

BUILDING A PLATFORM FOR EXPANSION AND GROWTH

In summary, NCNB's aggressive move into Texas was a strategic and tactical success, and became an important building block in its future expansion and growth. NCNB's stock was trading at roughly $23 per share when the deal was announced; one year later, the price had more than doubled to $53 per share. NCNB continued to champion the cause of nationwide banking and in July 1991 signed a deal to acquire the troubled Citizens and Southern National Bank of Georgia, becoming NationsBank. Eventually, after several other smaller bank mergers as well as some key nonbank acquisitions to fill out its product offering, NationsBank merged with Bank of America in April 1998 and took the BankAmerica name. Market capitalization for the bank had grown to $105 billion, from $2.3 billion a decade earlier, in 1988.[10] At year-end 2001, BankAmerica was the largest U.S. bank in terms of deposits ($360 billion) and the third largest based on assets ($640 billion).

Managing Unique Banking Risks

CHAPTER 6

Driving Successful Bank Turnarounds

Over the past ten years, McKinsey & Company has worked with more than forty bank turnarounds in Europe, North America, South America, and Asia. They run the gamut from money-center banks operating in New York to smaller retail banks in Southeast Asia. We have served private sector executives in turnaround situations—helping them reduce costs, work out nonperforming loans, build capital, develop new lending skills, drive new performance standards, and restore profitability—and we have served public sector banking officials as well on the unique challenges they face.

From these experiences, we believe that we understand what the best practices are for successful bank turnarounds. In our view, a turnaround is successful if a bank is restored to sustainable liquidity, solvency, performance (including needed skills), and profitability in a way that allows it to be competitive in the long run. There are important lessons, not only for bankers and private equity investors, but also for governments, which usually wind up in a stewardship role for which they typically are unequipped and underprepared. Moreover, the turnaround actions of both the private and public sectors in banking give early signs as to whether a nation is serious about laying the foundations for sustained economic recovery.

In synthesizing our experiences with bank turnarounds, we have arrived at two major conclusions. First, the architecture of successful turnarounds worldwide is very similar. While the details of various turnarounds may vary, the fundamentals that drive successful turnaround programs are surprisingly alike. Thus, the lessons learned from these turnaround cases are generally transportable to other parts of the world, regardless of whether developed or emerging markets. Second, the requirements for success are relatively obvious and straightforward. It is the execution that determines the chances for success.

In this chapter, then, we first examine seven management areas that are critical to successful bank turnarounds. Next, we describe in detail the successful turnaround story of Mellon Bank, led by experienced turnaround experts Frank Cahouet and Keith Smith; we highlight a similar story of Christiana Bank in Norway; and then we contrast these cases with the complete failure of Ecuador's Filanbanco. Finally, we examine the unique role that governments must play when they inherit failing banks during a financial crisis; many governments simply are unprepared when the need arises.

ENSURING TURNAROUND SUCCESS: SEVEN MANAGEMENT ACTIONS

In our experience, successful turnarounds are based on neither exotic formulas nor financial magic. Rather, they are based on the disciplined and continuous execution of seven vital management actions:

1. Install new management
2. Revamp credit risk management processes
3. Tightly manage the treasury function
4. Downsize the bank
5. Focus relentlessly on results
6. Add new capital
7. Manage nonperforming loans (NPLs).

Since managing NPLs well is such a critical management action to restore a troubled bank to health, Chapter 7 is devoted entirely to this necessary task.

Action 1: Install New Management to Ensure Success

We have seen few successful turnarounds that did not require a wholesale renewal of the team at the top. The reason is simple: To be successful, the top management team must have the right mindset and capabilities.

Incumbent management teams are impeded typically by two problems. First, they are entangled and obstructed by their past decisions. Unless they develop amnesia, they will waste time and resources revisiting old decisions. The old adage "a new broom sweeps clean" is borne out by our experience, and we believe that asking incumbent managers to leave is the correct course of action.

A critical milestone, in fact, is passed when the management team has been replaced. This is relatively easily accomplished in developed economies, but in developing nations finding the right individuals to replace a management team can be difficult. Some members of the new team may have to come in from outside the country. From our experience, we believe that it is better to hire some people from the outside—even if they are unfamiliar with the local culture and language and sometimes make mistakes because of that—than to be short of experienced hands.

In the past, we have helped clients in Korea, Indonesia, Jamaica, Colombia, Ecuador, and other countries to recruit turnaround-savvy executives. These executives are the banking equivalent of the French Foreign Legion, battling bank failures worldwide. Since they are outsiders, they are often preferable to permanent or long-term hires, even if they typically are more expensive in the short run. They are not entangled in the past mistakes and bad decisions of the banks. Moreover, since they are emotionally uninvolved, they can be brutally honest. These individuals also can be sent in quickly and removed just as easily when the assignment is over, avoiding the need for permanent bureaucracies. Two experiences in Mexico demonstrate this point. At Bancomer and Serfín, the true turnaround phase was marked by a wholesale renewal of the management teams. NCB in Jamaica was also turned around eventually, although it might have returned to health more rapidly had the board acted more decisively to renew the bank leadership.

The new management team is typically comprised of five key positions.

1. The CEO, as team leader, is the most critical new player. This position is sometimes reserved exclusively for local talent, especially in politically charged situations. This person is the most visible sign that a break with the past is being made. Hence, a fresh face is always needed.

2. The CFO is another critical appointment, one that will work to ensure capital adequacy, asset-liability management, and performance management. Since the CEO must have the trust and allegiance of the CFO, we recommend a new person in this role as well to ensure the quality and veracity of financial reporting.

3. The chief risk management officer should be replaced, signaling that the portfolio and the credit approval process will be reviewed thoroughly. Although the new person should be brought in immediately, the former officer may be retained in a staff role to help review the portfolio's past history. Our experience, however, is that these individuals rarely want to remain with the institution unless they can continue to oversee the granting of credit. They will ask for this lending authority to confirm faith in their past decision-making skills. We strongly recommend denying this request. The officer may be blameless in the past indiscretions of the banks; still, this is the time when credit decisions and renewals will be delicate and difficult, and it will require a fresh perspective.

4. The chief distribution officer or head of the retail network is almost always replaced. His or her position is of great importance to the ongoing franchise value of the bank. The chief distribution officer will be asked to perform a minor miracle. First, battling turbulent conditions to retain as much of the deposit base as possible, and second, simultaneously reducing frontline operating costs and finding a better mix of deposits. This person must be highly motivated and possess the technical and people skills to get the job done effectively and efficiently.

5. The chief accountant, who generally reports to the CFO, knows where the bank has financial resources and reserves that can be converted into capital, and more importantly, which bank accounts understate hidden weaknesses. This critical information will help management steer the bank through a successful turnaround. While the CEO needs a chief accountant that he or she can trust, the institutional memory of this individual is perhaps even more important. For this reason, it is preferable to keep the incumbent chief accountant, at least initially, unless there are issues about the veracity or accuracy of the financial reports.

Action 2: Revamp the Credit Process and Portfolio Strategy

When a bank falls into serious lending trouble, we have found that some banks will continue to lend to valued customers under new terms and conditions while revamping their credit policies, while others choose to stop making new loans altogether. In this latter case, the bank probably does not have the capital to continue lending. In fact, it is probably so short on capital that it starts recalling loans. There is no reason to give the officers who booked the bad loans an opportunity to book new loans in an even riskier environment, without a wholesale revamping of the credit process and skill enhancement. Rather, we generally recommend canceling all unused credit lines, reevaluating and marking-to-market every loan on the books, reassessing credit policies and centralizing credit decisions, and suspending loan rollovers, pending a vigorous senior management and board review.

We have seen firsthand the damage that can be done when inept loan officers continue to lend. At Workers Bank in Jamaica, for instance, the loan officers inflicted continuing damage on the bank through their lending practices, even after it was taken over by the government. The same thing was true in Ecuador's Filanbanco.

To be sure, probing the lending practices of a failing bank may surface some unpleasant surprises. For instance, we once advised a Mexican bank to cancel its credit lines and call in its short-term loans. We felt that management needed to know how large the bank's evergreen portfolio was—and whether some part of the short-term portfolio was actually funding longer-term investments. We were not surprised, however, when the probe revealed that a significant proportion of the portfolio's value was impaired and would never be recovered fully. We discovered that part of this supposedly short-term loan portfolio was actually funding fixed assets and other nonliquid investments.

Although many of these loans had to be restructured, the bank was finally able to uncover the real extent of its problems. Testing the real liquidity of its customers forced the bank to create reserves and reprice many of its loans. It also focused management on the right credit issues and kicked off a loan recovery process that might have taken longer to start if these measures had not been taken. This drastic action not only made the bank the very first in the country to admit the full extent of its problems, but also the first to clean up its NPLs. By moving fast, the bank was able to improve the condition of many of its loans, and thus minimize its write-offs.

In every bank turnaround situation that we have seen, recovering the NPL portfolio has been one of the most important profit improvement opportunities. If reserves had already been taken on these loans, then these loan recoveries drop straight to the profits column, shoring up the capital base of the bank and restoring its ability to book fresh loans under new policies and procedures. Even if this is not the case, bank managers should act as if all loans are impaired, if only to reflect the possibility that in turbulent times the value of collateral typically falls.

For this reason, banks should contact their customers immediately to review their status and take possible preventive action. Doing so will preserve the bank's portfolio, and will boost its institutional value. Most corporate borrowers are also sizeable depositors, so stopping lending could easily trigger a deposit run; hence, the need for a clear and actionable customer lending strategy. While banks in crisis may not return to renewed lending at previous levels for a while—if at all—they nonetheless need to reevaluate their loan strategies—reviewing and redesigning the loan-granting process—when they do. They also need to ensure that a decent loan rating system and review process are in place. Significantly improving their credit skills is typically a top priority before any new lending on a suitable risk-reward basis can begin.

Action 3: Tightly Manage the Treasury Function

Turning banks around also requires the tight control of the treasury, first to ensure adequate liquidity to keep the bank open and operating, and later to optimize the scarce available funds. During the first days of a banking crisis, the demand for liquidity inevitably surges: Domestic depositors will be demanding their money, or at least moving their resources into short-term deposits, where they can find shelter if conditions in foreign exchange (FX) and domestic money markets become too turbulent.

For this reason, the bank must closely monitor its own liquidity conditions, while simultaneously keeping a vigilant eye on FX and money markets. Since foreign exchange and interest rates will be erratic, any mistakes during the early period of a crisis could be costly, even deadly. For instance, in Mexico's money markets, daily interest rate swings surged by hundreds of basis points in the early days of the 1994 crisis. In Indonesia, BCA set up a special task force to monitor liquidity and depositor movements daily during the turbulent crisis period in 1998. Money market managers and treasurers always remember the dark days and weeks immediately following a banking crisis, the times when contagious bank failures are prevented only through the close collaboration between the commercial banks and the central bank.

In one case that we experienced, a lack of coordination between the fiscal authority, which was placing debt in the market, and the central bank, which was very tightly controlling the money supply, led interest rates to soar, much to the horror of the local money markets.

On another occasion, when a bank's own treasury requirements coincided with new financing requirements of the government, the market reaction was so extreme that near panic started in the market. Despite the extremely attractive interest rates available in domestic money markets, depositors interpreted these spikes as signs of additional uncertainty and panic, leading to rapid cash withdrawals and a renewed run against the local currency. Following this bout of depositor and investor panic, the government and the central bank sought ways to better coordinate their access to the market, and since our bank client played such an important role in money and currency markets, it too was included in this coordination process.

When a crisis has passed, bank CFOs, in some cases bank treasurers, need to step back from the frenetic pace they had assumed during the crisis when liquidity was desperately thin. More specifically, they should focus on new goals.

1. Restoring access to liquidity. In a banking crisis, access to domestic and foreign sources of liquidity dries up and is provided temporarily by central bank credit lines or nothing at all. With a relative return to normalcy, bank CFOs must restore credit lines with correspondent bank lines—both domestic and foreign. Generally, access to foreign credit is dependent upon the negotiations with creditors. Banks whose turnarounds are proceeding on schedule can also act as a weathervane, signaling the return of more normal financial conditions for the country. During a crisis in the interbank market, when gossip is omnipresent, one bank's liabilities are another bank's assets. Often, only the central bank can see the whole pattern and is in a superior position to manage it. Individual banks, therefore, must work closely with the central bank before the turnaround really can begin.

2. Managing ongoing liquidity conditions. Bank CFOs should also hold daily or eventually weekly asset and liability reviews as part of the new management of internal liquidity. These meetings are to ensure that assets and liabilities become increasingly matched. The meetings are meant to anticipate liquidity requirements, but they are also held to make sure that the line officers recognize the liquidity needs of the bank and the impact that large withdrawals can have.

3. Optimizing cash availability by carefully monitoring discretional spending and cash disbursements. Delaying cash disbursements on projects with long-term cash returns, as well as postponing spending on systems, advertising, and other discretionary items, is advised. Even if the returns of such investments are high, the cost of alternative funding relative to maximizing retained earnings during the crisis can be prohibitive. Banks also can manage liquidity in a crisis by selling assets to other, stronger banks or, in some cases, securitizing them.

Action 4: Downsize the Bank

We have yet to see a turnaround situation that did not require significant personnel cuts, typically in the range of 20 to 30 percent of total employees. In 1998, over 30 percent of the employees in the Korean banking sector, for instance, lost their jobs after the first year of the Korean crisis. Given the expected loss in earnings from NPLs, executives have to right-size the bank: The bigger the amount of NPLs, the more operating expenses that have to be cut by management to save the bank.

Sometimes, though, even bigger cuts are demanded by reality. In the Ecuadorian crisis of 1998–1999, for example, both the shift in the exchange rate from sucres to dollars and the drop in loan interest margins resulting from Ecuador's subsequent dollarization diminished the asset base of most banks. For that reason, the staffing cuts required to turn a bank around successfully went well beyond the typical range, and eventually amounted to about 40 percent. For more details on the best way to downsize, see Box 6.1: How to Downsize Successfully Before Growing Again.

BOX 6.1: HOW TO DOWNSIZE SUCCESSFULLY BEFORE GROWING AGAIN

Downsizing has to be driven by a relatively "rough-and-ready" process, involving the following chronology:

1. Use simple, top-down algebra to determine the right-sized bank: Typically, banks must first downsize before they can earn their right to grow again. Benchmarks, and the size of the profit gap, are key determinants. Savings in the range of 20 to 30 percent are typically required and can be achieved.

2. Quickly identify high-potential cost-reduction areas, including:
   - Noncontributing branches/distribution system components
   - Stacked/redundant organizational structures: focus on cutting management lines and simplifying structures. It is useful to keep in

(continued)

mind that in most emerging markets, management can be ten to fifteen times more costly than front-line personnel
- Low-value or delayed-value staff areas (e.g., chauffers, personnel services, training).

3. Announce staff downsizing targets and offer voluntary retirement programs to induce departures.

4. Eliminate prestige spending (fancy dining rooms, expense accounts, new autos, company airplanes) both to reduce the cost of bank operations and to maintain morale and discipline.

5. Rapidly cut staff, making deeper cuts than first quantifications suggest are needed.

Rightsizing the bank after a crisis is difficult, but it is also inevitable. Experience has taught us that spending a long time analyzing the situation is generally a way of avoiding the unpleasantness. Turnaround specialists generally have reputations for being tough-minded and driven by the numbers to restore the bank to prosperity, but in fact, their moves are rational and required, and compassionate in the final analysis. As the Filanbanco experience shows, procrastination can cause banks to fail that might have been saved. Rightsizing *is* right.

Action 5: Focus Relentlessly on Results

Operating improvements and bottom-line results are the marks of successful bank turnarounds. To get there, you must define your turnaround strategy early. Goals must be set that can be measured frequently with clear metrics. Management's focus must be on results and not excuses. Performance rewards and transparent sanctions including dismissal must be in place. Execution becomes the watchword. Strategy must be reevaluated continually, and management needs to adapt tactics accordingly depending on strategic shifts and changes in the external environment.

For instance, the CEO of Mexico's Banco Internacional, Jaime Corredor, would meet weekly to review a highly complex cost-reduction process under way in the distribution system that required relentlessly pursuing a systems relocation and simplification agenda that was the critical path for needed cuts in the system's costs. After several false starts, Corredor recognized that without this weekly review the timetable would slip and the cost-cutting discipline would be lost. Eventually, Corredor drove a successful cost-cutting program that was fundamental to the turnaround of this troubled bank.

Action 6: Add New Capital

As soon as management can tell a credible turnaround story, it is time to start raising fresh capital, which combined with new credit skills, is required to restart lending and earnings growth. Mellon Bank Corporation based in Pittsburgh, Pennsylvania, for example, was a U.S. bank whose turnaround was so impressive that it began to raise capital simultaneously with writing down its bad loans.[1] In fact, for executives in any country looking for a total success story that includes the actions listed above, there is no better story than Mellon's.

MELLON BANK'S SUCCESSFUL TURNAROUND

The five-year turnaround of U.S.-based Mellon Bank is one of the most successful cases anywhere in the world, and it provides managers with universal lessons learned that can be applied in any country.

Founded in 1869 in Pittsburgh, Pennsylvania, by retired Judge Thomas Mellon and his sons, Andrew and Richard, Mellon Bank had a distinguished and prosperous history for more than a hundred years as a pillar of the U.S. financial landscape. By the mid 1980s, Mellon Bank Corporation had transformed itself into a growing money-center bank. It was the fifteenth largest bank in the country, with a product reach that spanned not only the lucrative trust business and industrial financing in the Midwest, but also real estate and energy lending in the Southwest, and even extensive lending to less developed countries (LDCs).

In late 1986, however, Mellon Bank's board of directors began to be concerned about the rapid growth and concentration of the bank's portfolio in areas of the economy that were showing signs of strain. In the first quarter of 1987, Mellon Bank reported its first quarterly loss, with management blaming the bank's rapid expansion program for this unprecedented loss. The bank posted a $65 million loss, made a $175 million provision for future loan losses, and cut its dividend to shareholders in half. The future of the bank looked bleak. It was time for the board to act. It fired the CEO and replaced him temporarily with a veteran board member until a search committee could find a suitable replacement to turn the bank around and save it from potential failure.

By June 1987, Frank V. Cahouet, the former CEO of Crocker National Bank in California, was brought in to turn Mellon around. He was joined by W. Keith Smith as CFO, who held the same position at Crocker, as well as Anthony (Tony) Terracciano from Chase Manhattan Bank, as president, a position he held until January 1990. Each of these managers had long, successful careers in banking in other U.S. institutions, and together they brought their collective turnaround expertise and experience to Mellon

Bank. As they joined the bank, Mellon was about to announce a second quarter loss of roughly $566 million with a loan loss provision of $533 million. At the time, Mellon's market capitalization was roughly $750 million, and without fast action it was at risk of failing.

The three executives had their most challenging times ahead of them and went to work immediately to revitalize the corporation and return it to profitability. Like talented jugglers, they had to keep three synchronized streams of work moving simultaneously to be successful: They had to stabilize the bank immediately and stop the bleeding from life-threatening credit losses and unsustainable expenses; they had to refocus the vision and strategy of the bank in a way that its internal and external stakeholders—employees, customers, creditors, investors, and regulators—could readily understand and support; and finally they had to recapitalize the bank not only to make up for the huge credit losses that were mounting but also to position Mellon appropriately to leverage its brand and other strengths for the competitive future that lay ahead of them.

Stabilizing the Bank to Stop the Losses

The most immediate task was to stabilize the bank, stop the credit losses, and preserve its cash flow. The new team immediately saw problems that were similar to Crocker: destabilizing credit losses; excessive operating expenses with inadequate controls; a basic lack of focus on profitability and misunderstanding of what the numbers actually meant; a management team that was not prepared to recognize or trained to manage problems, especially problem credits. For example, they found that the controller knew more about the quality of the loan portfolio than the lending management, and much of the basic financial analysis presented to them was only surface deep.

By July, they had a stabilization plan in place that consisted of a number of basic tools used to stop the hemorrhaging. They instituted a cost reduction program that would result in a layoff of roughly 15 percent of Mellon's workforce within six months to save on operating expenses. They renewed early retirement incentives for three hundred employees. They continued to wind down Mellon's international banking department, closing half of its international offices and laying off two hundred out of seven hundred employees by October. They moved quickly to empower people and encouraged employees to bring them fresh and novel ideas to save money and improve internal processes, requiring them to drive down deep into minutiae at all levels of the bank.

One award-winning idea came from a long-term employee who noticed that Mellon was consistently paying high fees to the local fire departments whenever the balloons they used to celebrate hitting sales targets in the branches set off the fire alarms when they rose to the ceiling. The employee's idea was to call the fire department ahead of time, tell them about the branch party and the balloons, and ask them not to send their trucks when the false alarm rang. While obviously a tiny savings compared to the magnitude of the bank's problems, they used this story successfully to convey two larger messages: First, every single idea—no matter how small—was needed; and second, for the first time, management was listening to the frontline, and employees' ideas were being taken seriously as the senior executives probed everywhere for creative ways to rebuild the bank.

The team set out to change the management group and culture as well. They organized their own immediate management team—with many of whom they had previously worked and whom they trusted—and effectively did their own version of a hostile takeover of management, which helped to change both the players and the culture deeper in the company. They were joined by Richard H. Daniel as vice chairman and chief credit officer, Martin G. McGuinn as general counsel, Jeffrey L. Morby as vice chairman for strategic planning and corporate banking, and Steven G. Elliott as executive vice president of finance, who among others formed the nucleus of the leadership team to drive the bank forward.[2] They encouraged employees to surface problems sooner rather than later, something that had been a contributing cause of Mellon's credit problems in the past; they made it clear that they would not "shoot the messenger."

These executives led by example, starting their days at 6:00 A.M. and working sixty-hour weeks. The entire top management team met twice a week, Mondays and Fridays, from 7:00 A.M. to 9:00 A.M., to ensure the necessary two-way communication up and down the ranks, to break down the traditional territoriality among individual managers the next level down, and to start to build a climate of trust and real teamwork among the senior management team.

These experienced turnaround artists also recognized the value of being nimble and moving swiftly in a crisis situation. Together with other executive committee members, they made decisions quickly and didn't agonize over their decisions once made. To move at the speed they needed to move, they also recognized that they would make some mistakes along the way, but that was part of their management process. As a team, they could fix mistakes later and learn at the same time.

To be successful, the senior management team had to have the full confidence of Mellon's board of directors as well as its regulators—and they did. They held monthly board meetings throughout their tenure, relied heavily on a strong audit committee, and worked hard to ensure excellent communication with their board and major shareholders. "We wanted the board to cheer for us from the stands, and occasionally sit with us on the sidelines as we rolled out our game plan," Cahouet explains, "and that was appropriate, but we didn't suit them up and send them on the field—that was our job. They understood the difference between a governance role and an operating role."

They also began to reorganize the bank early to send the right message throughout the organization. From their perspective at this point, there was no built-in resistance to their new strategy and operating style anywhere in the company that they couldn't control. They also brought in a new head of human resources, an individual with a strong industrial background, to help complete the transformation. Performance reviews were conducted three times a year to get their message across to all senior employees.

Part of their early efforts also focused on "educating many of our managers on the simple math of the banking business," according to Smith. They forced their managers to get serious with numbers, worrying less with hitting volume targets and paying more attention to margins and return on invested capital. They implemented monthly budget reviews, where the business unit managers had to explain and defend three sets of numbers: their original operating plan for the year, the actual monthly results, and their revised projections for the year. Management focused on the absolute numbers as well as the changes month-to-month. Mellon leveraged its existing technology with some modifications to enable business unit managers to be able to report net income and return on equity within a few days of the monthly closing of its books. All business units had their own finance officers, who reported directly to the CFO, to ensure that there was no gamesmanship with the numbers. If business unit managers reported an 8 percent ROE when their target was an 18 percent ROE, then they had a problem with management. As former and current CFOs, Frank, Tony, and Keith knew numbers, and they imposed this rigorous financial discipline throughout the company.

Another key ingredient to the immediate task of stabilizing the bank was securing the cooperation of the bank's regulators who could have taken almost total regulatory control in 1987. Thanks to the credibility that the team had built with the regulators in their past positions, the Federal Reserve (the regulator of Mellon Bank Corporation) and the Comptroller of the Currency (the regulator of its national bank charter) were supportive. Rather than being forced to sign a restrictive supervisory agreement with the agencies, the executives instead sold them on their developing strategy and business plan to turn the bank around, which they reviewed with the agencies on a periodic basis. As a consequence, no formal regulatory plan was required, which ultimately saved both parties a tremendous amount of time and energy.

The years 1987 and 1988 marked the low point in Mellon's history, with losses of $844 million and $65 million respectively. Profitability of $181 million would not return until 1989 and even then Mellon faced a larger than normal fourth quarter provision for credit losses.

Refocusing the Bank for the Future

In his role as CEO, Cahouet knew that Mellon had been following a failed strategy in its pursuit of becoming a money-center bank. Almost every new lending area that the bank had entered—commercial real estate, mortgage banking, energy, and LDC loans—was a source of the bank's credit problems. As soon as the immediate cost savings tactics were set in motion, he turned to resetting the bank's vision and strategy.

"In every bank turnaround situation, the CEO needs a strategic plan and a good story to tell right out of the starting gate," advises Cahouet. Knowing that the analysts and the press would be all over them soon, within forty-five days the new team began publicly describing its new strategic direction.

Instead of staying the course as a money-center bank, Mellon would downsize and redefine itself as a super-regional bank following a strategy of balance focusing on wholesale, middle-market, and retail banking as well as fee service businesses where they had competitive strength. Mellon had a significant advantage over most other commercial banks at the time with its higher level of fee income, which rose to 50 percent of total income by 1992. It was this focus on fee income, especially in Mellon's sizeable trust operations and other service lines, that would play a key role in its future strategic shift.

By the end of 1990, Mellon had progressed sufficiently to begin to engineer another defining strategic moment: the back-to-back acquisitions of The Boston Company and the Dreyfus mutual fund group between 1992 and 1994. Both of these companies played to Mellon's historical but underdeveloped strength as a trust and asset management company, and helped to leverage Mellon's considerable but largely untapped brand strength. "These acquisitions unlocked Mellon's mentality to enable us to do new things and think outside the box," says Cahouet. "From that point forward, we were no longer just another super regional bank, but we had entered the national scene on our terms in our own way." These moves would pave the way for more M&A and business development, a deeper appreciation by Wall Street for where the new Mellon Bank team was heading, and even more degrees of freedom for significant strategic shifts in the years ahead.

Recapitalizing the Good Bank by Creating a Bad Bank

It was not enough to start the cost savings and reset Mellon's strategy; they also had to find a way to recapitalize the bank before it was too late. Cahouet and Smith had to devise an asset disposition and recapitalization plan that would convince the markets of their long-term viability and save them from potential regulatory intervention. They didn't have much time, and they needed about $500 million in fresh equity capital.

While at Crocker, they used a plan where their foreign parent provided capital to transfer nonperforming loans to a workout company. Mellon didn't have a foreign parent, and short of selling the bank, they had to come up with an alternative solution—and soon. Working with E.M. Warburg Pincus & Co., a New York venture capital group, they crafted a unique plan to tap into the junk bond market to finance the creation of a bad bank, known as Grant Street National Bank (GSNB). The plan was to transfer roughly $1 billion (book value) of Mellon's nonperforming assets to this new subsidiary of the parent holding company, using the proceeds of two types of common stock offerings totaling $525 million to offset the loss in the transfer of the loans and the other bad assets at market value and to inject some much needed new capital into Mellon.

As part of the transaction, they were able to spin off GSNB to Mellon's existing shareholders, and provide a class of stock for Grant Street directors as incentive compensation. Grant Street had also entered into a management contract with another Mellon Bank subsidiary, Collection Services Corporation, to collect the bad loans on a "cost plus 3 percent of collections" basis working under the direction of the Grant Street directors and management. This unit had a staff of more than fifty people with strong workout skills.

While a bit complicated financially, GSNB was a straightforward and relatively simple means of selling the bad loans quickly on a non-recourse basis in one lump sum, and simultaneously bringing fresh capital into Mellon Bank, thus allowing management to focus on its strategy, core businesses, and return to profitability. A positive first sign was the fact that Mellon Bank did as much new business in the fourth quarter of 1988—its first real operating quarter after the restructuring—as it had in the previous three quarters of 1988. The creation of Grant Street also gave Mellon employees a psychological lift; with the bulk of the problems now separated from the remaining bank, employees clearly could see the light at the end of the tunnel and project that optimism to their customer base.

It did take a lot of hard work on the part of investment bankers, lawyers, and accountants to make this novel plan a reality. By all accounts, GSNB was a complete success: It was structured well and had the right incentives with a strong workout team who would return to Mellon Bank once their job was done; it completed its mission and returned its bank charter to the banking authorities ahead of time; it paid off its debt early; it repaid the preferred stock held by Mellon and returned essentially all of the common equity invested in GSNB to its shareholders. Mellon's own stock immediately went up once GSNB was unveiled and contributed significantly to the fact that from July 1987 to December 1998 Mellon's total return to shareholders compounded at a 21.3 percent rate per year.

Mellon's Postcript on the Future

From our perspective, the work of the Cahouet team not only saved Mellon Bank from potential failure but also will go down in financial history as one of the great turnaround success stories of all time. After five years of hard work, the bank turnaround effort was mostly over and they could focus on repositioning Mellon Bank for the future and finding new ways to generate fee income and increase shareholder value. When Cahouet and Smith retired in December 1998, the market capitalization had risen to roughly $18 billion.

As a postscript, the new management team, led by Marty McGuinn, veteran of the turnaround and the current chairman and CEO, has advanced the Cahouet strategy significantly, building on strong fee businesses—currently generating 87 percent of all income—to transform Mellon Bank once again into a leading global financial services provider. In July 2001, McGuinn announced the sale of Mellon's retail branches for $2 billion to Citizens Financial, the U.S. unit of the Royal Bank of Scotland Group.

Consistently one of the highest-performing U.S. banks in terms of ROE, Mellon now provides private banking services, trust and custody, benefits and consulting administration, shareholder services, and a comprehensive list of services to affluent individuals, institutions, and corporations. As of early 2002, it had close to $3 trillion in assets under management, administration, or custody.

CHRISTIANA BANK'S SUCCESSFUL TURNAROUND

Christiana Bank was established in 1848 as Norway's first commercial bank. As the second largest Norwegian bank throughout the 1980s and 1990s, Christiana Bank was hit hard by the financial crisis that struck Scandinavia in 1991, and saw its losses mount to $1.2 billion within the first nine months of 1991.[3] Despite a government infusion of capital in August 1991 of $395 million, Christiana was unable to recover on its own, and became insolvent in October of that year.[4] Trading was discontinued on the Oslo Stock Exchange, and the government took full ownership of the bank through the Statens Banksikringsfond—the Government Bank Insurance Fund (GBIF).

Installing New Management Committed to Success

As the full weight of the Norwegian financial crisis hit, Christiana took bold actions to try to turn its financial situation around. In August it ousted top management as well as most of its board. Borger A. Lenth, formerly the managing director of Eksportfinans, took over as managing director in

August.[5] Over the course of 1991 and 1992, with several infusions of government capital totaling $1.3 billion, Lenth led Christiana through a turnaround effort that would return Christiana to profitability by the first quarter of 1993.

Tightening Its Operations

When the government took control of the bank, the new management and the GBIF agreed on a strategy to reduce non-interest expenses by at least 15 percent between June 1991 and June 1992. In actuality, top management exceeded these goals, reducing costs 21 percent over this time period.[6] These results were accomplished through several efforts aimed at downsizing, tightly managing the treasury function, and revamping the credit process and portfolio strategies.

A crucial aspect of Christiana Bank's turnaround was its downsizing effort, which Lenth began as soon as the government took ownership in 1991. This included a reduction of almost 1,200 employees over 1991 and 1992, equivalent to 21 percent of its 5,513 employees at the end of 1990.[7]

Simultaneously, Christiana began revamping its credit processes. One of the first things that the new management team did in the fall of 1991 was to review all nonperforming loans, and begin to mark them to market.[8] As a result, it wrote off $319 million in restructuring costs and doubled its loan loss provisions in November 1991.[9] It established a Loan Loss Recovery and Corporate Restructuring Area, and supplied it with considerable resources to monitor and work on loan loss exposures. Additionally, it focused on increasing its knowledge of credit policy, increasing its competence within the credit function, and strengthening its overall risk monitoring practices. Finally, Christiana took moves to protect its investment exposure by substantially reducing its equity investments and real estate holdings.

Changing Strategic Direction and Focusing on Results

Throughout Lenth's tenure as CEO, Christiana tailored its strategy to increase the bank's effectiveness at serving its customers. In 1991, it launched an effort to tailor and better motivate its sales and distribution network to its customers' needs. In fact, with fewer branches, Christiana was actually able to increase its customer deposits 7.5 percent ($694 million) by the first quarter of 1992.[10] Moreover, it was able to return to profitability by the first quarter of 1993, reporting $31.3 million in profits.[11]

This trend to increase performance continued with admirable success over the following years. Most impressive was the growth in Christiana's core financial suite of products: Under its new credit policies and procedures, net loans to customers increased at an annual rate of 13.2 percent over the same period, and life insurance premiums increased 36 percent annually from 1993 to 1996. While Christiana maintained its overall market position as the second largest bank in Norway, it gained market share in several of its key products, including life insurance and lending.[12] This successful growth at the individual product level contributed to operating success for Christiana as a whole. From an ROE of –98.3 percent in 1992, Lenth returned Christiana to levels averaging 25 percent over the period from 1993 to 1998.[13]

Adding New Capital for Growth

Christiana's turnaround effort would not have been possible without increased access to capital. Christiana achieved a capital infusion in late 1993 by regaining the trust of investors and of the government, which enabled it to issue stock offerings (both restricted and free shares) totaling $266 million. This move led to the relisting of Christiana on the Oslo Stock Exchange, and reduced government ownership to 69 percent.[14] Christiana's growth was also aided by its acquisition strategy. Its first post-crisis acquisition was of Norske Liv, a life and pension insurance corporation, in 1993. This was followed by the acquisition of Vestenfjelske Bykreditt AS in 1994, and Norgeskredit AS in 1996.

By 1999, Christiana was looking to build on its successful turnaround strategy, with aims at further acquisitions, increases in operating efficiency, and an increased product mix.[15] This acquisition strategy was halted, however, in September 1999, when Christiana was acquired by Nordea AB, a Swedish bank, for $2.9 billion (a 1.62 price-to-book value), creating the first pan-Nordic bank, with operations in Sweden, Norway, Denmark, and Finland.[16]

FILANBANCO'S FAILED TURNAROUND

If the case studies of Mellon's and Christiana's turnarounds are a successful road map for executives facing a similar situation, then the story of Ecuador's failed Filanbanco is the exact opposite. It is a classic case of how *not* to turn around a bank.

Filanbanco was Ecuador's second largest bank when it failed in late 1998. Based in the coastal city of Guayaquil, Filanbanco had close political ties to the opposition party at the time, which complicated the larger political solution for resolving failing banks in general. In another political context, Filanbanco might have been closed and liquidated, with the remaining franchise—branches, deposits, and the remaining "good" assets—going to the highest bidder. Given the deep political divisions in Ecuador throughout its crisis, however, Filanbanco was allowed to remain open for business. Its ultimate failure can be traced to a lack of vision and strategy for turning around the bank, a lack of corporate governance, and an inability to fundamentally change its operations and performance.

Lack of Vision and Strategy

Filanbanco's first shortcoming was a lack of vision and a turnaround strategy. Unlike other banks that had failed in the past and been turned over to the central bank for resolution, Filanbanco was the first bank to fail that was managed by Ecuador's new, untested, and understaffed Agencia de Garantía de Depósitos (AGD) that was established just as the bank was failing. The AGD did install new management at the time, but did little else to oversee the rehabilitation of the bank even though it had injected roughly $800 million in government bonds into the bank. Unlike the case of Korea or Indonesia, there was no rigorous business plan required by the government nor was there a clear timetable for fulfilling business objectives. The AGD did not tie its investment to any kind of strict performance contract by which to measure Filanbanco's success or failure. The AGD simply injected funds, without having its own vision or strategy for the successful rehabilitation of one of Ecuador's biggest banks.

Moreover, the new management team lacked a vision and strategy of its own, other than adopting a "business as usual" approach. Filanbanco simply continued to take in deposits, including deposits transferred by the AGD from other failed banks, and make even more bad loans, with no turnaround plan of its own.

Lack of Corporate Governance

Filanbanco is a classic case of the complete lack of corporate governance and accountability. The AGD was the bank's largest shareholder after its failure, but failed to provide the necessary guidance and oversight of its largest problem bank. Much of this was due to the larger political stalemate over the banking system crisis going on in the country at the time, but it was also due to AGD's inexperience and inability to act as a normal government bank restructuring agency.

AGD did not have all the resolution powers of the U.S. FDIC, for example, and furthermore its employees were subject to civil and criminal penalties for any repercussions from their official duties. Try to take the necessary corrective steps to restructure the bank, and you could be sued personally, your personal assets—your home, your savings—ultimately could be taken away, and you could face criminal prosecution. Many former AGD officials had to move their assets out of the country and seek a safe haven in

Miami to avoid what was largely political, but also legal, prosecution after their tour of duty.

Nor did the new board of directors make any attempt on its own to impose world-class corporate governance on the bank. One insider at the time described it as a "decorative" board, not a decisive one. Unlike the example of Korea, there was no effort to impose new corporate governance standards in line with observed best practices from around the world. There was no independent oversight of management; there was no truly functioning audit committee in place. Management did not have a budget in 2000, for example, and neither the board nor the AGD did anything about it. On the other hand, even minor decisions had to pass through the board to the highly politicized AGD for final approval, further complicating and needlessly delaying the turnaround.

Lack of Operation and Performance Improvements

As if these failings were not enough, there was no real attempt to improve the bank operationally and make the necessary performance enhancements to position the bank for a role in Ecuador's post-crisis banking system. It was clear there was no turnaround plan from the start.

When the fourth largest bank in Ecuador, Previsora, also failed, the AGD combined its newest failure with Filanbanco in mid-1999. It was not until January 2000 that a post-merger management study was commissioned in an attempt to salvage the newly combined, troubled bank, and even then the management team failed to implement the recommended turnaround vision and strategy. It took about two months to agree who would be CEO of the combined bank, and the situation worsened during this period when efforts should have been well under way to turn the combined banks around. Moreover, this was the first turnaround plan that the AGD had seen since the bank failed in late 1998.

During the interim period, there was no attempt to start the serious workout effort required to manage and collect on NPLs or sell bad assets. There was no effort to improve the bank-lending skills or impose new risk-reward processes and metrics; the bank simply continued to make loans in the same way that contributed to its initial downfall. Filanbanco even took part of the government bonds that were to be used for its capital adequacy, sold them on the secondary market, and then used the proceeds to keep lending as it had before its takeover. Since there was no investment contract between bank management and the AGD, there were no management incentives in place to support a successful turnaround effort.

As if this situation were not bad enough, there was little effort to reduce the costs of the combined banks, a prerequisite in almost every other successful bank turnaround. It was clear that it was more expensive to keep the bank open than it was to close it and liquidate it.

Management continued to spend on marketing and advertising, without regard to taking obvious costs out of the combined banks. When Previsora was merged into Filanbanco, the new bank had to accept the more generous and costly labor union contract of Previsora, instead of renegotiating both contracts in an effort to reduce costs to save the bank. Moreover, although it reported a small profit of roughly $18 million in 2000, 10 percent of which was shared with employees under their labor contract, a closer inspection by an independent consultant showed that the bank actually had approximately $150 million in *negative* cash flow, due to faulty loan loss provisioning in its loosely audited financial reports.

With these problems, it is not surprising that new management was introduced again in November 2000, after the previous management had been indicted on embezzlement charges as well. The AGD brought in a seasoned Ecuadorian banker, Antonio Bejarano, to make one last attempt to salvage its biggest problem bank, but the bank was simply too far gone by then. Too much collective damage had been heaped on top of the previous two combined failures. In January 2001, management was again replaced by AGD; in March 2001, the bank failed—again—and is now in the process of being liquidated.

GOVERNMENT STEWARDSHIP OF TROUBLED BANKS

From the Mellon Bank and Christiana Bank success stories, we clearly can see what a group of dedicated and skilled executives can do with a private sector turnaround strategy for a troubled bank. It *can* be done. Yet, in many cases, banks are taken over first by governments. The decision to save an institution or let it fail, in these cases, is made by government agencies, and not by markets and turnaround experts. This dilemma creates a host of special questions that normally are not faced when markets are entrusted with these tasks. Suddenly, and often without fully appreciating the warning signs, governments are forced to answer some tough questions. How to determine which banks should be saved, which should fail, and what to do with the banks in the middle? What should be done to protect the depositors of failed banks? What role should the government play in managing bank turnarounds?

Which Banks Should Be Saved?

Over the years, we have seen many banks that should be saved, due to their significance to the payments system or their importance to the economy— such as Banca Serfín in Mexico, National Commerce Bank (NCB) in Jamaica, Hanvit Bank in Korea, or Bank Central Asia (BCA) in Indonesia.

We have also seen banks that have been kept alive for purely political reasons, or because the government had taken them over but had not decided what to do with them. Many small banks fall into that category.

Insolvency is usually the reason that banks fall into the hands of the government, but not all situations are equal. Some banks with solvency issues can be turned around, such as Mellon Bank, Bank of America in the mid-1980s, and Banca Serfín and NCB in the late 1990s.

Yet, many other troubled institutions are often beyond repair. They should be eliminated expeditiously from the system. They are what one of our Korean clients called "vampire banks"—banks that prey on the lifeblood of healthy or recovering banks. Vampire banks will pay above-market rates to attract deposits, then use the funds to gamble on high-risk and typically bad, uneconomic loans, often issued to friends and political cronies.

Experience has taught us that banks that lack a distinct competitive advantage—and have failed once—should not be given a second chance. Time and again, we have seen banks that lack economies of scale and a distinctive set of banking skills fail again shortly after they have been put back on their feet.

More often than not, these banks are kept alive for very questionable reasons. Consider the following cases.

1. In Ecuador, one of the reasons for reviving inept banks was the regional rivalry between the cities of Quito and Guayaquil, with each wanting the biggest bank. In this case, political influence triumphed over good sense. As a consequence, banks that had failed miserably once, such as Filanbanco and Previsora, were given a second chance. They revived just long enough to fail again, at an enormous cost to the Ecuadorian taxpayer.
2. In Mexico, political rivalries between Comisión Nacional Bancaria e de Valores (CNBV), the banking sector regulator, and Instituto para la Protección al Ahorro Bancario (IPAB), the entity in charge of minimizing the resolution costs of the banking crisis, led to an impasse. This delayed critical decisions in the resolution of such failing and failed banks as Banca Cremi, BCH, Bancrecer, Banco del Sureste, and others. This political rivalry among competing bureaucracies, in turn, caused the crisis resolution to drag on for years and increased the costs as a result.

It would be easy to cite many other cases where politics or flawed decisions contributed to prolonged banking sector problems due to ineffective turnaround strategies. Keeping vampire banks alive is simply a bad idea, not only for the health of the banking system but also for taxpayers. Often vampire banks rise again from the dead to create new problems and crises in the future. It is better to act rapidly, decisively, and responsibly.

Lamentably, our experience is that almost every failed bank has had a champion with political connections arguing for its survival. In most cases the technically correct decision is obvious, but political decisions obstruct the resolution process, delay effective action, and increase final resolution costs. At a minimum, the choice of whether to provide official government assistance must be considered carefully, as Brian Quinn, former executive director of bank supervision at the Bank of England, warns in his essay in Appendix 6.1: Building a Rationale for Official Support in a Financial Crisis.

In fact, there are choices between alternative costs: the cost of failure versus the cost of rescue. In a systemic crisis, or one that threatens the system, it may be necessary to save failing banks at least temporarily to prevent a higher cost if the system collapses.

Recognizing Banks That Should Be Closed

So, which banks should be closed? Growing pattern recognition is one of the benefits of having observed and studied financial crises in many countries. The details of each crisis vary, but in our experience, several basic patterns are repeated. Depending on the unique country circumstances we find, here is the action plan that we normally would suggest.

1. Small insolvent banks should be closed immediately. They almost always lack the intrinsic conditions for success. Examples of this type of institution are Workers Bank in Jamaica, Previsora in Ecuador, and Banco Industrial in Mexico, all of which were allowed to continue operating for long periods of time even after it was common knowledge that they were insolvent.

The reason that these banks should be closed is that they do not, and typically cannot, develop a sustainable competitive position. Hence, they distinguish themselves in the market through adverse selection—taking on counterparty and market risks that other banks have avoided, sourcing themselves at unreasonable costs, and maintaining asset and liability mismatches that later prove to be unsustainable.

Their size hurts these banks in other ways: first, by making it almost impossible for them to diversify credit risks; and second, by making it difficult for them to attract and retain individuals with the skills required to develop value-added capabilities that can help them to overcome their cost disadvantages. Governments rarely go wrong if they decide to permanently and rapidly shut down these small failing banks and transfer their depositors and distribution systems to larger, healthier institutions that have a better chance of surviving the crisis.

2. Banks with extreme insolvency problems are the second category of banks to be closed. Examples of this type include Chunchong Bank and

Kyunghi Bank in Korea, Filanbanco in Ecuador, or Banco del Pacífico in Colombia. Experience has taught us that governments rarely go wrong when they close institutions whose turnaround programs require unbelievably extreme improvements by untested management. These cases are generally easy to recognize, because their turnaround plan rests on implausible assumptions, questionable execution, and improbable results. In these cases, there is little to be gained by delaying the decision to resolve the bank through liquidation, sale to the highest bidder, or merger with another bank or financial institution that has the capital and skills required to rehabilitate the failing bank.

3. **Policy violations and fraudulent practices.** The third category consists of banks run by individuals who are in clear violation of bank supervisory policies or who have been implicated in fraudulent practices. In Jamaica, for example, several banks were allowed to continue operating, even though it was clear to authorities that their officers were violating banking regulations. In Ecuador, Banco Progreso, for example, continued operating for several months although its owners had violated banking laws by extending loans to related parties. In Indonesia, Bank Dagang Negara Indonesia and Bank Unum National were implicated in fraudulent practices in 1998. By the time the audits were finished and those banks were seized, there was almost nothing left of value from which to pay depositors.

Identifying Banks That Deserve To Be Rehabilitated

Just as we have developed a clear image in our minds of institutions that should be shut down and rapidly resolved, we have also developed a robust methodology to determine which banks deserve to be recapitalized. Our methodology for determining which banks can be saved is found in Box 6.2: Determining Which Banks to Save, and is based on work we have done in Korea, Thailand, Indonesia, Jamaica, Ecuador, Colombia, Turkey, and other countries.

BOX 6.2: DETERMINING WHICH BANKS TO SAVE

At McKinsey, we use two complementary methods to identify those banks that should be given a chance to play a continuing role in a country's banking system after a crisis.

Capital adequacy and strategic direction. In Korea, Indonesia, and Colombia, we developed a matrix-ranking based on our assessment of a

(continued)

bank's real capital adequacy, after a thorough outside audit by international accounting firms using U.S. or U.K. standards to determine a realistic view of the portfolio. We also required a strategic plan and detailed business unit plans to identify those banks with a high probability of either qualifying for a capital infusion from the government or surviving on their own without government assistance. In exchange for an infusion of government capital, banks were required to complete an investment contract that had tough but well-defined performance metrics. This agreement, which protects the taxpayer as much as possible, is a minimum requirement. Such memoranda of understanding (MOUs) were drafted for each institution receiving financial aid from its respective government.

Competitive importance. In Ecuador and Korea, we used sequenced and incrementally tougher questions to determine the bank's value and contribution to the new, post-crisis banking environment. Does the bank have sufficient scale to compete? Does the bank have a robust franchise value? Does it offer competitive and unique products and services that others do not? Is it an integral part of the nation's payments system? If the bank answers in the affirmative and with hard evidence and is backed by management's commitment and fresh capital, then it has a good chance of making a positive contribution to a country's post-crisis financial landscape.

Taken together, these two tests are fairly reliable. They determine which institutions have the highest probability of turning around and which will add the most value to the country's future banking, payments, and financial systems.

1. **Large scale relative to competitors.** This is not to say that large banks should be saved because of their sheer size, but rather that size can be leveraged in a turnaround situation due to the competitive and operating advantages of size. Often, these banks are core to the nation's payments system. Banks with scale, we have found, have a head start in a turnaround situation, as indicated by NCB in Jamaica, Banca Serfín in Mexico, Hanvit Bank in Korea, or BCA in Indonesia.

2. **Trust-based relationships with depositors, despite solvency issues.** Trust is an extremely valuable intangible asset in banking. While you actually will not find it broken out as a separate line item on a bank's balance sheet, it is a real asset nonetheless.[17] Trusted institutions, therefore, have a funding cost advantage that can be used in a turnaround, even in situations

where all bank deposits are insured. Serfín leveraged its deep-seated customer trust during its turnaround process, for example, as did Mellon Bank. The president director of BCA in Indonesia, Djohan Emir Setijoso, focused the bulk of his attention on making his employees feel secure, thereby helping his customers feel more secure. BCA actually increased its withdrawal limits for depositors during part of the crisis to reinforce people's confidence and trust in the bank.

3. **Possess tangible assets.** Banks with strong distribution systems and skilled personnel are also likely candidates, since both of these assets can be used to regain solvency and recover financial health.

Protecting the Depositors of Closed Banks

Even when the conditions cry out for it, closing down a bank is not a simple matter. The impact on the banking system of a poorly managed bank closure can be devastating. Careful consideration should be given to the question of what to do with remaining bank assets, including NPLs, and the orphaned depositors who are at risk in a closed bank situation. We will discuss NPL recoveries in the following chapter, but the issue of orphaned depositors is real and significant, especially during a run on the banking system in the early days of a crisis.

The last thing that financial sector authorities want is to have depositors who feel uncertain about how they will be treated. We have seen a lot of street rioting as angry depositors try to retrieve their life savings. In a crisis, therefore, bank managers cannot risk further aggravating those who may touch off a run on the bank, a flight of capital, and a permanent erosion of the country's savings. Mexican depositors still recall the losses they suffered when their dollar deposits were forcibly converted to pesos in 1982. This act still motivates them to keep part of their savings outside of the country. As we write this book, Argentina faces similar issues, as well as the specter of ongoing long-term capital flight.

Moreover, liquid savings—cash withdrawn from banks—is often moving around the economy rapidly in the midst of a banking crisis and adds to the turbulence and feeling of panic. Argentina is experiencing this very same problem in 2002. Hence, government policy vis-à-vis these depositors should focus on dual objectives: first, to restore the confidence of depositors in the health and stability of the banking system by treating them fairly, consistently, and professionally; and second, to maintain intact valuable banking relationships, which are part of the residual value of the bank that can be transferred to the surviving or acquiring bank.

Best practices for managing the transfer of orphaned depositors, therefore, involve avoiding any disruptions in the availability of their funds and, wherever possible, the maintenance of normal distribution channels (e.g., branches, ATMs, account executives and relationship managers, and Internet banking facilities). These should be held at the same level of functionality as before the crisis, especially during the transition as the successor bank takes over for the failing bank.

The message that these practices should convey is that the funds are safe and available—with the same liquidity as before the crisis. Therefore, depositors have no reason for panicky withdrawals. To be believed, the transition from one institution to another must be executed proficiently and smoothly.

Since bank failures are generally uncommon in many countries before the crisis hits, few governments and banks have any experience in achieving this kind of seamless transfer. Yet, in the heat of the moment, they have to get it right.

We have found that the secret of transfers is to keep things simple. Branches and frontline personnel should remain intact until all accounts have been transferred and operational stability has been guaranteed. When the forerunner of BankAmerica—NCNB—took over the failing FirstRepublic Bank in Texas in 1988, for example, it stationed its highly trained troops of young professionals in each bank branch to ease the transition, religiously following the bank takeover blueprint that it had used successfully many times before.

During the transition period, furthermore, the banking systems of the failing and acquiring banks should be run in parallel until they are operating in sync. To emphasize the message of continuity, critical customer contacts should also be maintained during the transition. The only external change that customers should notice in the early days of a crisis is potentially a change of brand, but nothing else of practical consequence. Wherever possible, healthy loans should be transferred along with the deposit relationships, although distinguishing between impaired and healthy loans at this time may be difficult. Hopefully, customers in the long run should experience better service and more valuable products and services from the new owners.

Merging the deposit customers of two banks is always daunting, and at no time more so than in a financial crisis. During the S&L and banking crises of the late 1980s–early 1990s, the FDIC developed what is considered world-class best practices for seizing insolvent banks and resolving them quickly. Even then, many depositors commonly reacted with confusion, anger, and dismay, underscoring the difficulty of the challenge. For more information on the FDIC's methods, see Box 6.3: Copying Weekend Intervention Best Practices: The FDIC Model.

BOX 6.3: COPYING WEEKEND INTERVENTION BEST PRACTICES: THE FDIC MODEL

The U.S. Federal Deposit Insurance Corporation (FDIC), which has a long, distinguished history of taking over and resolving more than 2,000 banks from 1934 to 2000, has proven itself as one of the best government models of bank intervention and resolution.

Typically, a team of FDIC supervisors would appear at an insolvent bank at the close of business on a Friday, work furiously over the weekend with the help of the bank employees, who become temporary FDIC employees, and then reopen the bank for most business transactions on Monday morning.

Upon reopening, the bank's deposit and other transaction services (such as loan servicing) would be available, but new loans would be suspended pending the final resolution of the bank. In these operations, the team has full power to take over the bank and its branches. It is responsible for ensuring that security is in place—so that valuable assets don't walk out the door—for the continuation of information and reporting systems, and for the identification and monitoring of all the bank's assets.

There are several aspects to a bank closing. First, the intervention team must show up a few days in advance, maintaining a low profile, to prepare for the takeover; simply having bank examiners in and around the bank can lead to information leaks about the forthcoming bank closing and unnecessarily cause mini-runs on banks. Second, the bid package ideally should have been prepared in advance, if there was interest in the bank's franchise, so the bank can be sold quickly and efficiently. Managing communications with bank employees and customers following the closure is another important function. Controlling the physical premises, securing files, and restricting access to the bank is another.

Asset management involves securing the control and conducting the inventory of all bank assets, including the loan portfolio. Collateral, if held by the bank, must be secured. At this point, assets must be transferred, either to the succeeding government institution (e.g., KAMCO in Korea, IBRA in Indonesia) or the assuming institution, which temporarily includes the FDIC.

Deposit management is another function, and one that is most immediate for bank customers. Inventory and a balance of deposits are required, as is a strategy for the handling of deposits when the bank reopens. Typically, the FDIC would make all deposits available

(continued)

Monday morning, regardless of whether the bank was being liquidated (in which case a straight payoff would occur), assumed temporarily by the government, or purchased by a private sector buyer. Knowing which deposits are insured and which are not is another critical item to consider.

Some of the worst recent examples we have seen have occurred in Ecuador and Venezuela, where depositors were denied access to their funds for months. In Ecuador, for example, a deposit freeze was imposed at the height of the weeklong bank holiday. Had a deposit payoff/transfer process been in place similar to that of the United States, depositors could have received their money on Monday, and a great amount of panic and lost wealth could have been avoided.

The intervention of an entire banking system, if done according to best practices, is not unthinkable. Korea is a good model, one in which a deliberate process was put in place to evaluate all of the banks, so that they could be sorted out as to which should be rehabilitated with government finances and banking reforms, and which should be shut down.

GOVERNMENT'S ROLE IN BANK TURNAROUND STRATEGIES

We strongly believe that governments are not the best owners of banks, and that they should be extremely reluctant to own, manage, and run them for any period of time. Governments have different objectives, which often are at odds with good banking and managing efficient and profitable banks. Government-owned banks have experienced too many failures worldwide, at too great a cost, for anyone to believe that governments are better than the private sector at running banks.

Moreover, government-owned banks are plagued by agency problems, regulatory capture risks, and incompatible incentives for low-paid civil servants, which hamper them from delivering world-class customer service on a par with globally active banks. The French government's failure to turn around a number of its state-supported commercial banks serves as an example, as does the failure of the Turkish government to run its state-owned banks efficiently and profitably. The above notwithstanding, however, governments can occasionally be fine stewards of commercial banks. For example, in the decade following bank nationalization, Mexico ran its banks so proficiently that taxpayers actually profited from its intervention. Similarly, the Norwegian government successfully enabled the turnaround of Christiana Bank in the mid-1990s.

Nevertheless, governments should rapidly privatize institutions that end up in their control. Best practices include setting firm timetables for privatization. Independent governance bodies should be installed to support interim management, and should work toward the short-term actions that will maximize the institution's value at sale. Where possible, interim management should be rewarded in proportion to the value that it has added during the period of government ownership.

Experience has taught us that for the first few years after a crisis erupts, economic turbulence and recession may make an effective privatization nearly impossible. Hence, the government must be the steward of the banks during this time. It has three critical tasks:

1. Set governance methods and structures for the interim period
2. Provide clear turnaround mandates to the board
3. Ensure that a process is in place for the final privatization of the entity.

Setting Required Governance Structures

Recent events in the United States in 2001 and elsewhere have reminded the world that anything less than excellent governance practices will damage shareholder interests. Under normal circumstances, good governance emerges from negotiations between majority and minority shareholders, which ensures that the minority is not abused by the majority. Yet, even in some highly developed capital markets, minority shareholders run significant governance risks.

Four mechanisms have emerged over time that provide protections for minority shareholders. Two of these—disclosure rules and accounting and audit practices—are legally defined and defended in most countries, while the remaining two—board structures and processes and institutional investor oversight—normally result from codes setting forth the elements of sound corporate governance and sometimes listing requirements on the stock exchange.

In the United States and Europe, institutional investors play a critical role in protecting the small investor. They do this by representing the minority interests in governance and performance. In developed capital markets, then, a combination of these four elements protects minority investors. Furthermore, in developed capital markets, the price of shares acts as an additional incentive for good governance.

Governments, on the other hand, have neither the benefit of negotiations between minority and majority shareholders nor the opinion of the capital markets. Instead, governments are forced to be the steward of the taxpayers who in effect have become the new shareholders and have assumed the risks. The risk-pricing market failure is thus complete: Those who bear the risks—the taxpayers—have no way to reward or sanction those in charge of the banks. There is also an enormous free-rider problem; individual shareholders have little capability and few opportunities to become involved in any risk-mitigating actions.

Under these circumstances, the bank's board of directors provides the best and sometimes only line of defense. In our experience, board appointments are never more important than in these cases: They fulfill a critical fiduciary responsibility on behalf of depositors and shareholders who are otherwise not represented.

The individuals appointed to serve on these interim boards must possess five key characteristics:

1. Integrity, so that they can be trusted to be responsible stewards of the wealth of others. For this reason, potential board members should be subjected to a full "fit and proper" evaluation, ensuring that they meet minimum ethical standards. Any directors with conflicts of interest should be removed. Sadly, this is infrequently pursued. The pool of talent from which to draw these individuals, particularly in emerging markets, may be small. We have learned from experience, however, that the integrity of these individuals should be completely nonnegotiable.

2. Competence is another nonnegotiable characteristic that board members must fulfill. During the turnaround program in Korea, for example, advisors and board members were drawn not only from domestic sources, but from outside the country. These experienced individuals included, for example, Timothy Hartman, the retired vice chairman and CFO of Nations-Bank; and Mike Callen, the former vice chairman and head of corporate banking at Citibank.

3. Motivation and involvement are also required. Consequently, while participation on the board of one or more of these banks is positioned as an "honor," more tangible rewards should be provided. Given the fiduciary responsibility that the board plays and to ensure that they fulfill expectations, in fact, substantial economic rewards should be made available, as with publicly traded corporations in major capital markets. Our experience is that if compensation is seriously deficient, so is a sense of motivation and duty on the part of the board members. In Ecuador, for example, the government assumed that the prestige of being on the board of a failed bank was enough incentive. In truth, that attitude created boards marked by poor performance and a lack of independence and accountability.

4. Independence and objectivity are other critical traits. The ideal board should owe its allegiance to the taxpayers, not the individuals who appointed members to the board. Consequently, the board members should be drawn from across the political landscape and valued for their independence in support of the new "shareholders"—that is, the taxpayers. By representing all key constituencies, independent board members lend greater objectivity and legitimacy to the turnaround.

5. **Courage** is the fifth and final characteristic. Individuals who have well-established business reputations and who have been board members in other companies are prime candidates. Their voices at board meetings will guide and give courage to others as they share their knowledge and opinions.

Provide a Clear Turnaround Mandate

Boards of directors should fulfill a simple turnaround mandate: Ensure that bank management is executing strategies that will maximize the value of the institution at the time that it is privatized. The bank board should see that this wealth-building strategy is being pursued effectively. To do so, the board must be:

1. Fully informed of, and in agreement with, the bank's turnaround strategy
2. In possession of the necessary information to oversee the successful execution of the turnaround strategy. The board must also be involved in major strategic decision-making, including major loan commitments
3. Ready to empower management and make it accountable for the execution of the turnaround program. The board must define and monitor the metrics that will be rigorously tracked to ensure success. Korea's Financial Supervisory Commission (FSC), for example, issued frequent memos to its bank management teams, clearly stating performance goals and incentives.

Keep Privatization on Track

Keeping to a timetable is another imperative. The government should set "sunset provisions" up front, so that management and the board aren't tempted to think of their roles as permanent. Privatization should proceed as rapidly as possible—in a matter of months in an ideal world—but more typically up to two or three years under normal conditions. Unfortunately, what often slows down the process is the reluctance of investors to buy banks until the uncertainty of the financial crisis has abated and the government appears to have a grip on macroeconomic conditions.

Moreover, it is not just the turbulence of the crisis that has to be considered. Preparing a privatization process is laborious and requires several months of planning. There are many tasks to execute, including:

1. Preparing the privatization process itself—and ensuring that it meets the rules that govern the disposition of national assets. Our experience

is that this process takes at least two months, and frequently requires the authorization of both the executive and legislative branches of the government.

2. Identifying and hiring the accountants, lawyers, investment bankers, consultants, and others to carry out the privatization. Each of these professionals will have to interact in the design and execution of the process, documentation, due diligence, and business case for the bank. Government procurement processes are generally quite complex and bureaucratic; hence, this process generally takes three or four months—and unfortunately can take even longer.

3. Ensuring that progress is being achieved in the turnaround program, so that the privatization business case is believable. To do so, the board and management should be in place to provide the needed leadership and independent oversight.

4. Identifying potential buyers and setting aside two or three months for due diligence and the execution of the sale.

Experience has taught us that these steps can rarely be achieved in less than two years. Too ambitious a plan, therefore, may not be optimal, but neither is one that is too lax. The best plan is to continue to exert pressure on all stakeholders to privatize as rapidly as possible, while accepting the fact that the entire effort may take longer than expected to achieve the maximum value possible under the circumstances of the crisis.

■ ■ ■

There are many examples of successful bank turnarounds, and many examples of failures, regardless of where they occur. There are no secrets in these processes, but there is a common set of actions. Bank turnarounds can produce abundant rewards that await those investors and managers who move most rapidly, thoroughly, and aggressively. Whatever the country or the situation, this is the incentive for success.

APPENDIX 6.1: Building a Rationale for Official Support in a Financial Crisis

By Brian Quinn
Former Executive Director for Bank Supervision, Bank of England

In the great majority of cases, a financial crisis takes the form of an imminent or actual bank failure: discovery by, or notification to, the bank supervisory authority that one or more banks are unable to meet their obligations as they fall due. Too often the authorities are given little time to prepare to cope with the consequences. Decisions have to be made under great pressure and with imperfect information. In emerging markets in particular, choosing the correct course of action can be very difficult; and the judgment whether to apply public funds in a rescue operation—among the most taxing even in mature financial systems—becomes especially complex.

There is no manual to guide the authorities through this experience. Each case calls for difficult judgments. Nevertheless, there are some guidelines, drawn from the experience of a number of countries, which can give shape to the process of deciding whether to provide official financial support to banks in trouble.

The first strategic question, and almost always the most important, is whether the failure is systemic, affecting a significant part of the banking system or the financial system more widely, or whether it is confined to one or a relatively small number of banks. The answer may not be clear, either because information does not reveal the real scope of the problem, or because what begins as an isolated case later spreads as the economic and financial environment deteriorates.

Because of these uncertainties, the answers to a particular set of tactical questions can help in making the judgment.

1. Just how pervasive is the problem? Is it likely to affect a large number of institutions of different size and categories? Is a large, brand name affected? Are several regions of the country or a particularly important region affected?
2. What is the role of the bank or banks affected? Is it a "lender of first resort" (i.e., a central and significant clearing bank, acting for others in the payments system or money markets)? Does it have a key role in other financial markets, such as the foreign exchange or government securities market?
3. Is it a "clone" for other banks funded predominantly from a particular source (e.g., interbank market), or concentrated on the asset side (e.g., real estate or agricultural lending) and one of many with a similar balance sheet profile?
4. Who are its counterparties on both sides of the balance sheet? Are they important commercial or classes of individual counterparties whose failure would create widespread problems in the economy or financial markets?
5. Is the bank active and important in certain overseas markets? Would its sudden failure constitute a risk to the functioning of those markets? Could serious diplomatic or political repercussions follow from a sudden closure of the bank?

6. Does the bank have subsidiaries or affiliates, domestic or located overseas, whose future would be placed at risk by failure? Do these subsidiaries or associates share the same name?
7. What will be the effect of a decision to close or not to close the bank on the reputation of the home base, particularly if there are ambitions to develop it as a global or regional financial center?

A second strategic issue is whether the bank is suffering a liquidity or solvency problem. Once again, the answer may not be clear in the timeframe in which an answer is needed. Seeking a rescue from the private sector may not resolve this question since other banks are commonly unwilling to run the risk of contagion, whether the underlying risk is a deficiency of capital or liquidity. As a general rule, central banks are the correct vehicles for providing, or organizing, liquidity support, but not for providing risk capital. Creating doubt about the capacity of the central monetary authority to withstand losses—as has been the case recently in countries such as Jamaica or Ecuador—is scarcely likely to restore confidence and stability to the system.

Where the problem is systemic and takes the form of a shortage of liquidity, the response of the authorities should normally follow the lines long established by Walter Bagehot: The central bank should supply liberal amounts of liquidity on market terms to restore confidence and enable the economy to continue to function during times of systemic threats (e.g., the stock market crash of 1987).[1] In those cases where the problem is a temporary shortage of liquidity in an individual bank and where another bank will not assume the responsibility of helping meet that shortage, the central bank may choose to supply liquidity adequately collateralized on penal terms to give the recipient an incentive to minimize its dependence on official support; but the terms should not be so severe as to damage the bank's capacity to survive.

There are occasions, however, when it is not clear that the bank in difficulty has a viable future. In these circumstances the correct course may be to allow the bank to go into liquidation, or apply for the appointment of a receiver or administrator while some residual value still remains in the bank from which creditors may be paid in full or in part. Particular problems arise if the liquidity shortage is in foreign currency, raising questions not only about access to a country's foreign exchange reserves, but also about the effect on confidence abroad.

If the problem is solvency in a single bank, then the normal response would be to apply for resolution by the relevant authority. Bank failures are an integral part of a properly functioning market system, and the discipline engendered by an occasional failure can make a significant contribution to a safe and sound banking system. The difficulty is in knowing that the total social and economic costs of such a failure fall below the cost of a rescue;

unfortunately, that fact can never be established beyond doubt either before or after the event.

Where the whole banking system, or a significant part of it, is insolvent, however, that calculation is conceptually if not quantitatively clear. In those circumstances, an exercise of a different scale and scope is necessary.

One further important strategic question is whether there exists any form of deposit insurance, explicit or implicit. The expectations of depositors are crucial in assessing the likely effects of a decision whether to mount an officially funded rescue and can set limits to the authorities' commitment of funds.

■ ■ ■

Financial crises do not come in prepackaged form, complete with instructions on how to respond. It is trite but accurate to state that each one throws up problems that differ in their nature, scope, and complexity. All that can be stated is that the authorities should base their response on a set of presumptions that:

1. Systemic liquidity problems are met with ample, officially supplied liquidity on market terms
2. An individual bank experiencing pressures due to temporary mismanagement of liquidity should be provided with support on moderately penalized terms
3. Individual banks that are insolvent or appear likely to become insolvent should be sold to a market buyer or permitted to fail without unnecessary delays
4. Generalized insolvency problems call for a major reconstruction of the banking sector, typically involving significant contributions from taxpayers and substantial reform based on commonly accepted global standards.

Nevertheless, the judgments underlying each of these cases are difficult and frequently second-guessed in hindsight by others, ranging from other government officials and politicians to the multilateral financial institutions.

CHAPTER 7

Minimizing Costs Through NPL Recovery Excellence

When the great hurricane of 1900 swept through Galveston, Texas, it demolished the city, killing six thousand people in a massive storm and tidal surge, becoming the worst natural disaster in U.S. history. Galveston's story did not end that night, however. The survivors dug out from the storm and rebuilt their city, ensuring that it would prosper again.

In financial storms, however, the wreckage is not made of wood or twisted metal: It consists instead of an enormous pile of nonperforming loans (NPLs) and failed banks with significant bad assets that need to be managed as companies and economies begin to rebuild. After a crisis strikes, in some cases, loans are restructured and respectable margins restored to the bank's portfolios on a new risk-adjusted basis. In many other cases, however, NPLs are left buried in banks or the economy, broken and smoldering.

The NPL wreckage can be enormous. During the mid to late 1980s, for example, more than eighteen hundred U.S. banks and S&Ls with $700 billion in assets failed, due primarily to credit quality issues that wiped out investors' equity in those institutions.[1] In Scandinavia in the early 1990s, the NPLs ranged from 5 percent to almost 8 percent of total loans, but these were severe enough to drive most thinly capitalized banks into insolvency; in Norway, for example, NPLs amounted to 134 percent of available bank capital.[2]

In several major European nations today, some of our colleagues have estimated that NPLs amount to roughly $900 billion, and have cost a staggering total of 98 percent of total bank profits over the past five years.[3] In Asia, the Ernst & Young 2001 report on NPLs mentioned earlier estimated unresolved NPLs at $2 trillion, with the bulk of them in Japan and China.

Unfortunately, our starting operating assumption is that in most countries NPL problems will get worse before they get better, because the management and political will to actively and aggressively manage NPLs is often lacking until it is too late. In one Asian country where we worked in 2002, we estimated that roughly 15 percent of the loans in one critical segment of the banking industry were nonperforming and that new NPLs were growing in the range of 6 to 12 percent annually due to ineffective management. Left unmanaged, these NPLs—and the underlying businesses and assets—will deteriorate over time, further eroding the financial system's capital base, increasing costs, and leading to significant lost economic growth in that country. For private commercial banks, therefore, NPLs that are left unmanaged and get out of control can lead quickly to a change in management and significant losses for investors, even complete failures where investors lose everything.

Over the past decade, we have helped more than 75 private banks and governments manage their NPL problems. In so doing, we have found that managing NPLs effectively can translate into a difference of as much as 25 percent in terms of additional value recovered. For a large bank in a turnaround situation, this can represent tens of millions of dollars. For example, a European bank with a $2 billion portfolio could realize potential savings of $35 million to $50 million per year by improving its recovery performance by 10 percent.[4] For countries with an economy the size of Mexico's, for example, this difference in NPL recovery improvements can easily represent several billion dollars—and the sums can be even greater, depending on the specific circumstances of each crisis. The difference between managing NPLs effectively and ineffectively, therefore, is so significant in terms of costs to either shareholders or taxpayers that managers in both the private sector and government need to fully understand the importance of managing credit workouts aggressively and quickly.

In this chapter, we first outline the management steps required to develop world-class excellence in NPL recovery capabilities. These steps include: diagnosing and segmenting the NPL portfolio; developing tailored strategies for credit recovery; and building the organization to recover NPLs. Next, we address the special issues with respect to governments that step up to the NPL challenge by establishing an asset management corporation (AMC) and that simultaneously want to maximize the recovery value of the NPLs they inherit from failed banks. Special governmental issues include the mandate, governance, oversight, accounting, transparency, performance management metrics, and legal issues affecting AMCs. In the final section, we explore key management lessons from interesting bad bank case studies in Sweden and Norway during their financial crises in the early 1990s.

In every case, unfortunately, there is the unavoidable cost to both the private and public sectors during the time it takes to develop an adequate

NPL response. It takes time to understand the full magnitude of the problems facing an individual bank or, even more daunting, an entire economy and then assimilate these facts and develop a strategic plan to manage the NPL problem. It also takes time to create a new workout unit or agency with new and distinctive capabilities to manage those NPLs aggressively.

Based on our experience, crisis managers cannot afford to wait months to get new NPL workout units up and running while assets waste away, or worse yet, to wait even longer periods for remedial legislation to be enacted. It is useful to have preventive legislation in place before a crisis hits and system-threatening NPLs appear. For example, since the creation of the FDIC, the United States has had remedial legislation in place to manage failed banks and resolve their nonperforming assets. Moreover, these preventive measures are updated on a regular basis to factor in lessons learned from the latest episode of banking failures. The 1991 FDIC Improvement Act, for instance, was designed in part to respond to the new issues raised by the banking and S&L crises of the late 1980s.

In Ecuador, for example, we estimated that it cost taxpayers about $600,000 for each day that the government delayed creating an effective and fully functioning AMC with the appropriate capabilities to manage NPLs and resolve other bad assets. Furthermore, the cost of delayed NPL resolutions only adds an even greater burden on top of the already embedded NPL losses. Thus, shortening the time needed to create the operational capabilities for managing NPLs effectively is crucial to minimize the overall costs imposed on either shareholders or taxpayers. Time clearly is money with respect to NPL resolution. We believe that preplanning a cost-effective NPL recovery effort as much as possible before the problem gets out of control—as soon as the warning signs that we discussed in Chapter 3 are seen—will more than pay for the upfront investments that management teams in both the private and public sectors are required to make on behalf of either shareholders or taxpayers.

DEVELOPING WORLD-CLASS NPL RECOVERY CAPABILITIES

Some of our clients have described the task of managing their individual NPL problems as trying to sail a ship through a stormy sea filled with potentially destructive icebergs floating in their path. The known NPL portfolio represents only the tip of the iceberg that is visible to the ship's captain—the CEO steering the bank through unchartered waters—who must navigate around its hidden mass, not fully aware of what danger looms just below the surface and threatens to sink the ship potentially without warning. The NPLs on the surface are relatively easy to see, and can be managed accordingly.

Usually lurking further beneath the surface, however, are more serious credit challenges from ongoing and poor lending practices that need to be managed aggressively to prevent the problems from spreading to the entire loan portfolio and sinking the ship.

Unfortunately, many banks face a number of internal and external pressures when trying to resolve their NPLs. Credit risk management may fall short of best practices, with inaccurate or unclear tracking of cash flows or the failure to apply robust analytical models. Relationship managers are incented to continue providing loans, and their key performance indicators often are driven by volume. Or loan administration may be hampered by poor documentation (flawed or missing agreements and promissory notes) or poor loan and collateral tracking. Finally, there are the common political pressures that typically arise, which include government "priority" projects and mandated restructuring initiatives, and even corruption and graft in some cases.

Depending on the first moves executed by management, however, different dynamics can be established. If either a company or the government acknowledges its NPLs and takes visible, tangible steps to resolve them, as we saw in Chapter 4 with respect to Alfa Bank in Russia or in Chapter 6 in the turnaround success of Mellon Bank, then in fact it can create greater trust and a positive working attitude with its credit customers. If, however, debtors perceive that attempts by creditors to recover NPLs are ineffective, then they typically change their behavior in response to the new reality, as we have seen in Jamaica, Ecuador, and Colombia, among other countries. In Mexico, for example, the weakness of the initial NPL recovery effort was so glaring against a background of skyrocketing interest rates that debtors formed a cartel in 1995 called El Barzón to neutralize creditors' efforts to collect their loans.

In this section, we will describe a method that we have used successfully to help managers maximize the recovery value of their NPLs. For management, this method actually starts at the end of the credit process and not the beginning, focusing on credit workouts to stop the hemorrhaging before turning to the task of improving credit origination and underwriting (Figure 7.1). However, as we mentioned in Chapter 6, it is critical that the bank focus on fixing the credit origination and underwriting functions quickly as well, or the bank will continue to "grow" more NPLs that will contribute to a later downward spiral.

More specifically, our experience has taught us that excellent NPL recovery depends on three key management tactics:

1. Diagnose and segment the NPL portfolio.
2. Develop tailored strategies for NPL recovery.

FIGURE 7.1 NPL credit recovery starts first at the end of the process.

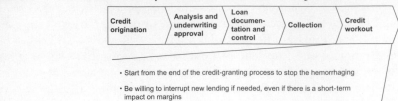

• Start from the end of the credit-granting process to stop the hemorrhaging

• Be willing to interrupt new lending if needed, even if there is a short-term impact on margins

• Create focused, specialized, and centrally controlled workout units differentiated by loan segment

• Don't rely on branch managers, current account executives, or loan officers to solve the NPL problem

3. Build a dedicated NPL recovery organization, either a bad bank or an AMC.

1. Diagnose and Segment the NPL Portfolio

The first tactical step in managing a large NPL portfolio is to accurately diagnose the extent of the problem. Although the NPL situation varies by each company and country, we have found that most nonperforming loans can be managed effectively by asking a common set of questions, employing similar methods, and tailoring them to local needs as necessary. Thus, the purpose of this initial diagnostic in most situations is to answer three basic questions. First, how serious is the credit problem; that is, what is the current net present value, or NPV, of the portfolio? Second, how should management prioritize loans to focus its efforts? Third, what strategy and tactics can management use to maximize the NPV of its problem portfolio?

When determining the expected NPV of the NPL portfolio, management must examine each loan by type of credit, credit originator (or business unit), geography, and major industry and customer group. This in turn requires a further segmentation of the NPL portfolio to design optimum workout strategies. Segmenting the portfolio enables managers to triage the part of the portfolio that cannot be recovered economically, to prioritize which loans require more urgent attention than others, and to focus on those loans that have the greatest likelihood of recovery.

The analyses required to do this are not simple, but they are necessary and highly time-sensitive. We have found that the best way to set up the analysis is to differentiate the loans by size and past-due period, the position of the bank vis-à-vis the debtor, and the quality of the loan documentation. They can then be sub-segmented by originator, industry sector, and type of collateral.

The initial differentiating factor is size. Managing small versus large loans requires different responses. Analyzing very small loans requires a careful budgeting of time and effort to remain cost-effective. Since the recovery value of certain types of loans—credit cards, auto loans, unsecured working capital loans to small companies, and so on—can be very low, we recommend that this part of the portfolio receive only cursory attention using sampling techniques to determine likely recovery values for the entire small loan portfolio. Even in the analytical phase of the recovery process, virtually any effort that is expended on this part of the portfolio is likely to be economically unattractive.

At one Mexican bank, for instance, it was quickly apparent that the expected net present value of a large number of its small loans was negligible. Making a significant effort to recover these loans would distract management's attention from more significant opportunities. Instead, the bank used the information about this part of the portfolio to define a semi-industrialized loan recovery process that rigorously defined the resources that could be invested to recover small loans. Still, the recovery process was focused only on loans that had a positive expected value. The remaining loans were culled ruthlessly, and after reserves had been created, they were sold to the highest bidder for only a few cents on the dollar.

Put simply, management should follow the 80/20 rule and spend more time on the larger loans that will have the biggest positive impact on the bank. Only with NPLs, the 80/20 rule really is 80/20. Depending on a bank's circumstances, effectively managing even 10 or 20 corporate accounts can make a substantial difference.

The portfolio of larger, more recently lapsed loans warrants deeper scrutiny and more ambitious recovery plans. Three factors weigh most heavily in recovering these NPLs. The first is the length of time from when the loans became nonperforming and when recovery efforts first began. In Jamaica, for example, some failed banks allowed hotel loans to lapse for several years before investing in significant recovery efforts. By the time these loans were transferred to the Financial Sector Adjustment Company (FINSAC), the problems of these hotels were so advanced—hotel maintenance had stopped and the hotels consequently had fallen into disrepair, which in turn drove customers away—that many of the NPLs were almost completely worthless, as were the deteriorating assets that served as collateral.

The value of NPLs deteriorates rapidly for several reasons. First, the value of the collateral securing these loans usually declines with time (e.g., automobiles, boats, factory equipment, computers); second, because of the time value of money itself (i.e., money today is worth more than the same amount of money in the future); third, other creditors are waiting to capture the residual value of the loans by moving early to seize a first mover's advantage; fourth, crisis conditions can undermine the cash generation ability of debtors, thereby further eroding the value of the loan; and fifth, bad debtors become harder to find over time; in fact, given enough time, elusive debtors even find ways to hide or transfer personal assets that could have been used to cover their outstanding loans.

The second key determinant of value is the position of the bank vis-à-vis its clients and other creditors. This is a qualitative measure that includes factors such as competitive position, client attitude, and the labor situation. It is important that a bank determine how much power it has in a negotiating situation relative to other creditors. If other banks are already moving to recover loans from a common borrower, bank executives need to ask how they can best maximize value; for example, by selling their position to other banks, forming a syndicate of banks, or going solo. Perceived client attitude also affects expected value and recovery strategies. If the bank believes its client is sincerely trying its best to make payments, the tenor of collection efforts will differ widely from if the bank believes client managers do not intend to pay or are hiding information. Finally, the bank needs to be sensitive to the labor situation, which can limit the options available to bank and client managers, and greatly influence the outcome of loan recovery efforts.

The third core determinant of value is the quality and availability of documentation and loan files. In Mexico, for instance, one of our banking clients had fairly good files, and was therefore able to determine whether its customers had used the loans as documented. What the bank found, however, was that many of the loans—which had been recorded as working capital loans—in fact had been used for other purposes, such as the purchase of company cars. The bank's knowledge and ability to substantiate this fact in court greatly enhanced its position during litigation.

Unfortunately, such success stories are rare. In Ecuador, Korea, Indonesia, Jamaica, and Mexico, recovery agencies have struggled with exactly the opposite set of circumstances—files so poorly compiled and maintained that they could not serve as the basis for successful litigation. In one instance in Korea during an M&A due diligence review, seventy-five loan certificates at the target corporation were discovered that had been filed without specifying either the interest rate or the maturity date. Later, it was discovered that the target company considered this a "normal" credit practice.

It typically takes a bank about three months to conduct a thorough diagnostic of its NPL portfolio. Despite the amount of time required, we believe it is critical that management do so as soon as possible. However, since managers usually have a fair sense of just how deep the problem is, they typically do not need to wait until all of the final analyses are completed. Even as initial results come back, management can start to move on other aspects of the NPL recovery process—such as designing its strategy, or building an effective organization and its skill portfolio—that ultimately are unlikely to be affected greatly by the final NPL analysis.

2. Develop Tailored Strategies for NPL Recovery

Generally speaking, a bank really only has three general, strategic options for resolving its NPL portfolio. First, it can attempt to improve the recovery value of the loans through loan restructuring, by playing with the terms and conditions of the loan contract. The bank might give the debtor some breathing room by extending a grace period, adjusting the term or rate structure, or relaxing deal covenants. Although the changes here appear limited, it is easy for a bank to destroy significant value by erring on the side of too much leniency if it does not have a good grasp of the condition of the NPL.

Second, the bank can pursue broader financial restructuring by looking at the entire set of outstanding loans. For example, it might reduce overexposures and stop rolling over certain loans, or extend fresh loans earmarked only for certain purposes.

During the Asian financial crisis, for instance, CEO Jung-Tae Kim told his staff at H&CB to closely review the institution's key debtors. What worried him was the thought that the bank had been lending a great amount of money to a large and troubled chaebol, Daewoo, but no one could tell him how much. Each department—corporate banking, foreign exchange, capital markets, and treasury—knew its own exposure to Daewoo, but there was no aggregated figure for the bank. As it turned out, the outstanding loans totaled approximately $2 billion, representing about 20 percent of the bank's corporate loan portfolio. Acting as swiftly as possible, Kim stopped rollovers on maturing loan contracts—trading in its securities and ceasing any new lending—thereby reducing the exposure of H&CB to Daewoo to less than $350 million, or 4 percent of the corporate loan portfolio on secure terms. The following year, Daewoo Group became the largest bankruptcy in history. In retrospect, Kim calls this decision one of the best that he made during the crisis.

Finally, if the bank believes that the borrowing company in question can be salvaged through major operational changes (change management with external assistance), it can pursue business restructuring. In this case, the bank makes it clear that the company's lines of credit are contingent upon a substantial improvement of its businesses. In the case of an airline company, for example, the bank may ask it to sell its planes, cut existing leases, or cut back on certain routes.

Across these three options, the bank may choose to liquidate loans and other assets, especially where there is no viable management plan or bank ownership and liquidation is the least-cost solution. The bank can sell assets either through swift bulk sales, when pressure requires getting the loans off the books as soon as possible, or through a more orderly liquidation process such as an auction, when current market conditions might make it unattractive to sell assets quickly out of fear of further depressing market prices.

Devising Segment-Specific Workout Strategies   Within these general strategic options, management can design more highly tailored NPL sub-strategies to more closely target the needs of its different customer segments. In Italy, for example, some small banks recover 20 percent more on their NPLs than the average competitor by tailoring their recovery strategies and processes to the type of NPL in question and by working closely with debtors.[5] Consider the case where a bank is devising workout strategies across four broad market segments: large corporate, middle market, real estate, and retail (Figure 7.2).

Large corporate NPLs, for instance, require a deal-by-deal evaluation process because of the high risk concentration associated with each deal. These loans usually involve complex loan structures and high stakes on each loan. Managing these loans frequently requires negotiating collaborative agreements with other lenders, with one bank taking the lead and the others agreeing not to seek foreclosure during negotiations. This process, however, can be difficult since there is a free-rider problem. To improve the creditor's position vis-à-vis the client, asset swaps with other lenders may make sense, although these swaps can further concentrate write-off risks.

Credit workouts in the middle-market segment also may justify case-by-case solutions because subtle differences in loan structures and client situations can be leveraged to produce substantially improved outcomes. In the middle market, however, vigorous triage of the portfolio is necessary to deploy workout resources efficiently.

Workout strategies for real estate loans should be evaluated individually but organized around several factors, each of which contributes significantly to the probability of recovering loans: debt-to-collateral market value ratio; debtor payment capacity; and type of underlying real estate (residential or

FIGURE 7.2   Segment-specific strategies are needed to work out NPLs.

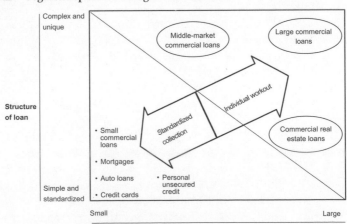

commercial). It is usually a good idea to pursue asset sales so the workout unit can recover the outstanding loan balance. Refinancing might be a better option sometimes, if the debtor repayment capacity and the asset value warrant such action. Depending upon the type of real estate, assets can be sold in bulk or packaged into real estate investment trusts (REITs) for resale in secondary debt markets.

Finally, retail segment workout processes (e.g., credit cards, consumer, and small business loans) are different from the first three segments since they require highly standardized or industrialized workout formulas for each asset class, given the large number of cases typically involved. This substrategy may involve selling a specific category of NPLs to a third-party firm. Unlike large corporate workouts, retail credit workouts should be based on predetermined decision rules, such as the debtor's ability and willingness to pay outstanding debts.

Who Are the Natural Owners of NPLs?   The analytical phase is not finished before determining who are the natural owners of the key segments of the NPL portfolio. In other words, is the bad bank or AMC currently charged with recovering the NPLs the natural or best owner of these same assets? If not, would it be better to transfer these assets to another entity that is capable of extracting a higher value from the portfolio, such as a bank, private equity group, collection agency, or third-party turnaround expert?

This question is critical to both individual companies and countries because most owners of NPLs are not necessarily the best equipped to actually work out the loans. The successful strategy implemented by the U.S. Resolution Trust Corporation, for example, demonstrated that outsourcing all or part of the portfolio to the most highly qualified workout specialist available, on a competitive basis, can be an economically attractive alternative, especially if other workout alternatives are expected to move slowly or if there are potential conflicts of interest in the way.

In our experience, a handful of banks always seems to survive crises, usually because they have better credit and collections skills, which they often develop into a profitable and freestanding business line. Hence, selling loans to these banks or using them as collection agents can shorten the time needed to jump-start the workout process and increase the ultimate recovery rate through shared incentive clauses. By not having creditors compete with each other for the remaining assets, moreover, further erosion in the value of the loan portfolio can be avoided. Consolidating the workout process in the hands of a single institution with the strongest workout capabilities is usually an efficient NPL strategy.

There are other players who can contribute, however. The list of potential workout specialists should also include certain private equity investors and turnaround specialists.

Private equity investors that specialize in distressed assets (e.g., GE Capital, Lone Star) typically show up early during a crisis, attracted by the opportunity to buy assets at bargain basement prices. They usually bring three scarce resources to the table: capital, and loan collection and business restructuring skills. Because they assume significant risks when they take on the NPLs, however, these parties invariably are also tough negotiators. To avoid losing most of the residual value of the loans to these investors, the entity in charge of resolving these assets should set up a bidding process that makes these "vulture" funds compete for the assets and requires them to forfeit any subsequent legal claim, as opposed to one-on-one negotiations that invariably lead to lower sale prices. Personal negotiations may cause critics to question the process and even raise charges of corruption.

Individuals and institutions that specialize in turnarounds usually appear as well when there are sizeable NPLs to be managed and recovered. Their value proposition is different, however. They bring financial and operating skills to the table, and are interested in turning the failing business around. In doing so, they preserve and try to maximize the value of the NPLs. In most cases, these individuals invest against the promise of a large reward at the conclusion of a successful restructuring process. For this reason, they sit on the "same side of the table" as the owners of the distressed assets during the workout process, though they are certain to require a handsome reward for their time and capabilities.

All of the above suggests that the unit managing the NPLs during a financial crisis should remain open to "renting"—rather than owning—its workout capabilities. A mix between owning and renting will be driven by a combination of national and local circumstances as well as particular resource constraints. We believe, however, that some amount of outsourcing will strengthen and speed the NPL recovery process and help to lower total resolution costs in the long run.

Kickstarting an Effective NPL Strategy   It is never too early to start devising a strategy to manage NPLs. It obviously helps if managers can identify and address deteriorating loans *before* they reach the point where they are officially classified as nonperforming. Based on our work with banking clients in Korea, for example, we believe that banks can capture between 50 and 70 percent of the value of "pre-NPLs," compared to the 20 to 30 percent that they typically recover from regular NPLs. By identifying and prioritizing these pre-NPLs early and executing their sub-strategies effectively to maximize the value, banks can sharply reduce their total loan loss provisions over time.

Yet, regardless of whether managing pre-NPLs or actual NPLs, management still faces the same challenge of getting their NPL recovery effort up and running in as short a time as possible. With a segment-specific strategy in place, management also needs to ensure three other end products as part of this phase of the process. The first is a road map that clearly defines the gap between the required resources to manage the NPLs and those that are currently available, and then charts the course for closing that gap. We have yet to experience a workout situation in which the initial resources were fully sufficient, either in quantity or quality.

The second end product required is a plan for action and established timetables—based on the strategic recommendations and resource assessment—which includes clear milestones, hard deadlines, and a sufficient budget to maximize the recovery effort.

The third end product is a segment-specific business plan, defining expected returns over time and targeted recovery levels. Almost always, identifying, recruiting, and hiring professional staff defines this critical path, so moving rapidly is also critical. Ninety days is the fastest that we have ever seen a bank reach this point, as management attempts to build a whole new organization to manage its NPLs, and this case happened in the relatively supportive NPL recovery environment of the United States.

3. Build a Dedicated NPL Recovery Organization

Based on our experience, there is no substitute for excellent execution. Once management has estimated the NPV of its NPLs and devised both general and segment-specific workout strategies to maximize their value, it can turn to the task of building a dedicated organization to execute its loan recovery strategies. Managers in charge of an NPL workout unit need to think creatively, creating the conditions for success in four critical areas: a separate and optimum organization structure; clearly defined processes and appropriate skills; performance-based incentive programs that attract the best NPL recovery talent; and MIS systems to support the overall effort. The anecdote about "The Russian" collection agent in Box 7.1 illustrates this need to be creative across all dimensions of NPL recovery.

BOX 7.1: DEFINING GENEROUS INCENTIVES PROGRAMS

Generous incentives are an important motivator for workout teams. Pursuing debtors is arduous and confrontational and few find pleasure in it. Therefore, to maintain motivated teams and encourage relentless effort, a significant portion of compensation should be tied to individual and group performance. At FAMCO, a U.S. "bad bank," senior case officers could make up to 150 percent of their base pay in bonuses.

(continued)

Later, to encourage even higher levels of productivity and reward exceptional achievement, the 150 percent cap was removed.

Individuals who work in successful workout groups expect to earn considerably more than they would in comparable jobs. The best performing workout organizations offer the opportunity to earn egregiously large incomes.

These incentives stimulate creative workout strategies. One of the most successful workout officers in Jamaica was nicknamed "The Russian." This gentleman relentlessly pursued individuals to collect on their debts. In a country where courts moved slowly and many NPLs were secured by personal guarantees, the best results usually came from negotiated settlements with debtors.

"The Russian" would go into the neighborhoods where debtors lived, and loudly and publicly announce his arrival and why he was there. He followed debtors to stores and reminded cashiers that they should be wary of accepting checks or credit cards from the debtor because he/she owed significant sums elsewhere. "The Russian's" reputation was so well-established that debtors would willingly meet with him in the workout group's offices just to avoid his dreaded visits to their neighborhoods.

Creating a Separate Organization Structure   Based on the cases we have seen, one of the major reasons for poor NPL execution is the fact that banks and existing government agencies are unprepared and ill-suited to manage NPLs in the first place. Too often, banks and governments do not assign or find the best talent to work on recovery strategy and tactics. In addition, NPL workout officers typically manage an excessive number of loans, sometimes on the order of four hundred to five hundred each. Finally, these officers typically also attempt to manage loan recovery on a part-time basis, on top of their other management responsibilities. Add to these process issues any number of substantive credit risk management or loan administration issues, and it is not surprising that many initial NPL recovery efforts are troubled from the very beginning.

To be successful, we believe that it is absolutely essential to establish a separate workout organization—either a bad bank or an AMC—to give the loans the management focus and attention that they require to maximize the recovery effort. In addition, a separate organization offers the benefit of separating the problem from its origins (e.g., account executives), as well as the freedom to implement radically different compensation schemes that would otherwise create problems if the entity coexisted within the standing structure.

These incentives, in turn, allow the bank to hire the particular breed of aggressive, transaction-oriented "workout bankers" needed to resolve NPLs (as opposed to more traditional, relationship-oriented bankers).

For these reasons, the structure of an NPL workout organization should closely reflect the composition of its portfolio. In some cases, management may wish to set up a bad bank, as executives at Mellon Bank did, where divisions are organized around the different kinds of loans to be worked out. For example, the president of a bad bank might have five direct reports: large corporate workouts; middle corporate workouts; real estate workouts; retail workouts; and repossessed assets. How each division is organized and supported by legal and other support functions (e.g., technology, finance) will differ depending upon the individual company circumstances. Regardless of whether a new bad bank is created or the workout process is carried out inside the existing company, it is important for management to set aside separate, dedicated resources to manage the NPLs to maximize returns.

Changing Senior Management   The most common mistake we have seen in twenty years of experience is when boards and senior management do not act to put in fresh and qualified leadership to lead the NPL workout process. Workout areas are highly dependent on the technical skills of the individuals who comprise them. Lack of risk management skills, especially credit skills, is what usually get banks into trouble in the first place, so replacing former senior credit managers is a top priority. Moreover, this step means creatively finding new, more qualified people, even sometimes from outside the country, to restructure the entire credit-granting process, not just the NPL recovery effort.

To be sure, this action will be tough, particularly when politically minded opposition mounts, as it usually does—especially when governments are forced to intervene to manage the NPL problem to prevent systemic threats. We have seen many situations in which governments intervene in failing banks, but then fail to actually remove existing managers of these banks due to political pressures. In these cases, new NPL teams try to take over the loan workout area, but subsequently find instead that they are thwarted from doing their jobs effectively by the old management team that has been left in place by regulators and, by definition, has a conflict of interest. Nowhere is this issue more delicate than in resolving NPLs, which lose their value rapidly, unless fresh thinking and new approaches are rapidly introduced and old management is completely replaced.

Ultimately, however, all of this rests upon the determination of the bank CEO. No matter how many changes take place at middle or even senior management levels, all of this will collapse if the leader at the top buckles to the enormous external pressures associated with working out NPLs. At one Asian bank, management ran into stiff opposition from a particular debtor that it was in the process of classifying as an NPL. The company's business portfolio was comprised primarily of companies in slow-growing or stagnant growth industries, and even though it was already substantially leveraged, it wanted to borrow more money to acquire a company in a new industry. The bank laid out its position in no uncertain terms: If the debtor even made overtures to acquire the target company, the bank would cut off all of its credit lines completely. Management began to receive phone calls from political and backdoor connections, pressuring the bank to extend fresh loans. Finally, the bank CEO stared down the debtor company and said, "You manage your business the way you want to; let me run my bank the way I need to." It takes this kind of gumption and determination by the CEO to defend a bank's bad loan strategy.

Independent Analysts   Successful workouts also require tough, reliable, and independent analysts to accurately gauge the NPV of a portfolio. From the start, they must assume that there are serious problems with all of the credits in the NPL portfolio, especially with any large loans made to related parties or bank shareholders. As a consequence, these analysts must be free of the pressures that bank managers typically can exert on their subordinates. This is especially important to ensure that the NPL portfolio is transferred over to a separate entity at the best equivalent "market" price.

In the previous chapter we argued that the first step toward a bank turnaround is to sweep out previous bank managers, freeze most new lending, and thoroughly review lending policies and procedures before new loans are made. Similarly, we believe that individuals who are unencumbered by the past and are totally objective should analyze the portfolio. We have learned the hard way: We have rarely been able to obtain the support that we need from incumbents, especially those who had a role in booking the NPLs that now have to be recovered.[6]

This is true even when all loans were booked following strict guidelines and with lenders of the highest integrity. In Mexico, for instance, we encountered stiff resistance from line officers of a commercial bank that hired us to set up an internal "bad bank." The line officers were not worried that we would uncover corruption; instead, they were concerned that we would reveal evidence of sloppy analysis and haphazard loan administration. In fact, as we highlighted in this same Mexican bank case in Chapter 3 (Figure 3.9), roughly 71 percent of the NPLs were due to problems in origination (policy violations, inadequate structuring, insufficient analysis), 24 percent to poor monitoring of the borrower, and only 5 percent to problems out of the bank's immediate control (e.g., problems in the macroeconomy).

Credit Committee Governance   Finally, NPL recoveries must be governed carefully, and for two reasons: first, to ensure that workout teams employ the best recovery strategies; and, second, to ensure the fair and consistent treatment of debtors, which is especially important in highly politicized environments.

To ensure impeccable governance, a credit committee should be assigned to oversee the workout process. At the highest levels, this group should include individuals with legal skills and persons knowledgeable in NPL recovery. Highly respected third parties, ideally taken from the board of the parent company or the bad bank, should be part of this review group charged with recovering assets. These credit committees should focus particularly on workout proposals for the larger commercial loans that will have the greatest impact on the company's results. Frequent meetings are normally required at the start of the workout effort so that officers and team leaders are calibrated to the expectations of the credit committee.

Wherever possible, clear decision rules should be defined. This requirement allows medium- and smaller-sized cases to be reviewed on an exception-only basis. If the decision rules have not been defined, the credit committee will have to meet more frequently; however, as rules begin to emerge, they should be codified so that decision making can be delegated to others. The workout unit head and the credit committee should also monitor the overall performance of the group by loan segment and by workout team to identify teams or segments whose performance may need further assistance. An effective loan-tracking system is essential for managing collections.

Developing Workout Processes and Critical Skills   We have discussed the importance of devising segment-specific strategies to maximize the value of the NPL portfolio. Depending on the strategy selected, management also needs to define processes and skill requirements. These actions, in turn, along with the size of the portfolio, help set targets on how many specialists are needed. In Sweden during the crisis of the early 1990s, for instance, this number varied from about fifty specialists at one of the larger banks (with assets greater than $40 billion), to about ten specialists at one of the smaller banks (with assets less than $20 billion).

Large credit workouts usually imply the need for targeted recovery teams. Each team is dedicated to a small number of cases (usually one to three), with specialized legal support as a constant backup. One of our clients in Mexico had a team led by a senior bank executive dedicated to working out the loans to an airline company that was in serious trouble. The principal of the loans amounted to several hundred million dollars, much of which could still be recovered, but only if the process was carefully managed and coordinated with other creditors. The airline was eventually turned around and the bank recovered most of its capital at risk, amply justifying the deployment of such valuable resources.

Teams working these types of loans need to understand and manage complex business issues related to cash flows, collateral, and contracts.

They also need to read the character of debtors accurately to design appropriate workout strategies. In Italy, we have learned that the "soft skills"—relationships and negotiations—matter as much as the "hard skills," such as knowledge about the business, technology, or industry. Due to the high stakes at risk, proposed workout strategies for these cases should be reviewed by a central credit committee and discussed thoroughly, to understand fully the implications of the decisions being made, and to create "case law" that can be extended to other situations.

Middle-market workouts are structured differently, usually by region. In Mexico and Jamaica, our clients created teams of four to five persons each, with each team handling twenty to thirty cases. In the middle-market segment, the team leader must have solid skills in analysis, communications, and risk negotiations. To leverage the team leader's time more effectively, and to provide training for less seasoned talent, about four more junior professionals should support the team leader. It often makes sense to set up a team of asset, credit, industry, and other specialists (such as legal, marketing, and investment banking) to support multiple loan workouts. As with large corporate loans, middle-market loans should also be examined on a deal-by-deal basis, with only the largest cases going through the credit committee, and the rest left up to the prerogative of each team.

The structure of real estate workout efforts differs from large commercial and middle-market loans. Depending on the size of the mortgage loans, real estate workout teams can be organized in cells working out of call centers, with each agent handling up to 150 cases, using preapproved workout formulas to guide their work.

If telephone account representatives are added, each agent can manage up to three hundred cases. Best practices also call for the establishment of restructuring offices where agents can meet face-to-face with customers to negotiate conditions or close deals. This configuration can be complemented by sub-contracting external agencies to locate and contact customers, with information about how to become current on their loans. Working out this type of asset frequently involves the creation of a network of external legal and repossession firms that manage foreclosures and repossessions, and must be tightly controlled.

Large commercial real estate loans, however, require an approach similar to large corporate credit workouts, with more individual attention. At one Scandinavian bank during the early 1990s, the top twenty loans (only 2 percent of the number of loans, but 15 percent of the total value, and typically more than $20 million each) were assigned roughly three employees each, whereas the remaining 98 percent of the loans (most less than $2 million each) were bundled in groups varying from five to twenty loans for each employee, depending on the size of the loan.

As with most real estate workouts, retail credit workouts also typically depend on a team of telephone account representatives, each handling many cases, and using a highly automated workflow system that processes individual cases rapidly and uniformly. The automated system should combine automatically generated warning letters with system-prompted phone calls. To realize economies of scale, this kind of organization must be highly centralized and its caseload must be large to defray the fixed costs of call centers. Door-to-door collections and recovery can occasionally work, but decision makers need to be aware that to be cost-effective, complex logistics and well-defined decision rules are required.

Creating Performance-Based Incentives With the appropriate strategies and skills in place, management needs to ask what resources are required to maximize the expected net present value of the different NPL segments, and how well this matches with existing capabilities.

Of all the resources required, by far the most significant is skilled loan workout specialists. In virtually every emerging market situation in which we have worked, skilled specialists of this sort are rare. Consequently, the cost of identifying, recruiting, and compensating these individuals is likely to be surprisingly high. Almost invariably, the compensation requirements of these individuals fall outside the realm of what is considered normal banking compensation in local markets. Hence, if overly restrictive compensation packages are offered to workout specialists, then it will be much more difficult to attract the kind of skilled talent that is needed to manage the NPL portfolio.

Creative problem solving is sometimes necessary, not only for companies hiring these individuals, but also—where governments have seized failed banks—for government agencies that face exacting government procedures that de facto prevent them from hiring the best workout specialists available. To get around these issues, some of our government clients have hired workout specialists into the banks that they have intervened. In this way, the skilled specialists receive higher incentive compensation through the bank than through direct employment by the government.

Some of the most effective compensation schemes that we have seen link a significant proportion of compensation, as much as 40 percent, to performance (Figure 7.3). Potential economic drivers include, for NPLs, the percent of losses on NPLs, workout costs, the collection rate, and duration of the recovery process. This is especially important for large commercial loan workouts, where specialized skills are in greater demand than for smaller loans. To ensure that the incentives of workout officers are aligned with those of the loan recovery entity, some of these packages pay only when the cash is received, as opposed to on the basis of accrued recoveries,

FIGURE 7.3   Incentive-based compensation system can enhance results.

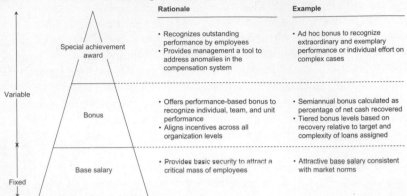

	Rationale	Example
Special achievement award	• Recognizes outstanding performance by employees • Provides management a tool to address anomalies in the compensation system	• Ad hoc bonus to recognize extraordinary and exemplary performance or individual effort on complex cases
Bonus	• Offers performance-based bonus to recognize individual, team, and unit performance • Aligns incentives across all organization levels	• Semiannual bonus calculated as percentage of net cash recovered • Tiered bonus levels based on recovery relative to target and complexity of loans assigned
Base salary	• Provides basic security to attract a critical mass of employees	• Attractive base salary consistent with market norms

which could take many months or years to collect, if they do not fall through entirely. Valuing the loans appropriately is key to compensation, because the revised value of the loan acts as a baseline cost to measure performance.

Ensuring Adequate IT/MIS   There are a number of analyses for which the workout team needs to rely upon its IT/MIS-related systems—from loan segmentation to estimates of the expected recovery value—but the most important is the loan-tracking system. The loan-tracking system used for workout groups should be more flexible than most standard loan-tracking systems found in banks. To meet the needs of workout groups, the system needs to perform standard interest calculations for different financing situations. It must also be able to account for penalty charges and accommodate balloon payments. In addition, it must have features for performance reporting that standard loan-tracking systems seldom have. For example, the system should be capable of reporting new target balances while storing original records in order to be able to track expected recovery as conditions evolve. The system must also be capable of reporting loans by teams so their progress can be reviewed regularly.

Kickstarting the Organization   There is no time to waste with setting up the organization, since the value of the bad loans will decline precipitously as the crisis continues. Under these conditions, managers should err on the side of building a recovery unit designed for quick, decisive, and complete loan resolution. This advice may seem counter-intuitive, especially in light of the fact that political and economic conditions might make rapid action seem sub-optimal, but it is necessary to protect shareholders or taxpayers from a worse outcome. Rapid action can also help to prevent contagion from spreading from one sick bank to others.

To abbreviate the time needed to get up and running, it is a good idea to leverage existing infrastructures, which include: a banking license, since loans will probably have to be transferred from the originating institutions to the entity charged with managing loan recoveries; a well-designed logistics process for pulling together the loan files and documentation, with adequate support from top management; a system to calculate interest payments and track loan repayments; a physical location for workout officers and walk-in debtors to visit; and finally, and perhaps most importantly, a competent management team and experienced workout staff.

The rest of the process can take two or three months. Hiring staff usually is the most time-consuming activity, but it can vary. Bancomer, a Mexican commercial bank, was able to do everything in about three months, thanks to the fact that licensing was not an issue. This result was because the workout area was part of an existing bank, and because senior executives gave the initiative their full attention and support.

Unfortunately, when governments decide to create their own workout units, time drags on due to typical bureaucratic procedures and clearance as well as safeguards in the procurement process designed to avoid corruption. When time is critical, these same safeguards can also be costly. Hence, it is important to apply common sense and minimize the time required by using best practices, which we have found generally include the following:

1. Using the name and license of an existing financial institution that has already been intervened, or alternatively asking the banking regulator to expedite the process as much as possible
2. Using existing facilities that are already equipped with vaults and systems in which to store valuable loan documentation
3. Beginning workout efforts using loan-tracking systems that are already up and running, even if that means eventually migrating to more sophisticated NPL loan-tracking systems
4. Booking the NPLs at estimated market values, rather than face value, even if these values are approximate. This avoids overstating the value of the assets and creates realistic recovery targets as the process kicks off.
5. Hiring the NPL unit head immediately and then quickly building teams under him or her
6. Hiring experienced local team leaders to abbreviate the period needed to fully understand the situation and economic interests of critical debtors. Again, care should be taken, however, to avoid having these individuals work cases that they had a role in originating. In fact, a criterion for hiring should be that individuals have not participated in making decisions leading to cases that must be worked out. Put your best noncontaminated people inside the workout organization as soon as possible, because finding the right people takes time. In some cases, it

may be advisable to retain several people who know "where the bodies are buried"

7. Beginning the workout process as soon as one to two team leaders are in place, loans have been transferred, and a rudimentary tracking system has been implemented.

The workout unit should be built at the same time that the loans are being worked out. Mistakes inevitably will be made, with regard to the size, cost, and functionality of the NPL unit; but these mistakes are typically small compared to the larger costs of moving too slowly.

SPECIAL ISSUES RAISED WHEN NPLS ARE MANAGED BY GOVERNMENTS

NPLs can be just as damaging for countries as they are for individual companies. In Mexico, for example, NPLs were estimated at 14 percent of GDP in the most recent 1994–1995 crisis, and IPAB has since been charged with recovering roughly $80 billion of bad loans through 1999.

Half-buried piles of bad debt and failing banks threaten not only the viability of individual banks and the companies to which they lend, but also the health of entire economies. Unresolved NPLs can weigh down an economy for years, and stand in the way of having otherwise productive assets being returned to the real economy. From our perspective, one of the reasons why countries such as Korea, Sweden, and the United States enjoyed such a rapid rebound in GDP and commercial bank credit is in part due to their effort at NPL recovery and bad asset management. If NPLs are not managed aggressively, they leave the economy more vulnerable to another crisis, and mortgage the well-being of future generations.

Special issues arise, however, when governments are in charge of managing loan recoveries. These issues have undermined the recovery efforts of the agencies in Mexico, Indonesia, Jamaica, Ecuador, and Colombia, to name just a few. Governments often lack the will to confront debtors and make them pay their debts. They also have shown a disparate range of loan recovery rates across various markets, ranging from lows of 26 percent and 27 percent in Mexico and Indonesia, respectively, to recovery rates at the end of the third year of a crisis as high as 86 percent in the United States (Figure 7.4). To avoid transferring huge costs to taxpayers, AMCs must be specially designed, with an eye to making them accountable for successfully achieving their mission of minimizing the resolution costs borne by taxpayers.

In this section we address these design challenges, describing the five conditions that most influence this outcome: defining a clear and stable mandate; creating appropriate governance structures; ensuring transparency

FIGURE 7.4   AMCs show varying degrees of success with recoveries, disposals.

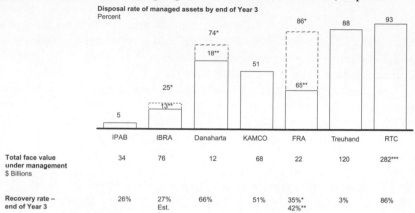

Disposal rate of managed assets by end of Year 3
Percent

	IPAB	IBRA	Danaharta	KAMCO	FRA	Treuhand	RTC
Total face value under management $ Billions	34	76	12	68	22	120	282***
Recovery rate – end of Year 3	26%	27% Est.	66%	51%	35%* 42%**	3%	86%

*Loans restructured and disposed
**Loans and assets disposed and recovered
***RTC acquired assets gradually, i.e., $282 billion is the amount of assets acquired by year-end 1991
Source: McKinsey research; interviews with other institutions; agency Web sites

and accountability; defining conditions that stimulate high performance; and ensuring supportive legal systems.

Defining a Clear and Stable Mandate

Agreeing to establish the asset management corporation is often the easy step. The decisions taken to define its mandate and scope of activities often can determine the new corporation's success or failure. We have worked with a range of these institutions, and have noticed several successful models that merit attention.

We earlier described the success of the U.S. Resolution Trust Corporation (RTC) in managing the S&L crisis of the late 1980s. The RTC was limited to a narrow mandate: It was charged with managing the resolution of failed thrifts, paying off depositors or transferring deposits to viable banks, and working out and disposing of the assets of these failed S&Ls. Its mandate was clear, narrow, and strictly related to minimizing crisis costs by implementing strategies that would maximize NPL recovery. The RTC did not have a role in defining general policies for the U.S. financial system, nor was it expected to influence banking legislation or regulatory conditions.

In Scandinavia during the early 1990s, two different models were employed by Sweden and Norway. Sweden generally followed a more supporting role, whereas Norway followed a second, more active model. In

Sweden, the State Bank Guarantee Fund was set up to make sure that the banks were capable of working out their bad loans and had enough funding to continue operations. Its interest was supporting and helping the private sector to resolve its bad loans. In Norway, the state took a much more hands-on approach by assuming control of the assets of troubled banks, and implementing the good bank/bad bank approach.

In the late 1990s, Malaysia and Thailand structured their institutions on similar models. Their agencies were able to focus their energies on narrowly defined goals, which helped them in fulfilling their mission by avoiding risks related to stretching limited workout talent across contending priorities.

In most democratic countries, broad policies addressing certain issues—such as whether banks should be sold to foreigners to attract needed capital and skills—are best left to legislative bodies and other government areas whose function it is to make political tradeoffs on behalf of the society they represent. If these questions are left to the workout agency to define, the asset management corporation inevitably will become involved in political battles that will reduce its effectiveness and independence. Ideally, the AMC should focus all of its energies on operating effectively, and defining loan recovery processes that are objective and apply to all debtors fairly and equally. Sheltering the recovery corporation from politics serves the purpose of setting the conditions for clear accountability and transparency.

Once the mandate of the new corporation has been defined, it is a relatively easy matter to establish operating policies and coordination mechanisms that are consistent with the institution's objectives. The next step is to develop an appropriate governance structure to oversee its functions.

Designing an Effective Governance Structure

A restructuring agency operates much like a corporation, but in an environment that is far more complex. Many stakeholders are involved. Some of these stakeholders may hold decision-making authority over the corporation (such as government officials or legislators), while others will have operational or influencing relationships that also need to be managed, and all have interests in what the AMC is doing.

The AMC's governance structure needs to take these stakeholders into account. The key attributes that the corporation's governance structure must fulfill are: transactional independence in line with the policies determining the institution's mission; a single oversight board that governs the corporation's performance and makes important decisions; accountability to the government, but not to individual ministries; openness and transparency in its operations and communications; and, finally, professional management responding to clearly defined performance objectives.

If the processes and structures of the AMC are well-defined, there should be no reason to override its operational autonomy, thus ensuring that it remains focused on executing its mission in a politically neutral fashion. The poor results observed in Mexico, for example, by FOBAPROA, are the direct result of too much political interference in the institutions' operations. Care should be taken to avoid repeating Mexico's experience, although similar mistakes have been made in Indonesia, Ecuador, and Jamaica. In these cases, the objective of maximizing the recovery value was not clear.

To discourage political meddling, openness and transparency are indispensable. It is also important that the AMC not report to individual ministries to prevent ministry officials from considering the corporation as part of their domain. This implies that the AMC's budget should be pre-funded with an infusion of public funds initially and subsequently self-funded as much as possible by the resources obtained from ongoing NPL and bad asset recoveries, subject of course to close public scrutiny and government intervention if necessary in extreme cases on policy grounds.

Moreover, operational autonomy and transparency should also apply to key transactional decisions, which could affect the local or national economy. Large, complex decisions, however, can have far-reaching policy implications. In practice, finding that fine line between making policy decisions and maintaining transactional autonomy will be difficult, especially when political agendas are highly charged during crisis conditions. For these reasons, the RTC in the United States, Danaharta in Malaysia, and FRA in Thailand developed policies early and fine-tuned them along the way, thereby creating acceptable conditions for their relative operating independence.

Creating an Oversight Board

Just like private corporations, government workout and restructuring corporations need an effective oversight board. The board has two critical roles: first, making critical strategic decisions; and second, monitoring the corporation and holding it and its leadership accountable for fulfilling the organizational mission.

The board should involve itself only in significant transactions and operational decisions; smaller decisions and authority should be delegated to management. This means that the board must take on a selective but hands-on role, meeting frequently enough to fulfill its mandate (e.g., the Thai FRA board met twice a week). There are almost no examples of a fully independent board,[7] and this is probably as it should be. Government representatives must be present to define operating policies and help hold what is still a government-owned corporation accountable. In addition, decision making related to resolution targets and defining new policies can be streamlined by having the government represented on the board. Including the minister of finance or central bank governor on the board may not be necessary, or even desirable, if operating policies are well-defined and generally accepted. Instead, senior civil servants and experts, who may have the advantage of more focused expertise and lack an overt political agenda, can play the needed role in driving policy decisions and ensuring accountability.

Ensuring Accountability

The AMC must be accountable to its citizens. This should be achieved by setting performance targets and, especially in a democracy, by having the government represented on the oversight board.

Accountability can be ensured by setting targets for the number of cases to be resolved and the amount of cash to be obtained from workouts. These targets should be determined by the AMC developing the strategic plan and corresponding budget, and then negotiating these plans with the appropriate stakeholders. Completing the work of the AMC is the ultimate target, so it is appropriate to set a date by which all cases must have been resolved, prior to winding up the corporation. The enabling legislation creating the corporation should also define a sunset clause for its existence. This will prevent it from staying alive longer than necessary and ensure that the troubled assets are effectively managed and quickly recycled into the economy.

Maintaining Transparency

Transparency can be achieved through internal and external audit functions. The results should be reported to the audit committee of the oversight board. The corporation also should fulfill other reporting requirements as mandated by its enabling legislation, including outlining its strategy, targets, operating performance, and the roles and responsibilities of its managers.

The corporation must also regularly report progress and plans, using press conferences and other means to operate in the "sunshine." This step includes publishing minutes of the board and other decision-making bodies. The corporation's key processes, such as auctions for asset disposals, should also be well-publicized and open to all qualified bidders. A full communications office and online information availability are minimum requirements for effective transparency.

Implementing Performance Management Incentives

To ensure successful execution, hard targets should be defined and managers held accountable for meeting them, just as other corporations do. The process for arriving at these targets should begin bottom-up through budgeting and strategic planning. An independent top-down process can also be used to challenge the organization and set stretch targets.

Once targets have been set, they need to be managed. There are three critical elements for this process, including a review process that formally evaluates progress at least every quarter; management incentives in the form of positive rewards (increased responsibility, public acknowledgement) and negative consequences (micro-management, remedial coaching, demotion, or even firing); and, finally, compensation that has variable components based on performance. In a government setting, the last point is certain to be viewed as radical, which is one more reason why the corporation needs to be independent.

Ensuring an Effective Legal Foundation for NPL Recovery

Countries whose laws support creditors' rights with effective enforcement mechanisms usually have higher recovery rates. Countries with poor laws and/or slow-moving courts usually do not. In these cases negotiating settlements out of court generally maximizes value. Following a financial crisis, emerging market legal systems in particular are tested and frequently found lacking in some of the necessary components to ensure rapid economic recovery after a crisis. The agenda for legal reform is usually obvious *after* a financial crisis.

A country's bankruptcy statutes, for example, may leave unanswered important questions, such as how courts are to hold valuation hearings, or which court has jurisdiction over matters involving debtors. Sometimes the problem is simply that the statute defines mechanisms that do not work well in practice. In other cases, the laws may be well written, but the mandated remedies are simply not enforceable due to defects in the law (e.g., ambiguities about what qualifies as a debt or which consumer assets are exempt from creditor claims). Defects in the written law are relatively easy to fix; there are several model bankruptcy codes and certainly many experts worldwide; intellectual obstacles are not a serious impediment to this kind of reform—political will, however, often is the limiting factor.

The defects that concern creditors the most in emerging markets are not just limited to the written bankruptcy law, but include how lawyers, judges, and government bureaucracies administer written laws. Sometimes these flaws are limited to bankruptcy law; more often, however, these failings extend throughout a country's legal system. Bolstering the bankruptcy regime therefore may require far-reaching reforms of the legal system. We examine these in more detail in Chapter 8.

Working with clients in several countries whose legal systems leave ample room for improvement, we have learned that it is frequently useful not only to seek negotiated outcomes for problem loans, but that creative problem solving, working within the current legal system, can make a big difference. For instance, one of our clients found that the simple expedient of ensuring that one of her employees was always physically present and carrying a cell phone in a critically important court made it possible to turn administrative processes around more rapidly in that same court. The role of that employee was as expediter, making sure that files that could be found were found, that their case files made their way to the top of the court's case load, and that simple bureaucratic procedures, such as affixing stamp taxes, did not slow down the progress of litigation.

Another client, recognizing that courts were understaffed and overloaded, arranged to take over many simple administrative processes that were distracting qualified court staff from higher, value-added tasks. Something as simple as investing in improving the procedural skills of the legal staff so that pre-litigation work is well prepared can greatly accelerate cases through crowded court dockets.

In the end, these solutions are not substitutes for legal reform when and where that is necessary. We have learned the hard way that sometimes the issue is not the quality of law, but the simple availability of court personnel to handle the surge of cases that invariably follows a banking crisis. This limitation slows things down to a crawl. Working with the courts, it is possible to craft solutions that optimize processes and greatly improve caseload productivity. Ruthlessly triaging cases that have little hope in court is another way of lightening the caseload.

MANAGEMENT LESSONS: GOOD BANKS/BAD BANKS IN SCANDINAVIA

Both Norway and Sweden suffered severe financial crises in the early 1990s, and provide interesting case studies for managing NPLs. These crises were seen as the worst those OECD countries had experienced in the previous twenty-five years. Interest rates rose dramatically; in the fall of 1992, Swedish interest rates on ninety-day treasury bills moved from 12 to 24 percent over the course of two months, with the overnight rate climbing as high as 500 percent. Both the Swedish and the Norwegian kroner depreciated by as much as 20 percent. Bad debts or nonperforming loans reached a range of 5 percent to just under 8 percent of total loans, but this was enough to impair bank capital on a systemic basis, reaching about 134 percent of bank equity in Norway. Consequently, banks failed and the governments had to intervene to prevent a complete breakdown of the banking systems and protect the domestic economies.[8]

These crises were driven largely by a massive credit boom, fueled by the banks and finance companies, which pumped credit into the economy when the government lifted price and volume controls (e.g., fixed interest limits) in the mid-1980s. The credit portfolio grew rapidly at first, but the significant economic slowdown in the late 1980s revealed problem loans. As elsewhere, poor lending practices and the absence of sound credit management processes made the financial systems of both countries vulnerable. Once economic growth slowed down, business bankruptcies increased, leading to significant pressure on all financial institutions—but most particularly the nonbank financial institutions which had been taking the most aggressive risks—to gain market share.

The real estate market also collapsed in both countries, further exacerbating the situation. A large-scale government rescue was launched that involved significant injections of new capital and liquidity loans. The largest commercial banks in Norway, for example, became de facto public banks, owned and indirectly controlled by the central government. In fact, both governments were forced to inject significant amounts of capital into the banking system, announcing "guarantees" to depositors to stem a bank run. At the worst point in the crises, two-thirds of the existing financial institutions were technically in default.

The Norwegian and Swedish governments followed broadly similar approaches in successfully managing their bad debts; some of the key players involved learned from the U.S. experience managing the S&L and banking crises in the late 1980s. Both countries pursued programs that had six core common components to them.

1. Immediately establishing a dedicated government advisory body to manage the financial crisis. In Sweden, a dedicated group of five professionals was established to advise the government (in particular, the Finance Ministry) over the course of several years. These professionals provided guidance on a broad range of issues related to the crisis, but the most important role this working group played was in designing and monitoring the overall crisis management approach.

2. Establishing a special government fund and process to provide capital and liquidity to the financial system. Funds such as these have played a range of roles, from immediately seizing failing and failed banks and taking over the bad asset workout processes, as was the case of the U.S. RTC, Sweden, and Norway, to providing turnaround support for troubled banks (e.g., liquidity, capital injections). This latter role often involves the fund asking the troubled bank to split itself into a "good bank" and "bad bank" with the fund supporting the bad bank workout process.

Both Norway and Sweden committed capital to support the financial system and outlined a process by which the financial institutions could get public assistance. Norway took control of troubled banks' assets and implemented very strong workout procedures and processes within the banks, including internal bad bank/good bank units for selective classes of loans. Sweden followed a process where the State Bank Guarantee Fund certified that institutions were able to continue operating after a review by bank examiners, auditors, and outside experts. This fund also forced the surviving bank to segregate bad debts or underperforming assets that the state had guaranteed into a separate legal entity within the surviving bank (the bad bank).

3. Setting overall objectives and criteria by which the success of the financial workout would be measured. Decisions were made as to which bank stakeholders (taxpayers, shareholders, borrowers) the government would protect and to what extent, and what level of foreign ownership/ participation would be allowed. Without establishing these parameters and developing consensus among the concerned stakeholders, a comprehensive turnaround plan would not have been possible since the individual players had conflicting interests.

4. Introducing the "good bank/bad bank" concept. Separating the good bank from the bad bank was copied from several of the large commercial banks, such as the successful Mellon Bank example, in the late 1980s, when the number, size, and severity of potential large bank failures rapidly outstripped the interest from potential acquirers.

Sweden implemented a solution that closely mirrored the bad bank approach used in the United States. Troubled banks' portfolios were segregated in two categories. Performing assets and all the deposits were placed in the good bank. The nonperforming assets (e.g., repossessed real estate, loans more than ninety days overdue) were placed in a bad or special asset bank. This bad bank liquidated the special asset portfolio and used the cash flows to repay various creditors' claims. The good and bad banks were structured as separate legal entities, but reported to either a separate subsidiary board or an independent board, which was different from the approach followed in many U.S. cases, including Mellon Bank, whose bad bank had its own board of directors.

5. Proactively consolidating and rationalizing the financial services industry to strengthen the overall financial system and minimize the government capital contribution. The special advisory group estimated the potential annual cost reduction value from consolidating the industry. These cost savings came from such actions as combining banks' sales and distribution networks and core retail and commercial processing functions like loan servicing, payments processing, and other back-office functions. In Norway, our colleagues estimated at the time that these consolidation savings were roughly $3 billion per year.[9] The net present value from such moves could be used to significantly offset large parts of the total banking sector losses. Consideration also was given to a better understanding of global forces at work in other countries with respect to consolidation and convergence (e.g., a single financial institution being allowed to sell a wide range of financial products like deposits, consumer loans, securities products, life and property and casualty insurance). This move was designed to ensure that a restructured banking industry would be able to keep pace with global trends and be competitive in the future at world-class standards.

6. Instituting world-class credit risk management skills. A major reason for the credit crises in Scandinavia was poor credit skills throughout the banking system. As part of an institution's rehabilitation, putting in place strong credit skills and processes was a key requirement.

The major difference in each government's approach was the degree to which the government took an active, ongoing ownership role or relied more on the private sector. There were also some differences in the legal structuring of the good bank/bad bank concept. For instance, by providing capital to all of the major banks that were in trouble, Norway's government ended up owning most of the banks. It then proceeded to carry out a good bank/bad bank initiative where appropriate, and restructured the overall industry. Sweden, on the other hand, decided to provide support more selectively, making decisions on a case-by-case basis, with a bias toward a private sector solution. Sweden focused only on the seven major banks and left the finance companies to be resolved through market forces.

We do not believe that there is a single right solution to managing an economy successfully through a financial crisis. However, we do believe strongly that there are common building blocks and design principles, particularly in managing the bad debt problem.

■ ■ ■

Aggressively managing NPLs is an imperative for minimizing the total resolution costs stemming from financial crises. Maximizing recovery rates, restoring as many NPLs to a performing basis as possible, and effectively redeploying valuable assets into the real economy is as important to CEOs for their shareholders as it is to public officials on behalf of taxpayers.

To ensure that the costs of NPLs and failed banks are minimized, tailored strategies are needed once the basic diagnostic and portfolio segmentation is done. Building a separate and efficient AMC or bad bank is also a key requirement for success. Moreover, governments have a special responsibility and special challenges that they need to address when they are required to step in and manage NPLs at a systemic level.

To minimize the impact of failed banks and NPLs in the future, more work is needed in the arena of strengthening system safeguards. Enhancing corporate governance, building capital markets, improving accounting and transparency, upgrading financial regulatory regimes, and ensuring effective legal foundations are required as well, topics we turn to in Chapter 8.

Building for the Future

CHAPTER 8

Strengthening
System Safeguards

When the California Public Employees' Retirement System (CalPERS) announced in February 2002 that it would no longer invest in four Southeast Asian economies, the news sent shock waves throughout emerging markets. CalPERS is the world's largest pension fund, with assets of more than $170 billion in 2000. It was not so much the withdrawal of CalPERS money that made news, however. It was the message that CalPERS was sending.

In its press release CalPERS said that it would no longer invest in economies that it felt were suffering from bad corporate governance and other omissions of good global standards. "For more than 10 years, CalPERS has made constructive attempts to improve corporate governance in the United States and abroad," said CalPERS President William D. Crist. "Enron has taught us that in spite of these efforts, shareholder value can be destroyed by faulty corporate governance. It clearly is time for us to tighten the screws."[1]

By "tightening the screws," CalPERS meant that henceforth it would institute a new rating system for its emerging market investments. The system would weight half its ratings on country-specific issues—such as political stability, labor standards, and financial transparency—and the other half on market factors, such things as the nation's market liquidity and volatility, market regulation and investor protections, capital market openness, and settlement proficiency and transaction costs. Under this new review, Argentina, Brazil, Chile, the Czech Republic, Hungary, Israel, Mexico, Peru, Poland, South Africa, South Korea, Taiwan, and Turkey were among the countries in. Newly out, however, were Indonesia, Malaysia, the Philippines, and Thailand.[2]

CalPERS' decision demonstrates the increasing influence that the private sector has in shaping global standards. The message sent by CalPERS, in fact, both frightened and assured investors. It frightened some who had commitments in the four adversely affected nations, of course. Yet, it also reassured others, who saw CalPERS' actions as necessary steps in bringing emerging markets into closer alignment with the standards that are important for the prevention of financial crises. In the final analysis, the standards need to be embraced by both international and domestic investors and intermediaries to be successful.

We get similar messages from investors as well. Investors tell us through a series of McKinsey & Company's investor opinion surveys that they will pay up to a 30 percent premium in many emerging markets for well-governed companies (Figure 8.1).[3] As part of our Firm-funded research, we also evaluated 188 companies from 6 emerging markets along 16 elements of corporate governance and found clear evidence that good governance is rewarded with higher market valuation: Companies that have a higher score on our corporate governance index have higher price-to-book ratios.[4] Both investors and managers can reasonably expect a 10 to 12 percent increase in their company's market valuation (Figure 8.2) by moving from worst to best along the critical elements of effective corporate governance that we outline in Appendix 8.1: Sixteen Elements of Good Corporate Governance. Those companies with better financial fundamentals due to their reliance on world-class standards, in our view, are better prepared to weather financial storms than their competitors who ignore such standards.

Standards and their enforcement, therefore, do make a difference.

Based on our client work, we believe strongly that the right set of standards can safeguard against future financial crises. More importantly, we

FIGURE 8.1   Investors in emerging markets pay more for well-governed companies.

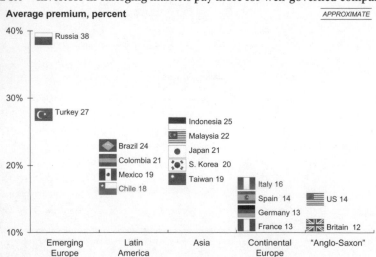

Source: McKinsey Investor Opinion Survey, 2002

FIGURE 8.2   Moving from worst to best in corporate governance improves market value.

Percent change in price/book

	Country	Industry	Effect
	India	Chemicals	10.6
		Textiles	12.4
	Korea	Auto parts/equipment	10.0
		Textiles	9.8
	Malaysia	Building materials	10.4
		Engineering/construction	10.0
	Mexico	Food	11.8
		Retail	11.8
	Taiwan	Electronics	10.7
		Food	10.7
	Turkey	Building materials	12.0
		Food	12.2
		Textiles	11.8

Source: McKinsey Global Strategy Practice

believe that the private sector—particularly investors and financial interme
diaries—can exert considerable influence along all three levels of what we
refer to as a crisis prevention safety net (Figure 8.3). We have found it useful
to think of standards and safeguards in three distinct but interrelated tiers:
self-governance; market supervision; and government regulation. All three
tiers play a unique role in crisis prevention, financial stability, and economic
growth. To be clear, we are not advocating a limited role for government; to
the contrary, governments play a unique and necessary role in preventing

FIGURE 8.3   Implementing a 3-tier crisis prevention safety net: strengthening system
safeguards.

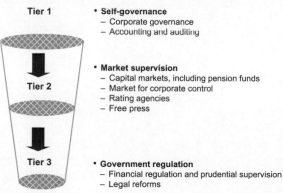

Tier 1
- **Self-governance**
  - Corporate governance
  - Accounting and auditing

Tier 2
- **Market supervision**
  - Capital markets, including pension funds
  - Market for corporate control
  - Rating agencies
  - Free press

Tier 3
- **Government regulation**
  - Financial regulation and prudential supervision
  - Legal reforms

Source: McKinsey practice development

financial crises. We nonetheless believe that the private sector can step up its role considerably and do more to help prevent financial crises in the future.

There is much that the private sector can do in self-policing and living by the spirit of the law, not just the letter of the law or standards: ensuring sound corporate governance and transparent accounting at the first level. There also is a well-defined role for the private sector in market supervision at the second level: promoting capital market development and actively participating in the market for corporate control. Finally, there is government regulation at the third and final level: strengthening financial sector supervision and surveillance as well as ensuring enforcement of predictable legal regimes and competition law. In this last tier, the private sector can play a contributing role as well; for example, collaborating with regulators on supervising new products, exchanging market information, and cross-pollinating people to enhance skills.

Moreover, at each one of these three levels, the private sector has an important role to play, not only in asserting its views and lending its expertise, but also in ultimately helping to shape the necessary crisis prevention standards and safeguards. In our view, the private sector in many ways can champion the necessary changes faster, better, and more cost-effectively in the long run than the public sector can on its own. At each level, the private sector needs to work closely with officials in the public sector to ensure that all three levels of the crisis prevention safety net are implemented fully and working harmoniously.

The instinct of many observers is to think first about a government-only solution to a crisis. For example, we frequently hear that "the problem is poor bank supervision," or "the government needs to bail out the banks." While the government has a critical role to play, we believe that crisis-related costs can be minimized (bad asset and credit workouts) and change realized faster (bank restructuring and turnarounds) with the private sector playing a leading role. While governments do play an important safety net role—for example, in the form of central bank liquidity lines or deposit guarantees—they are neither the first nor the only line of defense.

Furthermore, both companies and governments have a choice about the path they choose to prevent future crises. Often, this is done only implicitly without a clear strategy in place. Our recommended path is to move as aggressively as possible to install the necessary safeguards at each level of our safety net as a means of preventing or reducing the impact of crises in the future. The second path, one that we strongly advise against, is to delay the response and implement crisis prevention safeguards only marginally and incrementally. The first path is designed to prevent future crises and increase the chance for sustained economic growth; the second one only increases the risk that crises will recur in the future and growth will be impaired.

Executives in the private sector often shy away from trying to shape the standards and safeguards that directly affect the competitive environment in which they compete. Often they do not even enter the debate about which path to take. "Regulation and standards are beyond my sphere of influence," "The politics of public policy debates are messy," and "Even if I had the time, I wouldn't have much impact on getting the kinds of standards or enforcement we really need to restore investor confidence," are common refrains. In some cases in some countries, these observations are undoubtedly true.

Upgrading corporate governance can help to spot problems sooner rather than later, in addition to enticing investors who are willing to pay more for a company's stock. Adopting the right set of accounting standards can help to make the real economic value of a company more transparent to investors and help gain access to lower-cost capital in the world's financial hubs. Enhancing domestic capital markets, for example, not only can act as a safety valve for problems in the banking sector but also they can help to lower the cost of a company's capital. Reforming pension funds with greater private sector involvement is an important initiative in the development of local capital markets. Improving bank regulatory and supervisory systems can help to promote greater competition and add a final layer of oversight and risk management. Needed legal reforms can ensure more certain investor and creditor protection.

More importantly—as the case of Singapore's 1998 financial center development shows—the private sector can make a difference in driving and shaping a new financial regime: There is a valuable policy input role for the private sector to perform that can leverage its expertise. Private sector input can affect how and where companies compete, as well as the standards and safeguards that will ultimately govern their behavior. Obviously, the private sector must work hand in hand with the public sector to ensure that proper standards and safeguards are in place. For a more complete view, see Appendix 8.2: Singapore's Development as an International Financial Center.

We have found that the right time to initiate a comprehensive strengthening of basic system standards and safeguards is just as the overt crisis is subsiding, sometime after the first hundred days in most cases.[5] To illustrate our thesis in this chapter, we have selected five critical elements spanning our three-tier crisis prevention safety net:

1. Corporate governance reform
2. Accounting reforms
3. Capital market development
4. Financial regulatory improvement
5. Legal regime enhancement.

In each case, we first review why these building blocks are important for crisis prevention, and then explain what elements should matter most to CEOs and their senior management teams as well as policymakers. Because of the wide disparity among different countries' starting points, we will not attempt to offer suggestions about how these standards and safeguards can be implemented in any one particular country.

MOVING TO GLOBAL STANDARDS FOR CORPORATE GOVERNANCE

The financial crises in emerging markets over the last five years have produced at least one consensus point: Publicly stated strategies mean little to investors if a company lacks disclosure, transparency, management accountability, and—ultimately—a strong commitment to shareholder value through sound corporate governance. As a consequence, there is renewed interest in improving corporate governance structures and practices in many countries around the world, not only as a means to enhance value but also as a first line of defense to help prevent future crises.[6]

Why Corporate Governance Matters for Crisis Prevention

When financial problems arise, it should be management and the board of directors that identify them first, long before government examiners or other officials arrive on the scene. Protecting minority shareholder rights is a necessary first step to attract discerning investors that have a vested interest in the value and growth of the company. Introducing truly independent boards that can oversee a company's management team, strategy, organization, risk management, and auditing can go a long way toward preventing small problems from later manifesting themselves as systemic problems. Ensuring greater transparency can facilitate better risk-reward trade-offs by investors, which in turn sends strong signals to management. The illustrative list of effective corporate governance elements that we assess when we work with clients is found in Appendix 8.1.

Korea in particular stands out as a country that recognized the value of corporate governance reform (e.g., board responsibilities and shareholder rights) in the early days of its crisis to reduce the threat of future financial crises. Korea led the governance reform efforts after the Asian crisis. The Financial Supervisory Commission (FSC) mandated, among other things, that the major banks and chaebol appoint a majority of outside directors and establish committees and transparent board responsibilities. It removed ceilings on foreign ownership, thus sparking competition, and lowered the threshold for a group of shareholders to sue the board if it failed to protect their interests.

Strengthening Standards to Protect Investors

Emerging market companies that adopt sound corporate governance practices not only will be rewarded by investors for strengthening their own standards—effectively leapfrogging ahead of their competitors—but also they will help to insulate their companies from the chill of future financial storms. To augment our evaluation of the 188 emerging market companies, we also conducted more rigorous research on eleven companies in those same countries that had improved their corporate governance practices substantially in recent years. As expected, their performance improved as well: For example, each of these companies beat their respective local market indices by at least 20 percent over the sample period. Of course, market valuation is driven by many factors, and without the statistical work above, we could not draw firm conclusions about the impact of governance on valuation. Still, a closer look at our case studies shows some of the ways that good governance translates into higher value and a stronger foundation should a financial crisis strike in the future.

We find that good corporate governance enhances company performance in many different ways that coincide with effective crisis prevention measures. Disclosure and transparency of financial results allow a company to set clear targets and hold employees accountable for results, all the way from top management to the newest employees. An audit committee is an essential check on the CFO and can bring a much needed market perspective to risk management strategies and techniques; a management compensation committee is critical for creating the right incentives for managers. Independent, outside directors can bring a broad shareholder view as well as a fresh, objective, and disciplined perspective to the company and its committees, which is critical for decisions that may be counter to the interests of company insiders.

Thus, there is a useful coincidence of economic self-interest—enhancing a company's value—and crisis prevention—encouraging more rigorous oversight of a company's performance and risk management.

Consider the case of Infosys, an Indian software company. Infosys and competitors Wipro and Satyam all adopted relatively similar strategies in the same locations, with the same comparative operating performance. However, Infosys has gone the farthest in improving corporate governance, which has resulted in at least three distinct strategic advantages that we can identify. As one local bank analyst with a global firm explained, "Infosys is trading at a premium to its peers . . . due to its strong fundamentals and its corporate governance—you need both."[7]

The first advantage is purely economic. Infosys had a slightly higher return on invested capital in 2001 (54 percent compared to 45 percent for Satyam). More compelling, however, is the fact that Infosys had more than a

2:1 advantage with respect to its market-to-book ratio (24.0 for Infosys compared to 10.3 for Satyam), signaling market appreciation for its governance, strategy, and future earnings potential.

The second advantage is its command in the war for talent. Because of its superior performance, Infosys is better positioned to compete for—and retain—the talent it needs to compete in an industry where talent is a key strategic weapon. Where the attrition rate in the software industry is 25 percent in India, it is only 10 percent at Infosys.

The third advantage that Infosys enjoys is a lower cost of capital, created by its ability to list shares on the U.S. Nasdaq stock exchange. Without putting in place the necessary financial reporting and transparency measures, Infosys would not have been able to list its shares there. Listing on Nasdaq, in turn, has allowed Infosys to create many global partnerships with companies such as Nextel, Microsoft, and Franklin Templeton Investments.

These analyses and our experience suggest that good governance pays off with greater market strength and access, which can lessen the impact of a crisis for those companies that adhere to high standards. Should a financial crisis ever hit India, where warning signs are already apparent as we discuss in Chapter 3, a company like Infosys will be better prepared to weather the storm than many of its competitors. The question is thus not whether emerging market companies should start improving their governance practices. Rather, the question is how many CEOs and shareholders understand their financial self-interest in enhancing their corporate governance standards, and how fast can they put the necessary safeguards in place before the next crisis hits.

ADOPTING BETTER ACCOUNTING STANDARDS

The collapses of Enron and WorldCom—the largest bankruptcy cases in U.S. history—have cast a spotlight on a whole range of accounting issues in such a way that the tone and level of debate on standards and safeguards may have permanently shifted in the United States and elsewhere. Many companies have been hit with charges of inadequate financial reporting. As we write *Dangerous Markets*, we may be witnessing the beginning of a regime shift on accounting issues that frankly transcends a single company and has deeper implications for crisis prevention.

We are management consultants, not accountants. We admittedly are not experts in the complexity, intricacies, and technicalities of different national and international accounting standards. However, from our crisis work in both the private and public sectors, we do know that accounting issues have a direct and sizeable impact on the recognition, timing, and ultimate cost of a crisis, and we have several observations about the need for certain accounting standards that can enhance crisis prevention. Our observations fall into three areas: the need for greater transparency about the real economic value of companies; the need for common accounting definitions and more globally uniform standards like the International Financial Reporting Standards (IFRS—formerly known as the International Accounting Standards or IAS); and the need for a transition from old national accounting conventions to more accepted international market standards and safeguards.

Need for Greater Transparency

In every crisis country where we have worked, problems with transparency in both the real sector and financial sector are abundant. The lack of a deep and functioning capital market usually is an indicator of a lack of transparency. Standard calculations of ROIC over WACC are often thwarted by the lack of adequate, reliable data, although approximate estimates can be made as we discussed in Chapter 3. Such opaqueness makes it challenging to analyze individual companies and entire industry sectors to arrive at an informed opinion about the value destruction or creation occurring in an economy.

Understanding real cash flows has been elevated to an art form in many countries, requiring intense reviews of accounting appendices in annual reports to come close to having an informed point of view. You have to dig pretty deeply into annual reports to find that companies can generate negative cash flows, including dividend payments, for years. Even determining simple interest coverage ratios can at times be a challenge, and not something that is routinely reported in a user-friendly format by companies, although combing through an equity analyst's report helps to decipher some of the pertinent information needed to make informed investor and creditor decisions.

The lack of transparency is probably nowhere more apparent than in the ephemeral world of bank NPLs. From our perspective, this area is one of the greatest travesties of the accounting world from both a crisis recognition and cost perspective. In terms of crisis prevention, it is one of the priorities that we would tackle first as a means of reducing ultimate resolution costs.

Not recognizing nonperforming loans, i.e., effectively hiding them in the hopes that a company or the economy may turn around, is perhaps understandable from a human perspective—no one wants to be the messenger of bad news—but it is usually devastating from a financial perspective. In the United States, "regulatory accounting principles" allowed the S&L industry in the 1980s to underreport the true nature of their NPLs and therefore cover up their real problems. Thousands of S&Ls later became insolvent and the artificial accounting treatment that was used only delayed recognition of their true economic value; these same S&Ls failed and cost the U.S. taxpayers roughly $200 billion dollars. While we obviously cannot judge how much of this cost was directly attributable to regulatory accounting conventions and lax accounting treatment, we do know that they were contributing factors to the continuing widespread problems of the savings and loan industry until corrected.

The lack of transparency of NPLs in much of Asia is still a huge problem that is only being addressed slowly and reluctantly by countries and companies. For years, China, for example, restricted the write-off of NPLs to just 1 percent of total loans per year—just by regulatory fiat and without regard to the reality of their problems. It is no surprise, therefore, that NPL problems mushroomed over time. Moreover, there was no incentive to even think about imposing a real credit culture in the banking system, given the formulaic nature of loan loss recognition, which itself creates perverse incentives that perpetuate bad lending decisions. Today, as China enters the WTO and begins to transform its accounting practices, reforms are under way, but it could be a long march to reach acceptable accounting standards. Even during this accounting transition, the tax treatment of NPLs still gets in the way of recognizing and resolving bad loans, since China's tax code only gives companies credit for 1 percent of their NPLs annually.

We saw this transparency problem firsthand in Ecuador in 1998 as we discussed in Chapter 6 in the case of Filanbanco. Not only did the local Ecuadorian accounting practices mask the mounting problem of systemic NPLs, but the lack of transparency even affected the bank supervisor and central bank, neither of which had good information on the true state and seriousness of the problem. Bank annual reports were virtually worthless and the information used by the bank supervisors was outdated, often incomplete, and not much better than the publicly available information. In several noted cases, the banks' reports to their regulator were more than a year out-of-date and incomplete. When asked to explain this delay in transparency, we were told by one central bank official that "several of the banks had computer problems and they promised to get back to us later . . ."—a promise that failed to raise our comfort level about the accuracy of any of the bank numbers we were asked to analyze.

The only real comfort we got was when we actually had a chance to get inside some of the banks that had failed and been taken over by Ecuador's AGD, the deposit insurer and bank restructuring agency. What we found poignantly demonstrated the real cost of the lack of transparency and its eventual impact on all Ecuadorian depositors and taxpayers. Just prior to their failure and seizure by AGD, the failed banks were reporting NPLs in the range of 7 to 17 percent of total loans. The legacy accounting practices in place at the time delayed recognition of the problems and therefore exacerbated their ultimate resolution cost in the long run. The stark reality was at the other end of the NPL scale, however. The true NPLs ranged from an estimated 12 to 55 percent of total loans and in fact fully explained the bank failures. Filanbanco's true NPLs were 43 percent higher than reported, more than 25 percent of its loan portfolio. This problem was endemic to Ecuador's entire banking system, which consequently experienced a depositor panic, a bank holiday, and a full-blown financial crisis in early 1998.

If we had any doubts about the value of transparency before we arrived in Ecuador, those doubts rapidly vanished. Even recognizing that greater transparency cannot single-handedly prevent future crises, we are convinced that greater transparency for NPLs and other issues can help to minimize the significant costs that the lack of transparency imposes on a society. When we see the staggering estimates of real NPLs in Asia as a percentage of GDP—far above the currently reported ranges—we are deeply concerned about how the different societies will bear those eventual losses when they are finally made transparent and recognized as such.

Need for Common Definitions and Greater Convergence of Standards

One of the frustrating facts we constantly face is the lack of common definitions country-to-country that we think should be simple to define from a practitioner's perspective. For example, it makes a great deal of common sense to us to define a nonperforming loan as one whose payment of interest and principal is 90 days overdue for purposes of loan provisioning and write-offs. Yet, we find that practice and nomenclature vary greatly from one country to another—with disturbing, unintended consequences.

China's accession to the WTO is forcing a welcomed change in accounting practices in that country, but one of its legacy problems is the fact that the current accounting practices require the recognition of unpaid interest due as revenue until it is over 180 days old. Chinese accounting rules then allow for write-offs only in very specific situations, such as when the borrower becomes bankrupt in the case of a company or dies in the case of an individual. With respect to interest due, loan provisioning, and bad debt write-offs, IFRS allows for management discretion to present a full and fair picture of a company's financial condition. In contrast, the mechanical accounting treatment of regulatory rules and the use of definitions that stretch reality far beyond reasonable management discretion only compound and delay the resolution of problems, leading to increased crisis costs. They also make crisis prevention much more difficult.

The convergence of different standards—IFRS, U.S. GAAP, and U.K. GAAP in particular—into a truly globally accepted standard is still a long way off and, as realists, we don't underestimate the time and effort it will take for different national standards to converge, either to something close to the existing IFRS or to some incarnation of new, more transparent standards. Again, as non-accountants, we undoubtedly do not understand all the complexities and nuances of getting from here to there. We only understand the value of common definitions and the convergence of standards from a crisis prevention and crisis management perspective.

One way around these issues in the meantime is for companies to use prospectively two different accounting standards, one local and one global, effectively going to the trouble of keeping two separate sets of books and reporting both ways. Companies that are globally active already do so today, such as Infosys and Kookmin Bank. While some countries may complain that the use of more internationally recognized standards casts doubts on their own domestic accounting practices, many companies see the value in adopting this dual reporting approach and have built it into their corporate strategy as a means of giving them a competitive edge. Ultimately, one set of financial reports should emerge based on internationally accepted norms.

Infosys is a good example. From its early days, it saw the strategic value of moving swiftly to U.S. GAAP standards as one of the requirements to list its stock in the United States and consequently lower its cost of capital. It also had to report under Indian accounting practices because it was an Indian-domiciled company. In the absence of a globally recognized standard, management consciously chose to keep two sets of books to enhance its transparency and improve its access to lower-cost capital outside of India. Furthermore, should a crisis ever hit India, we would argue that Infosys is far better prepared to weather the storm than most other companies that only report according to local practices, simply because it has to be more transparent to global investors and therefore more diligent about its financial position.

The Need for a Transition

While we see the need for changes in accounting practices in many countries as a means of enhancing crisis prevention and we realize that a transition period is necessary, it is time to get on with needed reforms. Therefore, we favor starting the transition now and shifting to a new accounting regime that focuses on the crisis-related issues that we have raised.

As a means of prevention, whatever costs are associated with moving from here to there in terms of accounting standards would be miniscule on an individual country basis, compared to the actual and potential costs involved if and when a crisis should hit. We applaud the efforts of China to move away from its legacy accounting system and toward more modern and credible standards under its WTO commitment. We know that this effort will take time, but it is a good example of moving deliberately in a noncrisis environment.

Crises also afford unique opportunities for a radical regime shift that otherwise is not possible before a crisis. For example, Korea used its crisis as a reason to change not only its corporate governance regime but also its accounting regime to converge more fully with U.S. or international standards. At the height of the crisis, it required all commercial banks to be audited within sixty days by an internationally recognized accounting firm, as a precondition to receiving any government assistance. The results of those audits were a factor not only in determining the true financial health of the banks but also whether or not the government would inject funds to keep a potentially viable bank afloat. Since then, a new body, the Korean Accounting Institute, has been established to ensure that Korean accounting standards in a few years be fully consistent with, or in some cases be more stringent than, IFRS.

Individual companies can also start their own transition without waiting for common standards to emerge. Like Infosys, there often are no real hurdles in most countries that would prevent management from deciding on dual reporting to gain the benefits—such as listing access on foreign stock exchanges that demand greater transparency—that flow from such actions. For now, dual reporting under both traditional national and more market-oriented international standards may be the best transition possible.

DEVELOPING CAPITAL MARKETS

Recent financial crises have served as needed catalysts to spur financial market development—particularly capital market development—in many countries.[8] As the chairman and CEO of the U.S. National Association of Securities Dealers (NASD), Robert Glauber, has stated:

> *Strong, well-functioning equity markets provide the fuel to grow businesses and produce jobs. As we have seen with Nasdaq in the United States, most jobs are created by new, small businesses—today most often high-tech businesses—and it's here that equity capital plays the biggest role. Startups and small, growing businesses can't rely on debt financing; they feed on equity. Moreover, private equity investors need healthy markets where they can sell IPOs to take out their investments. This is true for the United States, for other developed countries, and for developing countries as well.[9]*

Specifically, the Asian crisis has once again highlighted the lack of reliable domestic funding sources, the result of underdeveloped capital markets, and the heavy dominance of bank financing. The Asian financial crisis also created greater urgency for improving Asian and other capital markets, and increased public willingness to accept policy changes necessary to strengthen markets. Crises are not the only factor forcing capital market development. Pension system reforms of the sort adopted early by Chile and being emulated throughout Latin America and other parts of the world are helping create deeper capital markets, providing substantial long-term financing. After all, more than $35 trillion in investment funds worldwide is available, and it is growing rapidly.

Developing effective capital markets is necessary to improve performance in the real sector and prevent the reappearance of pricing and asset allocation imbalances which, when abruptly reversed, accelerate and deepen real economy and financial market crises. As we noted in Chapter 2, for example, we can see the strong correlation between the depth of capital markets (i.e., the greater reliance on capital markets compared to bank financing) and economic development in general; that is, those countries with the deepest capital markets have the highest level of economic development.

Effective capital markets benefit the real economy in a variety of ways. First, they channel funds to the most appropriate investment (i.e., best return for risk). Second, by having a benchmark or a risk-free yield curve—typically a government debt rate across a maturity spectrum—they provide for better pricing of different risks and more timely and efficient repricing of financial assets. Third, they provide access to local currency funding. Fourth, they also help to provide more diversified and higher returns for domestic savings. Fifth, debt markets allow changes in risk and market conditions to be reflected in price rather than volume, which is how bank loans adjust. Moreover, this continuous repricing of financial assets minimizes any buildup of structural imbalances and reduces the risk of financial crisis. Sixth, they help to provide the necessary infrastructure where secondary markets can develop and new hedging instruments (e.g., swaps, currency futures) can be used. Seventh, they attract a mix of different types of investors that play different roles (short-term versus long-term investors). Finally, the development of robust capital markets has the added benefit of ensuring better financial reporting and scrutiny in both the financial and real sectors of the economy.

Why Liquid Domestic Markets Matter in Emerging Economies

Emerging economies derive three other major benefits from developing their capital markets. First, a solid capital market spurs economic development and profitable growth in the real sector by directing capital more efficiently to creditworthy companies. Second, developed capital markets are conducive to the long-term development of more stable financial systems because they reduce the dependence on bank financing in favor of more investors with longer-term interests. Finally, emerging economies with developed capital markets will integrate more efficiently into the emerging global market. The earlier these markets become nodes in the global market, even small nodes that meet the necessary standards, the sooner companies in these economies will enjoy the benefits of larger and cheaper access to capital.

Over the long term, the benefits of integration in the global market, in our view, will far outweigh the risks, even though as we stated in Chapter 3 there will be cases of only partial or poorly executed liberalization. Some emerging economies, however, focus almost exclusively instead on the risks of globalization and erect barriers (e.g., capital controls in Malaysia) to protect their markets. A deep and developed capital market, however, is the best "protection" against external shocks commonly associated with globalization and volatile capital flows in particular. Also, as we explained in Chapter 2, countries with a deeper domestic capital market have stronger and less volatile portfolio flows. This is the result of a deeper domestic investor base, which provides more stable and longer-term funding sources for the domestic economy.[10]

Companies in emerging economies should tap the emerging global markets not only for capital, but also for people, standards, and practices. Developing markets should leverage developed markets' experience and skills to speed market development. Indeed, most emerging economies will not be able to rapidly adopt best practice mechanisms and support (e.g., IFRS, trading practices) without leveraging external resources. For example, Singapore drew upon other developed economy market mechanisms and support models, and leveraged "excess capacity" (e.g., skills and capital) from international markets. It also pressured domestic players to develop by exposing them gradually to international competition.

Creating a Virtuous Cycle of Capital Market Development

Given how the real and financial sectors benefit from strong capital markets, an economy with access to a well-functioning capital market will have competitive advantages over its trading partners, and its companies will be more competitive. For example, a country's corporates will have more efficient access to deeper capital pools, enabling them to enjoy well-priced, long-term, fixed-rate capital. Thus, it is essential for executives to understand the five major steps that governments have to take to create a positive cycle of capital markets development.

1. Issue government debt through a series of tranches and maturities on a regular basis, even through surplus years. Government debt issuance is key to market development.[11] It is now widely recognized that having a benchmark asset is critical to market development. Such a yield curve helps price other assets and risks, provides the ability to develop hedging mechanisms, and creates a core financial market in which financial market participants are most likely to participate. Domestic markets worldwide demonstrate that—except for temporary exceptions—a liquid government debt market is the best way to create this benchmark asset because it is the only credible risk-free asset. Government debt in local currency is also attractive to domestic savers and reduces their exclusive reliance on banks.

2. Develop a vibrant investor base in domestic markets by creating or revamping existing, defined-contribution pension systems and promoting the development of highly active traders. Governments can boost a market's liquidity by encouraging the growth of a deep and broad investor base. With over $35 trillion in the markets in 2001, there basically are three different investor types, as determined by their investment strategy. *"Buy and hold investors"* (e.g., pension funds, insurance companies) typically have a very long-term investment horizon. They provide depth in the market since they represent the largest investment pool—more than $23 trillion in 2001. *"Buy and turn investors"* (e.g., mutual funds) have a shorter investment horizon and need to match performance to a predefined benchmark, typically a stock index. They are also very large—$12 trillion—and since they frequently need to adjust their asset allocation, they provide liquidity in the market. Finally, *"dynamic investors"* (e.g., proprietary trading desks and hedge funds) are a much smaller pool of investors, with an estimated $0.5 trillion in unleveraged assets in 2001. They look for market anomalies and discrepancies and use a variety of trading and hedging techniques to achieve the highest possible absolute returns.[12]

Each investor group brings a set of benefits and potential risks to market liquidity. From our perspective, pension fund reform is closely related to capital market development and is an important corollary to helping prevent crises by bringing greater private sector market discipline to bear on more financial, mostly nonbank, assets.

Around the world, pension fund reform is under way in both developed countries and emerging markets for the simple fact that many existing "pay-as-you-go," government-sponsored plans are underfunded and highly leveraged, imposing severe strains on future fiscal deficits. In many cases, this debt is proving to be unsustainable from a macroeconomic perspective, as many aging populations lead to an equally unsustainable and falling contributors/beneficiaries ratio. Consequently, pension fund reform can help to take the pressure off increasing fiscal debt and deficits, which by themselves may not be a major cause of a financial crisis as we explained in Chapter 3, but which certainly contribute to the depth and duration of a crisis.

When we look at examples such as Chile, we find a concerted effort in the early 1980s to move from an unsustainable pay-as-you-go plan to a free-standing, defined-contribution plan, the Administradoras de Fondos de Pensiones (AFP), which invests heavily in domestic companies thereby increasing the source of longer-term, privately-available capital needed for economic growth. Pension funds make the actual investments subject to strict state guidelines. It is no coincidence to us that Chile's capital market development and pension reform efforts have contributed to its economic stability and financial strength while other Latin American countries were going through their own financial crises.

As we write this book, changes in the U.S. 401(k) private pension plans are unleashing a vast sum of private capital, reaching more than $1.7 trillion in 2002 according to the Investment Company Institute, the trade association of mutual fund companies—funds that are available for investments in U.S. and other markets, funds that otherwise would have been held primarily in government securities. The bulk of 401(k) funds are placed in mutual funds run by Fidelity, Merrill Lynch, Vanguard, and many others, which help to diversify risk and thus indirectly help to prevent financial crises. Since mutual funds reprice daily in most markets where they exist, the problem of excess funds winding up in banks—that make illiquid loans that adjust wrenchingly by volume during a crisis—is also avoided.

Singapore and Hong Kong have used pension fund reforms to bolster their capital market efforts and thus their economic development as well. Singapore launched its plan to become an Asian financial center in 1998, and revamped its Central Provident Fund, a free-standing, defined-contribution plan, as an important corollary to help realize its dream of becoming a favored financial hub. Rules governing the investment of Central Provident Fund savings were liberalized, helping to attract more private asset managers to Singapore, and enhancing its economic prospects and strengths in the region compared to its surrounding neighbors.[13] Hong Kong's MPF, created in December 2000, is an employee-based, defined-contribution plan that allows beneficiaries to select and switch between investment choices provided by an employer-selected service provider.

Thus, while pension reform may seem a bit distant from preventing future financial crises, there is an important link between capital market development and pension fund reforms. From our perspective, the combination of capital market development and pension fund reform can bring more private sector discipline and diversification of risk to financial flows and investments that in the long run can help to minimize future crises.

3. Promote competition between intermediaries and leverage foreign talent and skills. Developing talent in emerging economies takes time, and therefore inducing foreign talent should be encouraged. In fact, domestic market development will be hampered by any regulations that constrain the activities of foreign firms—especially intermediaries, rating agencies, and law firms. For example, restricting foreign intermediaries to sub-markets or international markets is likely to be counterproductive. Similarly, restricting the hiring of foreign talent by domestic firms, as in Malaysia, will limit the pace of market development. Additionally, these restrictions will put domestic firms at a formidable disadvantage against potential competitors who enter when the domestic market eventually opens to foreign competitors.

4. Set market development and international integration visions that reinforce each other. As we explained in Chapter 2, a global financial market is currently emerging, initially as a network of individual domestic markets linked to each other through a hub and spoke system, with London and New York as the main hubs.[14] Initially, emerging economies' capital markets can serve as efficient nodes of this network. Given the increased role of global markets, emerging market companies, investors, and policymakers can no longer consider domestic market development and global market integration independently. Instead, officials must design their domestic markets to smoothly integrate into global markets to fully benefit from globalization. Specifically, they must adopt international standards (e.g., operating procedures, products, reporting, and rating systems) to allow foreign players and talent to operate in the domestic market and create links to global markets.

5. Implement required infrastructure support and market mechanisms to create liquidity. In most emerging markets, improving support and market mechanisms is essential to creating liquidity and greater market efficiency, and the improvements required are proven and well understood. From a macroeconomic perspective, low transaction costs are important. Managers need to address market mechanisms and microstructure, such as the preferred regulatory approach, accounting and transparency requirements, legal framework, technology platform and payments and settlement infrastructure.

RESETTING REGULATORY REGIMES

Financial sector standards and safeguards have been affected throughout the past decade by a combination of relentless market forces, widespread liberalization, the growth of new local and global competitors, and the inevitable policy reactions to financial crises. In all countries, financial regulators and the institutions they supervise are forced to adapt to these changes. Market liberalization is often required to reset a nation's regulatory regime because the old regime has failed to protect depositors and investors or encourage real economic growth, one of our themes from Chapter 3.[15] The challenge, therefore, is to ensure that the new regulatory and supervisory standards and safeguards are effective, efficient, and in line with basic market principles.

In this section, we use our three-tier safety net model to discuss needed standards and safeguards specific to financial regulatory regimes. Because of the importance that financial sector regulation plays in any economy, we develop our safety net model further into a matrix, as illustrated in Figure 8.4, by adding the three basic pillars of financial regulation that cut across all levels of the safety net: competition and market conduct; risk management and prudential supervision; and consumer protection and service. We briefly explore why financial regulation and supervision are necessary to avoid crises along each component of the matrix. Next, we discuss what standards and safeguards are needed to reset a regulatory regime after a financial storm hits.

Why Regulation and Supervision Are Important to Prevent Future Crises

We find it useful to discuss the importance of financial sector regulation for banks and other kinds of financial institutions across the three pillars we noted above.

1. **Competition and market conduct regulations** are needed to ensure the fair and smooth functioning of financial markets as well as the efficient delivery of quality products and services to consumers.
2. **Prudential supervision and surveillance** of financial institutions and markets ensures that risk management policies and processes are adequate, and that no financial institution's weakness poses a threat to the financial system. Prudential supervision also protects against excessive

FIGURE 8.4   Strengthening the financial system safety net.

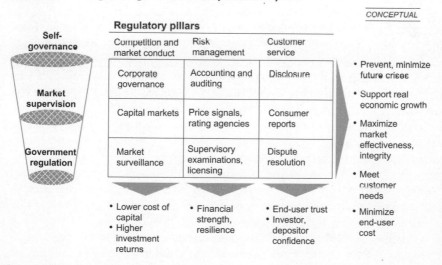

Source: McKinsey practice development

exposure to moral hazard. Above all, it protects individual depositors and investors.

3. **Customer service regulation** is needed to ensure complete and timely information so that consumers can make educated financial choices about the investment, savings, credit, and transactional products and services they require.

If any of these regulatory pillars is weak by global standards, then financial systems will be vulnerable to crisis, real economic growth potentially will be impaired, and consumers will be poorly served. Conversely, strong regulatory regimes that work with, rather than against, market forces can strengthen financial systems, bolster sustained economic growth, and serve customers better. Resetting regulatory regimes across all three pillars and tiers of our safety net can help to ensure that a virtuous cycle is set in motion. While all three are important, we will use the matrix in Figure 8.4 to focus on only the first two pillars given their relatively greater importance in the prevention of financial crises.

Understanding What Regulatory Standards Are Needed

The first step in resetting a regulatory regime is to understand precisely what changes are required either as precautionary measures to avoid future crises or to restore needed confidence in the aftermath of a financial crisis. We will review the first two pillars along each one of the three levels of our crisis prevention safety net.

1. Competition and Market Conduct   *In the first pillar at the first tier of our safety net, a financial institution's board of directors and senior management team play an important first-level function in setting and monitoring the vision and strategy that meets the demands of global competition and uses reputable business standards, including ethical codes of conduct.* Another part of their responsibility is to monitor compliance with regulations in spirit, rather than mechanistically or, worse yet, opportunistically. Investors increasingly demand that corporate governance policies and practices meet world standards to ensure that companies are well-run and consequently have access to the lowest possible cost of capital.

The second tier, market regulation, includes a combination of three basic elements: an effective market for corporate control; a thriving analyst community; and an active business press. An effective market for corporate control, permitting both friendly and hostile takeovers by competitors and new entrants, is perhaps the single most effective mechanism to supervise a thriving and healthy financial system. Market participants play an important role in rewarding winners and penalizing losers. Collectively, they influence the cost of capital, help decide who can acquire whom, govern the ability to expand into new markets, and determine who should exit the financial system.

Market indicators like market-to-book ratios and debt pricing can also signal a company's strengths and shortcomings well in advance of official government data, examination reports, and supervisory actions. The investor and analyst community, both local and global, plays an important role in commenting on financial trends and individual companies' competitive performance and future prospects. Standard and Poor's, for example, launched a corporate governance rating system in 2001, which provided an overall score of one to ten on four key dimensions of corporate governance, and is based on a rigorous, in-depth analysis. In fact, many equity analysts are now assessing companies' corporate governance practices. The business press also helps by reporting on individual institutions and by reaching consumers who may not have easy access to analyst reports.

The third tier, government regulation, is important as well to protect against potential market gaps and failures. Governments typically set basic entry requirements to obtain a financial institution license, which should include minimum equity capital requirements and "fit and proper" standards for the new management team. There should also be stringent standards for ongoing business practices such as insider dealings, ethical and fraudulent behavior, and anticompetitive practices (e.g., collusive pricing). Finally, the government also should set an explicit exit policy to resolve weak and failing institutions. These policies include certain liquidity and solvency requirements and should also include transparent intervention standards so that all stakeholders understand when the institution is at risk and what are the stepped-up penalties when a takeover is imminent.[16]

2. Prudential Supervision and Surveillance *The second regulatory pillar in Figure 8.4 is risk management and prudential supervision. At the first tier, self-governance comes again in the form of world-class corporate governance.* Hiring the right managers, putting stringent risk management policies and procedures in place (e.g., having a separate and independent credit review committee), having an independent internal auditor reporting directly to the board audit committee, and making risk profiles completely transparent through effective disclosure to investors and the markets are just some of the critical elements needed for effective self-governance.

Market supervision also counts significantly in the second tier. Capital markets in particular are demanding and play a critical role in determining a company's cost of debt and equity capital. Market indicators and signals are also useful for counterparty and other business decisions. Credit rating agencies, loan and deposit pricing reports, and investment analysts again play an effective market review role that commands the attention of senior management and boards of directors. External auditors have an important function to ensure that companies and investors have accurate and timely data with which to make informed business decisions.

Significant market incentives and penalties exist, contributing equally to overall market discipline on management. Strong performance gets rewarded and reinforced in a higher share price or lower cost of capital, while poor performance is reflected in lower prices and higher financing costs. Market incentives come in the form of higher market capitalization and greater acquisition currency, and therefore earn the right to be the natural owner of a larger pool of customers. Market penalties include lower market capitalization and greater degrees of difficulty in making acquisitions and growing. Market discipline can be faster, better, and cheaper than government regulation alone.[17] In the final analysis, the prudent conduct of business leads to market rewards.

To augment the first two tiers in prudential supervision and surveillance, the government plays a key role in supervising risk management at financial institutions at the third and final level (e.g., capital adequacy, asset quality, management capabilities, earnings quality and quantity, liquidity, and risk management systems and controls). In many emerging markets, where market supervisory mechanisms are nonexistent or ineffective, there is a premium on ensuring that government supervision is aligned with best global practices. Minimum bank capital standards set and refined periodically by the Bank for International Settlements (BIS) in Basel, Switzerland, are an accepted practice; the new Basle II standards are being phased in over a period of several years and their impact will be closely observed. Offsite reporting between onsite exams and interim analyses are utilized as well. Timely enforcement of regulatory orders and effective judicial remedies are other important parts of comprehensive government supervision.[18]

Government supervision can also include a set of regulatory incentives to reward good market performers and punish poor ones. For example, strong market players can be granted expedited product-approval processes, easier acquisition procedures, less intrusive examinations, lower examination fees, and lower deposit insurance premiums. Conversely, explicit penalties can be established against weaker players who pose a potential threat to the financial system. Such penalties can include a more rigorous and intense approval process for new products, rejection of acquisition applications until management is deemed to be fit and proper and in full control, more intense onsite and offsite examination, and higher deposit insurance premiums to compensate for a higher risk profile.

■ ■ ■

The three pillars of financial sector regulation and supervision can be analyzed across our three-tier safety net to design the appropriate standards and safeguards for each country to prevent future crises and help to support a return to sustained economic growth. Striking the appropriate balance among the various components of this matrix approach is a key success factor—before, during, and after a crisis. Finding an appropriate mix of standards and safeguards may take the private and public sectors several months of working together during a crisis and even years afterwards to implement fully and effectively.

BUILDING AN EFFECTIVE LEGAL FOUNDATION

At the base of effective and efficient financial system safeguards is a strong legal system. During the 1990s, while foreign bankers and asset managers were pouring billions of dollars into emerging markets, the law was not much on their minds. With currencies relatively stable, exports booming, and asset prices appreciating, why worry about the legal system that was hosting all that money?

The Asian financial panic of 1997 brought that complacency to an abrupt end. Many foreign lenders and shareholders stumbled upon an awkward reality: When a deal comes undone between arm's-length, often-anonymous parties, the law is the only protection that an investor may have. Foreign and domestic creditors turned their attention to the legal remedies available. In many crisis-stricken countries, they found those remedies weak and lacking. For example, the speed and efficiency with which distressed assets could be managed and redeployed into the real economy hinged on the effectiveness and efficiency of bankruptcy laws and procedures. Attracting needed capital and skills to manage failing companies requires changing old laws on corporate control to facilitate market solutions and reduce official resolution costs; see Appendix 8.3: The Discipline of the Market for Corporate Control: Issues for CEOs.

Why Law Is a Critical Foundation for the Future

An open, market-oriented financial system cannot flourish without a robust legal system. That is as true for capital markets as it is for foreign direct investment (FDI). In either case, the absence of close-knit ties between savers and borrowers demands that an objective entity referee the disputes between them. Therefore, building a modern financial system without shoring up the legal foundation is pointless.

For a legal system to be effective, we have found that it must ultimately rest upon three basic pillars of law. First, the content of the laws themselves is critical. A market-oriented financial system cannot function without well-drafted, transparent, and neutral statutes and codes for general business law, creditor rights, and financial transactions. Second, the laws must be effectively administered. Without sound administration, written laws are little more than words that have no practical impact if they cannot be implemented. Last, laws must provide protection against the state. In any modern economy, the state's hand can be everywhere. Consequently, there must be curbs against its abuse by ensuring adequate judicial review.

A financial system then can be judged against three goals: ability to attract capital from savers for business investment; ability to allocate it to the most efficient uses (distributing risk to the most efficient risk bearers); and minimizing the overall costs of those transactions. Law is central to achieving all three objectives. It is the private agreements between market participants—and their enforcement and dispute resolution mechanisms—that are the foundation behind modern finance.

Law's chief role in market-driven finance is to govern conflicts among private parties: creditors and debtors, owners and corporations. To do so, law must make clear who owns what (property rights), protect property against theft and destruction (criminal and tort law), and provide rules to govern and enforce private agreements and conflicts that arise. The law must also settle claims with efficiency and dispatch.

The empirical record confirms our view that a well-functioning legal regime is critical to a nation's financial health. Our research shows that deeper capital markets are correlated with higher GDP per capita, but the legal system is the only statistically significant explanatory factor. If you want to build a robust financial system, you *must* have a strong legal system. The world's leading international financial centers—New York and London—have one, based on common law. McKinsey analyzed the impact of various factors on the depth of capital markets in forty-four countries (depth was defined as total public bond and stock market value, divided by GDP). Besides the size and liquidity of public debt markets, legal protection for investors proved the *only* significant factor.[19]

The cost of a poor legal system goes beyond weak financial development to slow economic growth overall. If the cost of doing business is higher because the rule of law is absent, less business gets done and growth consequently lags. The World Bank estimates that inadequate legal systems have imposed huge costs on Latin America, for instance. According to their modeling, a strong legal system would boost economic growth per capita in Argentina by 2 percent a year, Brazil by 1.5 percent, and Bolivia by more than 3 percent.[20]

For a financial system that has fallen into crisis, the injury of legal failure is even more stark. A lethargic legal system prolongs a crisis with higher ultimate costs. Since 1997 in some Southeast Asian countries, for example, NPLs have festered as debtors hide behind opaque, feeble legal proceedings. The result is to scare off domestic and foreign investors, who will send their capital to more attractive investments in more inviting locations, just as CalPERS has done in exiting some countries in Southeast Asia.

The law must also do more than enforce private agreements with speed and efficiency. It must ensure that the state itself acts within the law, that state officials use their power in a manner that is neutral, fair, and pursuant to the goals of state policy. The law does so chiefly by constraint. It confines administrative policy and decisions to predefined limits and procedures (e.g., striking down a regulator's decision where he has exceeded his power or mandate). It halts uncompensated government seizures of private property (i.e., expropriation). Moreover, it suppresses political corruption—namely, by guaranteeing an independent, fair-minded judiciary and regulatory bureaucracy. In many countries, the judicial system needs to exert even greater pressure against corruption in the future.

What Standards Must a Legal Regime Achieve?

Just as a city needs its power grid, a market-oriented financial system needs a robust and resilient legal infrastructure. The best way to assess this infrastructure is from the perspective of those whom it serves: the private parties to a transaction. What a supplier or user of capital wants is to know in advance how the legal system will treat a business deal that, for whatever reason, falls apart. The issue is no more complex than questions such as: "Can the other parties sue? Will I win fairly? Can I collect my judgment?"

How can the investor or executive diagnose problems with the law? The answer lies in the one key function a legal system must perform for the investor: to explain how the law will treat the parties in a transaction that goes sour. To do so, the legal system must meet three standards: predictability, fairness, and efficiency.

Predictability. If the law is unpredictable, then it cannot define the investor's expectations—and he or she is thrown back into the informal, nonlegal mechanisms that do not work well in a modern economy. Often in emerging markets, the substantive law is unclear and incomplete, as with Chinese bankruptcy law. Or the judges are poorly trained, as in Indonesia. Or local authorities simply refuse to execute court judgments from elsewhere within the same country (as with Chinese interprovincial rivalries). In any of these circumstances, the law cannot tell the investor what to expect if a deal goes wrong.

Fairness and nondiscrimination. This is a question of neutrality toward the participants. For a legal system to meet this condition, it should produce the same outcome, no matter who the parties are. Of course, in reality, no legal system is perfect. American courts on the whole are of high quality, but it is possible to find state courts biased against nonlocal businesses (which is why the U.S. Constitution guarantees foreigners a trial in a more neutral federal court).

Efficiency. To be efficient, a court system must be speedy and cost-effective. Common problems are an understaffed judiciary (as in Korea and Indonesia), or elaborate and prolonged appeals and shortages of qualified private lawyers (as in Japan).

Suppose that executives judge the legal system to be deficient based on their business perspective. What can they do? Unfortunately, there are few quick fixes. Because it is one of the most basic applications of the state's power, law is wedded to a nation's political culture. Beyond the task of rewriting some basic statutes after a crisis, the needed legal reform is also a matter of strengthening institutions (e.g., courts, lawyers' associations, legal education) as well as building a consensus in civil society supporting the basic rule of law.

As an empirical matter, there is a rough but revealing way to test a legal system: Do foreign investors willingly submit to its jurisdiction and substantive law? Even when an investor is placing money in one country, he or she may be able to withdraw any potential disputes from a suspect jurisdiction and submit them to another. Some countries forbid or encumber exiting the legal system in this way, but this in itself ought to give the investor or policy-maker a reason to be concerned. Foreigners investing in China routinely insist on arbitration clauses, for instance. Even if investors trust the judges of one jurisdiction (for example, Korea), they may still opt to apply the substantive law of another jurisdiction (for example, New York). In fact, New York and London are the preferred jurisdictions and substantive law for financial agreements worldwide whether or not American or British parties are involved.

This legal "sniff test" tells us whether there is a problem, not why. In our experience, an effective way to dig deeper is to administer a quick, simple benchmarking survey to a group of local, private lawyers and others familiar with local and foreign jurisdictions. We recommend focusing on the three pillars of law noted above. We have developed a legal benchmarking template that subdivides each pillar into constituent parts. The administration of the law, for instance, hinges on the quality and competency of three institutions—the judiciary, the regulatory bureaucracy, and the private bar. By requesting grades on each constituent part on a scale of one to five, and then aggregating the weighted figures, executives can benchmark the legal system and develop their own informed perspective of the most pressing problems.

What about the need to harmonize national laws with evolving global international standards? This is chiefly a question of aspirations. For managers interested in achieving a working domestic financial system, harmonization is helpful, but not essential. Adopting legal standards familiar to foreign investors will reduce transaction costs and allow funds to flow more freely. Yet, a country does not need to adopt U.S.- or U.K.-style practices on a wholesale basis; the financial systems of Continental Europe have fared decently without it. As long as investors believe the local system to be reliable, fair, predictable, and protective of their rights, then investors will tolerate some legal differences.

■ ■ ■

In summary, the private sector has an undeniable self-interest in fully understanding and helping to drive the crisis prevention standards and safeguards being implemented at the national and global levels. In fact, there are initiatives that executives can take across the first two tiers of our three-tier crisis prevention safety net that not only can enhance their own value but also put them in a superior long-term position to weather the next financial storm.

Moreover, the private sector also can work with the public sector to ensure that the regulatory and supervisory policies at the third tier include the most effective set of market-enhancing standards and safeguards possible, particularly with respect to financial sector regulation. Strengthening standards and systemic safeguards are urgent tasks for everyone, but, as we explain in the final chapter, we also believe strongly that those who have the greatest self-interest can do even more to help build a new, market-based global financial architecture to help prevent future crises.

APPENDIX 8.1: Sixteen Elements of Good Corporate Governance

Drawing upon the work of the corporate governance team in McKinsey's Global Organization and Leadership Practice, as well as other useful codes for corporate governance (e.g., ICGN, IIF, OECD), we have identified sixteen elements of good corporate governance that we typically analyze in the course of our client work. Best practices include:

Dispersed ownership structure and protection of shareholder rights
1. **Dispersed ownership.** Although the presence of a large or majority block-holder is not necessarily a negative governance issue, a more dispersed ownership structure normally tends to be more attractive to investors. Most important, a company should have no single shareholder or group of shareholders who have privileged access to the business or excessive influence over the decision-making process.
2. **Transparent ownership.** A company's actual ownership structure should be transparent, providing adequate public information on breakdown of shareholdings, identification of substantial/majority holders, disclosure

on director shareholdings, cross and pyramid holdings, and management shareholdings.

3. **One share/one vote.** A company should offer one share/one vote to all of its shareholders, and have only one class of shares. All shareholders should receive equal financial treatment, including the receipt of an equitable share of profits.

4. **Anti-takeover defenses.** The company should not have any share-, capital-, or board-related anti-takeover defenses.

5. **Meeting notification.** Shareholders should be notified at least twenty-eight days prior to each general shareholder meeting to allow overseas investors to participate, and online participation should be available for shareholders.

6. **Other rights.** Shareholders should enjoy other rights, such as the receipt of an equitable share of profits and equal treatment when shares are repurchased.

Independent corporate boards and committee structure

7. **Board size.** The board should be neither too large nor too small. Experience suggests that the optimal board size is from nine to twelve members.

8. **Limits on inside directors.** Less than one-half of the directors should be executives of the company.

9. **Independent directors.** More than one-half of the directors should be independent, nonexecutive outsiders without any other links to the company (e.g., no consulting contracts, no cross-shareholder arrangements).

10. **Written board guidelines.** A company should have its own written corporate governance rules that clearly describe the board's responsibilities. Based on these rules, directors and executives should be fairly remunerated and motivated to ensure the success of the company.

11. **Board committees.** The board of a company should also appoint independent committees to carry out critical functions such as auditing, internal controls, and top management compensation and development.

Frequent and credible disclosure and transparency

12. **Disclosure.** At a minimum, a company should provide disclosure on financial and operating performance; business operations and competitive position; corporate charter, bylaws, and corporate mission; and board member backgrounds and their basis of remuneration.

13. **Accounting standards.** A company should use an internationally recognized accounting standard (U.S. GAAP, U.K. GAAP, or IFRS) for both annual and quarterly reporting.

14. **Independent audit.** A company should perform an annual audit using an independent and reputable auditor reporting directly to the board committee.
15. **Broad disclosure.** A company should offer multiple channels of access to its information, including both online and offline access. Information should be in both the local language and English.
16. **Timely disclosure.** Information should be disclosed in a timely manner to conform to standards at the listing stock exchange.

APPENDIX 8.2: Singapore's Development as an International Financial Center

In late 1997, while the Asian financial crisis was raging all around Singapore, the central bank, known as the Monetary Authority of Singapore (MAS), saw an opportunity and made a fundamental strategic decision to make Singapore an attractive financial center. To the financial community, Singapore was literally an island of stability in large part due to the tough, highly principled regulation of its financial institutions. Within two years, Singapore was well on its way to becoming a major financial center, rivaling Hong Kong as the leading financial center in Asia.

Much of the success that Singapore experienced was due to the unique vision of senior government and business leaders, the subsequent leadership demonstrated to implement that vision, the embracement of global standards and willingness to jettison sacred cows, the rigorous, multi-year project approach they took, and the way in which executives from the private sector were leveraged to drive many of the recommendations.

Deputy Prime Minister Lee Hsieng Long personally led this far-reaching initiative and used much of his political capital, putting his own reputation as the head of the MAS on the line. He established a Financial Sector Review Group (FSRG) that led that change. Private sector working groups each focused on a set of initiatives including general debt issuance, equity markets, fund management, treasury/risk management, corporate finance/venture capital, insurance/reinsurance, and cross-border electronic banking; and they had a secretariat from the MAS to support their deliberations. An actual diagnostic, benchmarking Singapore against the leading global centers and then the regional centers, and a strategy study were also commissioned. After a period of six months the deputy prime minister announced the new strategy, together with a set of implementing initiatives and overall milestones.

Within a year Singapore had a well-functioning debt market with some international players, such as the World Bank, raising tranches of debt in

Singapore dollars. Singapore's commitment to issue a series of long-range debt securities (e.g., with term structures of ten, fifteen, twenty years)—despite having a current budget surplus—was critical to success. This debt issuance created a yield curve to ensure that there would be a reference point (i.e., risk-free price) to price other more complex products like high-yield debt, which had great, untapped demand in the region. For years, many countries in Asia have studied, debated, and analyzed the benefits of establishing a debt market, but only Singapore has made real progress from a very small base.

Similarly, recognizing the crucial importance of asset managers in driving much of the related activity in financial centers and attracting service providers such as investment banks, the MAS aggressively pursued the top asset managers in the world to locate their Asian headquarters in Singapore. By 2000, Singapore ranked third behind Japan and Hong Kong in terms of percent of assets managed in Asia, with a compound annual growth rate of 29 percent from 1997 to 2000.

Singapore prodded its local banks to prepare for greater competition with foreign players, opening up the market progressively and encouraging in-market consolidation. They brought in a highly respected, foreign banking executive from JP Morgan, John Olds, to revolutionize and run the largely government-owned bank—Development Bank of Singapore (DBS). They opened up the legal profession to foreign firms to help upgrade skills in financial services, and they merged their cash and derivatives exchanges into a single equity exchange under the leadership of a foreign-experienced CEO brought in from the U.S. The speed, openness, and commitment to becoming an established financial center were truly remarkable, as have been the results so far.

One of the key success factors from our perspective was that Singapore, under the leadership of the deputy prime minister and the MAS, effectively leveraged the private sector by creating multiple private sector committees to recommend changes on the best way to promote Singapore as a financial center. The recommendations of the private sector committees were completely transparent and published in simple tables in *The Straits Times*. With the help of external consultants, the MAS also interviewed more than a hundred intermediaries and investors in and outside Asia to assess their competitive position and develop their recommendations. This reliance on market input and private sector advice throughout the process was the only guarantee that intermediaries would embrace them.

APPENDIX 8.3: The Discipline of the Market for Corporate Control: Issues for CEOs

By Mark Wiedman

In developed capital markets, with dispersed shareholdings of most major firms, a powerful device for driving senior managers to perform is the market for corporate control—the prospect that some investor(s) may buy control of a company, bring in new management, and take charge over important strategic decisions. In markets that have effective corporate control, the ever present prospect of being replaced helps to discipline managers so they are constantly finding ways to enhance shareholder value, not necessarily their own.

In many emerging markets, this market for corporate control is virtually absent. Based on our work, however, we believe that emerging market CEOs can maximize the value of their firms by operating as if such a market existed. By applying the same discipline on themselves that an outside raider would exert where an effective market for corporate control did exist, CEOs will be forced to focus on critical strategic issues such as which businesses add value and truly belong in their portfolio and which businesses should be either fixed, restructured, or sold.

A DISCIPLINE FOR EMERGING MARKET CEOS

Investors will try to buy the valuable asset of control if they think that they, or their hired managers, can run a company better than the incumbent management. Some managers may be holding on to underperforming businesses, investing fresh capital in unpromising projects, or failing to seize profitable opportunities.[1] New ownership, however, can bring new skills or strategy, or a value-creating fit with other businesses in the investors' portfolio. Investors' typical tools are mergers and acquisitions, divestitures and spinoffs, and leveraged and management buyouts.

Such effective markets are lacking in many emerging market countries. Family ownership dominates; shareholdings are concentrated in a few hands; and laws typically inhibit control transfers to protect incumbent management. Isolated instances exist, often involving foreign buyers. In these countries, the basic foundation for an effective market for corporate control simply does not exist: a deep capital market; dispersed shareholdings; laws that support the maximization of shareholder value; and the presence of investors willing and able to exert control.

Despite the absence of a market for corporate control, emerging market CEOs should not overlook its lessons. Global capital and product markets increasingly demand that emerging market CEOs make sure they own and control only those businesses where they can maximize value creation. If a company in Chile wishes to tap international capital, it must provide returns in line with the other global opportunities investors enjoy. The same holds true for global consumers, who will demand the best value.

Put simply, CEOs should develop their corporate strategy as if an effective market for corporate control already existed. Whether in Boston or Bangkok, CEOs must decide where they, their management team, and their businesses possess a distinctive advantage in creating value. What are their aspirations? What are their capabilities? Where can they best turn those capabilities into revenue-generating intangible and tangible assets? When do you change management? Do you ever seek a buyer? What businesses should they hold? Buy? Divest?[2]

The answers for an emerging market CEO may differ from those for his or her peers in a developed market. Emerging market firms cannot rely on a full set of market institutions, like liquid public offerings and deep private equity pools, or a flexible labor market for skilled workers. The strategic questions that all CEOs must answer, however, remain the same.

BUILDING THE FOUNDATIONS FOR A ROBUST MARKET

Shareholders are not the only potential beneficiaries of an effective market for corporate control. The benefits for an emerging market nation can be even greater. The discipline it imposes on corporate managers ensures that they deploy scarce capital as efficiently as possible. Faster economic growth and higher standards of living are the result. As Alan Greenspan, chairman of the U.S. Federal Reserve Board of Governors, recently said, "Such changes in corporate leadership have been relatively rare but, more often than not, have contributed to a more effective allocation of corporate capital."[3]

To realize the full financial potential of a market for corporate control, CEOs and policymakers need to build or strengthen its underlying prerequisites in three key areas:

1. Develop or link to efficiently functioning capital markets with publicly traded shares and transparent financial disclosure
2. Ensure a market-oriented legal framework that encourages maximizing shareholder value, with strict fiduciary responsibilities for directors and managers, and laws that allow takeovers despite management obstructions
3. Welcome the presence of investors willing and able to exert control to extract higher shareholder value from companies under their control.

CHAPTER 9

Designing a New, Market-Driven Financial Architecture

We are convinced that the stakes in financial crises are now higher for everyone—investors, financial intermediaries, corporates, and individuals—than they were even a few years ago. While global financial markets will continue to grow in importance and evolve in ways that provide great benefits to society, they also unfortunately have unintended and sometimes negative consequences that manifest themselves occasionally as financial crises.

Because crises can be devastating financially and linger for years, the private sector needs to be better prepared to manage in the event of future financial crises. As we argue in *Dangerous Markets,* we believe that there is a great deal more by way of prevention that individual companies and firms can do on their own in anticipation of financial crises, since many of the underlying causes are at the microeconomic level, not just the macroeconomic level, as we explained in Chapter 3.

International organizations such as the World Bank, IMF, and BIS historically have played a vital public sector role in financial crises, and have made important contributions to promote higher standards and new safeguards through the financial and technical assistance they provide. Despite these efforts, we believe frankly that market forces have overtaken them and will continue to diminish the impact that they can expect to have alone in the future. Largely missing from the discussion table is the private sector. Many thoughtful observers have been frustrated at the lack of progress to date by individual governments and multilateral organizations. Moreover, based on our observations of what is going on around the world as we write this book, we believe that now is the time for private sector action, before the next wave of financial storms hits.

In this final chapter, we sketch one way that the private sector's agenda and a new market-driven financial architecture could evolve, building significantly on some of the varied private sector initiatives and market mechanisms already in place.

More specifically, we think that some version of a global, member-driven, market-based self-governing organization (SGO) of investors and intermediaries should be considered and debated within the private sector. Since it is the private sector that drives huge amounts of capital flows, it is the private sector that should drive and monitor standards and safeguards across multiple dimensions—not just corporate governance, but also transparency, capital market integrity and surveillance, effective markets for corporate control, regulatory efficiency and effectiveness, accounting, business conduct, investor protection, and other areas that are in the greatest self-interest to members. This private sector SGO could also play an important clearinghouse function for information, the ratings of companies and even countries, and the transfer and development of necessary skills to improve risk management and prevent future crises.

RECOGNIZING THE LIMITATIONS OF CURRENT STANDARDS AND APPROACHES

There certainly is no shortage of international standards for financial stability today, some of which are useful building blocks for the kind of private sector initiative that we advocate. Many of these international standards have been advanced by the international public sector—for example, the IMF, BIS, and OECD—at the country and macroeconomic levels. One of the best sources for a broad set of these standards is the catalogue of the twelve main standards prepared by the Financial Stability Forum (FSF)[1] (see Appendix 9.1: FSF Compendium of Standards).[2] While not all of these standards have direct applicability in the private sector, such as the IMF's Code of Good Practices on Transparency in Monetary and Financial Policies, others clearly do. For example, the BIS bank capital adequacy standards and the OECD's Principles of Corporate Governance are useful building blocks for crisis prevention standards in the future.

From our perspective, however, there are three major problems with these public standards from a pure prevention perspective. First, many of them are not universally accepted: Not all countries buy into the standards, while others only pay lip service to them. Second, many of them fail to address some of the underlying causes of crises in the microeconomy and the financial sector. Third, many of these standards are well-intentioned, but they lack any means of uniform accountability and practical enforcement—in other words, they have no teeth. Had the proper standards been in place universally and enforced on a global basis in both developed and emerging markets, in our view there would have been fewer crises of lesser intensity over the past decade.

Most of the public organizations that have crisis prevention as part of their perceived mission unfortunately cannot keep pace with the world's financial markets. For the most part, these large bureaucracies have laudable objectives to promote financial stability or to rid the world of poverty, but they are not focused strictly on preventing financial crises.

Despite their good intentions, these multilateral institutions are often far removed from markets, from customers, from investors, and from creditors—that is, they are far removed from those most directly affected when a financial storm sweeps across the landscape. Market participants, if they can agree, have a much closer vantage point from which to set their own standards of conduct and behavior. They also have a greater sense of urgency and higher degree of self-interest in ensuring that markets work effectively and efficiently without the kind of market interruptions that financial crises imply. As we have said, they also control most of the capital flows.

From our perspective, the private sector is a more important factor in global financial flows than multilateral organizations or governments, a point that George Soros, among others, has illustrated. Consequently, the real, demonstrable power to manage financial systems and contain crises is shifting from governments, and by extension the multilateral organizations, to market participants. This fact is a direct result of the relentless advance of globalization and the rapid erosion of national economic and financial sovereignty that we discussed in Chapter 2. Governments and international organizations such as the IMF and World Bank increasingly will be less able to contain or manage financial crises in the future.

Since it is the private sector that has the raw financial power—roughly $35 trillion in the hands of large investors in 2002—it is the private sector that needs to take a more visible and vocal leadership role to ensure that the proper standards and safeguards are in place globally and then work to drive those same standards down to the national level.

Moreover, as we explained in Chapter 3, the sources of crises are found more in countries' microeconomic behavior than in their macroeconomic performance, and neither governments nor international financial organizations have much of a track record at this level. Companies in the real sector can quietly destroy value, in part because no entity systematically collects and reports data on the health of critical sectors in the real economy. The capital markets may not be developed enough to reward and punish managers to respond appropriately. Banks, which should not be lending to certain companies due to their lack of creditworthiness, are weakened as a result, and NPLs grow undetected. Boards of directors sometimes fail to provide rigorous shareholder oversight, while bank regulators often look the other way or are caught off-guard when problems arise.

Crises, therefore, are allowed to build up largely because of a lack of transparency, standards, and early market discipline on laggard companies and economies. Thus, new market mechanisms are required to help make needed corrections sooner and consequently minimize the economic impact of future crises: better information flows between suppliers and users of funds, and their intermediaries; more effective ratings of companies, their corporate governance, and the countries in which they operate along multiple new dimensions; and more effective markets for pricing and corporate control that allow troubled companies to be taken over and turned around before crisis conditions fully emerge.

ENHANCING THE PRIVATE SECTOR'S ROLE IN SETTING STANDARDS TO REDUCE THE RISK OF FUTURE CRISES

Fortunately, we are beginning to see signs that the private sector is starting to step up to fill in the gaps. Of greatest initial interest, perhaps, are those existing standards where the private sector already has played a lead role and had some impact on crisis prevention and management. Take corporate governance for example. Manuals to help guide board members have been around for years in developed markets, which can serve as models for emerging market executives.[3] Most of the standards for good corporate governance apply universally, but obviously some elements may have to be tailored to specific individual country situations.

The International Corporate Governance Network (ICGN), for example, whose members in 2002 have more than $12 trillion in assets under management, has been dedicated since its founding in 1995 to advancing corporate governance practices in the private sector. ICGN has amplified the OECD code by promulgating its own ten standards and then developing a practical working kit to aid with their implementation: (1) corporate objectives; (2) communication and reporting; (3) voting rights; (4) corporate boards; (5) corporate remuneration policies; (6) strategic focus; (7) operating performance; (8) shareholder returns; (9) corporate citizenship; and (10) corporate governance implementation.[4]

Moreover, it is not just large investors that have recognized the importance of corporate governance as a required standard. Coming on top of the sharp fall in net private capital flows from the developed world to the emerging markets—from $169 billion in 2000 to $115 billion in 2001—the Institute of International Finance (IIF), a global trade association of the largest banks in the world, issued its own corporate governance guidelines that closely track the ICGN work and which it believes are critical to strengthening capital flows to emerging markets in the future.[5] We wholeheartedly agree with the IIF assessment of the great need to link capital flows with sound corporate governance and other needed reforms.

While the IIF code will look familiar to many observers, what is striking at this critical time in global finance is the fact that this leading group of international financial providers has stepped up with its own road map for securities regulators, stock exchanges, corporate boards of directors, and management teams in emerging markets, where many of its members are significant providers of financial services. Among other things, the IIF code advocates actions to "strengthen minority shareholder rights, enhance the responsibility of boards of directors in monitoring the decision-making authority of corporate managers, and increase transparency and disclosure to ensure adherence to internationally recognized public accounting standards," according to IIF Managing Director Charles Dallara.[6]

CalPERS, as we discussed in Chapter 8, has gone one step further by pulling out of several Southeast Asian markets because these countries do not meet its criteria on transparency and market discipline, among other factors. On one level, this is just a single company attempting to exert market discipline in recalcitrant countries that fail to meet its explicit standards, but on another level this action is a strong signal to other market participants to beware of investing in those countries until standards are enhanced and safeguards upgraded. While CalPERS is relatively small in emerging markets, its action does exemplify a new attitude on the part of large global institutional investors and will send clear signals to others. Of course, just how much this kind of action coalesces to more proactive and collective activities by major providers and intermediaries of funds remains to be seen.

Because the stakes are so high, the private sector has an undeniable self-interest and should play a lead role in preventing future crises by actually helping to design a new, market-driven financial architecture that acts as a safety net for the global economy. In Chapters 4 through 7, we explained how private sector executives could do more individually on behalf of their shareholders to anticipate, prepare, manage, survive, and ultimately prosper when a financial storm strikes—one of our recurring themes throughout *Dangerous Markets*. In Chapter 8, we reviewed how individual companies could work to strengthen the standards that govern their competitive conduct and industry structures.

What Standards and Safeguards Do We Need?

If there are some basic standards in place today but little accountability and no real enforcement, what more can the private sector do to ensure effective safeguards, ones that reward good conduct and appropriately discipline bad behavior?

As we stated in Chapter 1, we can imagine a set of high-integrity, market-oriented standards for business conduct that would become the cornerstone of a new financial architecture embraced by the major global providers and intermediaries of funds. We can imagine a greater harnessing of private sector energy on nonlegal, market standards—such as business conduct and financial reporting—that are enforced by greater transparency and the use of existing and new market mechanisms. Legal and quasi-legal rules at either the national or international level—such as requirements for bank closures and bankruptcy codes—are also important, and the private sector can intervene here as well to effect needed change to conform legal and regulatory regimes to new market realities.

Focusing on the voluntary, nonlegal market standards is where the private sector could bring the most resources to bear and potentially have the highest impact. Therefore, that is the area where we would recommend that executives set their priorities and strategy and focus their resources to establish high standards—a company's "ticket to play"—across several dimensions noted below. While it would be up to the leaders to set the precise standards and safeguards and then agree on their details and the mechanics to implement them, we can imagine an agenda that starts with the following items to review and prioritize along the three-level safety net we described in the last chapter.

1. Self-Governance

World-Class Corporate Governance   Codes for sound corporate governance are already well-established. International organizations, such as the ICGN or IIF, and even national groups, such as the Thai Institute of Directors, are operating and using them. These groups should be encouraged more actively, to ensure that the fundamentals of sound corporate governance are applied universally, even though local nuances may have to be recognized. We applaud Standard & Poor's recent move into the business of rating corporate boards, for example. Such actions will help to drive and further enforce these standards, and turn "words" into entrenched "behaviors." Experienced board directors should play more of a role in training and coaching newly formed or reconstituted boards of directors.

Prudent Business Ethics   Industry codes of ethical behavior for fair and open competition and rules against price fixing and fraudulent behavior are necessary for effective market operations. For example, bribery and corrupt practices is an area where investors could develop their own set of standards to be applied globally and then work with national officials and companies in specific countries to enact them into national laws that are enforced by public authorities. In its most recent *World Development Report,* the World Bank makes the case quite clearly in our view: Higher levels of corruption are associated with lower levels of growth and lower levels of per capita income. Relatively "cleaner" countries attract more investment funds than "dirty" ones.[7]

Transparency   More work can be done to ensure that pertinent market information gets to fund suppliers, intermediaries, and end users on a timely basis. Information that is not easily available today on a comparable basis—

such as corporate sector value creation/destruction, cash flow calculations, interest coverage ratios, and key signaling rates (interbank, deposit rates, bond prices)—should be more transparent to investors and creditors. We can even imagine rating agencies for the accuracy and completeness of user-friendly financial statements (quarterly and annual reports), a service line that goes well beyond what the U.S. Securities and Exchange Commission currently requires.

2. Market Standards and Supervision

Market Integrity and Capital Market Development   Standards for the development of local capital markets, stock exchange listings and de-listings, market integrity, investor protection, and efficient links to global financial markets, similar to the ones we outlined in Chapter 8, need to be in place to ensure access to capital at the lowest possible cost. We are excited by the prospects we see developing in Italy's STAR exchange for high-quality, mid- and small-cap stocks, and Brazil's Novo Mercado within the Bolsa de Valores de São Paulo (BOVESPA), which are designed to become a higher-quality, premium valuation marketplace within existing exchanges for companies that meet tougher requirements for corporate governance, transparency, and liquidity.

Effective Markets for Corporate Control   Many countries lack an effective market for corporate control, where publicly traded companies can be bought and sold relatively freely and in a way that does not amount to market abuse, as a means of replacing management teams that are not serving their shareholders' best interests. An effective market for corporate control allows natural owners with the right skills, management talent, and capital to extract higher value on behalf of investors. The ability to do hostile takeovers is also a minimum required condition, even if the private sector has to drive needed legal changes at the local level to ensure that the proper degrees of corporate freedom are available.

Accounting   International financial reporting standards already exist in addition to various national accounting standards, which can vary greatly from country to country, making global comparisons difficult. More certain and effective standards are needed in critical areas such as definitions of nonperforming loans, meaningful disclosure of real risks (on and off the balance sheet), and cash flow analysis, among other areas.

3. Government Regulation

Minimum Entry Licensing   The ability for fund suppliers and financial intermediaries to enter the financial markets in any significant way should be subject to certain minimum and uniform standards overseen by the appropriate national supervisors. These entry requirements include minimum capital levels to operate and, more importantly, requirements for management to meet tough "fit and proper" tests to do business nationally or globally.

Bankruptcy and Exit Conditions for Failing Companies   Failing and failed companies should be forced to exit the market in an expeditious and orderly way. For banks, a swift and certain administrative process is needed to resolve insolvent companies that pose a threat to their shareholders and/or depositors and taxpayers, either through sales, merger, or liquidation. For nonbanks, an equally swift and certain bankruptcy code for voluntary and involuntary resolution of troubled corporates is needed on a globally accepted basis.

For example, just as the IMF's first deputy managing director, Anne Krueger, has advocated a mechanism for addressing sovereign bankruptcy,[8] we see a role for a global corporate bankruptcy code within the private sector. In the case of both sovereign and corporate bankruptcies, the growing number and type of creditors make restructuring agreements difficult to achieve. Different creditor motivations (e.g., the long-term relationship of a bank versus the short-term goal of a vulture fund) make this doubly so. Corporate restructuring difficulties arise in multi-jurisdictional cases in large part because there is no official way to compel different creditor parties to reach an agreement. Within a jurisdiction with sound bankruptcy codes, the mere presence of a court can help to compel the parties to reach agreement on their own. Within the U.S., experience shows that many creditors are motivated to agree on terms outside of court out of fear that a bankruptcy judge might impose a less attractive settlement.

On the international level, we believe the presence of a universal and enforceable bankruptcy code would have much the same effect. Reaching agreement should be easier as a result. Bankruptcy experience within a nation's borders makes it clear that quick resolution of bankruptcies is almost always in the interest of creditors and the companies themselves. With the proper support and standards in place, we believe that a global bankruptcy code could have much the same effect.

Increasing the Private Sector's Role in Setting Standards and Enforcing Safeguards

We think that global financial markets have reached a juncture in economic history similar to the time of the rebuilding of Europe and the world's financial architecture after World War II. A new, market-oriented effort would be as broad and as sweeping as the old Bretton Woods Agreement among countries, but unlike that agreement it would be designed, implemented, and monitored by the leading private sector participants with the most at risk, and enforced by current and potentially new market mechanisms, not just by nation states. To ensure fairness, self-interested, private sector leaders should come together from developed as well as emerging markets to set these standards and agree on the best way to implement them.

While the general goals would include preventing future crises, promoting financial stability, lowering the cost of capital, and promoting economic growth, the specific goals could be centered on better corporate governance, more timely and meaningful disclosure of crisis warning signs, and promoting and monitoring market integrity and investor and depositor protection.

Since the suppliers and intermediaries of funds have the most to lose when a crisis hits, it follows therefore that they also have the most to gain from crisis prevention in the long run. Our goal would be to have these self-interested parties join forces to do five things:

- **Set standards and define best practices.** First, clarify and define best practices and explicit standards by which they—and those with whom they do business such as end users, creditors, and suppliers—intend to operate and conduct themselves. These standards, for example, could be derived from the agenda outlined above and augmented as the need arises.
- **Build a private sector SGO.** Second, in a marked departure from business as usual, create a small but globally recognized, transparent, and member-driven SGO, with a small executive secretariat, that would be held accountable by its members for developing, promoting, transferring, and monitoring acceptable standards for private financial flows between private sector firms at both the national and global levels. The sharing of best practices and noncompetitive coordination among institutions to set high standards and guidelines of conduct would be an overarching objective. Helping to replicate in other countries what is going on in Italy's STAR exchange or Brazil's Novo Mercado is just one example of the important knowledge transfer role this SGO could play.
- **Transfer and develop skills.** Third, we also think that such an organization could play a critical clearinghouse role for the skills transfer and development that is needed to prevent future crises. There is a vast need for general management, risk management, legal, accounting, communications, and other skills that are required to prevent future crises. Based on our client work, we know that there is a largely untapped reservoir of talent in the form of retired and experienced executives who can play the role of coach, mentor, consultant, or board member to other companies, especially in the emerging markets. The potential for capable individuals like Frank Cahouet and Keith Smith of Mellon

Financial Corporation, Timothy Hartman of NationsBank, Brian Quinn from the Bank of England, or Patrick Hylton of Jamaica's Finsac to transfer their knowledge to other markets to help build better capabilities to avoid future crises is invaluable, and could be the start of a continuous skill-transfer effort. We find that effective knowledge transfer for critical standards such as corporate governance or asset-liability management are best carried out by knowledgeable, experienced, private sector individuals who can work with boards to make change really happen, as opposed to simply holding conferences and giving speeches.

- **Act as an information clearinghouse and rating organization.** Fourth, develop a research capability to rate both leading companies and countries on their adoption of these standards. This private sector SGO, as an information clearinghouse, would at first mostly promote transparent disclosure and encourage ratings along multiple dimensions. This role could be done internally or outsourced externally to either existing private sector companies (e.g., ratings agencies such as Standard & Poor's, Moody's, Fitch, Economist Intelligence Unit), groups of private sector players (e.g., ICGN, IIF), or new ventures.

- **Encourage more coordinated market supervision and discipline.** Greater transparency at the national and global levels (e.g., through ratings), and the subsequent market rewards or discipline that result, would be the primary "supervisory" tool—shining the spotlight on both good and unacceptable behavior. In the final analysis, these standards would be "enforced" through private sector market discipline and mechanisms, just as they are to a large degree today (e.g., access or denial to certain markets and exchanges, higher or lower risk spreads and financing costs, rejection or granting of funding with different conditions attached), but in our model the very public, global spotlight and rating function would result in better crisis prevention on an ongoing basis through more rapid corrections, resulting in lower financial costs over the long run. Such measures also would lead to a better understanding of why these actions are important for companies, regulators, and the public at large. We would expect that the biggest impact would be in those national markets and societies that do not currently have any viable alternatives to greater transparency and more accepted ratings functions.

While this may sound like an idea whose time has not yet arrived, we disagree. Now is precisely the time when the private sector needs to step up to help drive the new financial order and architecture for the twenty-first century. The private sector can act more quickly than the public sector and—assuming the right players come to the table—can frankly carry more weight given their distinct advantage in market presence. While we obviously recognize that there is an important role for the public sector to continue to play in some areas, we also strongly believe that there is great merit in having the private sector take the lead initially and work with the public sector later when necessary to ensure an optimal balance.

While internationally and nationally active companies obviously would be bound by the current laws of the countries in which they operate, we argue that there is also much they could do to promote and enforce even higher standards and safeguards, which others would—and be forced to—follow. In effect, they could set their own crisis prevention rules that in all likelihood would be superior to existing national laws.

How Can We Effectively Implement Needed Standards and Safeguards?

How can we accelerate this trend and ensure market standards and safeguards that will work to prevent future crises? In our view, those companies in the private sector with the greatest self-interest and the most at risk from future financial crises need to start analyzing the benefits and costs of some of these ideas now. We understand that the motivations of the major players are varied, complex, and not necessarily straightforward, which complicates such an initiative. We also understand the real potential for a "free-rider" effect, where nonparticipants get some of the same benefits—less dangerous markets—as participating members.

Nevertheless, from our perspective, we think the timing is right to start the discussion of creating a member-driven, private sector SGO that could be the engine driving the design of a new global financial architecture and reinforcing the required standards through its members' investment decisions. For now, we refer to it as the Financial System SGO or FSSGO. We believe the new FSSGO could build on many of the appropriate standards already in place—such as ICGN or IIF corporate governance principles—and then develop its own agenda and comprehensive set of operating standards and safeguards across our three safety net dimensions: self-governance; capital market supervision; and government regulation. We can even imagine the ICGN—representing mostly large investors—and the IIF—representing large financial intermediaries—partnering to explore the design feasibility and initial implementation of this initiative.

Moreover, there is a successful model from which we can extrapolate, even if it has to be adapted to the realities of the global financial system: There is a precedent, it has been tested for years—and it works effectively.

In the United States, the National Association of Securities Dealers (NASD) is a private sector, member SRO with the primary responsibility for protecting securities investors and market integrity. It tests and licenses all of the participants to ensure that they achieve minimum levels of market knowledge and skills; regulates the Nasdaq and American Stock Exchange; sets compliance standards including new forms of self-compliance; examines members on a regular basis; offers training and dispute resolution services to its members; and can provide other services to those with whom it contracts (e.g., information services, database management, back-room support, compliance software). It has its own privately funded budget and a relatively small staff, considering its mission of setting standards and taking the necessary enforcement steps to protect U.S. capital markets. Its members pay a nominal fee in exchange for these services.

One of the great strengths of the U.S. capital markets is the unique form of member self-regulation that is close to the markets—with high standards for market integrity and investor protection. If this kind of SRO can work at the national level and be a key element in the financial success of one of the world's financial hubs, then it stands to reason that a similar SGO can work in an amended form at the global level as well—if self-interested stakeholders want to embrace this vision, devise a strategy, make the necessary commitment, and provide sufficient resources to make it work.

There are clear differences between NASD and the FSSGO that we envision that would need to be addressed, such as NASD's mandated membership and enforcement capabilities. NASD also reports to the Securities and Exchange Commission (SEC), a U.S. government agency with the final responsibility for overseeing securities markets and their participants—including NASD. If the SEC does not like what NASD is doing or not doing, then the SEC can intervene. That direct reporting relationship to, and ultimate control by, a government agency is an obvious departure from our model. In our view, the FSSGO would not "report" to the IMF or the World Bank or any other multilateral organization for example. Instead, we believe that the market itself would be the ultimate "supervisor," with tough transparency requirements and more frequent and timely market corrections, which have the additional benefit of avoiding cultural overtones and political interference.

Properly designed, much of the FSSGO's functions would be focused on analyzing the potential warning signs of crisis—for example, monitoring and reporting value destruction by economies, industry, and companies on a quarterly basis, keeping an eye on rapid loan growth and rising funding rates by major banks (deposits and other liabilities). We can imagine the FSSGO building alliances with national private sector organizations with similar interests, such as Thailand's Institute of Directors, which has just launched a multi-year effort to rate companies and do peer comparisons for corporate governance standards. Clearly, there is a role for the FSSGO to work closely with—without being subservient to—a host of other official organizations, all of whom have responsibility for bits and pieces of crisis resolution, but lack a comprehensive view and clear mandate.

Moreover, we can imagine the FSSGO working closely with rating agencies such as Standard & Poor's, Moody's, Fitch, and others to play an important role in the development of efficient markets and market infrastructure standards at the national and global levels. Not only should these standards apply to all market participants, but we can imagine taking this to the next level in the very near term under the FSSGO with the development of more universal ratings for corporate governance and transparency—much as Standard & Poor's is starting to do today, for example—and eventually even moving to enhanced market ratings of capital adequacy and risk management systems, as well as ratings of national bank supervisory systems' adherence to the BIS core principles and national stock exchanges. Much of this could be competitively outsourced to existing or new rating agencies.

We also can imagine how this FSSGO could potentially evolve over time. While membership among leading investors and intermediaries would remain voluntary, the ticket to participate could escalate over time in line with members' wishes and the need to keep pace with rapidly evolving markets. For example, membership could evolve to a point where members had to make a greater financial or nonfinancial commitment to join and remain a member in good standing. A nonfinancial commitment could go well beyond the initial voluntary approach to include, for example: accepting binding arbitration under New York state law, as many companies do today; only doing business in countries that have been rated by the FSSGO, or its designated third party, as fully protecting minority shareholder rights; or giving up the right in advance to be sued in your home country if the local law discriminates in favor of domestic over international competitors. Moreover, as time evolves, we can imagine that credit insurance companies and other entities that hedge risks would start to set new standards at the global level, which rise above national legal standards, that not only become the de facto operating standards but also strengthen the quality of a comprehensive safety net. We can even imagine a group like this, representing a significant portion of global capital flows, ultimately providing advice and counsel to a country like Vietnam that is just now beginning to plug into the global financial system.

Getting Started

How would private sector executives start to design and establish such an SGO? Because of the urgency we see, we can imagine a meeting in the very near future, where leading fund managers and intermediaries in both the developed world and emerging markets—institutional investors and pension fund managers, commercial and investment bankers—get together to start the process. After more discussion and prior syndication, we can envision signing a binding charter membership agreement—an "admission ticket"—among like-minded fund suppliers and intermediaries, to embrace prudent standards for corporate governance, accounting, transparency, and bankruptcy—to name a few priority areas where a consensus could form. Part of this voluntary agreement would also have to confirm a high-quality, committed management team and permanent funding for a small organization that would become the FSSGO. Measures would have to be taken to ensure that entry was not restricted and the FSSGO did not behave as a cartel.

From this point, the FSSGO would start its work to gain agreement on further standards and safeguards across all levels of the crisis safety net, identify the market incentives and penalties, and begin to build a system of transparency and market surveillance. Being a member of the FSSGO could be the equivalent of being a "certified, trusted global player" with the collective force of standards and safeguards standing behind all members in good standing. Whatever costs would be involved with setting up and running the FSSGO would be a small fraction of the costs that result when a financial crisis strikes. Furthermore, belonging to such an SGO could also be viewed as being a smart insurance policy to operate nationally or globally, since adherence to the organization's standards would be a key prerequisite for continuing membership in good standing in the organization. This institution could then act as a force to get the other players to the discussion table to reform the global financial system architecture, including reassessing and redefining the role and strategy of organizations like the IMF and the World Bank in light of new market realities.

Moreover, from our client experience, we know that it only would take a handful of thoughtful, forward-looking CEOs to embrace the idea and then start a process of contacting other like-minded executives to make the SGO a reality. This effort would probably start small, and grow over time, as more and more players better understood their economic self-interest in belonging to their own SGO. It could begin as a side meeting before the next gathering of the World Economic Forum in Davos, Switzerland, since many fund providers and intermediary executives attend that meeting.

The first formal meeting would launch the FSSGO officially. After several months of preparatory and logistical work by a smaller organizing and leadership group made up of globally representative investors and financial intermediaries from both developed and emerging markets, this charter meeting would be convened by the sponsoring members and begin to get down to real work. A small secretariat and senior management team would have to be approved and installed, and articles of association authorized. Membership requirements, annual dues, and a multi-year operating budget would need to be put in place. A vision statement, guiding principles, and multi-year work plan for the new organization would need to be debated and approved. A preliminary strategy that fulfills the vision and guiding principles also would need to be discussed and adopted. Working groups could then be formed that would start the process of implementing the portfolio of initiatives that would flow from the organization's new agenda items. We can imagine agenda issues such as ensuring more widespread adoption of good corporate governance, promoting better coordinated market surveillance through greater transparency, and enhancing information flows, knowledge sharing, and skill development and training, but the working group agenda obviously would be set by the members themselves based on their view of the organization's priorities and committed resources.

To achieve this high aspiration, real vision, leadership, and an aggressive strategy are required to be successful. Such an effort requires strong management will and experienced skills, just as it demands a substantial commitment of resources and time. Executives need to understand that no one is going to solve the problem of future financial crises for them, so they had better take the necessary precautions to start solving it on their own—now.

We recognize that some players may not share these interests since they profit directly from market anomalies and discrepancies in standards and practices among countries. We understand some of the obstacles of this kind of initiative, but we frankly wonder what the practical alternatives are to more universal involvement of the private sector in setting higher standards and doing more in the future to prevent and minimize the impact of financial crises.

The number of companies and countries that in our view would benefit from this approach outweighs those arbitrageurs and others who have a different set of economic interests. We are convinced, however, that those executives who understand their self-interest in lessening the impact of financial storms, strengthening a new financial architecture for sustained economic growth, and avoiding dangerous markets in the future can come together to better manage the significant economic impact of financial crises, wherever they may strike.

APPENDIX 9.1: FSF Compendium of Standards

Please refer to the Glossary for the complete names and Web site addresses of the organizations listed below. This table was taken from *International Codes and Standards to Strengthen Financial Systems*, Financial Stability Forum (April 2001).

Policy	Subject	Key standard	Issuing organization
• Macroeconomic policy and data transparency	• Monetary and financial policy transparency	• Code of Good Practices on Transparency in Monetary and Financial Policies	• IMF
	• Fiscal policy transparency	• Code of Good Practices on Fiscal Transparency	• IMF
	• Data dissemination	• Special Data Dissemination Standard/General Data Dissemination System*	• IMF
• Institutional and market infrastructure	• Corporate governance	• Principles of Corporate Governance	• OECD
	• Accounting	• International Financial Reporting Standards (IFRS)	• IASC
	• Auditing	• International Standards on Auditing	• IFAC
	• Payment and settlement	• Core Principles for Systemically Important Payment Systems	• CPSS
	• Money laundering	• The Forty Recommendations of the Financial Action Task Force	• FATF
• Financial regulation and supervision	• Banking supervision	• Core Principles for Effective Banking Supervision	• BCBS
	• Securities regulation	• Objectives and Principles for Securities Regulation	• IOSCO
	• Insurance supervision	• Insurance Supervisory Principles	• IAIS

* Economies with international capital market access are encouraged to subscribe to the more stringent SDDS, while all other economies are encouraged to adopt the GDDS.

endnotes

CHAPTER 1 Introduction to *Dangerous Markets*

1. We take a much more expansive view of a safety net to include the private sector playing an active role, especially along the first two levels. Traditionally, a financial safety net is viewed as simply providing temporary liquidity facilities through central banks in times of economic distress or deposit guarantee schemes to small savers.

CHAPTER 2 Recognizing New Global Market Realities

1. "The Man Who Broke the Bank of England—George Soros," *The London Times,* October 26, 1992.
2. Gerard Caprio and Daniela Klingebiel, *Episodes of Systemic and Borderline Financial Crises,* report published by The World Bank, October 1999 (World Bank report). For purposes of this study, our definition of a financial crisis is found in Box 2.1.
3. Gasprombank, the bank of the state-controlled gas monopoly, placed €150 million worth of two-year bonds in 2001. Alfa Bank, one of Russia's largest private sector banks, was reported to be issuing a €200 million Eurobond in 2002 as of this writing, its first foray into the capital markets since the crisis.
4. Glenn Hogarth, Ricardo Reis, Victoria Saporta, *Costs of Banking System Instability: Some Empirical Evidence,* Bank of England, 2001.
5. Ernst & Young, *Nonperforming Loan Report: Asia 2002,* November 2001.
6. This estimate reflects the difference between historical growth and the observed growth rates.
7. World Bank report, op. cit.
8. For more on the globalization of capital markets, see Lowell Bryan and Diana Farrell, *Market Unbound—Unleashing Global Capitalism* (New York: John Wiley & Sons, 1996).
9. Martin Baily, Diana Farrell, and Susan Lund, "Hot Money," *The McKinsey Quarterly,* Number 2, 2001.
10. *Capital Flows to Emerging Market Economies,* Institute of International Finance, January 30, 2002.

11. "All Bets Are Off: How the Salesmanship and Brainpower Failed at Long Term Capital," *The Wall Street Journal,* November 16, 1998; "Long Term Capital Lost $4.4 Billion," *USA Today,* October 22, 1998; Nicholas Dunbar, *Inventing Money—The Story of Long-Term Capital Management and the Legends Behind It* (New York: John Wiley & Sons, 2001).

12. Guy Longueville, "The False Start for Private Investment in Emerging Markets and the Consequences for Country Risk," *Economic Newsletter,* Banque Nationale de Paris, October 1999, p. 4.

13. *State Regulator Seizes Two Banks,* Economist Intelligence Unit Brief on Turkey, November 1, 2000.

BOX 2.1: What Is a Financial Crisis?

1. World Bank report, op. cit.

CHAPTER 3 Using Crisis Dynamics to See Growing Risks

1. Pasuk Phongpaichit and Chris Baker, *Thailand's Boom and Bust* (Silkworm Books, 1998), pages 105 and 112.

2. "Thailand: Bond Payment—Bangkok Land Asks for a Delay," *Southeast Bangkok Post,* October 29, 1997.

3. Phongpaichit and Baker, op. cit., page 316; *Thailand Annual Report,* International Monetary Fund, 1997.

4. Experts also missed the signs of crisis in Indonesia, Korea, and Malaysia. In Indonesia, Moody's maintained a BBB rating until shortly after the Thai crisis broke, at which time it was downgraded to BBB– in October 1997. It was not until after the crisis hit that the rating was further downgraded, first to BB+ and then subsequently down to CCC+– over the course of the next six months. In Korea, Moody's credit rating was A– when the crisis hit; in October 1997, for example, Moody's downgraded Korea's foreign currency for long-term bank deposits from A1 to A2 with a negative outlook. ("Moody's Lowers Korea's Ratings," *The Korea Times,* October 29, 1997.) Finally, in Malaysia, the Moody's rating was also at A– when the crisis hit, decreasing to a BBB– rating when spreads on U.S. Treasury bonds peaked in September 1998.

5. We have examined the following crises: Argentina, 2002; Ecuador, 1998; Colombia, 1998; Jamaica, 1998; Mexico, 1994; United States, 1986; Sweden, 1992; Turkey, 2001; Thailand, 1997; Korea, 1997; Indonesia, 1997; Chile, 1983; and Russia, 1998. We have also examined the situation of several other countries whose financial sectors are threatened by many of the same underlying conditions discussed in this chapter, including: China, 2001; Japan, 2002; India, 2000; Taiwan, 2000; Guatemala, 2001; Nicaragua, 2001; Venezuela, 2001; and

Honduras, 2001, as well as a few others which at the time of our reviews were in a situation intrinsically healthier and more stable: Brazil, 1999; Peru, 2000; and El Salvador, 2001.

6. Lending restrictions prior to 1985 included: restrictions on interest rates; limitations on lending to the private sector; obligations for all banks to invest in government securities and mortgage bank securities; and a ban on foreign bank participation. The removal of these restrictions was coupled with the addition of state subsidies for housing construction, increasing the demand for real estate lending.

7. "Government Lifts Restrictions on Ownership of Foreign Shares," *Reuters News,* January 19, 1989.

8. Sveriges Riksbank (Central Bank of Sweden).

9. If EBITDA stays constant but interest rates double, which can easily happen due to issues that are external to the corporate sector, then the debt-service ratio has fallen to a barely breakeven level. While such sharp interest rate rises are relatively infrequent, they are not unheard of in emerging market economies and are usually accompanied by plunging companies' EBITDA. Hence, corporate sector ICRs of 2.0 signal distress in the economy and the likelihood of major upcoming problems.

10. *Financial Statements Analysis,* Bank of Korea, Annual Information.

11. By nonperforming loans (NPLs), we typically mean loans that are ninety days past due for principal and interest, which is the standard used in the United States for the full value of the loan. One of the problems with country-by-country comparisons is that different countries use different NPL definitions. For instance, in some countries, the NPLs would be defined for the full principal of the loan, whereas in other countries only the portion past due would be reported as nonperforming. This fact also would affect the reserves that have to be created and has further consequences for the capitalization level of banks. Throughout this book, we are using NPLs as defined by each national supervisory authority. Because of the complexity involved, we have not adjusted the figures to U.S. GAAP, so NPL figures are not homogeneous in the countries covered by this book.

12. In a normally capitalized commercial bank, whose loan portfolio is also a normal proportion of total assets—70 percent—an NPL portfolio of 1 percent of total assets signifies probable write-offs of about 10 to 15 percent of bank capital.

13. McKinsey interview.

14. Superintendencia Bancaria de Colombia.

15. Stock Exchange of Thailand.

16. Bank of Thailand.

17. Degrees of overvaluation vary and are subject to differences when using different methods of calculation.

18. In most emerging markets, these foreign-denominated liabilities are often unable to be hedged, so banks and corporates alike are left exposed to currency risk.
19. Baily et al., op. cit., page 99.
20. A bank holiday is when the government closes all banks for a period of time until liquidity can be restored to the banking system. One of the most notable bank holidays occurred during the Great Depression in the United States, which eventually led to the creation of the Federal Deposit Insurance Corporation in 1933.
21. For example, both the Argentine and Russian governments defaulted on their debt.
22. They were present in Sweden, Japan, Jamaica, Thailand, and, to a lesser degree, Argentina.
23. "The Non-Performing Economy," *The Economist,* February 16–22, 2002, page 24.
24. Ernst and Young report, op cit.

BOX 3.3: Japan: The Rising Cost of Delayed Reforms

1. *Establishments and Enterprises Census,* Japan 2001; *Creditreform— Wirtschaftsdatenbank,* Destatis Unsatzsteuerstatistik; U.S. Small Business Administration; Administrative Office of the U.S. Courts, 1998.
2. "The Non-Performing Economy," op. cit.
3. Mary O'Mahoney, *Britain's Productivity Performance 1950–1996: An International Perspective,* OECD; Ministry of Labor, Japan; Bureau of Economic Analysis.
4. Ernst & Young, op. cit., page 6.
5. Japanese Bankers Association.
6. "The Non-Performing Economy," op. cit.
7. Ibid.
8. Ministry of Finance, Japan.
9. "Wrap: Ratings Agencies Warn Japan to Reform or Face Decline," *Dow Jones Capital Markets Report,* March 6, 2002.

BOX 3.4: China: Plugging into the Global Economy

1. *China Statistical Abstract, 2001.*
2. Joe Studwell, "Glossing over China's Economic Woes," *The Asian Wall Street Journal,* February 22, 2002.
3. Ernst & Young, op. cit., Executive Summary.
4. Bankscope.com; *Almanac of China's Finance and Banking.*
5. Economist Intelligence Unit.
6. Joe Studwell, op. cit.

BOX 3.5: India: Seeking a Second Generation of Reforms

1. "India Seeks New Life in 'Second Generation' Plan," *The Financial Times,* February 25, 2002.
2. "A Survey of India's Economy," *The Economist,* June 2, 2001, page 20.
3. Centre for Monitoring Indian Economy; Prowess database.
4. Reserve Bank of India.
5. Ibid.
6. Center for Monitoring Indian Economy, December 1998.
7. "A Survey of India's Economy," op cit.
8. Ibid.
9. Currently, state-owned banks are required to pay 9.5 percent interest rates on deposits for small savers. "India Seeks New Life in 'Second Generation' Plan," op. cit.

APPENDIX 3.1: Ten Warning Signs of a Financial Crisis

1. "IMF Splits over Plan for Global Warning," *The Washington Times,* May 2, 1998, page A-11.
2. Methods to estimate these parameters are described in Appendix 3.2: Estimating Value Destruction in the Economy.

APPENDIX 3.2: Estimating Value Destruction in the Economy

1. Cost of debt is a more conservative number and hence a more acceptable figure to determine if value has been destroyed or created.
2. The cost of foreign funding should be adjusted for local currency devaluation, calculated as $(1 + \$ \text{ rate})$ *multiplied by* (average exchange rate Y_n/average exchange rate Y_{n-1} (exchange rate = local currency/$; currency mismatch risk should be placed in the equity side).

CHAPTER 4   Managing the First Hundred Days

1. *The New Straits Times,* December 13, 1998.
2. Ibid.
3. McKinsey interview.
4. Ibid.
5. The lease contracts were payable in Indonesian rupiah but were set to an amount in U.S. dollars. That amount was converted at the prevailing spot rate at the time of each payment. Source: McKinsey interviews; company annual reports.
6. Figures are from company financial statements.
7. For service providers such as telecom companies with high fixed costs, the optimal pricing strategy for their outputs may be to lower prices aggressively to maintain asset utilization.

8. McKinsey interview.

9. More information on changes in the competitive landscape during financial crises is discussed in Chapter 5.

10. In Argentina, for example, delayed central bank approval of foreign exchange transactions has led to a massive reduction in business transactions during the 2002 crisis. See *The Economist,* March 2, 2002.

11. Alarko followed a similar approach with its suppliers, ensuring that they had proper warning about sales irregularities to help avoid inventory buildups and unnecessary cash outlays. Source: McKinsey interview.

12. To convince suppliers not to raise their prices, Ramayana guaranteed that volume would increase, which actually occurred. Also, as noted earlier, Ramayana received rebates from suppliers in exchange for early payments. According to one manager, gross margins would have likely fallen even further without the rebates, to somewhere around 18 to 20 percent. Meanwhile, net profit margins over the same period (1996–1998), although still high compared to peers, declined from 9.5 percent to 7.3 percent. Source: McKinsey interviews; company annual reports.

13. Doosan Group's total debt was $4.9 billion in 1996, compared to $2.1 billion in 1992. The Group includes all KSE- and KOSDAQ-listed, registered, and statutory-audited subsidiaries. Total debt includes all IBDs, i.e., short-term and long-term borrowing, CPLTD, and corporate bonds. Source: KIS-LINE.com.

14. Doosan was ranked twenty-seventh among the top thirty chaebol in terms of debt-equity ratio. Eventually, seventeen of the top thirty chaebol were either forced to change ownership or to enter court-mediated workout processes.

15. *The Korea Herald,* February 26, 2002; McKinsey interview. Today, Doosan is widely recognized in Korea as a success story and model company. In subsequent reform phases since the crisis, the company has completely restructured its balance sheet from a debt-equity ratio of almost 700 percent to less than 150 percent in 2002. Cash flow from operations has dramatically shifted from being well below the level of their interest payments (an interest cover of less than one) to well above. ROE, which had not been regularly monitored before the crisis and had in fact been negative, has increased to over 18 percent. Its portfolio of companies has gone from twenty-three (listed) affiliates to sixteen, mostly in consumer and industrial goods, and its ranking among Korea's largest conglomerates has gone from twenty-seventh to eleventh in size.

16. Obviously, this list of stakeholders is not exhaustive and managers should evaluate their own specific circumstances when creating their communications strategy. In one case, a company worked closely with the local militia during the crisis, on the theory that its protection in the event of future riots would help save local jobs. The militia conse-

quently became more protective of that company's stores whenever the specter of riots appeared.

17. *The Business Times* (Singapore), July 2, 1999.
18. Alfa Bank company reports.
19. *Business Week,* July 3, 2000.
20. *Chosun Ilbo,* March 4, 2002.
21. We discuss Roust and its response to the 1998 Russian financial crisis in further detail in Chapter 5. Elizabeth Florent-Treacy, et al., "Roustam Tariko: Russian Entrepreneur, An Iconoclast in a Maelstrom," (Fontainebleau, France: INSEAD, 2000).
22. McKinsey interview.
23. McKinsey interviews.

BOX 4.3: Preparing for a Financial Storm—While the Skies Are Still Blue

1. McKinsey interview.

APPENDIX 4.1: Painting the Picture of a Financial Crisis

1. The Korean government led a group of private insurers to partially guarantee the securitization of multiple corporate loans and bonds issued by banks and investors. In doing so, the government reduced the risk borne by financial entities in extending credit and increased resources available to the private sector. The program was successful in part because it focused on improving risk perceptions, which is often a key factor hindering credit extension.
2. Based on our experience, an additional growth area to be examined for regulatory reform in emerging market economies is labor productivity. The key insight from our work is that most emerging economies have trapped labor (and other factor) productivity at low levels as a result of poorly conceived regulations and government practices. For instance, poor land use regulations frequently discourage investment because of restrictions on land's use and sale. The "solution" to this barrier to growth is particularly compelling because it does not require extensive government funding or other financing. Managers should think creatively about how they can benefit from changes in regulation that may enhance their productivity, as well as be aware of the impact of such changes on the financial position of suppliers and customers.

APPENDIX 4.2: How Companies Can Strengthen Funding Before a Crisis

1. Charles Knight, "Emerson Electric: Consistent Profits, Consistently," *Harvard Business Review,* January–February, 1992.
2. Dollar borrowing rate is based on LIBOR plus 100 to 150 basis points. The lending rate ranged from 12 to 15 percent in 1996, and from 14 to

25 percent in 1997. Source: *Lending Rates in Financial Markets,* Bank of Thailand.

3. Bank of Korea; news clippings.

CHAPTER 5   Capturing Strategic Opportunities After the Storm

1. Figures are highs and lows for the second half of 1997, between July 1 and December 31. By the end of 1998, the Malaysian ringgit had fallen even further, losing 118 percent of its value, and the Indonesian rupiah, 589 percent. Source: Thomson Financial Datastream.
2. Market capitalization figures are averages for February 2002 and December 1994, respectively.
3. Market capitalization figure is average for February 2002.
4. Asset figure is for year-end 2001.
5. Market capitalization figure is average for September 1998. Jung-Tae Kim was officially appointed CEO of H&CB on September 1, 1998.
6. Market capitalization figure is average for October 26, 2001, the last day of trading before H&CB merged with Kookmin Bank. Average market capitalization for Kookmin in February 2002 was $12.8 billion.
7. Based on interviews and the case study of Roustam Tariko by Elizabeth Florent-Treacy, op. cit.
8. *East European Business Law,* June 1, 1994. The value of the deal was estimated at $48 million. Source: Europe Information Service.
9. The total turnover of the Zagreb Stock Exchange in 1994 was limited to $270 million. Marko Skreb, *Banking in Transition: The Case of Croatia,* National Bank of Croatia, October 1995.
10. Other investments in Central and Eastern Europe include Bulgaria, Hungary, Romania, and Slovenia.
11. Market capitalization figures are averages for December 1998 and December 1988, respectively.
12. In fact, only one bank merger had ever occurred before the 1997 crisis, and that was seen as a failure since labor law restrictions eliminated any cost savings.
13. The Newbridge-KFB deal closed on January 20, 2000. Less than a year later, in November 2000, JP Morgan and the Carlyle Group acquired a 40 percent stake in KorAm Bank for $392 million. *American Banker,* September 20, 1999; and *The Korea Herald,* November 15, 2000.
14. Figures are from the Central Bank.
15. *FALIA News,* No. 32, April 2000; and *Nikkei News,* February 11, 2002.
16. Olympus Capital set up a joint venture with KEB Credit Card Company in November 1999, investing $119 million for a 45 percent stake. Warburg Pincus took a smaller stake in LG Capital, 23 percent, which it

purchased from LG Industrial Services for about $400 million in November 2000. *The Korea Herald,* November 26, 1999, and November 30, 2000.

17. During the 1994 Mexican financial crisis, for example, a look at the rankings of the top ten companies in that country shows that, in the three years leading up the crisis, there was an average of about four "movements," or changes in the rankings, each year. In the three years following the crisis, there was an average of seven movements. Similarly in Korea, the difference was an average of three movements per year during the three years leading up to the crisis, versus an average of seven movements per year for the three years following, based on rankings by revenue for the given year. Source: Expansion, *Financial Analysis of the Top 30 Chaebols in Korea,* New Industry Management Academy.

18. Banco Nacional was acquired by Unibanco in November 1995, and Banco Econômico was acquired by Excel in May 1996, which in turn was acquired by Spain's Bilbao Vizcaya (BBV) in May 1998. Bamerindus was acquired by HSBC in March 1997. Bamerindus was practically though not officially bankrupted, and sold for the equivalent of about one U.S. dollar. A fourth top-ten bank, BCN, although not bankrupt, was acquired by Bradesco in October 1997.

19. Austin Asis; Central Bank of Brazil.

20. Expert Rating Agency; Interfax.

21. Between 1999 and 2001, *Global Finance* named Alfa Bank the "Best Russian Domestic Bank."

22. Asset figure is for year-end 2001. Source: Expert Rating Agency; Interfax.

23. Asset figure is for year-end 2001. Asset rankings are from the Bangko Sentral ng Pilipinas (Central Bank of the Philippines) Factbook.

24. "Citibank Conquers Asia," *Business Week,* February 26, 2001.

25. Ramayana also had to cope with recovering from the May 1998 riots, during which the retail chain lost 19 percent of its store space in stores that were burned down. Combined with other store closures, total selling space for the retail chain contracted by 29 percent by the end of the year. Nonetheless, the company managed to beat revenue targets for the year by 30 percent, and increased sales year-over-year by 15 percent. Source: McKinsey interviews; company annual reports.

26. Figure for 2001 is estimated. Associação Nacional dos Bancos de Investmento (National Association of Investment and Development Banks, ANBID); balance sheets of financing companies.

27. In the previous organization, regional branch managers reported to the CEO, and product management was considered a cost center. The reorganization divided the bank by customer groups, retail and corporate, with the former subdivided into product and channel management, each with its own profit-and-loss responsibility.

28. *Survey on Korean Opinion on Foreigners Investing in Korea,* Korea Development Institute, 1994 and 1998.

29. *Dow Jones News,* January 18, 1998.

30. Ministry of Commerce, Industry, and Energy, Korea; *Foreign Direct Investment in Korea,* KPMG, September 2001; and "Pupil Who Has Learned Enough to Tutor," *Financial Times,* March 21, 2002.

31. "A Survey of Thailand," *The Economist,* March 2, 2002.

32. Although usually thought of as negative, there are instances where some customer groups actually benefit. In Indonesia, for example, the crisis led to demand for and the enactment of a minimum wage law, which has increased several times since. In this case, policy changes led to an improvement in the purchasing power of lower-income customers.

33. This survey question excluded borrowing to purchase a house.

34. Growth rates in 1996 and 1997 were 8 percent and 12 percent, respectively; and in 1999 and 2000, 28 percent and 23 percent. Source: National Statistical Office of Korea.

35. McKinsey interviews.

36. Mergers and acquisitions figure does not include Japan. Rajan Anandan, "M&A in Asia," *The McKinsey Quarterly,* Number 2, 1998.

37. "Hanging Tough," *Business Week,* April 22, 2002.

38. Thomson Financial Securities Data.

39. Following the 1994 crisis, a number of privatization deals—led primarily by Banco Itaú and others like ABN-Amro, BCN, and Bozano Simonsen—led to a decline in public bank assets from 52 percent in 1994 to 46 percent in 1998. The 1999 crisis accelerated this trend even further, with the same percentage decreasing from 46 to 37 percent between 1998 and 2000. Source: Central Bank of Brazil; press clippings.

40. Between 1997 and March 2002, Interbrew completed more than thirty acquisitions in over a dozen countries, with a number in Central and Eastern Europe and Asia. Source: McKinsey interview.

41. *The Wall Street Journal,* October 23, 1991. Interbrew acquired a 52 percent stake in Borsodi Sorgyar at an undisclosed price.

42. Debt and asset figures are from company financial statements. Workforce reduction and debt guarantee figures are from *Business Week,* February 28, 2000.

43. *Automotive News,* June 29, 1998.

44. *Automotive Engineering International,* August 1, 2000.

45. Based on industry interviews conducted during the crisis.

46. *Business Week,* op. cit.

47. McKinsey interview.

48. Jung-Tae Kim also had the confidence of other observers. In 1998, CEO Kim was named by *Business Week* as one of the top fifty leaders in Asia,

the same award given to Banthoon Lamsam at Thai Farmers Bank, in 2000. See "The Stars of Asia," *Business Week,* June 29, 1998.

49. Market capitalization figure is average for February 2002. BIS ratio figure is as of March 2002.

APPENDIX 5.1: Leveraging Strategic Opportunities in Financial Crises: The Successful Story of NCNB

1. Ross Yockey, *McColl: The Man with America's Money* (Atlanta: Longstreet, Inc., 1999). See also Howard E. Covington, Jr. and Marion A. Ellis, *The Story of NationsBank* (Chapel Hill: The University of North Carolina Press, 1993).
2. Wachovia and First Union eventually merged in 2001.
3. The only exception for "foreign" banks to enter new state-controlled deposit markets was through the acquisition of failing banks. Under the arcane U.S. law at the time, a North Carolina bank was considered a foreign bank in Florida—and most other states.
4. Federal Deposit Insurance Corporation, *Managing the Crisis: The FDIC and RTC Experience, 1980–1994* (Washington, D.C.: FDIC, August 1998).
5. The 1982 Garn–St Germain Act permitted out-of-state banks in the United States to acquire failing banks.
6. One of the two favorable tax rulings came on the eve of the FDIC's bid proposal date.
7. The FDIC owned 80 percent of NCNB-Texas National Bank, while NCNB owned the other 20 percent with an exclusive, nontransferable option for five years to buy the remaining 80 percent. The FDIC created one of the first bridge banks in U.S. history, which NCNB-TNB managed for it. NCNB-TNB owned and managed the $12 billion in problem assets, and segregated them in a separate asset pool after writing them down by roughly 30 percent to market value. The FDIC assumed the bridge bank's debt to the Federal Reserve. Ultimately, NCNB bought out the FDIC one year later in August 1989 for a total of $1.15 billion, producing a total gain to the FDIC of $275 million, including dividends.
8. Tim Hartman later became Chairman and CEO of NationsBank West.
9. Eventually this special asset unit became a separate profit-making subsidiary of the NCNB holding company, known as Amresco, operated as a third-party provider and manager for distressed assets of other banks, and eventually was spun out of the bank after a few successful years, since the distressed asset business was not part of NCNB's long-term growth strategy.

10. Market capitalization figures are averages for December 1998 and December 1988, respectively.

CHAPTER 6   Driving Successful Bank Turnarounds

1. Mellon Bank Corporation is now known as Mellon Financial Corporation to more accurately reflect the shift of its financial services strategy.
2. Marty McGuinn is now Chairman and CEO of Mellon Financial Corporation.
3. "Scandanavia's Banks Grapple with Crisis," *The Wall Street Journal*, November 1, 1991.
4. "Christiana Bank Final Results," *Regulatory News Service*, March 4, 1992; "Norway Kreditkassen Shares Seen Worthless," *Reuters News*, October 25, 1991.
5. "Kreditkassen Board Wants Lenth as New Bank Head," *Reuters News*, August 19, 1991.
6. "Christiana Bank's 2nd Quarter and Interim Results," *Regulatory News Service*, August 4, 1992.
7. Alfred Berg, "Christiana Bank: Focus on Internal and External Restructuring," ABN-AMRO, February 25, 1999.
8. "Nordic Banks Catch Cold as Recession Hits Sector Strongly," *The Sunday Telegraph*, November 10, 1991.
9. "Christiana Write-Off 180 Million in Restructuring Costs," *The Daily Telegraph*, November 1, 1991.
10. "Christiana Bank's 2nd Quarter and Interim Results," *Regulatory News Service*, August 4 and August 19, 1992.
11. "Christiana Bank Says It Returned to Profit During the 1st Quarter," *The Wall Street Journal Europe*, May 3, 1993.
12. Finansstatistik.
13. Alfred Berg, op. cit.
14. "Christiana Bank EGM Proposal re Share Capital," *Regulatory News Service*, November 18, 1993.
15. Alfred Berg, op. cit.
16. "Pan-Nordic Bank Business," *Tradewinds*, October 20, 2000. The acquisition became effective in February 2001, and following the acquisition, in December 2001, Nordea AB changed its name to Nordea Bank Norge ASA.
17. For a more detailed discussion of the value of intangible assets in general, see the recent book by our colleagues, Lowell Bryan, Jane Fraser, Jeremy Oppenheim, and Wilhelm Rall, *Race for the World—Strategies to Build a Great Global Firm* (Boston: Harvard Business School Press, 1999); see especially Chapter 7, "Building Intangible Capital," pp. 177–206.

APPENDIX 6.1: Building a Rationale for Official Support
in a Financial Crisis

1. Walter Bagehot, *Lombard Street*: *A Description of the Money Market* (New York: John Wiley & Sons, 1999; originally published London 1873).

CHAPTER 7   Minimizing Costs
Through NPL Recovery Excellence

1. *The FDIC and RTC Experience: Managing the Crisis,* FDIC (Washington, D.C.: August 1999), pages 5, 29.
2. Johan A. Lybeck, "Facit av finanskrisen," SCB, Central Bank of Sweden.
3. Michele Cermele, Maurizio Donato, and Andrea Mignanelli, "Good Money from Bad Debt," *The McKinsey Quarterly,* Number 1, 2002.
4. Ibid.
5. Ibid.
6. Determining the availability of such resources in local markets is essential for speedy intervention. In certain cases (smaller economies) it becomes necessary to bring in foreign management teams with experience in managing institutions in crisis. With the numerous occurrences of financial crises, a mini-industry of financial crisis management firms has emerged. These firms consist of retired bank executives and line managers who were used to assist in crises in the U.S., U.K., and other countries and can deploy resources quickly to institutions around the globe.
7. IPAB in Mexico is an exception with a five-member board that includes the executive chairman plus four independents.
8. SCB Bankerna.
9. McKinsey estimates.

CHAPTER 8   Strengthening System Safeguards

1. CalPERS press release, February 21, 2002.
2. See CalPERS, at www.calpers.com; Wilshire Associates, *Permissible Equity Markets Investment Analysis and Recommendations.* Preliminary, January 2002. Subsequently, CalPERS reinstated the Philippines. Press Release, May 13, 2002.
3. McKinsey & Company's Emerging Markets Investor Opinion Survey 2001. Conducted by the Corporate Governance team of McKinsey's Global Organization and Leadership Practice, this series surveys institutional investors on their views of corporate governance and, in particular, their willingness to pay for well-governed companies. In aggregate,

respondents managed approximately \$3.25 trillion in assets. Also, we surveyed attendees at the International Finance Corporation (IFC) Global Private Equity Conference (May 10–11, 2001); the forty-six respondents, all of whom are private equity investors, manage approximately \$5 trillion in assets, 90 percent of which is invested in emerging markets.

4. Carlos Campos, Roberto E. Newell, and Greg Wilson, "Corporate Governance Develops in Emerging Markets," *McKinsey on Finance* (Winter 2002). To ensure consistency in the ratings, we developed explicit criteria for how ratings should be assigned. To control for researcher bias, we directed local McKinsey teams to evaluate companies from each market. This result was statistically significant at the 95 percent confidence level.

5. In both crisis and noncrisis situations, McKinsey has worked on public policy and regulatory issues to strengthen financial systems, for example, in Australia, Canada, Jamaica, Korea, Singapore, Thailand, the United Kingdom, the United States, and other countries.

6. This section is adapted from "A Premium for Good Governance," by Roberto Newell and Greg Wilson, *The McKinsey Quarterly,* Number 3, 2002.

7. McKinsey interview.

8. A capital market in our definition includes a debt market (bonds), equities markets (cash and derivatives), and foreign exchange markets, and includes a broad variety of asset managers and investors (e.g., pension funds), intermediaries (e.g., investment banks, traders), and infrastructure (e.g., lawyers, accountants, IT systems, talent, and skills).

9. Remarks by Robert R. Glauber, Chairman and CEO of NASD, at NASD's Regulation Securities Conference, San Francisco, California, November 17, 2000.

10. Domestic pension funds and insurance companies are natural long-term investors in the domestic economy.

11. Robert Becker and Emmanuel Pitsilis, "A Case for Asian Bond Markets," *The McKinsey Quarterly,* Number 3, 2000.

12. ING Group, *Major Themes in Global Fund Management,* April 2001.

13. Singapore administers the CPF and invests the assets, with a limited number of state-approved investment managers.

14. Becker and Pitsilis, op. cit.

15. We use the terms "market liberalization" and "deregulation" interchangeably in this chapter, since both refer to changes in old, outmoded regulatory regimes. Deregulation does not, however, imply a lack of prudential regulation. To the contrary, when markets liberalize to meet the needs of end users and providers, new ways of supervising financial institutions that are more effective and efficient are required as well.

16. For example, U.S. banking law includes explicit guidelines for what has become known as "prompt corrective action" to resolve and, if

necessary, intervene troubled banks, based on an institution's capital levels and other supervisory factors.

17. See *Market-Incentive Regulation and Supervision: A Paradigm for the Future*, The Bankers Roundtable (Washington, D.C., April 1998); and *Building Better Banks: The Case for Performance-based Regulation*, The Bank Administration Institute (Chicago, Illinois, 1997).

18. For an excellent primer on an effective and efficient approach to modern regulatory frameworks and tools, see *A New Regulator for the New Millennium*, U.K. Financial Services Authority, January 2000.

19. McKinsey practice development. Higher GDP per capita and deeper capital markets are positively correlated. When legal variables are added in a multivariate regression, the only significant variables that remain positively correlated are the ones based on the legal system. GDP per capita, total GDP, the savings rate, size of government spending, and even the volume of capital inflows all proved statistically insignificant.

20. La Porta, Lopez de Silanes, Shleifer, and Vishny, *The Role of Law and Legal Institutions in Asian Economic Development, 1960–1995*, Asian Development Bank, 1998; www.adb.org.

APPENDIX 8.3: The Discipline of the Market for Corporate Control: Issues for CEOs

1. The seminal thinking on the market for corporate control comes from Henry Manne, "Mergers and the Market for Corporate Control," *Journal of Political Economy*, April 1965, 110–120.

2. Two excellent starting points for a corporate strategy are works from our McKinsey colleagues: Lowell Bryan et al., op. cit.; and Richard Foster and Sarah Kaplan, *Creative Destruction: Why Companies That Are Built to Last Underperform the Market—And How to Successfully Transform Them* (New York: Doubleday, 2001).

3. Hon. Alan Greenspan, Chairman, Board of Governors, Federal Reserve System, remarks on corporate governance at Stern School of Business, New York University, March 26, 2002.

CHAPTER 9   Designing a New, Market-Driven Financial Architecture

1. The FSF was established in 1999, with Andrew Crockett, General Manager of the BIS, appointed as its first chairman. It is the outgrowth of a 1998 G-7 finance ministers and central bank governors meeting, which agreed on the need to enhance international cooperation among supervisors, and it has played a leadership role in the cataloguing and publishing of twelve key standards in its *Compendium of Standards*. Its three objectives are: 1) to assess vulnerabilities affecting the international

financial system; 2) to identify and oversee actions needed to address these vulnerabilities; and 3) to improve coordination and information exchange among the various authorities responsible for financial stability.

2. Collectively, these standards are designed to promote financial stability and avoid financial crises at the macroeconomic level, but not, however, at the microeconomic level where they are most needed, as we explain in Chapter 3. Beyond simply issuing these standards, practical templates for actual self-assessment are also being developed—a step that we take as a positive sign of the kind of actions that we recommend. For a more complete listing of *FSF Compendium of Standards,* see Appendix 9.1.

3. See especially: Robert E. Barnett, *Responsibilities and Liabilities of Bank and Bank Holding Company Directors* (Chicago: CCH Incorporated, 1996, 4th ed.); *Pocket Guide for Financial Institution Directors,* Federal Deposit Insurance Corporation (Washington, D.C.: FDIC, 1997); *The Director's Book: The Role of a National Bank Director,* Office of the Comptroller of the Currency (Chicago).

4. ICGN is a collection of 250 large institutional investors, financial intermediaries, companies, academics, and other interested parties from twenty different countries, whose mission is to facilitate the exchange of information and development of guidelines on corporate governance practices internationally among its participating members. For more information on ICGN, see its website at www.icgn.org.

5. The IIF's corporate governance guidelines are similar to the OECD and ICGN guidelines.

6. "New Code Proposed to Strengthen Corporate Governance," press release, Institute of International Finance, February 12, 2002; www.iif.com.

7. "The Worm that Never Dies," *The Economist,* March 2, 2002, p. 12.

8. Anne Krueger, "International Financial Architecture for 2002: A New Approach to Sovereign Debt Restructuring." Address to the National Economists' Club Annual Members' Dinner at the American Enterprise Institute, Washington D.C., November 26, 2001.

AGD   Agencia de Guarantía de Depósitos (Agency for the Guarantee of Deposits), Ecuador's bank restructuring and deposit insurance agency; www.agd.gov.ec

ASEAN   Association of Southeast Asian Nations; www.aseansec.org

Asobancaria   Asociación Bancaria y de Entidades Financieras de Colombia; corporation founded in 1936, represents Colombia's financial sector; www.asobancaria.com

BCBS   Basel Committee on Banking Supervision; established by the G-10 Central Banks; refer to BIS Web site for more information

BIS   Bank for International Settlements; international organization which fosters cooperation among central banks and other agencies in pursuit of monetary and financial stability; www.bis.org

Bretton Woods Agreement   agreement signed in 1945 that established the International Monetary Fund (IMF) and the International Bank for Reconstruction and Development (IBRD, better known as the World Bank)

CPSS   Committee on Payments and Settlement Systems; established by the G-10 Central Banks; refer to BIS Web site for more information

FATF   Financial Action Task Force on Money Laundering; established by the G-7 Summit in 1989; refer to OECD Web site for more information

FDIC   Federal Deposit Insurance Corporation, the U.S deposit insurance, regulatory, and bank resolution agency; www.fdic.gov

FINSAC   Financing Sector Adjustment Company, Jamaica's bank restructuring agency; www.finsac.com

FOBAPROA   Fondo Bancario para la Protección del Ahorro, the former Mexican bank restructuring agency

Fogafín   Fondo de Garantías de Instituciones Financieras, Colombia's bank restructuring agency; www.fogafin.gov.co

FSC   Financial Supervisory Commission, Korea's unified financial services regulatory agency created in 1998; www.fsc.gov.kr

FSF   Financial Stability Forum; convened in 1999 to promote international stability through information exchange and international cooperation in financial supervision and surveillance; www.fsforum.org

GKO bonds Gosudarstvennye Kaznacheyskie Obiazatelstva; Russian state treasury bonds

IAIS International Association of Insurance Supervisors; est. 1994, represents insurance supervisory authorities of some 100 jurisdictions; www.iaisweb.org

IASC International Accounting Standards Committee, a private sector standard-setting body

IBRA Indonesian Bank Restructuring Agency

IBRD International Bank for Reconstruction and Development, commonly known as the World Bank; www.worldbank.org

ICGN International Corporate Governance Network; founded 1995, private sector network to promote good corporate governance; www.icgn.org

IFAC International Federation of Accountants, a private sector standard-setting body; www.ifac.org

IFRS International Financial Reporting Standards, the successor to International Accounting Standards (IAS)

IIF Institute of International Finance; est. 1983, the world's only global association of financial institutions; www.iif.com

IMF International Monetary Fund; www.imf.org

IOSCO International Organization of Securities Commissions; www.iosco.org

IPAB Instituto para la Protección al Ahorro Bancario, Mexico's current bank restructuring agency; www.ipab.org.mx

NASD National Association of Securities Dealers, the U.S. self-regulatory organization for securities brokers and dealers; www.nasd.com

NCNB North Carolina National Bank, the forerunner of NationsBank and BankAmerica

OECD Organization for Economic Cooperation and Development; international organization with 30 member countries committed to democratic government and the market economy; www.oecd.org

RTC Resolution Trust Corporation, the U.S. asset management corporation for failed savings and loan associations

SUPERBANCARIA Superintendencia Bancaria de Colombia; Colombia's financial supervisory agency founded in 1924; www.superbancaria.gov.co

WTO World Trade Organization; www.wto.org